CLINICIAN'S THESAURUS, 7TH EDITION

CLINICIAN'S THESAURUS

7th Edition

*The Guide to Conducting Interviews
and Writing Psychological Reports*

EDWARD L. ZUCKERMAN, PhD

THE GUILFORD PRESS
New York   London

Published by The Guilford Press
A Division of Guilford Publications, Inc.
72 Spring Street, New York, NY 10012
www.guilford.com

Printed in the United States of America

This book is printed on acid-free paper.

Last digit is print number: 9   8   7   6   5   4   3   2

The author has checked with sources believed to be reliable in his efforts to provide information that is complete and generally in accord with the standards of practice that are accepted at the time of publication. However, in view of the possibility of human error or changes in medical sciences, neither the author, nor the editor and publisher, nor any other party who has been involved in the preparation or publication of this work warrants that the information contained herein is in every respect accurate or complete, and they are not responsible for any errors or omissions or the results obtained from the use of such information. Readers are encouraged to confirm the information contained in this book with other sources.

Library of Congress Cataloging-in-Publication Data

Zuckerman, Edward L.
    Clinician's thesaurus: the guide to conducting interviews and writing psychological reports / Edward L. Zuckerman.—7th ed.
        p.   cm.
    Includes bibliographical references and index.
    ISBN 978-1-60623-874-5 (pbk. : alk. paper)
    1. Interviewing in psychiatry.   2. Mental status examination.   3. Neuropsychological report writing.   4. Psychiatric records—Terminology.   I. Title.
    RC480.7.Z83 2010
    616.89001′4—dc22

                                                                2010016504

About the Author

Edward L. Zuckerman received his PhD in clinical psychology from the University of Pittsburgh and continued there as an adjunct teacher of personality psychology and human sexuality for 14 years. He taught abnormal psychology at Carnegie Mellon University for 9 years and now consults to the Social Security Disability Determination Division. He was in the independent general practice of clinical psychology for more than 15 years and has worked in state hospitals and community mental health centers. He lives on a small farm in Pennsylvania with his wife and their horses, chickens, dogs, cats, geese, and ducks.

Contents

PART III. Useful Resources

Appendices

Acknowledgments
and an Invitation

I must first express my continuing appreciation to my editors at The Guilford Press, without whom this work would be much less clear, organized, and precise. I am very grateful for their expertise, experience, and enormous efforts. Anna Brackett's organizational skill, Marie Sprayberry's attention to detail and thoroughness, and, especially, Barbara Watkins's wisdom and grace have turned this collection of words into a highly useful tool.

I want to acknowledge, with thanks, Dan Egli of Williamsport, PA, who was coauthor of the list of medications in Section 28.1. With appreciation for their expertise and generosity, I am happy to give credit here to the following professionals for their contributions.

Dolores Arnold, MEd, NCC, of Lawton, OK
Judy Bomze of Wynnewood, PA
Renee F. Bova-Collis of Richmond, VA
Richard L. Bruner, PsyD, of Hightstown, NJ
Jeffry Burkard of Colvis, CA
Kathryn Elkins of Victoria, Australia
Joe Elwart, PsyD, of Royal Oak, MI
Patricia Hurzeler, MS, APRN, CS, of
    Bloomfield, CT
Mustaq Khan, PhD, of London, Ontario,
    Canada
Dorothy H. Knight of Jacksonville, IL
Bryan Lindberg of Portsmouth, RI
Susan G. Mikesell, PhD, of Washington, DC
Ilene D. Miner, CSW, ACSW, of New York, NY
Robert W. Moffie, PhD, of Los Angeles, CA

Fay Murakawa, PhD, of Los Angeles, CA
Michael Newberry, MD, of Palm Bay, FL
James L. Pointer, PhD, of Montgomery, AL
Joseph Regan, PhD, of Toronto, Ontario,
    Canada
Daniel L. Segal, PhD, of Colorado Springs,
    CO
Judith Shea, MA, of Lawrence, MA
Janet L. Smigel, RN, CD
Henry T. Stein, PhD, of San Francisco, CA
Frank O. Volle, PhD, of Darien, CT
Marcia L. Whisman, MSW, ACSW, of
    St. Louis, MO
Leslie J. Wrixon, PsyD, of Cambridge, MA
Nora F. Young of Sedro Wolley, WA

I must also clearly acknowledge my debt to many other colleagues, from whose clearest thinking and best writing I have borrowed liberally to fill these pages. More than 250 of you have furnished the more than 60,000 reports from which I have culled the thousands of unduplicated wordings incorporated here. Although you are too numerous to credit individually, please accept my gratitude and appreciation. While I have borrowed many of the words and phrases, I alone must assume responsibility for the content and organization of the *Clinician's Thesaurus*, whatever its merits or limitations.

Now, you are invited to contribute. What is missing from this book? What would you have put in or taken out? What have I gotten wrong? Please let me know by mail or e-mail, and—if your suggestions are adopted into the next edition—three good things will happen:

1. You will get **a free copy of the next edition.**
2. Your contribution will be fully acknowledged here.
3. You will receive my (and our fellow clinicians') sincere appreciation for adding to our knowledge, and for making our work easier.

Send mail to P.O. Box 222, Armbrust, PA 15616, and e-mail to *edwardzuckerman@gmail.com.*

＊　　＊　　＊

The following copyright holders have generously given permission to quote or adapt material from these copyrighted works:

CLINICIAN'S THESAURUS, 7TH EDITION

Getting Oriented
to the *Clinician's Thesaurus*

What Is the *Clinician's Thesaurus* and What Does It Do?

This book is more than a giant collection of synonyms; it is a treasury of the terms, standard phrasings, common concepts, and practical information clinicians use in their daily work. *In breadth and in depth, this book covers the language of American mental health.* It is organized to help you, first, collect the client information you need; second, organize those findings into a high-quality report; third, find the most precise terms to express your findings; and fourth, develop appropriate diagnoses, treatment plans, and recommendations.

If you write mental health evaluations and intakes, psychosocial narratives, testing-based reports, progress notes, managed care treatment plans, closing summaries of treatments, and the like, the *Clinician's Thesaurus* will ease your workload as it sharpens your writing because it does the following:

- Presents dozens of related terms to enhance the clarity, precision, and vividness of your reports.

- Offers behavioral descriptions for a range of psychopathology to help you document your observations, formulations, and conclusions.

- Suggests phrasings that can individualize and personalize a report or description.

- Stimulates your recall of a client's characteristics (we all can recall more when we prompt our memories by reading related terms).

- Suggests "summary statements" where only a brief indication is needed, such as when cognitive functioning is within normal limits.

- Contains extensive cross-references and a helpful index for ease in locating materials and ideas.

- Replaces the drudgery of narrative reporting with playfulness, spontaneity, and serendipity. (I know this is a big promise, but when you skim the book you will find both the familiar and the novel.)

In addition, because of its format and structure, the *Clinician's Thesaurus* can help you do these things:

- Structure an interview or assessment to ensure that you have not missed any important aspect.

- Organize your thoughts when writing or dictating a report to ensure that you have addressed all the issues of relevance for that client.

- Access the knowledge base you have built from your training and experience for use in treatment planning or other clinical decisions you have to make.

- Revise, elaborate on, or tighten up a report you have drafted. The wide diversity of terms offered allows you to refresh and vary your writing, even about a familiar topic or point.

- Learn, do, or teach report writing (see below).

The *Clinician's Thesaurus* can be thought of as an enormous checklist. It is designed to approximate your internal checklist—the one on which you draw to conduct interviews, understand and respond to questions, and construct your reports. However, because it is far easier to work from an external checklist, it converts the demanding free-recall task into a much simpler recognition task. You just have to read, weigh, and select the best wording for the task at hand.

How This Book Is Organized

The *Clinician's Thesaurus* is organized in the same sequence of actions you would take to approach a client, assess the client's functioning, and then construct the report. Part I covers conducting a mental health evaluation. Part II offers ways to begin, develop, and end the report; it includes all of the standard topics addressed in mental health reports, presented in the sequence they are addressed in a typical report. Part III offers treatment plan formats, alternative report formats, and other useful resources.

Part I offers a guide for interviewing, plus hundreds of questions and aids for eliciting specific kinds of client information.

- Chapter 1 provides pointers for conducting a valid and ethical interview and guidance for beginning and ending the interview.

- Chapter 2 covers all the traditional aspects addressed in a **Mental Status Evaluation (MSE).** It offers common questions (and many variations on them) for examining cognitive functioning.

- Chapter 3 offers hundreds of questions designed to elicit information about all kinds of **signs, symptoms, and behavior patterns,** including ones that are particularly difficult to address in the interview context (such as paranoia, dissociative experiences, and sexual history).

Part II of this book is designed to guide your writing of a report. It is organized in the sequence of the traditional evaluation report. (For more on this format and on constructing reports, see below.) The chapters offer a range of descriptors and phrases by topic area. Almost any report can be shaped from the terms and areas covered. Useful clinical tips and common wording pitfalls also appear throughout the text.

- Chapters 4–6 cover **introducing the report**: preliminary information; the reasons for the referral; and background information.

- Chapters 7–13 address **the person in the evaluation**: behavioral observations; responses to aspects of the examination; presentation of self; emotions/affects; cognition and mental status; abnormal symptoms; and personality patterns.

- Chapters 14–19 cover **the person in the environment**: Activities of Daily Living (ADLs);

social/community functioning; couple and family relationships; vocational and academic performance; recreational functioning; and other dimensions clinicians are often asked to evaluate.

- Chapters 20–24 cover **completing the report**: summaries, diagnostic statements, recommendations, prognoses, and professional closings.

Part III of this book offers useful clinical resources. These include the following:

- Formats for treatment plans.
- Formats for writing a wide range of reports and summaries.
- A brief list of treatment manuals for specific disorders and other treatment resources.
- A list of common psychotropic medications, by trade and generic names.
- Cues for recognizing the psychiatric presentation ("masquerade") of medical conditions.

In addition, there are Appendices containing useful abbreviations and an annotated list of readings in assessment, interviewing, and report writing.

Understanding the Style and Format of the Chapters

As just described, the three main parts of this book cover, respectively: questions for broad aspects of an evaluation (in Part I), wording for areas of a report (in Part II), and clinical resources (in Part III). The chapters within each part are then subdivided into more specific topics. For example, Chapter 10, "Emotional/Affective Symptoms and Disorders," has 13 main sections—each addressing a specific affective symptom or disorder, ranging from anger to depression to panic. Each of these main topics has its own section number (e.g., the third section in Chapter 10, "Anxiety/Fear," is numbered 10.3). Cross-references throughout the book are to these chapter and section numbers.

To find terms and descriptors for an anxious client, you could turn to the book's table of contents, find Chapter 10, see that Section 10.3 is "Anxiety/Fear," and then turn to that section for a full range of terms relating to anxiety and fear grouped by manifestation. You could also look up "anxiety" in the index and find other related sections.

Of course, not all section topics within a chapter will need to be covered in every report. The section topics represent a range of possible options across different types of clients and different types of reports. Select from these topics and terms those relevant to the particular client and type of report you are writing.

Types of Information in the Chapter Sections

Most of this book consists of lists and groupings of the standard terms used in North American mental health. Other kinds of useful information also appear throughout the chapters:

- Introductory and explanatory comments.
- Cross-references to related sections of the book.
- Practice tips, reminders, and cautions.
- References to the standard works in the field or area.
- Descriptors, terms, and phrases for wording reports.
- Sample "summary statements."
- Sample evaluation questions and tasks (primarily in Chapters 1, 2, and 3).

Figure 1 (see below) offers a quick visual guide to identifying these various types of information within the chapter format. It also illustrates many of the formats and typographic conventions described below. (Note that the figure represents a composite of several pages, so as to illustrate a wider range of formats. Some content has been omitted in this composite.) It is from the descriptors that you may select the ones most appropriate for incorporation into your reports. The format for these is explained below.

The descriptors and phrasings offered in this book are standard American English usage and are the conventional language of the mental health field. Because the terms offered are only rarely defined here, you may find useful a specialized psychiatric dictionary (e.g., Campbell, 2009; *Stedman's Medical Dictionary*, 2006; *Stedman's Psychiatry Words*, 2007).

As you will see in Figure 1 and throughout the book, the descriptors and terms may appear in different formats, such as in a paragraph, in a list, or as columns of words across the page. Some formats indicate that the terms have been ordered according to degree of meaning. Understanding the arrangements gives you further information about those terms. These formats are explained below.

Because so much valuable information is now available on the Internet, dozens of websites have been incorporated into this edition. Most of these web addresses can be easily typed into any web browser. Alternatively, entering the first few terms of the address into a search engine (like Google. com) will produce a collection of sites, including the one you seek.

Formats for Descriptors and Terms

The terms and descriptors offered in the *Clinician's Thesaurus* are always shown in the following font, suitable to set them off from other kinds of text. They may be arranged in one of four ways, from an unordered grouping of related words to increasingly ordered arrangements:

1. **Unordered groups of similar but not synonymous words and phrases** in a line or paragraph. Example:

   > Presentable, acceptable, suitable, appearance and dress appropriate for age and occupation, businesslike, professional appearance, nothing was attention-drawing, modestly attired.

   These words are often used as alternatives for each other. They are presented in a line or paragraph with no ordering principle. In the example above, the terms and phrases are all similar descriptors for "appropriateness" of clothing/attire.

2. An **ordered spectrum of words and phrases,** indicated by a double-arrow graphic ($\leftrightarrow$), in a line or paragraph. Example:

   > ($\leftrightarrow$ *by degree*) Awkward, clumsy, "klutzy," often injures self, "accident-prone," inaccurate/ineffective movements, jerky, uncoordinated, <normal>, purposeful, smooth, dextrous, graceful, agile, nimble.

   In the example above, a client's movement or activity is characterized along a spectrum of ability from uncoordinated ("awkward") to highly coordinated ("nimble"). The arrowheads (< >) enclosing the word "normal" indicate that it is the midpoint of the spectrum.

3. **Columns of words ordered by degree** ($\leftrightarrow$) across the page. Example:

Qualities of Clothing ($\leftrightarrow$ *by degree*)

filthy	rumpled	needing repair	plain	**neat**	**stylish**
grimy	disheveled	threadbare	out of date	careful dresser	fashionable
dirty	neglected	seedy	old-fashioned	clothes-conscious	elegant

Chapter number

Chapter title

Cross-references
by chapter
and section number

Introductory and
explanatory comments

A subsection of
"General Aspects of Mood
and Affects"

Columns sequenced by
degree across the page

Boldface: Most
commonly used term
in a cluster

Lines or paragraphs
staggered down the page
by degree of meaning

Slash mark (/):
Alternative word follows

Additional wordings
only "For a Child"

Underlining and
capitalizing initial letters:
An acronym

Quotation marks
(" "): Slang

Unordered, similar (but
not synonymous) words

✓ indicates comments,
advice, or suggestions

Spectrum sequenced
by degree

Braces { }: A term that
is obsolete, obscure,
or historical
Small caps:
A non-English term

10

Emotional/Affective Symptoms and Disorders

10.1. General Aspects of Mood and Affects

See Section 3.5, "Affect/Mood," for questions.

"Mood" refers to pervasive and sustained emotional coloring of one's experience, a persistent emotional trend (like the climate). It is usually self-reported (but is sometimes inferred). "Affect" is of shorter duration, such as what the clinician observes during the interview, . . .

Amount/Responsiveness/Range of Affect (↔ *by degree*)

flat	**blunted** (amount)	**constricted** (range)	**normal**	**broad**
affectless	apathetic	contained	**usual**	deep
bland	inexpressive	low-intensity	average	intense

Appropriateness/Congruence of Affect or Mood and Behavior

(↔) The following groupings are sequenced by degree of increasing appropriateness/congruence.

Indifferent to problems, floated over his/her real problems and limitations, LA BELLE INDIFFÉRENCE . . .

Affect variable but unpredictable from the topic of conversation, modulations/shifts . . .

A range of emotions/feelings, appropriate emotions for the ideational content and . . .

10.3. Anxiety/Fear

For a Child:

Fears of animals, ghosts, demons, "the bogeyman," darkness, getting lost, parental illness/disability/death/loss, punishment, being embarrassed/humiliated.

10.7. Depression

See Section 3.11, "Depression," for questions. See also Sections 10.11, "Seasonal Affective Disorder," and 12.26, "PreMenstrual Dysphoric Disorder."

Affective Facets

Anhedonia   *See also Section 10.1, "General Aspects of Mood and Affects."*

Absence of pleasure, loss of pleasure in living, "nothing tastes good any more," joylessness, lack of satisfaction in previously valued activities/hobbies, loss of interests, no desire/motivation/energy to do anything, no fun in his/her life, indifference, "couldn't care less," apathy, . . .

Behavioral Facets

Libido   *See Section 10.12, "Sexuality," for descriptors.*

✓ Remember that libido is sexual interest, not activity.

10.9. Mania

(↔ *by degree*) Gregarious, likeable, dramatic, entertaining, pleasant, vivacious, seductive, cracks jokes, prankish, naive, infantile, silly, {WITZELSUCHT}.

FIGURE 1. Reduced composite page illustrating various formats and typographic conventions.

The word columns above are sequenced along a spectrum of degree of the trait—in this example, from "filthy" to "stylish." Each individual column contains one or more unordered alternative terms with slightly different **shades of meaning**. However, when a word is a standard term used by clinicians for a cluster, it is presented at the top of the column in **boldface**. In the example above, the three words in the first column all indicate the same relative degree of "Qualities of Clothing," but have different nuances. "Filthy" is a standard term for this degree in quality.

4. **Lines or paragraphs sequenced by degree** (↔) and staggered downward across the page. Example:

> Unable to recognize the purposes of the interview/the report to be made …
> Indifferent, bland, detached, distant, uninvolved, uncaring …
> Dependent, sought/required much support/reassurance/guidance …
> Anxiety appropriate/proportionate to the interview situation …
> Understood the social graces/norms/expectations/conventions …

In the example above, each level represents a degree of the quality along an ordered spectrum. The words or phrases at each level are rough synonyms. In the example above, the quality of a client's response to the evaluation ranges from "Unable to recognize the purposes … " to "Understood … "

Typographic Conventions for Descriptors and Terms

- **Double arrow** (↔): Indicates that the terms or phrases are ordered along a spectrum of degree for the trait, quality, or behavior.

- **Slash mark** (/): Indicates that an alternative word or words immediately follow. Example:

  > Understood the social graces/norms/expectations/conventions …

  Here the terms "social graces," "norms," "expectations," and "conventions" are alternative descriptions, each of which can be used with the term "Understood" to indicate a quality of client response to the evaluation.

- **Quotation marks** (" "): Indicate that a word is slang or inappropriate in a professional report. Example:

  > Awkward, clumsy, "klutzy," often injures self, "accident-prone," …

  Slang and similar inappropriate words are frequently offered by persons being evaluated. They are placed in the *Clinician's Thesaurus* under appropriate headings to assist the clinician unfamiliar with such phrasings in understanding their meanings. For example, the descriptors for uncoordinated movement in the example above include "klutzy" and "accident-prone." Their placement indicates their meaning, but the quotation marks should alert you not to use the terms in your report.

- **Check mark** (✓): Indicates comments, advice, cautions, and clinical tips. These range from brief comments to tables of information; they are useful in understanding the client or phenomena, but are not to be borrowed for the report. Example:

  ✓ **Note:** If the client is incapable of providing this information, a family member or other informant should be sought.

- **Braces** ({ }): Indicate words or phrases that are obsolete, obscure, or only of historical interest. Example:

  > (↔ *by degree*) Gregarious, likeable, dramatic, entertaining, pleasant, vivacious, seductive, cracks jokes, prankish, naive, infantile, silly, {WITZELSUCHT}.

The descriptors above constitute a spectrum of terms relating to mania. The word "WITZEL-SUCHT" is now considered an obsolete description, and so it appears in braces. (Small capital letters in this case indicate the word's non-English origin.)

- **Underlining and capitalization of the initial letters of a phrase**: Indicate a commonly used acronym. For example, Activities of Daily Living are often referred to as ADLs. (Note that this convention is also used in a couple of chapter titles and elsewhere in text proper.)

- **Special headings**: Most wordings apply to both adults and children. However, words used only in the evaluation of children are listed at the end of each area where they apply, and are indicated by the heading **"For a Child."** Similarly, other uses are indicated, such as **"For a Disability Report."** Finally, in some instances sample sentences are provided to indicate how you might sum up a situation; these are indicated by the heading **"Summary Statements."**

Typographic Conventions for Descriptors and Terms at a Glance	
Convention	*Meaning*
↔	Ordered spectrum of meaning
/	Alternative word or words immediately following
" "	Slang or inappropriate for professional report
< >	Midpoint in a spectrum
✓	Comments, advice, cautions, clinical tips
{ }	Obsolete, obscure; historical interest only
Capitals Underlined	Indicates the acronym, as in Activities of Daily Living (ADL)

Notes on Grammar

For compactness and simplicity, adjectives, adverbs, verbs, and nouns are sometimes mixed in a listing. Just modify the word to suit the sentence you have in mind.

The **pronoun forms** used throughout this book are intended to lessen the sexist associations and implications whose harmful effects are well documented in this field. The book uses combinations such as "her/him" and "he/she" in varying order, or alternates in turn between "he" and "she," to avoid furthering gender associations. When pronouns of a single gender are employed, that phrasing should not be taken to imply any association of gender with behavior.

A Functional Guide to Report Construction

The Nature of Reports, the Steps of Their Construction, and the Corresponding Portions of the *Clinician's Thesaurus*

The purpose of a report is to communicate the results of your assessments (and, for therapy summaries, interventions) to someone who has a need for this information. To accomplish this purpose, you, the writer, must simultaneously attend to two tasks:

1. Create a coherent, integrated narrative. What you have to say should be relevant, should be important, and should fit within a familiar professional structure.

2. Focus the narrative on the needs of the reader. That reader may be a referrer, a supervisor, the client's next therapist, a court or lawyer, a teacher or school system, a physician, another professional, or the person examined and his/her family. Each will understand your words from her/his background and experience.

Keeping these two tasks in mind is essential to producing reports that communicate well and are useful.

The next few pages move from looking at the most general to the most specific aspects of a report's narrative. You will see how the flow of information is organized to produce a report whose ideas are of value to the report's reader(s), and whose expression is precise, tailored to the individual, and meaningful.

Report construction begins when you begin to collect relevant information about the client. You must then organize the information you have collected. In general, the sequence of topics in a report begins with old information, such as the client's history and the referral reasons. It proceeds to the new information you have gathered in the interview or assessment. It then presents the new understanding you have formed of the client, based on both the old and the new information. This integrated picture finally leads to new planning, which involves the generation of appropriate and effective interventions. This stepwise process corresponds to the main components of a traditional evaluation report, as seen below:

The process of constructing a report	*The main components of an evaluation report*	*Subdivisions of Part II of the* Clinician's Thesaurus
Old information	Introducing the report	A
New information—personal	The person in the evaluation	B
(New information—test results)	(Standardized samples of behavior)	(Not covered in this book)
New information—social	The person in the environment	C
New understandings and plans	Completing the report	D

The model above is an extremely general version of the logic of constructing reports. (Readers are referred to Braaten, 2007, for detailed guidance on how to report test results for children and adolescents.) Each of the four main components of a report covered in this book includes a range of specific issues or concerns that you can address, as shown in Table 1. Of course, no single report will include all of these. Rather, you must use the report's purpose combined with your clinical judgment to select those issues of most use to the reader of the report.

Now let us look more closely at these concerns (and their parallel chapters and sections of the *Clinician's Thesaurus*), so as to understand the nature of the clinical work involved in each. What is a clinician doing when he/she considers each area of personal and social functioning? What are the questions implicitly or explicitly asked by the report's reader that will help her/him to do what is best for the client? The chapters and sections of Part II of the *Clinician's Thesaurus* are designed to offer ways of framing the answers. The following discussion is intended to guide you in framing the questions.

A. Introducing the Report

BEGINNING THE REPORT: PRELIMINARY INFORMATION (CHAPTER 4)

The beginning of a report covers old information: facts and issues before this evaluation took place. Don't include every piece of historical information you may have. Rather, include only the information relevant to the goals of the report. Use the information to clarify why you are doing an evaluation or writing a summary.

Reports usually begin with identifying information (the client's identity, age, marital status, etc.). In addition, important aspects of your meeting with the client, such as the client's competence and consent to participate in the interview, are customarily included here although they are not historical. This is done to avoid interrupting the later flow of clinical information.

TABLE 1. Generalized Format for an Evaluation Report

Components of a report	Chapters/sections of the *Clinician's Thesaurus*
A. Introducing the report (old information)	
Preliminary information	Chapter 4
Could include these:	
Headings and dates	Section 4.1
Sources of your information about the client	Section 4.2
Identifying information about the client	Section 4.3
Self-sufficiency in appearing for the examination	Section 4.4
Statements of consent to be evaluated	Section 4.5
Reliability of the client/validity of the information	Section 4.6
Confidentiality notices about the report	Section 4.7
Referral reasons	Chapter 5
Could include these:	
Nature of the problem(s) faced by the client or the referrer	Section 5.1
Who referred the client, for what services, and for what purpose(s)	Sections 5.2 to 5.4
Background information and history	Chapter 6
Could include these:	
History of the presenting problem or chief concern	Section 6.1
Medical, family, social, adjustment histories	Sections 6.2 to 6.5
Using a genogram	Section 6.6
B. The person in the evaluation (new information—personal)	
Could include these:	
Behavioral observations	Chapter 7
Responses to aspects of the examination	Chapter 8
Presentation of self	Chapter 9
Emotional/affective symptoms and disorders	Chapter 10
Cognition and mental status	Chapter 11
Abnormal signs, symptoms, and syndromes	Chapter 12
Personality patterns	Chapter 13
C. The person in the environment (new information—social)	
Could include these:	
Activities of Daily Living	Chapter 14
Social/community functioning	Chapter 15
Couple and family relationships	Chapter 16
Vocational/academic skills	Chapter 17
Recreational functioning	Chapter 18
Other specialized evaluations	Chapter 19
D. Completing the report	
New understandings	
Could include these:	
Summary of findings and conclusions	Chapter 20
Possible psychiatric masquerade of medical conditions	Chapter 29
Diagnostic statement/impression	Chapter 21
New plans	
Could include these:	
Recommendations	Chapter 22
Prognostic statements	Chapter 23
Detailed treatment plan	Chapter 25
Closing statements	Chapter 24

Who are you? When, where, and from whom did you get this information? Who is the client? How well does the client understand the interview process and outcomes? (See Chapter 1, especially Sections 1.3 and 1.4, for assistance with explaining the purposes, consequences, and confidentiality of the interview to the client.) Were there any limitations on the interview? How reliable was the client?

REFERRAL REASONS (CHAPTER 5)

What is the nature of the problem(s) faced by the client or the referrer? Who referred the client, when, for what services, and for what purpose(s)? The greater the precision of this goal, the easier the report is to write, because you will always be returning to it. Spend as much time as necessary to refine your understanding of the referrer's needs.

BACKGROUND INFORMATION AND HISTORY (CHAPTER 6)

What led up to this evaluation? What do you know about this person's previous functioning and the context in which he/she has lived?

B. The Person in the Evaluation

The goal of the next main component of the report is to state how this person is doing in her/his life at present or in the recent past. This component, like the one that follows it, consists of *new information*—that is, information about the client's functioning in contact with you (during the assessment or therapeutic interviews).

What did you observe of this person's appearance, behavior, ways of relating to you, cognitive functioning, emotional reactions, symptoms, and personality? Your findings might be either test data for a psychological evaluation, or things you learned about the client's dynamics, personality, or functioning during therapy sessions you are now reviewing.

For each of the first three areas covered below, the central question is this: What do these observable behaviors indicate or illustrate about important aspects of the client's mental state and interpersonal functioning? Information irrelevant to these aspects should be excluded.

BEHAVIORAL OBSERVATIONS (CHAPTER 7)

In what ways might the client's appearance, clothing, movement, speech, etc., indicate phenomena of clinical interest?

RESPONSES TO ASPECTS OF THE EXAMINATION (CHAPTER 8)

How did the client relate to you and your questions or materials? How much effort and persistence did he/she demonstrate? How did the client respond to difficulties, failure, frustration, success, or feedback?

PRESENTATION OF SELF (CHAPTER 9)

How friendly or forthcoming was the client? How self-confident? How dependent or independent? How knowledgeable about socially appropriate behaviors? How warm or cold? How socially skilled?

The next four areas covered below are those usually seen as the most psychological: emotions; thinking; other signs, symptoms, and syndromes; and personality patterns.

EMOTIONAL/AFFECTIVE SYMPTOMS AND DISORDERS (CHAPTER 10)

What were the client's mood and affects? How did these change during the interview, in response to topics discussed or for other reasons? Did the client display or recount anger, anxiety/fear, depression, mania, guilt/shame, or other feelings?

COGNITION AND MENTAL STATUS (CHAPTER 11)

How well was the client able to think, to process information, to come to conclusions, to make decisions, and to take actions? Could she/he recall and integrate relevant information and exclude the irrelevant? Did she/he understand the world, her-/himself, and what was happening in common ways? Did he or she organize thoughts and words normally and communicate effectively? What evidence did you see of judgment, insight, and higher-level functioning? (See Chapter 2 for questions to evaluate all aspects of cognitive functioning.)

ABNORMAL SIGNS, SYMPTOMS, AND SYNDROMES (CHAPTER 12)

What other symptomatic behaviors (i.e., not purely emotional/affective or purely cognitive) have you been alerted to, observed, and investigated, and want to tell the reader about? How severe are these? How limiting? (See Chapter 3 for questions to evaluate abnormal and symptomatic behaviors.)

PERSONALITY PATTERNS (CHAPTER 13)

What enduring and cross-situational patterns of attending, thinking, feeling, and acting did you observe? What evidence did you see of traits or patterns of the better-known personality disorders and character patterns (e.g., aggressive, authoritarian, codependent, sadistic, self-defeating, etc.)?

C. The Person in the Environment

The third main component of the report continues with new information. Its purpose is to describe how this person functions in the larger world of everyday activities, close and formal relationships, and similar areas. The central question to be answered is this: How successful or impaired is this person in each area?

ACTIVITIES OF DAILY LIVING (CHAPTER 14)

Can this person take care of him-/herself? How well accomplished are the daily tasks of self-care, cooking, cleaning, child care, shopping, and getting around?

SOCIAL/COMMUNITY FUNCTIONING (CHAPTER 15)

What has the client or others told you about social and community relationships? How skilled and involved is the client? How much conflict and failure does she/he experience?

COUPLE AND FAMILY RELATIONSHIPS (CHAPTER 16)

What did the client or others tell you about more intimate and persistent relationships with the members of his/her family of origin, spouse/partner, and/or children? How effective or limited is this person in these areas? If you evaluated family members, how competent were they? What were their structural and systemic patterns?

VOCATIONAL/ACADEMIC SKILLS (CHAPTER 17)

What do you know of the client's academic and vocational adjustments and accomplishments? What are her/his current reading, mathematical, and vocational skill levels? What kinds of problems or conflicts have occurred?

RECREATIONAL FUNCTIONING (CHAPTER 18)

How does this person spend his/her free time? What activities are engaged in, and at what level of performance or intensity? How satisfying are they?

OTHER SPECIALIZED EVALUATIONS (CHAPTER 19)

You may be asked to evaluate the client's competence to manage his/her finances, make a will, cope with stress, or adapt to being a refugee, among other things. Or you may be asked to describe her/his spiritual or religious concerns, problems, and issues.

D. Completing the Report

The last main component of the report covers new understandings and the resulting new plans. Groth-Marnat (2009) says that a good report should not only integrate old information, but provide a new and unique perspective on a person. This is a daunting task. It requires an organization of the data around topics of interest, but there are a very large number of topics or ideas on which you can focus. If a report is to have value, it will be in the integration of the information and the formulation of accurate diagnoses, well-considered recommendations, and achievable plans for treatment.

New Understandings

SUMMARY OF FINDINGS AND CONCLUSIONS (CHAPTER 20)

Offer an integration of history, findings, and/or observations, and your understanding of the client's functioning in the areas most relevant to the referrer's or reader's needs. Condense this information into a paragraph: the relevant demographic information, referral reason, history, and your major findings most relevant to the referral question, treatment history, or any other purpose of the report.

Additional issues may need to be addressed at this point in some reports. For example, what additional information do you need and from whom? Also, might the psychological symptoms presented be due to a medical condition? (See Chapter 29, "Psychiatric Masquerade of Medical Conditions.")

For testing reports, findings can be organized by topic (integrating the results of different tests, such as cognitive functioning, emotional controls, interpersonal relations, etc., depending on the referral questions). A statement about the probable reliability of the findings is also needed (see Chapter 4, Section 4.6, "Reliability/Validity Statements").

DIAGNOSTIC STATEMENT/IMPRESSION (CHAPTER 21)

A diagnosis is professional shorthand that integrates many kinds of data. Generally you should include all five axes of a DSM diagnosis and any "rule-outs." Placing it here orients the reader to the recommendations and treatment planning that follow. ICD-9-CM is replacing DSM-IV-TR for some purposes; both are offered in Chapter 21.

New Plans

The last few elements of the report involve using your fuller and newer understanding of the client (generated above) to do new planning for services that are in the client's best long-term interest: recommendations and treatment planning (for more detail on the latter, see Chapter 25, "Treatment Planning and Treatment Plan Formats").

RECOMMENDATIONS (CHAPTER 22)

Are any further evaluations needed to clarify diagnoses or other points? What levels and areas of current functioning indicate the need for treatment? What supports might the client need? What kinds of treatment would best restore functioning? How motivated is the client for treatment? In general terms, what intensity of treatment, approaches, and methods would be best? (For creating a detailed treatment plan, again see Chapter 25. For a list of common psychiatric medications, see Chapter 28, "Listing of Common Psychiatric and Psychoactive Drugs.")

PROGNOSTIC STATEMENTS (CHAPTER 23)

What course do you expect for this client if she/he does not receive the recommended treatments and services? What course do you expect for this client if she/he does receive the recommended treatments and services?

CLOSING STATEMENTS (CHAPTER 24)

Thank the referrer, indicate your continued availability (if so), and sign the report.

Do not be afraid to do outlines and drafts (Ownby, 1997). You might start with summaries of the old and newly acquired information. You can then create a longitudinal picture: In your initial review of the client's life's trajectory, how do his/her background and history fit with the current findings (of a single slice of time) and lead to your prognosis and treatment recommendations? A later review should edit the materials into a tight narrative that clearly links the pieces of evidence to the conclusions drawn from it. Finally, use your understanding of the referral reasons or the readers' needs to pare down the report to focus only on answers to these needs.

Attributions

References to professionals may be phrased as follows:

> The clinician, therapist, psychologist, social worker, psychiatrist, nurse, counselor, behavior specialist, consultant, evaluator, interviewer, writer, undersigned, author, reporter, correspondent.

The professional can be said to do the following:

> Report, offer, observe, note, document, record, state, summarize, etc.

References to the client may be phrased as follows:

> The client, patient, claimant, {examinee}, resident, {subject}, individual, person, citizen, consumer, man, woman, child, student, etc.

The client can be said to do the following during an interview:

> Say, state, report, note, speak of, describe, indicate, mention, tell me, concede, present, disclose, elaborate, maintain, offer, deny, disavow, disclaim, exhibit, evidence, register, reveal, etc.

Or, for more legalistic language, you can use these terms:

> Allege, submit, claim, contend, aver, opine, certify, etc.

The use of first names, given names, or nicknames is unprofessional except for children. For adults, Mr. or Ms. (yes, even for married women who use their husbands' surnames) is the professional standard. Use "Dr." and other titles only where necessary to prevent misunderstanding or where they are relevant to the purpose of the report.

Further Guidelines and Advice on Report Writing

- Unlike reports of the past, which emphasized precise diagnosis and understanding of etiology, current models focus more on descriptions of the person and his/her specific behaviors.

Current report models have shifted away from a focus on symptoms, maladjustments, and areas needing change; they now emphasize assessing strengths and coping mechanisms.

- Use headings and subheadings to help the reader follow your thinking and understand when you change levels of analysis.

- Evaluation reports that need to include test results require that the results be both clearly available (usually by being set into tables) and integrated into the picture of the client being developed in the progress of the report. For a report of test results, Lichtenberger et al. (2004) summarize three common ways to organize the paragraphs of data: (1) these can move from one domain of functioning to another, with headings like "Intelligence," "Adaptive Functioning," and "Academic Achievement"; (2) they can report abilities under headings such as "Memory," "Judgment," and "Expressive Language"; and (3) they can report results test by test. In my opinion, these are most appropriate only for hasty and simple reports, because the goal of a good evaluation is the integration of test data into functioning and the understanding of the whole person. Another useful guideline for reports of test data is to move from the more global tests and findings to the more specific instruments and findings (Lichtenberger et al., 2004). For example, you might have IQs precede subtest scores, give Minnesota Multiphasic Personality Inventory–2 validity scores before two-point interpretations, and only then present the findings from the Rotter Incomplete Sentences Blank. Similarly, they suggest moving from the more standardized test results to the less formal, such as the facts of your or others' observations.

- Because of concerns with test security and copyrights, do not repeat the questions from standardized tests or the mental status questions in your reports, but only the responses you received. (Or refer to the question indirectly—e.g., the Wechsler "Brooks" proverb.)

- As to writing style, Ownby (1997) calls for a "professional style," by which he means avoiding jargon, using shorter words with precise meanings, writing short paragraphs focused on a single concept, and employing a variety of sentence lengths and structure to maintain readers' interest.

- Take into account how the intended readers of your report will interpret it. Consider their level of psychological sophistication, their theoretical or professional orientation, their decisions and options, and their relationship with you. Although reports are typically written at the writer's reading level (graduate school) and are addressed to peers, reports are now widely made available to parents, less trained or differently trained professionals, and clients. Therefore, they should be phrased for readers with 12th-grade or lower reading levels (Harvey, 1997). Use the readability tests of your word processor to check. It is preferable to use lower reading levels (as long as meaning is not lost), use shorter sentences, reduce acronyms, and omit passive voice. Brenner (2003) argues for reports that (1) are written for the consumer, (2) eliminate jargon, (3) fully respond to the referral questions, (4) individualize and tailor all findings, (5) emphasize strengths, and (6) make concrete recommendations. Segal and Hutchings (2007) offer a thorough checklist for making certain that an intake report is complete, well written, and professional.

- Only those details that are relevant and have meaning for the point/purpose of the report should be given.

- Do not report as facts what you have only been told. Instead, specify where the information came from. (For various phrasings, see "Attributions," above.)

- Remember to report negative (absent) as well as positive (present) findings.

- Avoid the unclarified use of acronyms, abbreviations, and names for local service providers and programs if the report is addressed to or might be used by those unfamiliar with such references. Instead, use the local language and then describe the program in general terms—for example, "TSI, a transitional community residential services provider" or "7 West, the alcohol detoxification ward."

- Where you are concerned about confidentiality and yet know you will be releasing the report to readers with whom you wish to maintain the subject's anonymity, you might use this method: Write the subject's name at the top of page 1 only, and use the subject's first (for a child) or last (for an adult) initial in all subsequent references to the subject. This way, you will have only one occurrence of the name to remove. (See also Section 4.7, "Confidentiality Notices.")

- For the prevention of tampering with and loss of the pages of a report, they can be numbered as "Page 1 of 6," "Page 2 of 6," etc.

- Make sure your statements are consistent. Don't make different judgments in the narrative and on a check-off form. Don't state different conclusions based on different data.

- Be neat and legible. Use correct spelling and grammar, and use a dictionary or spelling checker.

- Get feedback on your reports, no matter how intimidating this may seem. Ask peers and report recipients for their input.

- It is customary to write intake reports and similar contemporaneous evaluations (e.g., progress notes) in the present tense, and to use the past tense for events and experiences reported from the past (as in closing summaries and histories) and also for mental status results. Use careful phrasings with attributions in the present tense for past material that is controversial, potentially untrue, or slanderous, and for which you have no confirming evidence beyond the client's report. For example, phrasings like "The client describes her parents as being severely alcoholic" or "He reports having been sexually abused by a priest" are preferable to "Her parents were alcoholics" or "He was sexually abused by a priest."

Sattler and Hoge's (2005) advice on writing reports is worthwhile:

- Prefer the specific to the general, the definite to the vague, the concrete to the abstract.

- Do not take shortcuts at the cost of clarity.

- Avoid fancy words.

- Omit needless words. Make every word tell.

- Express coordinate ideas in similar form. The content, not the style, should protect the report from monotony.

- Use a clear order of presentation so that your ideas can be followed.

- Avoid the use of qualifiers. "Rather," "somewhat," "possible," "may"—these are the leeches that infest the pond of prose, sucking the blood of words.

- Put statements in positive form. Make definite assertions; avoid tame, colorless, hesitating, noncommittal language.

- Do not overstate. Avoid overgeneralization, overinterpretations, and "Barnum statements"—those so general as to be universally applicable.

Esser (1974) points out these common problems with reports:

- Failure to answer referral questions or provide desired information.

- Making the report too long or too short. The report should be the shortest way to convey the essential information. Balance brevity and thoroughness.

- Telling the referrer what he/she already knows, or, conversely, failing to use referrer-provided information.

- Providing just pure data: findings without interpretations, judgments, or impressions.

- The presence of contradictions in the report.

- Reluctance to provide realistic or negative findings.

- Making unrealistic plans for the client.

- Failure to back up recommendations and plans with facts and reasons.

- Failure to consider alternative recommendations, courses of action, and objectives.

- Giving a summary that isn't one: It fails to bring together the information and to create a composite picture from it.

Zimmerman and Woo-Sam (1973) offer other points:

- State the information simply and concisely.

- If you cite an authority, make certain she/he is qualified and neutral.

- Do not go beyond your data.

- Identify the substantiated bases of your cause–effect conclusions, and beware of fads in these interpretations.

Some Ways to Use the *Clinician's Thesaurus*

When You Interview

You can use Part I of this book to guide your interview. You might simply read some of the mental status or symptom questions to the client; you might copy out a few to ask; or you might use them to refresh your memory of the questions appropriate to the referral's concerns. In contrast to structured interviews, these chapters offer many questions for each area; if a particular question does not result in a satisfactory response, you will have many similar ones to use.

When You Write or Dictate a Report

As described earlier, Part II of this book is organized in the same sequence as the "classic" mental health report. If you are constructing other kinds of reports, you will find that you can select relevant sections to fit your needs and requirements for contents and structure. Each chapter is independent and can be seen as a module to be put to different uses. The individual chapter titles correspond to the major headings of standard reports, such as "Behavioral Observations," "Mental Status," or "Diagnostic Summary." Within each chapter, the numbered sections cover the aspects that are typically evaluated in that area. Paging through the major numbered sections within each chapter will remind you to address each relevant area in your report. If you need to do a very comprehensive evaluation, you can use all the numbered headings within each chapter as a checklist to make certain you haven't overlooked any important point.

The chapters in Part II contain specific words and phrases that reflect numerous ranges of meaning. From these, you can select the best descriptors for your patient in these areas. You can turn to a specific chapter and its numbered sections to focus on a particular topic for writing a more fine-grained description.

As you use the *Clinician's Thesaurus,* you may find it worthwhile to highlight in color, underline, or box the words or phrases that best suit your writing style and are most relevant to your practice and setting. You may find it practical to use the black thumb tabs on the edge of each page to access sections of the book more quickly.

When You Teach

As a teacher, you simply cannot offer your students more than a fraction of the behaviors a clinician must understand. When you focus on a few diagnoses or processes, students may miss the breadth they will need. If you discuss theory, your students may miss the concrete; if you offer cases, they may learn only a few examples and not the larger picture of the disorder. As a teacher, I have struggled with these choices myself. This book provides another option: All the aspects of each syndrome and pattern are in the *Clinician's Thesaurus*. The whole language of the mental health field is in here.

When students need to interview, the questions here will enable them to follow up (almost) any referral question. When they sit down to write up their findings, all the language options are here. They and you can concentrate on the higher-level functions—weighing, winnowing, and integrating—not on reinventing the standard language.

Students love this book because it both reduces their anxiety and makes them more competent. When they see that (almost) everything they will need is in this one book, they breathe a sigh of relief. The book does not replace their clinical education, but it does assist the process. It is equivalent to giving a calculator to a math student: The student can concentrate on the nature of the problem, not the details of the calculation.

When You Supervise

Less skilled professionals or students may sometimes fail to think deeply or may write glib reports. The usual supervisor's response to this situation is to interview the students, trying to pull from them observations of the patients that they probably never made because they lacked the terms for labeling the phenomena of interest.

When you supervise, try this instead: Refer such students to the appropriate sections of the *Clinician's Thesaurus* and ask them to find, say, three or more words to describe the cognitive aspects of a patient's depression. Not only does this make the supervision problem into a game instead of a contest over who is smarter, but also it puts the burden of discrimination on the students, where it belongs. Moreover, this process of weighing the alternatives trains a kind of clinical judgment that I find almost impossible to teach in other ways.

The *Clinician's Thesaurus* is not a "cheat sheet" or a crutch. Reports written by clinicians using it are not "canned." Few individuals have thousands and thousands of words and statements in mind to choose from, and there is no limitation on entering new ones into the book. It does not write reports for anyone; students still have to learn the words' meanings and evaluate their appropriateness for each client.

A Cautionary Note and Disclaimer

The entries of this book are presented simply as sample questions and lists of terms that have been used in the field. Their presence here does not imply any endorsement by the author or publisher. These wordings are offered without any warranty, implied or explicit, that they constitute the only or the best way to practice as a professional or clinician.

When individuals use any of the words, phrases, descriptors, sentences, or procedures described in this book, they must assume the full responsibility for all the consequences—clinical, legal, ethical, and financial. The author and publisher cannot, do not, and will not assume any responsibility for the use or implementation of the book's contents in practice or with any person, patient, client, or student. The author and publisher shall not be liable in the event of incidental or consequential damages in connection with or arising out of any use by purchasers or users of the materials in this book. By employing this book, users signify their acceptance of the limits of the work and their acceptance of complete personal responsibility for all such uses.

The author and publisher presume (1) that the users of this book are qualified by education and/or training to employ it ethically and legally, and (2) that users will not exceed the limits of documentable competence in their disciplines as indicated by their codes of ethical practice.

If more than the material presented here is needed to manage a case in any regard, readers are directed to engage the services of a competent professional consultant.

Part I

Conducting
a Mental Health Evaluation

1

Beginning and Ending
the Interview

1.1. Structuring the Interview

There are dozens of specialized interview methods (see Hersen & Turner, 2003) and numerous structured interviews, which should be used to increase reliability and validity over more open-ended approaches. An excellent guide for a clinician seeking this direction is Rogers (2001).

The format below addresses some points crucial to beginning all interviews, whether structured or unstructured. Because a client may not understand a question's goal, or the answer may not be as informative as you hoped, Chapters 2 ("Mental Status Evaluation Questions/Tasks") and 3 ("Questions about Signs, Symptoms, and Behavior Patterns") offer multiple questions under each topic so that you can ask a second or third question.

1.2. Introducing Yourself and Noting Possible Communication Difficulties

When you are interviewing clients for treatment, bear in mind that "When clients present for an evaluation, they are often in a great deal of emotional pain. They are often demoralized and hopeless because their efforts to address their problems have failed or had only limited impact. They can benefit by simply having an opportunity to share their story [*sic*] with a compassionate and attentive listener" (Segal & Hutchings, 2007, p. 115).

Make eye contact and introduce yourself to each client as follows: "Hello, I'm [Title] [Name]. And you are … ?" This format avoids breaching confidentiality by calling out a name. If the area is crowded, you can announce your name and ask, "Who is here to see me at this time?"

With each client, be alert to the client's possible **limitations of hearing and vision,** and inquire if you have any reason to suspect a disability. Ask about any need for glasses/contact lenses or hearing aids if not worn, and comment in your report on the effects on the client's performance. Ask the client for suggestions to improve conditions, such as minimizing the background noise or changing the lighting. Don't cover your mouth; be sure to speak clearly. When you are interviewing hearing-impaired clients or users of American Sign Language (who call themselves deaf), it is legally required by the Americans with Disabilities Act of 1980 (amended in 1990 and 2008), as well as clinically preferable, to obtain the services of a certified interpreter. Do not force clients to read or write in a language structure other than ASL or to lip-read. There are far too many examples of hearing-impaired people being misdiagnosed as mentally retarded or psychotic for any examiner to be complacent about this.[1]

Assess and report, with your conclusions, the presence of any of the following:

Visual impairment: Near-/farsightedness, astigmatism, cataracts, hemianopsia, blindness, etc.; totally/partially/not compensated for with glasses.

Hearing impairment: Total/partial deafness in left/right/both ears, necessitating hearing aids/ lip reading/signing/total communication/American Sign Language; understands amplified/ simplified/repeated conversational speech.

Limitations of movement (especially hands if you are doing testing) and ability to sit for periods of time.

Impaired speech. (See Section 7.4, "Speech Behavior.")

Unfamiliarity with the English language, English as a second language, non-native speaker. Use of or need for an interpreter (in the case of a client with either a hearing impairment or an English-language difficulty).

Literacy: Able/unable to read aloud/understand/rephrase a paragraph from a newspaper or common magazine, national news magazine; look up a location on a map; fill out a job application; understand the instructions for a prescribed medication; follow a recipe; etc. [Avoid using "grade-level" terms, because they are misleading and functionally irrelevant.]

✓ It may be hard for clinicians to understand that up to half their clients, depending on the setting, may lack basic literacy. However, because illiteracy is socially negative, few clients will acknowledge it when asked. Appropriate evaluation should be routine. Administering an instrument called the Rapid Estimate of Adult Literacy in Medicine (Davis et al., 1993) may be more relevant than having a client read aloud and summarize the content of a few paragraphs from a magazine. Low literacy and its resulting misunderstanding and low compliance should not be mistaken for resistance or low intelligence.

Lastly, consider all the known variables that affect interpersonal communication, such as age, gender, ethnic, socioeconomic, and "racial" differences; language use and style of communication; the demand characteristics of the interview situation; the unstated expectations of each person about the nature and purposes of the interview; and others for your particular situation.

1.3. Assessing the Client's Understanding of the Interview Situation

Ask early, especially if the client seems reluctant to raise the subject:

"What have you been told about this interview/our meeting?"
"What do you expect to happen here?"
"What did you think and feel before you came in here/met me?"

"Because I have spoken with _____/read reports from _____/know you from _____, I already know some things about you/why you have come here/why we are talking. However, I'd like to hear from you why you have come to see me/come here."

"I'd like to talk with you for a few minutes in order to _____."

---

[1] I am grateful to Ilene D. Miner, CSW, ACSW, of New York, NY, for this information.

1.4. Obtaining Informed Consent

See Section 4.5, "Consent Statements."

You must obtain fully informed, cognitively competent, and voluntary consent to the interview or evaluation.

Explain the purposes of the interview. Attend to the client's and examiner's perceived expectations of the referring agent; what information is to be gathered, by what means; what is then to be done; and, if a report is written or made, who will see it (e.g., Social Security Disability, workers' compensation, courts, and other agencies or parties to whom it may be forwarded without the client's additional authorization under the terms of the Health Insurance Portability and Accountability Act of 1996).

As you explain each relevant aspect, ask the client: "Would that be all right with you?"

Once some private fact is revealed, it cannot be ignored, so you must fully explain the likely consequences of your evaluation and subsequent report and then offer the client the opportunity not to participate and let him/her know he/she can stop participating at any point. I usually use statements such as "Consider what will be in your long-term best interests" or "If you have any reservations let us discuss them before we proceed any further." Do encourage questions if you detect or suspect any reluctance.

Of course, issues may arise as you proceed, in which case you might say something like "You can stop me at any time during our interview if you don't understand me or need to question what I am asking you to do."

For situations in which you are a consultant, you should explain that your interview will not be for treatment, you will not be their doctor or refer the client to other therapists, nothing is off the record, and the client may choose not to answer any of your questions.

When the assessment's purpose is to help the client qualify for some special educational service, get hired, or receive financial support, make it clear that your findings and report may not support this goal—and that even when they do, the final decision will be made by the relevant agency, not by you. On a more positive note, you can explain that even if the goal is not achieved, the results may provide useful information to the client about further activities or interventions.

Lastly, explain and have the client sign an authorization to release records for the evaluation. It may incorporate the points made above with a statement such as this: "I fully understand that no specific outcomes can be guaranteed as a result of this evaluation."

1.5. Other Points for All Interviews

Ask **everyone** about the following:

> **Current medications prescribed, taken:** Name(s), dosage(s), frequency.
> **All forms of abuse** *(see Sections 3.2 to 3.4).*
> **Major losses and grieving.**
> **All substances used** *(see Sections 3.28 and 3.29).*
> **Suicidal** *(see Section 3.30)* **and homicidal** *(see Section 3.31)* **ideation and impulse control** *(see Section 3.17).*

Raise any other issues that would arise because of the nature of your setting, population, providers, location, and other factors, and that would be unfamiliar to the average person.

1.6. Eliciting the <u>C</u>hief <u>C</u>oncern/<u>C</u>omplaint/Issue

See Section 6.1 for more on addressing the <u>C</u>hief <u>C</u>oncern.

"Would you please tell me why you are here/came to see me/are being evaluated?"
"What brings you to the hospital/the clinic/my office?"
"What concerns you most?"
"What has been going on?"
"What has happened to you?"
"What do you hope to have happen/come from our meeting?"

1.7. Eliciting the Client's Understanding of the Problem

See also Section 19.2, "Culturally Sensitive Formulations."

Some initial questions to elicit the client's understanding of the presenting problem (based on similar questions by Reimer et al., 1984) are as follows:

"What do you think caused your problem?"
"Do you have an idea of why it started when it did?"
"How severe is your problem/disorder/complaint/sickness?"
"How long do you expect it to last?"
"What other problems has your problem/disorder/complaint/sickness caused you?"
"What do you fear about your problem/disorder/complaint/sickness?"
"What kind of treatment do you think you should receive?"
"What results do you hope to receive from this assessment/treatment?"

1.8. Dimensionalizing the Concern/Problem

"For how long has this been happening?"   (Duration)
"How often does this happen?"   (Frequency)
"When it happens, how strong is it when it   (Intensity)
    starts, at its worst, etc.?"
"Think back to the last time this happened and
    tell me:

   "What led up to its happening?"   (Antecedents, cues, controlling stimuli,
                                                     latency, sequences, progression, chains)

   "What were you thinking and feeling?"   (Expectations, beliefs, meanings, affects)
   "Who else was around, and what did they   (Social support, persons who defined prob-
       think and feel?"   lem)
   "What happened next/afterward?"   (Sequences, reinforcers, consequences)
   "How typical was this occasion?"   (Development of the problem, intensity)
   "Was the first time it happened different?"   (Client's understanding of development)
   "What could have made a difference in   (Expectations of outcome, changeability,
       this incident?"   treatment, treaters, understandings of cau-
                                                     sation)

✓ **Note:** The causative factors for a problem may not be the same as the factors maintaining it.

1.9. Ending the Interview

It is best to develop a standard set of closing statements for your interview. These will ensure that potentially important information is not lost, that consistency across clients and occasions is maintained for reliability and validity, and that important legal or patient care issues are discussed.

"Is there anything else that you want to add/tell me/want me to know/understand?"

"Is there anything important/relevant/that matters that we have not covered?"

"Do you have any questions about what we have done today/about this evaluation/about the report I will be writing?"

"Do you have any questions about what the next step will be/what happens next?"

"The next step is that _____ will contact you about _____ by mail/phone, in _____ days."

"You will need to make an appointment with _____ to _____."

"I appreciate your taking the time to come to this interview and the efforts you made to provide the information I needed."

"Thank you for your time and efforts in coming here and talking to me."

"I expect that you will receive some benefit from all of this." Or "Although you will not benefit directly from what we have done today, you will be assisting in the training of professionals who will/in the collection of research data that will help others in your situation."

2

Mental Status Evaluation Questions/Tasks

The questions in this chapter are about **cognitive functions**. Questions about **symptoms** and **abnormal behaviors** are in Chapter 3.

2.1. Introduction to the Mental Status Questions

Over the years, clinicians have formulated questions for assessing mental status (especially cognitive function) and passed them down to their students. But with empirical examination, most of these have been found to lack reliability, validity, or both, and the whole area of interpreting the patient's responses is unstandardized. Therefore, for higher reliability, a number of standard brief mental status tests and short batteries are available, such as the classic Mini-Mental Status Examination by Folstein et al. (1975) (available at *www.3parinc.com*), and the Global Deterioration Scale by Reisberg et al. (1982). More recent screening tools include the Saint Louis University Mental Status Exam (available at *aging.slu.edu*) and the Montreal Cognitive Assessment (available at *www.moctest. org*). Both have sensitivity superior to that of Folstein et al.'s MMSE, especially for the detection of mild cognitive impairment/mild dementia (Smith et al., 2007) and for cognitive dysfunction in Parkinson's disease (Gill et al., 2008). The Cambridge Cognitive Examination—Revised also appears to be highly discriminating for mild cognitive impairment (Heinik & Solomesh, 2007). The NEPSY-II (Korkman et al., 2007) assesses children ages 3–16 in six domains.

You could, of course, use the questions from the age-appropriate sections of the Stanford–Binet, or the Wechsler subtests of Information, Arithmetic, Comprehension, Similarities, or Digit Span, for the advantage of precise scoring and interpretation of the responses. Even with these tests, however, norming and validity may still be less than desired for the important consequences that flow from MSEs.

The questions offered below may be suitable alternatives for clients who have recently been formally tested on the instruments cited above, or they may be used for other reasons. These questions are appropriately used only as screening devices; unusual responses must be investigated further with standardized tests, and patterns of unusual responses must be investigated with neuropsychological, neurological, or other appropriate scientific methods.

No assertion or implication of any kind of validity is made or should be inferred about the use of the questions presented here. As far as I know, no research has been conducted on them, and no published norms are available to guide clinicians in interpreting the responses obtained to the questions asked. The internal "norms" of experienced and well-trained professionals are the only basis for evaluating such responses. Although you will find guidance in almost any psychiatry text, the best books for learning to do MSEs are Trzepacz and Baker (1993) and Morrison (2008). The latter has a simple but excellent eight-page outline that integrates the process of data gathering and the formal structure of the interview. Rogers (2001) offers reviews of MSEs and structured interviews.

Also, bear in mind that your observations and conclusions about the client's thought processes ("symptoms") are entirely inferred from your observations ("signs"), as you have no direct access to these processes. Verbal and behavioral expressions can be affected by conditions such as sensory limitations, learning disorders, illiteracy, pain or other distractions, language limitations, or even dental problems.[1]

The numbered sections below cover areas of mental functioning in rough order of increasing complexity and demand on the client's cognitive abilities. For each subsection that asks about a specific cognitive function, such as memory, similarities, or social judgment, a cross-reference is included to the appropriate section of Chapter 11, "Cognition and Mental Status." There you will find the terms for describing the cognitive function.

2.2. Background Information Related to Mental Status

See also Chapter 6, "Background Information and History."

✓ **Note:** If the client is incapable of providing this information, a family member or other informant should be sought and identified in your report.

"How far did you go in school/How many grades did you finish in school/Did you finish high school?"
"In school, were you ever left behind a year/not promoted to the next grade/did you have to take a grade over again?"
"Were you ever in any kind of special classes/special education/classes for students with learning disabilities/mental retardation/social and emotional disturbances or disabilities?"

2.3. Rancho Los Amigos Cognitive Scale

This scale can be used to assess the level of function in carrying out purposeful behavior. Adapted from Hagen, Malkmus, and Durham (1979). Used by permission. See also the Rancho Los Amigos Scale on Levels of Coma (copyright 1997; see *www.waiting.com/rancholosamigos.html*; a more detailed version can be found at *www.northeastcenter.com/rancho_los_amigos_revised.htm*).

Level I	No response to pain, touch, sound, or sight.
Level II	Generalized reflex response to pain.
Level III	Localized response. Blinks to strong light, turns toward/away from sound. Responds to physical discomfort. Inconsistent response to commands.
Level IV	Confused–agitated. Alert, very active, aggressive, or bizarre behaviors. Performs motor activities, but behavior is nonpurposeful. Extremely short attention span.

---

[1]Thanks to Joe Elwart, PsyD, of Royal Oak, MI.

Level V   Confused–nonagitated. Gross attention to environment. Highly distractible; requires continual redirection. Difficulty learning new tasks. Agitated by too much stimulation. May engage in social conversation, but with inappropriate verbalizations.

Level VI   Confused–appropriate. Inconsistent orientation to time and place. Retention span/recent memory impaired. Begins to recall past. Consistently follows simple directions. Goal-directed behavior with assistance.

Level VII   Automatic–appropriate. Performs daily routine in highly familiar environment in a nonconfused but mechanical, robot-like manner. Skills noticeably deteriorate in unfamiliar environment. Lacks realistic planning for own future.

Level VIII   Purposeful–appropriate.

2.4. Glasgow Coma Scale

This scale can be used for more precise numerical rating of core mental functioning, particularly after brain trauma. It is for an older child (age 4 and up) or adult and is adapted from Teasdale and Jenvet (1974). It is used by permission. The GCS can also be found online (*www.northeastcenter.com/glasgow_coma_scale.htm*), as can a version for infants and younger children (*www.northeastcenter.com/modified-glasgow-coma-scale-for-infants-and-children.htm*).

Eyes:	Open:	Spontaneously	4
		To verbal command	3
		To pain	2
		No response	1
Best motor response:	To verbal command:	Obeys	6
	To painful stimulus:	Localizes pain	5
		Flexion–withdrawal	4
		Flexion–abnormal	3
		Extension	2
		No response	1
Best verbal response:	Oriented and converses		5
	Disoriented and converses		4
	Inappropriate words		3
	Incomprehensible sounds		2
	No response		1

Total (3–15): _____

✓ Generally, ratings of 12 or above indicate mild injuries, and ratings of 8 or less indicate severe injuries.

2.5. Orientation

See Section 11.15, "Orientation," for descriptors.

To assess and document disorientation and confusion after Traumatic Brain Injury more formally, the Galveston Orientation and Amnesia Test (available at *www.utmb.edu/psychology/adultre-*

hab/goat.htm) has been widely used. However, for those whose difficulties have other causes, the 10-item <u>O</u>rientation <u>Log</u> may be more appropriate (see *tbims.org/combi/olog*).

To Person

"Who are you?"
"What is your name?" [Pay attention to nicknames, childhood versions of name, hesitations, aliases.]
"Are you married?"
"What kind of work do/did you do?"

For a Child:

"What school do you go to?"
"What grade are you in now?"
"What is the name of your teacher?"

To Place

"Where are we/you?" (Setting, address/building, city, state/province.)
"Where do you live?" (Setting, address/building, city, state/province.)
"How far is this place from where you live?"

To Time

Observe whether the client wears a watch and, if so, whether the time indicated is correct and the client can read the time correctly. If the client wears no watch and indicates not knowing the time, ask for a guess or an approximation.

"What time is it? Is that A.M. or P.M.? Is it day or night?"
"How old are you?" "When is your birthday?"
"What day is today? Which day of the week is today? What month is it now? What is today's date?"
"What season is it? What year is it?"
"When did you first come here? How long have you been here? Have you ever been here before?" *(If yes:)* "How long were you here then?"

To Situation

"Who am I?"
"What am I doing here?"
"What is the purpose of our talking?"
"Why are you here?"

To Familiar Objects

Hold up your hand and ask, "Is this my right or left hand?" "Please name the fingers of my hand."
Hold up/point to a pencil, a watch, and eyeglasses, and ask the client to name each object, its uses, and its parts.

To Other People

"What is your mother's/father's/spouse's name?"
"What is your child's name/are your children's names?"

"What is my name?"
"What is my title/job?"
"When was the last time we met?"
"What are the names of some staff members?" [Ask about their titles, functions, etc., as well.]
"What are the names of some other persons here/patients?"

2.6. Attention (↔ *by degree*)

See Section 11.3, "Attention," for descriptors. For attention span questions, see Sections 2.7, "Concentration," and 2.10, "Memory."

The questions and tasks below, arranged in order of increasing difficulty, cover active information processing about a single or particular stimulus with filtering out of irrelevant stimuli.

"Please say the alphabet as fast as possible." (Note the time taken; normal speed is 3–10 seconds.)
"Spell 'earth'/'house.'" "And now please spell it backward."
"Repeat your Social Security number backward, please." [You may need to clarify this by adding "One number at a time, from the end." Note time needed and accuracy.]
"Tap a pencil on the table each and every time I say the letter C." (Present a series of random letters at the rate of about one each second, with the letter C randomly distributed but occurring about every three to eight letters.) [Normal performance is making one or two errors (not noticing a C) in 45 seconds/45 letters.]
Digit span, forward and reverse: In other words, ask client to listen to, repeat, then repeat in reverse an arbitrary series of single digits you say first. *(See Section 2.10, "Memory.")*
Name three objects and have the client repeat them. Record the trials until the client is able to repeat all of them accurately. [This can also be used for delayed recall.] *(See Section 2.10.)*
"Count and then tell me the number of taps I have made." (Tap the underside of the table, or in some other manner make several trials of 3–15 sounds out of the client's sight.)

2.7. Concentration (↔ *by degree*)

See Section 11.4, "Concentration/Task Persistence," for descriptors.

The questions and tasks here cover the maintenance of/holding of attention, or the performance of linked mental acts that require the excluding of irrelevant stimuli.

"Please spell your last name." "Now please spell it backward."
"Name the days of the week backward, starting with Sunday."
"Please name the months of the year." "Now please say them backward."
"Say the alphabet backward as fast as you can."
Ask the client to write a fairly long and complex sentence from your dictation.
Ask the client to tell you when a minute has passed while you talk/don't talk to him/her, and record the time taken.
Ask the client to point to/underline each A in a written list presented on a full page of letters: for example, B, F, H, K, A, X, E, P, A, etc.
Have the client do mental arithmetic problems. *(See Section 2.16, "Calculation Abilities," for examples—including the famous "serial sevens.")*

2.8. Comprehension of Language

Receptive

Receptive language abilities can be assessed by the responses to simple questions such as "Is my aunt's brother a man or a woman?" or "The lion killed the tiger. Which one is dead?" Next in complexity are the client's responses to a series of commands such as these:

> "Close your eyes. Open them. Raise an arm. Raise your left arm."
> "Show me how you brush your teeth/comb your hair."
> "Put your right hand on your left knee three times, and then touch your left ear with your right hand."
> "If today is Tuesday, raise one arm; otherwise, raise both."
>
> (A three-stage command:) "Pick up that paper, fold it in half, and put it on the floor."
>
> "Please read and obey this sentence." (Presented on a card: "Close your eyes for 5 seconds.")

Fluency

> "Please tell me as many words as you can think of that begin with the letter F. Don't give me names/proper nouns or repeat yourself, and keep going until I stop you." (Stop the client after 30 seconds, and perhaps repeat with the letters A, P, or S. Score is the total number of words meeting the criteria on each trial.)

Expressive

> Ask the client to read and explain some sentences from a magazine or newspaper.
> Show her/him a photograph (e.g., in a magazine) and ask for the name(s) of the item(s) depicted.
> Ask her/him to describe a picture that portrays several actions.

2.9. Eye–Hand Coordination/Perceptual–Motor Integration/ Dyspraxia/Constructional Ability

> Ask the client to:
> Pick up a dime with each hand from the tabletop.
> Spin a paper clip on the tabletop, using each hand.
> Touch each thumb to each finger as you name them (not in order).
>
> Ask the client to:
> Copy a design of two overlapping pentagons from an illustration on a card.
> Draw a house/a tree/a person/a person of the opposite sex/yourself. [These are known as the House–Tree–Person and Human Figure Drawing tests.]
>
> Ask the client to draw, from your dictation:
> a diamond   the outlines of a cross
> a smoking pipe   the edges of a transparent cube
>
> Ask the client to draw a clock face and then indicate the present time as he/she estimates it to be, or "twenty after six." [This is known as the Clock Test. See Juby, 1999; Heinik & Shaikewitz, 2009.]

2.10. Memory

See Section 11.12, "Memory," for descriptors.

If possible, it is probably best to use the <u>W</u>echsler <u>M</u>emory <u>S</u>cale–<u>IV</u> (Wechsler, 2009) or a similar validated test for accurate and precise evaluation.

Introductory Questions

"Has your memory been good?"
"Have you had any difficulty concentrating or remembering what you read/watch on television/ recipes/telephone numbers/appointment times?"
"Have you recently gotten lost/forgotten an important event/forgotten something you were cooking/left some appliance on too long?"
"Have you had any difficulty recalling people's names or where you know them from?"
"Have other people said to you that your memory is not as good as it was?"

Immediate Memory/Memory Span

Immediate memory covers a period of about 10–30 seconds in the experimental laboratory, or what was just said, done, or learned during the evaluation in the clinic.

"Digit span," both forward and reverse, is a common but complex task requiring perhaps more concentration than immediate memory.[2] Begin by telling the client:

"I am going to say some numbers one at a time. When I finish, please repeat them back to me. Ready?"

Start with two digits ("1, 7," not "17, 36," etc.). When the client repeats these correctly on a first or second attempt (with different digits), increase the length of the list by one digit until the client fails both trials/number sequences offered. Write the numbers down as you say them.

✓ Speak at a consistent rate of one digit per second; do not emphasize ending numbers with changes in your voice; and avoid consecutive numbers and easily recognizable dates or familiar sequences, or use your own Social Security number or telephone number.

Then say:

"Now I am going to say some more numbers, but this time I want you to repeat them backward. For example, if I said '6, 2,' what would you say?"

✓ The score is the maximum number of correctly recalled digits in correct order on either trial. "Five forward with one mistake" is four forward.

✓ Education (but not age) affects digit span, so be careful with interpretations. Normal digit span in adults is five to eight digits forward and four to six backward. A difference of three or more between forward and backward may reflect concentration deficits. Norms are available in the manuals for the Wechsler tests (Wechsler, 2003, 2008, 2009).

Short-Term Retention

Short-term retention covers a period from a few minutes up to 1–2 hours.

Name *(for auditory retention)* or point to *(for visual retention)* three related items (e.g., Broadway–New York City–taxi; book–pen–tablet; scissors–stapler–pad, apple–peach–pear). Tell the client that you will ask him/her about them later, and then ask for recall after 5 minutes

---

[2]I am grateful to James L. Pointer, PhD, of Montgomery, AL, for this clarification.

of interspersed activities. The score is the number recalled out of three without and then with prompting.

Offer four items from four categories (e.g., house, table, pencil, dictionary) and record the number of trials taken to learn the list. Ask for recall in 5 and 10 minutes. If the items are not recalled, prompt with category descriptions (e.g., a building, a piece of furniture, a writing tool, a kind of book). If they are still not recalled, ask the client to select the words from a list of four similar items (e.g., for pencil offer pen, crayon, pencil, paintbrush).

Give the client three colors or shapes to remember, and ask her/him to recall them in 5 minutes.

Tell the client your name and ask him/her to remember it because you will ask for it later. Ask in 5–10 minutes. If it is not correctly recalled, reinform and teach; then ask again every 5 or 10 minutes more, and note the number of trials to mastery or your abandoning the test.

Ask the client to read a narrative paragraph from a magazine or newspaper, and to produce the gist of the story upon completion without being able to refer to the source.

Ask about events at the beginning of the interview. (For example, were any other people present? What was asked first and next? Which history items were sought?)

Recent Memory

Recent memory covers a period from a few hours up to 1–4 days, and also today's events.

Ask about yesterday's meals/television programs/activities/companions (but only if these can be verified).

Ask about the route taken/distance to this office, your name (if not overused in the interview), events in the recent news.

Ask, "What clothes did you wear yesterday?"

Recent Past Memory

Recent past memory refers to the last few weeks and months. Ask the following questions only if the answers can be verified:

"What did you do last weekend?"
"Where and when did you take your last vacation?"
"What presents did you get on your last birthday/Christmas?"
"What were you doing on the most recent national holiday (July 4th, Labor Day, Christmas)?"
"Name any other doctors you have seen/any hospitalizations/tests received, when the present illness began/you first felt troubled/ill."

Remote Memory

Remote memory extends from approximately 6 months ago up to all of the client's lifetime, including the premorbid period (before symptom onset). Ask about the following:

Childhood events (in their correct sequence), places lived, schools attended, names of friends.
"Where were you born?"
"What is your birth date?"
"Your first memory?"
"What was the name of your elementary/grade/high school?"
"Please tell me the names of some of your friends in school."

Life history: parents' full names, siblings' names and birth order, family deaths, first job, date(s) of marriage, names/birth dates/ages of children.

More difficult alternatives: siblings' birthdays, dates of hospitalizations, names of doctors, school teachers' names, "How you dressed up for Halloween."

Activities on holidays about a year ago or on other dates that stand out.
Local historical events.
Historical events: Attack on Pearl Harbor (Dec. 7, 1941); Sputnik (1957); first men on the moon
(July 20, 1969); name of the U.S. president who resigned (Nixon, Aug. 9, 1974); U.S. presi-
dents during wars (WW II—F. D. Roosevelt; Korean War—Truman, Eisenhower; Vietnam—
Johnson, Nixon; Iraq and Afghanistan—G. W. Bush, Obama); *Challenger* disaster (Jan. 28,
1986); collapse of Berlin Wall (Nov. 9, 1989); Oklahoma City bombing (Apr. 19, 1995); World
Trade Center/Pentagon attacks (Sept. 11, 2001); etc.

2.11. Fund of Information

See Section 11.8, "Information," for descriptors.

Basic Orientation Information

"What is your birth date? Social Security number?"
"What is your phone number? Area code?"
"What is your address? Zip code?"
"What is your height? Weight? Shoe size? Dress/suit size?"

"Tell me the time." "What time will it be in an hour and a quarter?"
"How long will it be until Christmas?"
"How many days are there in a month/year?"
"Name the days of the week/months of the year."

"Where are we?" [Ask for state, county, city, hospital/building, floor, office.]
"Name the local sports teams."
"What is the capital of this state?"
"Which states border this one?"
"Name the five largest U.S. cities."
"How far is it from here to _____ (one of the large cities named above)?"
"How far is it from New York City to San Francisco?"
"In which country is Rome/Paris/London/Moscow?"
"Name three countries in the Middle East/Europe/South America."
"What is the current population of this city/state/the United States (about 308 million in 2010),
the world (about 6.8 billion in 2010)?"

Information about People

"Who is the current president? And before him? And before him? Name the presidents back-
ward, starting with the current one." (U.S. presidents since 1901 in reverse order: Obama,
G. W. Bush, Clinton, G. H. W. Bush, Reagan, Carter, Ford, Nixon, Johnson, Kennedy, Eisen-
hower, Truman, F. D. Roosevelt, Hoover, Coolidge, Harding, Wilson, Taft, T. Roosevelt.)
[**Note:** The failure to recall most of these is not pathognomonic.]
"Where does the president live?" (In the White House; Washington, D.C.)
"Who was the first president of the United States?"
"Who is the governor of this state/mayor of this city?"
"Who is . . . ?" [Name several present or past entertainers and/or sports figures that the cli-
ent would seem likely to know.]
"What was/is Booker T. Washington/Thomas Edison/Jonas Salk/Albert Einstein/Steve Jobs/Bill
Gates famous for?"
"Who invented the airplane?" (The Wright brothers, Wilbur and Orville.)
"What does a pharmacist do?"
"Who is/was John F. Kennedy/Martin Luther King, Jr./Fidel Castro?"

For a Child:

"Who is Mickey Mouse/Mr. Rogers/Big Bird/Ronald McDonald/Barney/Harry Potter/Sponge-Bob?"
"What are your teachers' names?"

The names in several of these questions can of course be varied depending on a client's age, gender, place of residence, and ethnicity, as well as on the current popularity or importance of various figures.

Information about Things

"Name five foods."
"Name five animals."
Ask about local geography: rivers, mountains, streets, downtown, parks, highways, stores, malls, schools.
"How many sides does a pentagon have?" (Five.)
"Name three animals beginning with C."
"Name three cities beginning with D."
"How many ounces in a pound?" (16.)
"What are houses made of?"
"Which is the longest river in the United States?" (The Mississippi.)
"In what direction does the sun set?" (The west.)
"Please identify these." [Show some coins and bills of common U.S. currency.]
"Who/whose face is on a penny/nickel/dime/dollar bill/five-dollar bill?" (Lincoln/Jefferson/F. D. Roosevelt/Washington/Lincoln.)
"At what temperature does water freeze?" (32 degrees Fahrenheit or 0 degrees Celsius.)
"From what do we get gasoline?" (Oil, crude oil.)

Information about Events

"What do we celebrate on the 4th of July/Christmas/Thanksgiving Day/Labor Day/Memorial Day/Easter/Passover/Ramadan/Kwanzaa?"
"Who won the last Super Bowl/World Series?"
"Please name some events/big stories that are currently in the news/that you have read about in the papers or seen on the TV news."
"What has happened recently in (specify a place)?"
"What did (person's name) do recently? What happened to (person's name) recently?"
"In about what years did the United States fight in World War II/Korea/Vietnam/the Persian Gulf/ Afghanistan/Iraq?" (1941–1945, 1950–1953, 1965–1975, 1990–1991, 2001–?, and 2003–?, respectively.) "Why did we fight that war?"
(For those over 75 years of age:) "What was the date of the attack on Pearl Harbor?" (Dec. 7, 1941.)
(For those over 55 years of age:) "What was the date President John F. Kennedy was assassinated?" (Nov. 22, 1963.)
What was the date of the attacks on the World Trade Center and the Pentagon? (Sept. 11, 2001.)

2.12. Opposites

"Please tell me the opposite of each of these words."
    Hard   fast   large   out   high   child

2.13. Differences

Use the format "What is the difference between a _____ and a _____?" or "In what ways are a _____ and a _____ different or not the same?"

lie–mistake	midget–child	kite–airplane
duck–pigeon	orange–baseball	water–land
boy–girl	hand–foot	tongue–nose

Ask: "Which of these is the different one and why?"

Desk, **apple**, chair, lamp. (Apple is not furniture, not artificial, is edible.)
Pottery, **statue**, painting, **poem**. (Poem is not tangible; statue does not begin with P, etc.)

2.14. Similarities/Analogies

Use the format "In what ways are a _____ and a _____ the same or similar?"

Pairs of words, grouped by difficulty, are listed below.

Easy *(because there is a commonly available word for an abstract commonality, but these still have concrete and functional levels)*

yellow–green	dollar–dime	apple–orange	scissors–saw
joy–anger	violin–piano	cat–lion	ship–airplane

Moderately Difficult *(because a word for an abstract commonality is not so easily available)*

truck/car–bus	bus–airplane	duck–chicken	elbow–knee
sun–moon	barn–house	socks–shoes	watch–clock

Difficult *(because the commonality is quite abstract and difficult to find)*

theater–church	wings–legs	work–play	prison–zoo
mountain–lake	telephone–radio	steam–fog	ruler–thermometer

✓ Question any vague responses until you obtain a clear estimate of the level of comprehension and abstraction involved. For example, "bus–airplane" can be interpreted on a spectrum of increasing abstraction: "Both have wheels/People ride in both/Both are means of transportation/Both are technological artifacts."

✓ In ambiguous cases, ask the client: **"Please tell me more about that."** If necessary, add: **"What type/ class of things do they belong to?"**

2.15. Absurdities

You can, of course, use Verbal Absurdities from the Stanford–Binet Intelligence Scales, Fifth Edition (Roid, 2003), or you might select from your experience examples tailored for the particular person being examined.

Ask the client: **"What is wrong with/is foolish/doesn't make sense about this?"**

"The doctor rushed into the emergency room, got out the bandages, and after eating a sandwich, bandaged the bleeding man."

"Bill's ears were so big he had to pull his sweaters on over his feet."
"An airplane pilot ran out of gas halfway across the ocean, so to be safe, he turned around, flew back, and landed where he took off."
"A man was in two auto accidents. The first accident killed him, but the second time he got well very quickly."

Only if you believe it useful, ask about absurdities/contradictions/paradoxes in everyday life:

"Please give me an example of 'Catch-22.'"
"Prevention is more effective than treatment, yet is underfunded."

2.16. Calculation Abilities

See Section 11.2, "Arithmetic," for descriptors.

The questions below require attention, concentration, memory, and education. On all math problems, make note of the actual answers given; the effort required/given; time needed; accuracy/changed performance when given a prompt, on the next correct answer in a sequence, or when given paper and pencil to perform the calculations; etc. Also note self-corrections, use of fingers to count upon, requests for paper and pencil, complaints, excuses, etc.

Basic Examples of Arithmetic Questions (↔ *by degree*)

"How much is 2 + 2? And 4 + 4? and 8 + 8?" [Continue in this sequence and note the limits of skill. More difficult versions are 3 + 3's and 7 + 7's.]
One-step: "3 + 4 = ?" "6 + 4 = ?"
Two-step: "7 + 5 − 3 = ?" "8 + 4 + 9 = ?" "4 + 6 + 3 = ?"
"Which is larger: ⅓ or ½?"

Verbally Presented Arithmetic Problems (↔ *by degree*)

"How many quarters are there in $1.75?" (7)
"If pens are priced at 2 for 18 cents, how much would half a dozen cost?" ($0.54)
"How much is left when you subtract $5.50 from $14.00?" ($8.50)
"How many nickels are there in a dollar?" (20)
"How many nickels are there in $1.95?" (39)

Serial Subtractions/"Serial Sevens"

See Section 11.4, "Concentration/Task Persistence," for descriptors.

"Starting with 100, subtract 7, and then subtract 7 from that, and continue subtracting 7."

✓ Normal performance is 1 minute or less in subtracting to 2 with two or fewer errors, not including spontaneous self-corrections. In reporting responses to this, it is clearer to the reader if you underline the errors, as in this set of responses: 93, 84, 77, 70, 62. Attend not only to accuracy but to speed and persistence.

Simpler Alternatives to "Serial Sevens"

Simpler alternatives to "serial sevens" include counting from 1 to 20 by twos, or counting to 39 by threes and subtracting "serial fives" from 100. More difficult are "serial fours" from 50, and "serial threes" from 31. For those for whom "serial sevens" is too easy, "serial thirteens" from 100 may be suitable.

2.17. Abstract Reasoning/Proverbs

See Section 11.17, "Reasoning/Abstract Thinking/Concept Formation," for descriptors.

Our interpretation of our clients' interpretation of proverbs should be circumspect and informed (see Gibbs & Beitel, 1995). The selection of which proverbs to offer depends on your initial assessment of the client's deficits and diagnosis. Some are more difficult to interpret satisfactorily, while others reveal coping strategies, the intensity of the cognitive dysfunction, or personalization.

Ask, "What do people mean when they say _____?", followed by a proverb such as the following:

"All that glitters is not gold"/"You can't judge a book by its cover." (Appearances can be deceiving.)

Make hay while the sun shines"/"Strike while the iron is hot." (Using an opportunity, taking initiative.)

"Don't cry over spilled milk." (Mature resignation and priorities.)

"The grass is always greener on the other side of the fence." (Optimism, pessimism, envy, regret, dissatisfaction.)

"Every cloud has a silver lining." (Optimism, hopefulness, trust, patience.)

"Rome wasn't built in a day"/"Great oaks from little acorns grow." (Patience, frustration tolerance, deferral/delay of gratification.)

"People who live in glass houses shouldn't throw stones." (Arrogance vs. tolerance, humility, guilt, impulse control.) (Or more casually: What goes around comes around.)

"Birds of a feather flock together"/"Like father, like son"/"The apple doesn't fall far from the tree." (The effects of history, genetics, or learning.)

"Don't count your chickens before they are hatched"/"A bird in the hand is worth two in the bush." (Caution, realistic hopes/plans.)

"The squeaking wheel gets the grease." (Excessive modesty vs. attention-seeking behavior, self-assertion.)

"When the cat's away, the mice will play." (Control and rebellion.)

"A rolling stone gathers no moss." (Either positive or negative interpretations of stones/moss/rolling.)

✓ An alternative is to ask, "**Do you have a favorite Bible story?**" If so, "**Tell me the story.**" Then ask, "**Why is it your favorite?**"

2.18. Paired Proverbs

These proverbs can be used to further evaluate the client's abstraction abilities. Present one on the left and then the paired one on the right. Ask the client, "What do people mean when they say ... " before each proverb.

✓ Note when and how the client recognizes the conflicts presented by the pairs. Does she/he fail to notice the conflicts; seem to notice but then ignore the conflict; make some joke; comment on human nature, proverbs in general, the examiner, or the examiner's questions; try to resolve the conflict at a higher level of abstraction; offer other conflicting proverbs?

"Don't change horses in midstream."	and	"If at first you don't succeed, try, try again."
"A bird in the hand is worth two in the bush."	and	"Nothing ventured, nothing gained."
"Look before you leap."	and	"He who hesitates is lost."
"Out of sight, out of mind."	and	"Absence makes the heart grow fonder."
"A stitch in time saves nine."	and	"Don't cross a bridge until you come to it."

"Haste makes waste." and "Strike while the iron is hot"/ "Make hay while the sun shines."

"Do unto others as you would have them do unto you." and "To each his own"/ "Different strokes for different folks."

2.19. Practical Reasoning

General Questions

"Why do we refrigerate many foods?"
"Why do we have newspapers?"
"Why should people make a will?"
"Who picked out the clothes you are wearing?"

Hazard Recognition (↔ *by degree*)

"What should you do before crossing the street?"

"Why shouldn't people smoke in bed?"
"What should you do when paper in a wastebasket catches fire?"
"What should you do if food catches on fire when you are cooking at the stove?"

"What should you do when you cut your finger?"
"What should you do if you smell gas in your house/come home to find that a broken pipe has flooded the kitchen?"

2.20. Social Judgment

See also Section 2.19, above; see Sections 11.13, 11.16, and 11.20 for descriptors.

The questions below require increasing social understanding (↔ *by degree*).

"What should you do if you lose/find a library book?"
"What should you do if you see a purse or a wallet on the sidewalk/in the street?"
"Why should people go to school?"
"What should you do if you are stopped by the police?"
"What would you do if you found that you had locked your keys in your car?"

"Why do we have to put stamps on letters we mail?"
"Why do people have to have license plates on their cars?"

"Please tell me of a situation/incident in which you made a bad/foolish/mistaken choice."
"Have you ever been taken advantage of/been a victim?"
"Have you ever made any bad loans?"

"What should you do if someone is very critical of a job you have done?"
"What would you do if someone threatened/tried to hurt you?"
"Please tell me the name of a close friend of yours/someone you would confide in/talk with if you had a personal problem/talk over a serious problem with."

"How would you spend $10,000 if it were given to you/if you won the lottery?"

"Who is or was the most important person in the world/history? Why?"
"What is the role of a free press in a democracy?"
"Why do we vote by secret ballot?"

"Why do people feel so strongly about the subject of abortion?"

"What do you think are the major differences between the Republican and Democratic parties?"

For a Child:

"If you could be any animal, which would you choose and why?"

"If you could have anything you wished for, what three things would you wish for?"

"If you could live anywhere in the world, where would you want to live?"

"What would you do if another student pushed/hit/teased you?"

"Do you think you have enough friends?"

"What would you do if someone you didn't know offered you a ride home from school/offered you a video game/wanted to show you a puppy or kitten?"[3]

"If you could change anything about yourself, what would you change?"

2.21. Decision Making

See Section 11.6, "Decision Making," for descriptors.

"Are you satisfied with the decisions you make?"

"Do you have a hard time coming to some decisions? Which are hardest? Why?"

"Do you decide too quickly or take too long to make a decision?"

"Have other people ever said you were indecisive/wishy-washy? Do you agree?"

2.22. Self-Image

For descriptors, see Section 9.3, "Self-Image/Self-Esteem."

"Which three words best describe you?"

"What are your strengths as a person?"

"How would you describe yourself?"

"What was the most important thing that ever happened in your life?"

"What would be written on your tombstone/in your obituary if you were to die today?"

"Has life been fair to you?"

"Please tell me about the turning points in your life."

2.23. Insight into Disorder

For descriptors of responses, see Section 11.9, "Insight."

"What kind of place is this? What goes on here?"

"Why are you here? What causes you to be here?"

"Why are you talking to me?"

"Do you think there is something wrong with you?" *(If so:)* "What? Do you think you are ill?"

"What do you think has caused your troubles/pain/confusion/being disabled/being hospitalized?"

"How well is your mind working?"

"What are your major problems?"

---

[3]Some of these questions are from Judy Bomze of Wynnewood, PA.

"What is your diagnosis?" "What does that mean?"
"Did you ever have a nervous breakdown/bad nerves/something wrong with your mind?"

"Do you think you need treatment?"
"Why did/do you need to take medicines?"

"What role or part do you think/believe you have played in this problem/your problems?"[4]
"What do you need to do to stay well."
"What are your suggestions for your treatment?"
"What changes would help you most?"

"How would you describe your childhood/family/earlier life?"

2.24. Strengths and Coping

This list is adapted from Tedeschi and Kilmer (2005).

Self-Efficacy

"How sure are you that things will work out for you when you have to try something new and challenging/someone counts on you to do something important/you're faced with a problem in an important relationship?"

Social Support

"How much can you count on your friends and family when you need them?"
"Do you have someone who really 'gets' you and understands how you feel?"
"Other than your family/folks, do you feel as though there are adults and people who care about you and will help you?"

Coping Strategies

"What do you tend to do when you're faced with a problem or stressful situation? How do you handle it?"
"What do you do when you are stressed?/When you are upset, what do you usually do?"
"What gets you through? What do you do then?"

2.25. Mental Status Evaluation Checklist

✓ In any evaluation of mental status, always consider variables that may be affecting the client's performance, such as current medications and illnesses, limitations of communication, and others. (*See Section 1.2, "Introducing Yourself and Noting Possible Communication Difficulties."*)

The checklist presented on the next two pages (Form 1) is adapted from my book *The Paper Office* (Zuckerman, 2008). The form is concise and helpful for recording the results of an MSE. You may photocopy and adapt it for your work with clients without obtaining written permission, but you may not use it for teaching, writing, or any commercial venture without such permission.

---

[4]This way to assess the client's degree of taking responsibility or blaming comes from Michael Newberry, MD, of Palm Bay, FL.

[Use the top of this page for your letterhead.]

Mental Status Evaluation Checklist

Directions: Rate current observed performance, not reported, historical, or projected. Circle the most appropriate descriptive terms in part C, and feel free to write in others. If an aspect of mental status was not assessed, cross out the heading. Write additional observations, clarifications, and quotations in part D.

Client: _____ Date: _____ Evaluator: _____

Highest grade completed _____ GED? _____ Special education for _____?

Primary occupation: _____ Other: _____

A. Informed consent was obtained about:

❑ The recipient(s) of this report   ❑ Confidentiality   ❑ Competency   ❑ HIPAA   ❑ Other: _____

B. Evaluation methods

1. The information and assessments below are based on my observation of this client during:

   ❑ Intake interview   ❑ Psychotherapy   ❑ Formal mental status testing   ❑ Group therapy

   ❑ Other: _____

2. We interacted for a total of _____ minutes.

3. Setting of the contact: ❑ Professional office   ❑ Hospital room   ❑ Clinic   ❑ School   ❑ Home   ❑ Work

   ❑ Jail/prison   ❑ Other: _____

C. Mental status descriptors (Circle all appropriate items)

1. **Appearance and self-care**

Stature	Average	Small	Tall	(For age, if a child)	
Weight	Average weight	Overweight	Obese	Underweight	# pounds: _____
Clothing	Neat/clean	Careless/inappropriate	Meticulous	Disheveled	Dirty
	Appropriate for age, occasion, weather		Seductive	Inappropriate	Bizarre
Grooming	Normal	Meticulous	Neglected	Bizarre	
Cosmetic use	Appropriate	Inappropriate for age	Excessive	None	
Posture/gait	Normal	Tense	Rigid	Stooped	Slumped	Bizarre	Other: _____
Motor activity	Not remarkable	Slowed	Repetitive	Restless	Agitated	Tremor

   Other notable aspects: _____

2. **Sensorium**

Attention	Normal	Unaware	Inattentive	Distractible	Vigilant
Concentration	Normal	Scattered	Variable	Preoccupied	Confused
	Anxiety interferes	Focuses on irrelevancies			
Orientation	×5	Time	Person	Place	Situation	Object
Recall/memory	Normal	Defective in: Immediate/short-term	Recent	Remote	
	Amnesia	Confabulation			

(cont.)

FORM 1. Mental Status Evaluation Checklist.   From Zuckerman (2008). Copyright 2008 by Edward L. Zuckerman. Adapted by permission in *Clinician's Thesaurus,* 7th ed., by Edward L. Zuckerman. Permission to photocopy this form is granted to purchasers of this book for personal use only (see copyright page for details).

3. **Relating**

Eye contact	Normal	Fleeting	Avoided	None	Staring	
Facial expression	Responsive	Constricted	Tense	Anxious	Sad	Depressed	Angry
Attitude toward examiner	Cooperative	Dependent	Dramatic	Passive	Uninterested	Silly

Resistant   Critical   Hostile   Sarcastic   Irritable   Threatening
Suspicious   Guarded   Defensive   Manipulative   Argumentative

4. **Affect and mood**

Affect   Appropriate   Labile   Restricted   Blunted   Flat   Other: _____

Mood   Euthymic   Irritable   Pessimistic   Depressed   Hypomanic   Euphoric   Other: ___

5. **Thought and language**

Speech flow   Normal   Mute   Loud   Blocked   Paucity   Pressured   Flight of ideas

Thought content   Congruent mood and circumstances   Incongruent   Personalizations
Persecutions   Indecisions   Suspicions   Delusions   Ideas of reference
Ideas of influence   Illusions

Preoccupations   Phobias   Somatic   Suicide   Homicidal   Guilt   Religion   Other: _____

Hallucinations   Auditory   Visual   Other: _____   Content: _____

Organization   Normal   Logical   Goal-directed   Circumstantial   Loose   Perseverations

6. **Executive functions**

Fund of knowledge   Average   Above average   Impoverished by: _____

Intelligence   Average   Below average   Above average   Needs investigation

Abstraction   Normal   Concrete   Functional   Popular   Abstract   Overly abstract

Judgment   Normal   Common-sensical   Fair   Poor   Dangerous

Reality testing   Realistic   Adequate   Distorted   Variable   Unaware

Insight   Uses connections   Gaps   Flashes of   Unaware   Nil   Denial

Decision making   Normal   Only simple   Impulsive   Vacillates   Confused   Paralyzed

7. **Stress**

Stressors   Money   Housing   Family conflict   Work   Grief/losses   Illness   Transitions

Coping ability   Normal   Resilient   Exhausted   Overwhelmed   Deficient supports
Deficient skills   Growing

Skill deficits   None   Education   Communication   Interpersonal   Decision making
Self-control   Responsibility   Self-care   Activities of daily living

Supports   Usual   Family   Friends   Church   Service system   Other: _____
Needed: _____

8. **Social functioning**

Social maturity   Responsible   Irresponsible   Self-centered   Impulsive   Isolates

Social judgment   Normal   "Street-smart"   Naive   Heedless   Victimized   Impropriety

D. Other aspects of mental status

_____
_____
_____

This is a strictly confidential patient medical record. Redisclosure or transfer is expressly prohibited by law.

This report reflects the patient's condition at the time of consultation or evaluation. It does not necessarily reflect the patient's diagnosis or condition at any subsequent time.

3

Questions about Signs, Symptoms, and Other Behavior Patterns

Questions here do not address **cognitive functioning** or **mental status**; those are covered in Chapter 2, "Mental Status Evaluation Questions/Tasks." For interviewing and evaluating **couples or families,** see Chapter 16, "Couple and Family Relationships."

3.1. Introduction to the Questions about Signs, Symptoms, and Behavior Patterns

The questions in this chapter address two kinds of phenomena: (1) signs and symptoms (such as anxiety, hallucinations, and mania) and the disorders with which they are associated; and (2) behaviors that are considered the province of the clinician but are not psychopathological (such as gay and lesbian identity formation, affects, and compliance with treatment).

These questions are generally open-ended and address the issues from several directions. This allows you to ask a second or third question about the same phenomenon, to get a fuller sense of it or allow the client to offer more information.

Some of the phenomena covered in this chapter are of great clinical importance, but formulating nonleading or nontransparent questions about them is most difficult. Examples of these include dissociative experiences, delusions, and sexual identity; this chapter provides questions that will make it far easier for you to address such topics. The chapter also includes full sets of questions for taking a sexual history and for assessing substance use of all kinds. Finally, most of the symptom sections here are cross-referenced to sections in Chapter 10, "Emotional/Affective Symptoms and Disorders," or Chapter 12, "Abnormal Signs, Symptoms, and Syndromes." In those chapters you will find the terms for describing your findings.

If you are engaged in screening persons for the presence of psychopathology, an efficient strategy is first to use a symptom checklist and then use an interview to follow up on what the screening checklist has found. There are hundreds of well-validated checklists for any kind of symptomatic behavior, and they are time- and effort-efficient. Expensive interview time should be reserved for in-depth evaluations of the severity, impact, development, dynamics, and duration of the psychopathology. As an interviewer, you might also use the referral question or historical records to select which topics to address with a client.

The questions about nonsexual and sexual abuse, substance use and abuse, suicide, and impulse control/violence are considered essential to the assessment of risk; ask them of *every* client you interview.

3.2. Abuse (Nonsexual)/Neglect of Spouse/Elder

See also Sections 3.17, "Impulse Control," and 3.31, "Violence." See Sections 12.1, "Abuse," and 12.5, "Battered-Woman Syndrome," for descriptors. For nonsexual abuse/neglect of a child, see Section 3.3, just below.

✓ It is a good idea to have a list of shelters and support programs ready, should you find evidence of abuse.

Opening Questions

Inquire of all patients about physical and sexual abuse, threats, fights, arguments.

> "How are things at home?"
> "Are you alone at home a lot?"
> "Are you afraid of anyone at home?"

✓ Neglect/abuse may show as weight loss, dehydration, withdrawal, etc.

Battering by Partner

These questions are based on similar questions by NiCarthy and Davidson (1989).

> "Has your partner ever[1] hit, punched, slapped, kicked, pushed, or bitten you/your children/ anyone else at home?"
> "Have you had bruises from being hit, held, or squeezed?"
> "Have you ever had to stay in bed or been too weak to work after being hurt?"
> "Have you ever seen a doctor because of injuries from your partner?"

Emotional/Psychological/Financial Abuse

> "Has your partner ...
>> 'tracked' all of your time?"
>> controlled all the money in the household and forced you to account for everything you spent?"
>> repeatedly accused you of being unfaithful when you weren't?"
>> bragged to you about his/her affairs with others?"
>>
>> interfered with your relationships with family and friends?"
>> prevented you from working or attending school?"
>> humiliated you, called you names, or made painful fun of you in front of others?"
>>
>> gotten very angry or frightened you when drinking or using drugs?"
>> threatened to hurt you or the children?"
>> threatened to use a weapon against you or the children?"
>> repeatedly threatened to leave you?"
>> punished the children or pets when he/she was angry at you?"
>> destroyed personal property or sentimental items?"
>> forced you to have sex against your will?"

---

[1]You can use "ever" for emphasis or to reduce denial.

A simple mnemonic for domestic abuse questions is Sherin et al.'s (1998): HITS: <u>H</u>urt? <u>I</u>nsulted? <u>T</u>hreatened with harm? <u>S</u>creamed at?

3.3. Abuse (Nonsexual)/Neglect of Child

See also Section 3.2, above, and Section 3.4, "Abuse (Sexual) of Child or Adult," below. For DSM-IV-TR/ICD-9-CM diagnoses, see V codes in Section 21.21.

✓ You must know your local legal definition of abuse and the threshold criteria for your legal responsibility to report abuse and to whom. Also, since a confession cannot be unsaid, you must advise a client of this before exploring any situations in which abuse may have occurred. If you have suspicions about injuries or risks, obtain experienced psychological, medical, and legal consultation immediately. You can usually call your local child protection agency on its hotline and discuss a case, using "hypotheticals" to help clarify your understanding, obligations, and options without breaking confidentiality. For more, see Section 3.9, "The Duty to Protect (and Warn)," in *The Paper Office* (Zuckerman, 2008).

Opening Questions[2] for a Child

"Are you a happy kid or not so happy?"
"How do you get along with your father/mother/caregiver?"
"Are your parents strict?"
"What happens when you get into trouble?"
"Are you afraid of anyone at home?"
"Do you have problems with a teacher/babysitter/minister/coach?"

3.4. Abuse (Sexual) of Child or Adult

See also Sections 3.2 and 3.3, above.

The relevant DSM-IV-TR and ICD-9-CM codes are complex. *(See Section 21.21, "V Codes, Etc.")*

✓ This is a specialty area; if you are not experienced and trained, get consultations or refer clients before going very far into the topic, in order to avoid contaminating the memories or interpretations. The note under Section 3.3 also applies here.

Initial Inquiry

✓ Sometimes, in the right context, a gentle inquiry like "What has happened to you?" will open the door to these issues. This is preferable to "What is your problem?", as sexual abuse may not be seen as a "problem."[3]

For a Child:

"What do you call your private parts? What do you call the other sex's private parts?"
"Who has touched your private parts?" [**Note:** Do not add "when you didn't want them to," as that may not have been true or may as yet be unrecognized.]
"How did that make you feel?"
"Whom did you tell? What did they do about it?"
Ask other "who, when, where, why" questions.

---

[2]This stepwise approach and wording are suggested by Nora F. Young of Sedro Wolley, WA.

[3]This sensitive approach is recommended by Nora F. Young of Sedro Wolley, WA.

For an Adult:

"Have you ever been forced into sexual acts as a child or adult?"
"Has any partner ever insisted on sex when you didn't want to?"
"Was your first experience with sex by choice, or were you forced?"

Sexual Victimization

"Did anyone ever touch you sexually when you didn't want them to?"
"Have you ever had a sexual experience with anyone who was also a relative of yours?"
"Have you ever been forced to have any kind of sex with anyone?" *(If so:)*
    "What happened? With whom?"
    "Where? When?"
    "How many times did it happen?"
    "Whom did you tell?" *(If no one:)* "Why not?"
    "What did you do about this?"
    "How did this affect you, etc.?"

Consider your legal and professional obligations under mandated reporting and duty to protect.

Sexual Offenses

"Have you ever forced anyone to have any kind of sex with you?"
"What happened? With whom? Where? When?" *(Continue with the questions under "Sexual Victimization," above.)*
"Have you had any kind of sex with anyone who was under 18 years of age?"

Activities of Daily Living   *See Chapter 14 for descriptors from which you can fashion questions shaped to the goal of the evaluation.*

3.5. Affect/Mood
    See Sections 10.3, "Anxiety/Fear," and 10.7, "Depression," for descriptors.

"How would you describe your mood today?"
"Are you happy, sad, or what right now?"
"Using a scale where plus 10 is as happy as you have ever been, 1 is not depressed at all, and minus 10 is as depressed as you have ever been, please rate your mood today." [Less educated persons may need a scale from 0 to 10.]

"What is your usual mood like?" *(If negative, ask:)* "When was it last good?"
"When are/were you happiest?"

"In the last month, how many times have you cried/yelled/been afraid?"
"How long does it take you to get over a bad mood/upset?"

"What was your mood like during your childhood/adolescence/earlier life?"
"Were there ever times when you couldn't control your feelings?"
"When do you swear? What do you swear at? What do you say?"

Alcohol Use/Abuse   *See Section 3.28, "Substance Abuse: Drugs and Alcohol."*

Anger   *See Sections 3.17, "Impulse Control," and 3.31, "Violence," for questions, and Section 10.2, "Anger," for descriptors.*

Anorexia Nervosa   *See Section 3.13, "Eating Disorders."*

3.6. Anxiety

See Section 10.3, "Anxiety/Fear," for descriptors; see Section 29.2, "Anxiety," for possible medical causes. For social anxiety/social phobia, see Section 3.23, "Phobias."

"Is there something you are very concerned about/afraid of happening?"
"What do you worry about?"
"How does the future look to you?"

"When you get frightened, what happens to you?"
"Do you ever have times of great fear or anxiety/panic attacks?" [If so, inquire about cues/triggers, frequency, duration, whether observed by others, specific physiological symptoms, the sequence of the symptoms, etc.]

"Are there any distressing memories that keep coming back to you?"
"Is there any situation you avoid because it really upsets/scares you?"

3.7. <u>B</u>ody <u>D</u>ysmorphic <u>D</u>isorder

See Section 12.6, "<u>B</u>ody <u>D</u>ysmorphic <u>D</u>isorder," for descriptors.

"Are you unhappy with the way you look?" (*If yes:*) "What are you concerned about?"
"Is there some part of your body that you consider quite unattractive, ugly, or deformed?"
"When you think about your appearance, do you become depressed? Anxious?"
"When you tell others about this defect, do they tell you there is nothing wrong?"
"How much time each day do you spend checking in a mirror, touching the area/picking at the defect, seeking reassurance from others, camouflaging the defect, or exercising/dieting/tanning/weightlifting?"
"How much does thinking about this defect interfere with your concentration, schooling/work, or daily activities such as shopping?"
"Do you avoid some relationships because of this defect?"
"Have you spoken to a dermatologist/plastic surgeon/dentist/other professional to correct something about your appearance?"
"Have you had surgery or treatment for this defect without any relief?"

Because of embarrassment, such symptoms will not often be reported without inquiry, so ask about BDD when the presentation includes referential thinking, social anxiety, depression/suicidal ideation, being housebound, and/or a history of unnecessary surgery or dermatological treatment.

Bulimia Nervosa   *See Section 3.13, "Eating Disorders."*

Child Behavior Disorders   *See Chapter 6, "Background Information and History," and Sections 5.2–5.4 (covering typical problems of children).*

3.8. Compliance–Noncompliance with Treatment

The relevant DSM-IV-TR and ICD-9-CM code is V15.81, Noncompliance With Treatment (DSM) or Noncompliance with medical treatment (ICD).

"What medications do you take every day? What medications should you be taking?"
"What problems have you had in getting treatment/finding an understanding doctor/taking the medicine as it was prescribed/keeping scheduled medical appointments?"
"Have you ever stopped taking medications prescribed for you before they ran out/because of some reason?" *(If so:)* "What was the reason?"
"Is there anything that makes you reluctant to take medications/get the treatments prescribed for you?"

3.9. Compulsions

See also Section 3.19, "Obsessions"; see Section 12.8, "Compulsions," for descriptors.

The questions below are based in part on similar questions by Goodman et al. (1989).

Initial Inquiries

"Are you a person who is especially careful about safety?"
"Is there anything in your house/at work that you have to check on frequently?"
"Do you ever have to do the same thing over and over, or in a certain way?"
"Do you have any habits/frequent actions/behaviors that you must/feel compelled to do in a particular way or very often?"
"Are there some things you must do in order to fall asleep/to get ready to go out?"

Cleaning/Contamination

"Are there any actions you have to do before or while you eat/go to the bathroom?"
"Do you have to be very careful about dirt/germs/disease?"
"How many times a day do you wash your hands?"
"Do you find that you need to change your clothing more than once a day?"

Checking/Doubting

"Do you find yourself checking and rechecking locks/doors/windows/lights/appliances?"
"Do you need to go back repeatedly to see that everyone is OK and you did not accidentally harm anyone?"
"Do you have to recheck to make certain you did not make a mistake?"
"Do you have to tap or touch anything several times?"

Hoarding/Collecting

"Do you find that you have a lot of items that you don't need but just can't discard?"

Arranging/Organizing

"Do you feel you have to arrange your clothes or personal items in a certain way, or you will feel very nervous?"
"Do you get upset when anything is not very tidy/disorganized/out of place/unsymmetrical/out of order?"

Repeating/Counting

"Are there any words or phrases you feel you have to say in a certain way or at certain times?"
"Do you find you have to count any items over and over?"
"Do you rewrite even simple lists over and over?"
"Do you find that the reassurances of others don't help you relax?"

Client Awareness of Excess/Irrationality

"Do you feel uncomfortable until these actions are done, even though you may know that they are unimportant/unnecessary/ineffective?"

"Do these actions seem reasonable to you or more than you should be doing? Do you spend more time on these than you would like to?"

"How does doing these things affect your life/routines/job/relationships/family members?"

"How much control do you feel you have over these actions? Do you resist them or yield to them?"

Conduct Disorder in Children   *See Sections 5.2–5.4 (covering typical problems of children). See Section 12.9, "Conduct Disorder," for descriptors.*

3.10. Delusions

See also Section 3.22, "Paranoia"; see Section 12.10, "Delusions," for descriptors.

Mind Control

"Did anyone ever try to read your mind/use unusual means to force thoughts into your mind/ try to take some of your thoughts away/stop or block your thoughts?"

Grandeur/Special Abilities

✓ Note the person's reports of a large number of cars or other possessions, exaggerated abilities, titles/degrees/education/high positions, dramatic or unlikely consumption of alcohol or drugs, or history of unlikely or criminal activities.

"What is unusual about you?"

"Are you an especially gifted person?"

"Do you have great wealth/unusual strengths/special powers/impressive sexual qualities?"

"Are you able to influence others/read people's minds/put thoughts into their minds?"

"Have you ever received personal messages from heaven/God/someone unusual?"

"Have you been in communication with aliens/dead people/God/Christ/the Devil/the Blessed Virgin/any Biblical persons?"

"Do you think you are immortal/cannot be harmed/hurt/killed?"

Imposter

"Are you a fake?" [Separate a delusion from beliefs of inadequacy based on low self-esteem— the "imposter phenomenon."]

"Do you think people recognize who you really are?"

"Are you concerned about being discovered/identified/exposed?"

"What is your real rank?"

Monomania

Is this person preoccupied with certain ideas, themes, events, or persons? Does all his/her conversation return to a single overvalued topic/false idea?

Nihilism

"Do you think everything is lost/hopeless/pointless?"

"Do you think that tomorrow will never come? Do you think that time has stopped?"

"Do you think that things outside no longer exist?"
"Do you suspect that nothing is real?"
"Do you still have all the parts of your body?"

Persecution   *See Section 3.22, "Paranoia."*

Reference

"Do people do things/do things happen that only you really understand/have special meanings for you/are designed to convey or tell you something no one else is to know?"
"Are things on the TV/the radio/in the papers especially meaningful to you/contain special messages just for you?"
"Have you ever been forewarned/known that something would happen before it did?"

Somatic/Hypochondriacal

"How is your health? How often are you ill? How often do you see a physician? Do you have many illnesses/medical or health problems?"
"Do you have a lot of pain or unusual pains?"
"Which medicines do you take regularly? Which medicines/herbals/supplements do you take regularly that don't need a prescription?"

"Is there some illness you are worried about getting, or some illness you already have, that concerns you?"
"How often do you think about it?"
"How does it make you feel when you think about it?"
"What do you do about it?"
"Do you think you might/do have some serious disease that hasn't been diagnosed correctly?"
"Do you think you have a serious disease, but haven't been able to find a doctor to treat it?"

Self-Deprecation   *See Sections 3.11, "Depression," and 10.7, "Depression."*

Depersonalization and Derealization   *See Section 3.12, below.*

3.11. Depression

See Section 10.7, "Depression," for descriptors; see Section 29.4, "Depression," for possible medical causes.

Screening Questions

"In the past 2 weeks, how often have you ...
    felt blue or down in the dumps?"
    felt slowed down or had lower energy?"
    blamed yourself too much or felt worthless?"
    eaten more than usual or less than your usual amount?"
    not been able to get to sleep or stay asleep?"
    had trouble concentrating or making decisions?"
    felt very pessimistic or hopeless about the future?"

Somatic/Vegetative Symptoms

"Has your health changed recently?"

"Has your appetite or eating habits or your interest in food changed recently?"

"How is your sleep?" *(If a client replies with anything but "Fine" or "No problem" ask:)* "**On how many nights in a week do you have trouble with sleep?**" *(See Section 3.27, "Sleep," for more questions.)*

"Have your bowel or bladder habits changed?"

"Has your interest in sex changed?" [Libido is desire, not performance.]

Affective Symptoms

"How are your spirits generally?"

"When was the last time you felt really down?"

"Do you ever get pretty discouraged/depressed/blue? Are you blue/feeling low now?"

"When you get sad or down, how long does it last?"

"Have you had a time when you felt very tired or very irritable?"

"Have you suffered some personal losses recently?"

"Do you think you are more depressed in the winter than the summer, or only in one season?" *(See Section 10.11, "Seasonal Affective Disorder.")*

Social Functioning

See also Chapter 15, "Social/Community Functioning," and Chapter 18, "Recreational Functioning."

"Do you find yourself avoiding being with people?"

"Do you go out less than you used to?"

"Have you given up any friendships/any social activities?"

Self-Deprecation

"Are you hard on yourself?"

"Have you been harder on yourself lately?"

"Do you think you are worthless/ugly/giving off bad odors?"

"Are there times when you call yourself names?" *(If so:)* "Which?"

"Do you think you are a wicked person/have sinned/have done something unforgivable?" *(If so:)* "Why?"

Suicidal Ideation

See also Section 3.30, "Suicide and Self-Destructive Behavior"; see Section 12.40, "Suicide," for descriptors.

"When people are depressed, they sometimes think about dying. Have you had thoughts like that?"

"Have you ever thought of hurting yourself?"

"What do you see for yourself in the future?"

"Do you think you will get well/over this problem?" *(If so:)* "How long will it take?"

Optimism–Pessimism

"What is the worst thing that ever happened to you?"

"What is the best thing that ever happened to you?"

"If you could have three wishes come true, what would you wish for?"

Anhedonia

"What do you do to enjoy yourself/have a good time/for fun?"
"Has your interest in this/these things changed?"

Assessment Scales

A great deal of information about psychological tests is available online at no cost. A prime resource is the website generously maintained by W. E. Benet, PhD, PsyD (*www.assessmentpsychology.com/tests.htm*; for specific depression tests, see *www.assessmentpsychology.com/onlinetests.htm*).

Commonly used scales for depression that are now available for free include the <u>H</u>amilton <u>R</u>ating <u>S</u>cale for <u>D</u>epression (Hamilton, 1960), at *healthnet.umassmed.edu/mhealth/hamd.pdf*; the Zung Depression Rating Scale (Zung, 1965), at *healthnet.umassmed.edu/mhealth/ZungSelfRatedDepressionScale.pdf*; the <u>C</u>enter for <u>E</u>pidemiologic <u>S</u>tudies <u>D</u>epression Scale (Radloff, 1977), at *counsellingresource.com/quizzes/cesd/index.html*; the Geriatric Depression Rating Scale, at *counsellingresource.com/quizzes/geriatric-depression/index.html*; the Goldberg Depression Questionnaire, at *counsellingresource.com/quizzes/goldberg-depression/index.html*; the <u>Q</u>uick <u>I</u>nventory of <u>D</u>epressive <u>S</u>ymptomatology—<u>S</u>elf <u>R</u>eport, at *counsellingresource.com/quizzes/qids-depression/index.html*; and the <u>E</u>dinburgh <u>P</u>ostnatal <u>D</u>epression <u>S</u>cale, at *health.utah.gov/rhp/pdf/epds.pdf*.

3.12. Dissociative Experiences

See Section 12.12, "Depersonalization and Derealization," for descriptors.

For standardized evaluation, you can use Ross et al.'s (Ross, 1997; Ross et al., 1990) Dissociative Disorders Interview Schedule, or Bernstein and Putnam's (1986) <u>D</u>issociative <u>E</u>xperiences <u>S</u>cale which is available and can be scored online (*counsellingresource.com/quizzes/des/index.html*). An updated version of the DES, DES-II, can be downloaded as a pdf (see *www.neurotransmitter.net/dissociation-scales.html*).

Dissociative Experiences

"Have you ever walked in your sleep?"
"Did you have imaginary playmates as a child?"
"Have you ever remembered a past event so vividly that it seemed you were actually reexperiencing it?"

"Have you ever suddenly realized that ...
 you don't remember earlier parts of the trip you are on?"
 you are in a place and have no recall of how you got there?"
 you are wearing clothes you would not have chosen?"
 some of your personal possessions were missing?"
 you have items you don't recall getting or buying?"

"Have you ever been greeted by people who call you by another name and really seem to know you?"
"Have you ever been unable to recall major events in your life?"
"Have you ever been unable to decide whether you actually did something or just imagined doing it?"

Depersonalization

"Are you aware of any significant change in yourself?"
"Do you feel normal/all right/natural/real?"

"Are you always certain who you are?"
"Did you ever feel detached/divorced from yourself?"
"Did you ever act in so strange a way you considered the possibility that you might be two different people?"
"Did you ever feel that you have lost your identity/like you were someone else?"
"Do you ever wonder who you really are?"
"Did you ever feel that you were becoming someone or something different?"

"Have you ever suddenly realized that you don't recognize your face/body in a mirror?"
"Did you ever feel that your self/body was different/changed/unreal/strange?"
"Have you ever felt that your body doesn't belong to your self?"
"Have there been times you felt your mind and body were not together/linked?"
"Do you ever feel like you were/your mind was outside/watching/apart from your body?"
"Do you ever feel like someone else is moving your legs as you walk/ever feel like a robot?"

Derealization

"Did you ever get so involved in a daydream that you couldn't tell if it were real or not?"
"Do people, trees, houses, etc., look as they usually do/always did to you?"
"Did you ever feel like you weren't really present?"
"Did you ever feel you were detached/alienated/estranged from yourself or your surroundings/everything around you?"
"Have you ever been in a familiar place but found it strange/peculiar/weird/unfamiliar/somehow changed?"
"Did you ever feel that things around you/the world were/was very strange/remote/unreal/changing?"
"Do things seem natural and real to you, or does it seem like things are make-believe?"
"Did things or objects ever seem to be alive?"

Drug Abuse   *See Section 3.28, "Substance Abuse: Drugs and Alcohol."*

✓ **Always ask every client** about past and present use of medications/street drugs/other chemicals, and especially alcohol (Ramsey et al., 2005).

3.13. Eating Disorders

See Section 12.14, "Eating Disorders," for descriptors.

✓ Evaluate weight, fat percentage, and proportion. Also evaluate self-efficacy, preoccupation, or hypervigilance around eating; terror over weight gain; body image; odd eating behaviors; etc. To evaluate anorexia nervosa, see Garner and Garfinkel (1979) for the 40-item Eating Attitudes Test (see also *www.medal.org*).

Opening Questions

"What is your present weight? The most you ever weighed? Your lowest weight as an adult?"
"Have you gained or lost weight in the last year or two?" *(If so:)* "How much?"

"What have you eaten in the last 24 hours?" [Explore for patterns, typicality, rationales, etc.]
"Do you think your eating habits are unusual?"
"Is your life a series of diets?"

"Do you have 'food binges' where you eat a large amount of food in a short time period?"
"If you have binged, was it on high-calorie foods such as sweets, desserts, or salty or fatty foods?"
"Have you stopped a binge by vomiting, purging, or sleeping, or because of pain?"

A British mnemonic for eating disorders is SCOFF:

"Do you make yourself Sick because you feel uncomfortably full?" *(Purging.)*
"Do you worry that you have lost Control over how much you eat?"
Have you recently lost more than One stone in a 3-month period?" *(One stone is 14 pounds. An American version might be F for Fifteen pounds, making the acronym SCFFF.)*
"Do you believe yourself to be Fat when others say you are too thin?"
"Would you say that Food dominates your life?"

The authors (Morgan et al., 1999) suggest scoring 1 point for every "yes," and believe that a score of 2 indicates a likely case of Anorexia Nervosa or Bulimia Nervosa.

Thoughts and Feelings about Weight

"How often do you think about your weight/eating/dieting?"
"How do you feel about your current weight?" [Note any disparity between client's statements and your judgments of appearance.]
"Do you feel you are too fat?" *(If yes:)* "How long have you felt that way?"
"Are you afraid of being/becoming overweight?"
"How much control over your eating do you feel you have?"
"Is your eating out of your control?"
"Do you avoid certain foods (foods with sugar, fat, salt, cholesterol, etc.)"?
"How would your life be different if you lost/gained the weight you want to?"

History of Food Restriction

"What kinds of diets have you tried?" [Take a diet history: dates; losses; time to regaining; kinds of restrictions used; weight at initiation, at termination, and at next diet; etc.]
"Have you ever gotten so upset or desperate about your weight that you have done something drastic?"
"Have you ever: gone on eating binges, vomited after you've eaten, fasted for long periods, used diet pills/cathartics/laxatives/diuretics/overexercising to lose weight, lost a great deal of weight, or felt guilty after eating?"

Alternative Questions

"Do you eat when you're not hungry? Do you eat to escape from worries or troubles?"
"Is your life dominated by thoughts of food?"
"Do you look forward with pleasure to the times when you can eat alone?" *(If so:)* "Do you plan these occasions?"
"Do you have a fear of becoming fat or losing control of your eating?"
"Do you feel guilt or remorse after overeating?"
"Do you eat sensibly when others are present and then binge when you are alone?"

"Is your life a series of diets?"
"Do you resent being told to 'use your willpower' to stop overeating?"

3.14. Gay and Lesbian Identity Formation

See also Section 19.5, "Homosexual Identity: Stages of Formation," and the "Sexual Adjustment" heading under Section 6.4, "Adjustment History."

Homosexuality is of course not pathological, but the strong social pressures and prejudices against it are stressors, and so it may require additional efforts for homosexual persons to form an adaptive identity. The questions in this section cover normative homosexual identity development.[4]

General Questions

"Did you ever have a sense of not belonging or of feeling sexually different from most people?"

"Do you know any gay men? Any lesbians?" *(If so:)* "What are they like?"
"What images of gay men and lesbians do you have?"

"Have you ever thought you might be gay?" *(If so:)* "When did you first think this?"
"What was it like to consider this idea/recognize such feelings?"

Attraction

"Do you find yourself attracted to gay/lesbian relationships or to specific gays/lesbians?"
"Have you ever acted on your feelings?" *(If so:)* "What did you do?"
"Have you tried to ignore or change these thoughts and feelings and/or convince yourself that you may not be gay?"

Understanding

"Why do you think gay people are that way?" *(Example: "They are born that way.")*
"Do you see yourself as gay and accept it without liking it?"

Identity Activism

"Tell me about the pressures from society you feel/are aware of."

"Are you out *(i.e., "out of the closet"—not concealing one's homosexuality)* to friends/family/coworkers/the public?"
"Are you considering coming out to them or others?"
"Are you involved in any gay activities—social, political, or otherwise?"

3.15. Hallucinations

See Section 12.17, "Hallucinations," for descriptors; see Section 29.7, "Psychosis," for possible medical causes.

✓ **Note:** Look for behaviors that suggest hallucinating: return of gaze to a spot, sudden head turning, staring at one place in room, eyes following something in motion, mumbling or conversing with no one else present, etc. If there is an indication of the presence of hallucinations, ask questions to discriminate those that are apparently due to entering or leaving sleep, delirium, alcohol or drug withdrawal or abuse, medications, etc.

---

[4]I am grateful to Leslie J. Wrixon, PsyD, of Cambridge, MA, for these questions and for guidance regarding the stages of identity development.

General Questions

"Do you have a vivid imagination?"
"Do you dream so vividly that you aren't sure it was a dream?"
"Did you ever think/act in really strange/odd/peculiar ways?"
"Have you had any uncanny/eerie/bizarre/unexplainable experiences?"
"Has your mind ever played tricks on you?"
"Did you ever see or hear things others did not?"
"Have you had visions/seen apparitions?"
(For any of these:) "Where did you first experience this?"

Auditory

"Were you ever surprised that you could hear some sounds other people couldn't hear (whispering voices, echoes, melodies, parts of conversations, people arguing/giving you orders, etc.)?"
"Have you ever heard noises in your head that disturb you?"
"Have you ever heard voices coming from inside your head?" *(If yes:)*
  "Was this like voices speaking your own thoughts or someone else speaking?"
  "Where do the voices come from?"
  "Whose voices? Men's or women's? How old were they?"
  "What did they say?"
  "When does this happen? How often do you hear them?"
  "When did this start?"
  "What brings these on?"

Visual

"Have you ever seen anything so unusual that other people didn't believe it?"
"Did you ever have visions/see apparitions/ghosts?"
"Did you ever see anything like in a dream when you were awake?"
"Have you ever seen things that no one else saw?" *(If so:)*
  "What? What did you feel then?"
  "What do you call these experiences?"
  "What causes these things to happen?"
  "When was the first time this happened?"

Kinesthetic/Tactile/Haptic

"Have you ever felt strange sensations (e.g., electricity)/odd feelings in your body/anything crawling on you (e.g., bugs)?"

Gustatory

"Have you ever felt strange tastes in your mouth (metal, electricity, poisons, etc.)?"

Olfactory

"Have you ever smelled strange odors that you could not account for (poisons, death, something burning, sewage, odd smells from your own body, dead spirits, etc.)?"

Other

"What was the strangest experience you ever had?"
"Did you ever visit another planet? Ever die and return to life?" *(If so:)* "How/why do you think these things come about?"

Homosexual Identity Development   *See Section 3.14, "Gay and Lesbian Identity," and Section 19.5, "Homosexual Identity: Stages of Formation."*

3.16. Illusions

See also the "Derealization"? heading under Section 3.12, "Dissociative Experiences"; see Section 12.18, "Illusions," for descriptors.

"Do you believe there is only one reality?"
"Does the world ever look very different to you?" *(If yes:)* "In what way(s)?"
"Do any things feel different, in some way, at certain times?"
"Do things ever seem to change size/look smaller or larger?"
"Do parts of your body ever seem to change in size or shape or texture?"
"Do things sometimes seem nearer or farther away than they should?"
"Does time ever seem to move very slowly or very fast?"

3.17. Impulse Control

See also Section 3.31, "Violence," for questions, and Sections 12.19, "Impulse-Control Disorders," and 12.41, "Violent Behaviors," for descriptors.

"Do you find yourself suddenly doing things before you have thought about or decided to do them?"
"Does money 'burn a hole in your pocket' until you spend it?"
"Do you feel compelled/driven to do things you don't want to do?"
"Do you feel unable to stop yourself from doing some things?"

"Have you ever been involved in sexual behaviors you regretted?"
"Do you ever steal/shoplift?"
"Please tell me about all the times you have had contact with the police."
"Have you ever been fired/evicted/arrested?" *(If yes:)* "Why did that happen?"

"What do you usually do when you get very upset and angry?"
"Do you have a bad temper/fly off the handle/flare up?"
"Have you ever thrown/broken things? Ever hit/attacked anyone?"
"Do you get involved in more fights than others in your neighborhood?"
"Do you have a list of people you just don't talk to any more because you always get into arguments with them?"

Insight   *See Section 2.23, "Insight into Disorder"; see Section 11.9, "Insight," for descriptors.*

Irritability   *See Sections 3.5, "Affect/Mood," and 3.11, "Depression."*

3.18. Mania

See Section 10.9, "Mania," for descriptors; see Section 29.5, "Mania," for possible medical causes.

"Was there ever a time when you ...
    stayed very excited?"
    were too happy without any reason?"

were too full of energy?"
talked too much and couldn't stop?"
phoned or visited too much?"
planned or started many things and couldn't finish any of them?"
did without sleep for a day or two?"
seemed to be oversexed?"
were overworked/held several jobs at the same time?"
spent money recklessly/spent money you didn't have/made extravagant gifts/gambled?"
"Have you ever found yourself pacing and couldn't stop/stop for long?"
"Was there ever a time when you were too impatient/irritable/couldn't concentrate/couldn't stop your mind's racing?"

(If yes to any of the above:) "When did this start? How long did this last? What happened because of this?"
"Were you ever treated for these conditions?"

✓ A large selection of screening tools and rating scales can be accessed at *www2.massgeneral.org/ schoolpsychiatry/screeningtools_table.asp.*

Munchausen's Syndrome   *See Section 12.20, "Malingering."*

Noncompliance   *See Section 3.8, "Compliance–Noncompliance with Treatment."*

3.19. Obsessions

See also Section 3.9, "Compulsions"; see Section 12.21, "Obsessions," for descriptors.

✓ Differential diagnosis must distinguish obsessions from depressive ruminations, anxious worrying, and delusions. For standardized recording, you can use the Yale–Brown Obsessive–Compulsive Scale (Goodman et al., 1989; *www.brainphysics.com/ybocs.php*). It covers contents, distress, time spent, insight, indecisiveness, avoidance, and resisting thoughts. A children's version is also available.

Initial Inquiries

"Are there any thoughts you just seem unable to forget/get rid of/keep out of your mind/stop thinking about?"
"What do these thoughts revolve around or continually come back to?"
"Are there any phrases/names/dates/slogans/rhymes/titles/music that continually run through your mind/you can't seem to control?"
"Are there any prayers/numbers/names/phrases you feel you have to repeat?" *(If so:)* "Which? When?"

Thoughts

"Is there any possibility that you keep thinking about/considering/mulling over/speculating about?"
"Are there any everyday decisions you seem unable to make or take too much time to make?"
"How often do you think about your health/how your body is working/whether you are sick?"

Client Awareness of Excess/Irrationality

"Do you think about these things more than you should/would like to/more than a sensible number of times a day? Do they take up a long time each day?"
"How does thinking these things affect your life/routines/job/relationships/family members?"
"Do you feel uncomfortable until you think these thoughts, even though you may know them to be nonsensical/unimportant/ineffective?"

"How much control do you feel you have over these thoughts? Do you resist them?"
"How do you try to get these thoughts out of your head/make them stop?"
"Where do you think these thoughts come from?"

Contents of the Obsessions

Somatic: Body parts, appearance, or illness.
Contamination: Bodily waste, dirt, germs, animals, etc.
Religious scrupulosity.
Repetition, counting, arranging, checking, hoarding/collecting, etc.
Sexual: "Perverse" or forbidden acts, incest, {homosexuality}, etc.
Symmetry, precision, balance, arrangements.
Violence: Self or other harm, horrific images, blurting out obscenities/insults, etc.

3.20. Organicity/Cognitive Disorders

See Chapter 11, "Cognition and Mental Status," for descriptors; see Chapter 2, "Mental Status Evaluation Questions/Tasks," for guidance in conducting an MSE.

Ask for a history of:

Sunstroke.	Head injuries.	Syphilis.
Near-drowning.	Major surgery.	AIDS/AIDS-Related Complex.
Electrocution.	Apnea.	High fevers/delirium.
Poisonings.	Vertigo/dizziness.	Seizures/convulsions/fits.

Exposure to toxic chemicals in the workplace/home/garden.
Substance use/abuse, intravenous drugs, overdoses. *(See Section 3.28, "Substance Abuse: Drugs and Alcohol.")*
Periods of unconsciousness/being "knocked out"/having fainted/being in a coma.
Episodes of alteration of levels of consciousness, "out cold," "weirded out," "falling out."

Do a complete MSE, and consider neuropsychological testing and/or neurological evaluations.

3.21. Pain, Chronic

See Section 12.23, "Pain Disorder/Chronic Pain Syndrome," for descriptors.

The usual medical interview asks these questions, using the mnemonic OPQRST:

Onset: "What brings it on?"
Palliative and Provocative: "What makes it better or worse?" (Time of day, cold, movement?)
Quality or character: e.g., "Is it throbbing or steady?" "Dull or sharp?"
Region and Radiation: e.g., "Is it located on one or both sides?" "Does it spread?"
Severity: Use comparisons (toothache, wound from a . . .) from the person's history.
Timing and duration: "How often do you get it?" "How long does it last?"

A good list is available at *www.painassessmentresources.com/resources/index/html* and then click on "Notes on psychological assessment tools."

"Do you frequently have pain somewhere in your body?" *(If so:)* "Where?"
"Has the pain affected your sleep?" *(If so:)* "How?"
"Has the pain affected your eating? Has your weight changed?"
"Has the pain changed your ability to think or concentrate?" *(If so:)* "Please explain."
"Do you have to lie down and rest because of the pain, or does it force you to keep moving?"
"Do you find that you are thinking about the pain a lot?"

"Tell me about your activities in a 24-hour day, such as cooking, laundry, shopping, cleaning, reading, exercise, hobbies, etc. When do you wake up?" (And so on.)
"Does the pain affect your ability to take care of yourself/your day-to-day needs?"
"What activities have you had to restrict or stop because of pain?"
"Do you need to use any assistance device? Anything to walk with?" *(If so:)* "When did you start using it? Which physician gave it to you?"

"How has the pain changed in the last year?"

"What medications do you take for the pain?" [Ask for names, dosages, over-the-counter or physician source.]
"How does the medicine affect the pain?"
"Do you get any side effects from these medications?"

"What other treatments have you had? (Chiropractor, physical therapy, other?) How well did they work?"
"Have you been treated in any pain management program or pain clinic?" *(If so:)* "When? Where? To what effect/with what result?"
"Have you ever been referred to a psychologist or psychiatrist to help you to learn to cope with the pain?" [Ask for name, dates, location, phone number, dates of treatment.]
"Do doctors seem to have helped or failed you?"
"Has some doctor said your pain was 'imaginary' or 'all in your head'?"
"Do you truly believe your case is hopeless?"

3.22. Paranoia

See Section 12.24, "Paranoia," for descriptors.

Being Monitored

"When you get on a bus/eat in a restaurant/enter any public place, do people notice you/turn around to look at you?"
"Have you ever been singled out for special attention/watched/spied on?"
"Do people sometimes follow you for a while?"

Suspicion

"Would you say that you are more suspicious than other people, perhaps with good cause?"
"Have you been attacked/been shot at?"
"Would you feel safer if you carried a gun/knife/Mace or hired a bodyguard?"

"Do you think there is someone or something out to get you?"
"Do you think anyone is against you? Do you have enemies?"
"Does any organization or group of people have it in for you? Is anyone plotting against you?"

"Is there anything about you that has made other people jealous of you/prejudiced against you/ out to get or harm you/want to damage your property?"

"Do people talk about you more than they talk about others?"
"Do people say things about you behind your back? What do they say?"
"Are people making insulting/derogatory/critical/negative remarks about you?"
"Do people laugh at you?"

"Do you believe you have to be extra careful/extra alert/vigilant around people?"
"Have you had to take any special precautions?"
"Have you changed your way of doing things to feel safer?"

Being Controlled (↔ *by degree*)

"Do people try to trick you/play tricks on you?"
"Are people doing things that affect you and that you do not understand?"
"Have drugs been put in your food or drinks?"

"Do other people seem to know your thoughts? Can other people read your mind?"
"Have you ever had thoughts in your mind that were not your own?"
"Are people controlling your thoughts or your mind?" *(If so:)* "What are they doing? How are they doing/attempting this? Why is this happening?"
"Is your mind controlled by others/thought waves/electricity/radio or television waves?"

3.23. Phobias

See Section 12.25, "Phobias," for descriptors.

"Are you afraid of any things that do not frighten most people as much?" *(If so:)* "What are they?"
"Is there any activity or any place that makes you very uncomfortable or anxious, and so you avoid it?" *(If so:)* "Tell me more about it or them."
"Do these fears/avoidance behaviors seem reasonable and appropriate to you?" *(If not:)* "How have you tried to overcome these fears?"

Social Phobia/Social Anxiety

"Are you often embarrassed? Do you limit the things you do so that you are not embarrassed?"
"Are you very afraid of giving speeches/appearing stupid/being observed/being criticized?"
"Do you avoid social gatherings like parties and talking to strangers because they make you anxious?"
"Do you blush easily/sweat/shake/tremble/get heart palpitations in public?"

3.24. Self-Injury

See Section 12.33, "Self-Injurious Behavior," for additional information.

"Have you ever harmed yourself to feel better or get some relief?"
"What was happening in your life at that time?"
"What did you do to yourself?" "How many times?"
"What did you feel as you did it or right afterward?"
"What happened afterward?" (Nothing, ignored, emergency room, surgery, psychiatric hospitalization, etc.)

When more rapport is established, you might ask more detailed questions about the methods involved: cutting/slicing, burning, rubbing/scratching, scraping, hitting with an object, punching, biting/chewing, picking/pinching, hair pulling, ingesting nonfood items (coins, nails, broken glass, etc.), inserting objects.

3.25. Sexual History

If a client presents with a sexual problem, see the "Sexual Adjustment" heading under Section 6.4, "Adjustment History," or Section 10.12, "Sexuality." If sexual abuse is suspected, see Section 3.4, "Abuse (Sexual) of Child or Adult."

This section is for a non-problem-focused history and is arranged in developmental order. See Kaplan (1983) and Ross et al. (2000) for how to take a very complete sexual history. Levine (2006) gives excellent guidance. A short outline can be found on the <u>C</u>enters for <u>D</u>isease <u>C</u>ontrol and Prevention website (*www.cdc.gov/std/see/HealthCareProviders/SexualHistory-H.pdf*). This is a sensitive area for everyone—especially for members of sexual and ethnic minorities, and for those who have been abused—so do get specialized training.

Always ask every client about a history of sexual abuse.

Childhood

"When were you first aware of the sexes' differences?"
"What toys did you play with as a child?"
"Were you ever called a 'tomboy' (for females)/'sissy' (for males)?"
"Did you ever wear the clothes of the other sex as a child?"

"What were your first sexual experiences/feelings? How old were you? What was the situation? What thoughts did you have then?"
"What sex games did you play with girls and with boys?"
"When did you first masturbate? How did you learn about masturbation? What did it feel like and what did you think when you started?"

"What sexual behaviors did you see between adults? What were your feelings and thoughts about these?"

Adolescence

"From whom or what did you first learn/learn the most about sex?"
"Did you have sex education classes in school?" *(If so:)* "What did you learn about?"
"Did you feel free to ask sexual questions in your home?" *(If not:)* "To whom/where did you go with your questions/for information?"
(For females:) Ask about age of menarche, regularity of menstrual cycle, changes in menstrual cycle, pregnancies/miscarriages/stillbirths/abortions/deliveries.
(For males:) Ask about age of puberty (voice cracking, nocturnal emissions, body hair, ejaculation/orgasm by masturbation, etc.).
"How and when did you learn about menstruation, intercourse, and pregnancy?"
"How prepared were you for menstruation/wet dreams/the changes in your body?"

"Have you ever engaged in voyeurism/watching someone get undressed, or exhibitionism/ showing off your genitals, sex with animals?"
"What erotic materials (or 'pornography'[5]), such as books, magazines, or videotapes, have you

---

[5]A useful distinction (made by Steinem, 1980) is as follows: Of all artifacts made by humans, some are designed to arouse viewers sexually—these are erotica. Some types of erotica show a large difference in power between the partners—these are pornography. Thus closeup pictures of intercourse can be erotica and beautiful (and likely harmless), while fully clothed depictions of rape can be pornographic and ugly (and likely harmful).

seen? What was shown in this material?" (Heterosexual or homosexual intercourse, oral sex, child sex, group sex, etc.)

"At what age did you start to date?"
"How many people have you dated and for how long?"
"What was your first experience with petting ('necking,' 'making out') like?"

"How old were you when you first had sex with another person?" [*Sex is deliberately not specific here.*]
   "Was this heterosexual or homosexual?"
   "What were your feelings and thoughts?" [Attend to issues of force.]

"What methods of birth control have you used?"
"Do you want to become pregnant/father a child?"
"How often do you have unprotected intercourse?"
"What sexually transmitted diseases have you had?"

Adulthood

"How many times in your life do you guess you have had intercourse without using a condom/birth control?"
"Have you had any kind of sexual intercourse with men, women, or both in the last 20 years?"
"Have you had a male sexual partner who has had sex with other men in the last 20 years?"

Based on the responses to these questions, consider asking for information on HIV risk:

"Have you ever shared or borrowed a needle to inject yourself with a drug, or do you think that someone you had unprotected sex with did this?"
"Have you ever had unprotected sex with someone who you knew, or later learned, was HIV-infected or had AIDS?"
"Are you at all concerned that you may have picked up HIV?"
"Have you ever had a test for HIV or AIDS?"

"What are your sexual fantasies about?"
"Do any of your sexual fantasies distress or frighten you?"

"Do you have any sexual problems now? Did you in the past?" (*If so:*) "Which?"
   (*For men:*) "When have you had difficulty with erection/'getting and staying hard,' or orgasm/ejaculation/'coming' too soon or not at all?"
   (*For women:*) "When have you had difficulty with arousal/'getting excited/hot,' or orgasm/'coming'/'climaxing,' or painful intercourse?"
"As you see it, do these problems affect you alone, mainly you, both you and your partner, or mainly your partner?"
"What have you done to try to overcome this/these problem(s)?"

"As you look back over your past history, what have been the sexual high and low points?"
"What things about your sexual development do you wish could have been different?"

For Women Only:

"How does your menstrual cycle affect your mood/attitudes/behavior/sexual desire?"
"Please describe all your pregnancies."

✓ **Note:** Because medications and illnesses affect libido and performance, ask about medications (prescription and over-the-counter), street drugs, and alcohol (by referring to Section 3.28), and illnesses (especially diabetes and circulatory diseases).

Relationships

"In each of your previous relationships, how was the sexual relationship?"
"What was the reason each relationship ended?"
"In your present relationship, how has the sexual adjustment been?"
"How attracted to your partner do you feel?"
"How attractive do you feel to your partner?"
"Are you satisfied with the frequency of sexual relations? Is your partner?"
"What images or fantasies do you think of when you are with your partner?"
"What conflicts do you have with your partner in any aspect of your sexual relationship?" (Oral sex—either kind; positions; frequency; amount of stimulation; the circumstances of sex; communication of preferences; initiation; etc.)
"What incompatibilities or conflicts exist in other aspects of the relationship?"

3.26. Sexual Identity/Transgender Issues

See also the "Sexual Adjustment" heading under Section 6.4, "Adjustment History."

✓ Distinguish transgender identification from transvestism, cross-dressing, dissatisfaction with one's body, and delusions.

"At what age did you first know you were a boy/girl?"
"Did you ever dress in the other sex's clothes/play with the other sex's toys?"

"Do you want to look like someone of the other sex?"
"Do you dislike your sex's clothes or bodies?"
"Do you think you really should have been/are of the other sex?"
"Do you want to marry a person of your sex?"
"Are your sex organs normal? Do you dislike them? Do you feel disgust at your genitals?"
"Have you ever sought to change your sex?"
"Have you ever tried to injure your genitals?"

For Females Only:

"Were you a tomboy? Are you still?"
"Do you feel more comfortable/better when you wear masculine clothing?"
"Do you stand up to urinate?"
"Do you feel like a man trapped in a woman's body?"

For Males Only:

"Do you dress in women's clothes or underclothes/use makeup?"
"When do you do this? How does it make you feel? What do you get from this?"
"Do you feel like a woman trapped in a man's body?"

For further information, see Brown and Rounsley (2003). Also, *wpath.org* offers the very educational "Standards of Care," and *www.firelily.com/gender/gianna* offers many readings for all aspects.

3.27. Sleep

See Section 12.37, "Sleep Disturbances," for descriptors.

Reports of minimal or problematic slevep may be exaggerated or erroneous. Completion of a sleep diary and practice of sleep hygiene are almost always appropriate. The Pittsburgh Sleep Quality Index is a standard measure of many aspects of sleep (it is available at *www.sleep.pitt.edu/content. asp?id=1484&subid=2316*).

SYMPTOM QUESTIONS

General Questions

"Do you have any trouble with your sleep?" *(If so:)* "What kind?" (Insomnias, parasomnias, nightmares, confusional episodes, sleep paralyses, awake frightened, vivid dreams, hypnagogic or hypnopompic hallucinations, cataplexy, sleep attacks, bruxism, etc.)
"How does this affect your life?"
"Has there been any change in the ways you sleep?"
"What time do you usually go to bed? Fall asleep? Wake up?"
"Are you sleepy during the day? Do you usually/have to take a nap during the day?"
"Do you wake up refreshed, or irritable and tired?" [Compute the client's total sleep time and compare it with that of age peers and the client's own lifelong patterns. This is more likely to be accurate than asking, "How much sleep do you usually get each night?"]
"What do you dream about? Do you have bad or unusual dreams?"
"Do you usually have the same dream every night for a while?"
"Are there dreams you dream over and over?"

Difficulty Falling Asleep (Initial Insomnia)

"What do you do just before you go to bed?"
"What do you do in bed?" (Watch TV, read, study, eat, use telephone, have sex, etc.)
"Typically, what time do you fall asleep?"
"How long does it take you to fall asleep after you go to bed?" [15–20 minutes is usual.]
"What keeps you awake?" (Activities, partner, rehearsing the day, conditions of bedroom, etc.)
"What do you think about before you fall asleep?"
"Do you see or hear or feel unusual things before falling asleep?"
"Do you do anything to help yourself fall asleep?/What do you do to fall asleep?"

Sleep Continuity Disturbance (Middle Insomnia)

"Are you a very light/light/sound/very sound sleeper?"
"Do you awaken in the middle of the night?" *(If so:)* "How many times, on the average?"
"Is there anything that wakes you so you can't sleep through the night?" (Need to urinate, bed partner's behavior, a needy child, street noises, etc.)
"How long is it before you fall back to sleep?"
"What do you think about as you lie in bed?"
"What have you tried to help you return to sleep?"

Early Morning Awakening (Terminal Insomnia)

"What time do you usually wake up/awaken?"
"Do you awaken too early in the morning and are unable to go back to sleep again?" *(If so:)* "What do you do then?"
"What do you think about as you lie in bed?"

Other

"How much coffee/cola/tea do you drink each day?"

"Do you use any caffeine-containing medications/over-the-counter medicines/drugs, such as Midol (for premenopausal females), Bufferin, Anacin, etc."?

"How many cigarettes do you smoke in a day?"

"What medications are you taking? Do you use any sleeping aid or sleeping pill?"

"What do you eat and drink before going to sleep?"

"Do you work shiftwork/changing/rotating shifts?"

"Are you under a lot of stress?"

"Did anyone in your family have problems with sleeping/similar problems?"

"Do you snore loudly?"

"Do you awaken gasping for air/with leg jerks/cramps/pain?"

For a Child:

Ask about regular bedtimes, fears (of the dark, of the "bogeyman," relatives, dangerous animals, violence, harm to caregivers), bedtime rituals, reluctance to fall asleep, need for lights/company, entry into parents' bed, bad dreams/nightmares/night terrors, sleepwalking, incontinence.

Social Phobia   *See Section 3.23, "Phobias."*

3.28. Substance Abuse: Drugs and Alcohol

See Section 12.39, "Substance Use, Abuse, and Dependence," for descriptors. See Section 3.29 for tobacco and caffeine use.

There are no sharp demarcations or agreed-upon criteria among use, misuse, and abuse, or between "problem drinking/drug use" and "alcoholism/drug addiction," because people now enter treatment at all stages/levels. In this section, abuse and misuse issues concern any of these substances:[6]

Alcohol in beer, wine, liquor, over-the-counter medications, nonpotable forms, etc.

Prescription/legal drugs, such as amphetamines, barbiturates, antidepressants, opioids, sedatives, hypnotics, and anxiolytics.

"Street"/illegal/unidentified/synthetic ("designer") drugs, including cannabis/marijuana/ "weed"/"grass"/"pot," etc., cocaine, crack, hallucinogens, narcotics.

Over-The-Counter medications such as stimulants.

Substances inhaled ("huffed"), such as glues, chemical thinners, gasoline.

Behavioral Signs of Substance Abuse

Sedatives/Hypnotics/Anxiolytics

INTOXICATION

Short attention span, mood lability.

Slurred speech, loss of coordination, ataxia with falling/bruises, nystagmus, small pupils.

Somnolence.

---

[6]Bernard (1991) provides a very complete checklist of substances-by-when-consumed, which can be used for screening.

WITHDRAWAL

Insomnia, disturbing dreams.
Restlessness, tachycardia, palpitations, diaphoresis' tremor, dilated pupils, hyperreflexia, nausea, vomiting, headache, aches and pains, seizure.
Feelings of unreality, hallucinations, disorientation, memory impairment.
Anxiety, irritability, depression, suicidal ideation, agoraphobia.

Depressants (Barbiturates, Benzodiazapines, GBH, Rohypnol)   *See "Alcohol," below.*

INTOXICATION

Reduced anxiety, feelings of well-being, lowered inhibitions.
Limited attention span, impulsivity, mood lability.
Slowed mental and physical functioning.
Disorientation, impaired judgment, bizarre thoughts, confabulation.
Discoordination, slurred speech, nystagmus, ataxia, seizures.
Dozing or prolonged sleep.

WITHDRAWAL

Irritability, depression, acute anxiety.
Nightmares, insomnia.
Weakness, restlessness, tremor, nausea and vomiting, headaches, seizures and risk of death.
Delirium Tremens: Disorientation, agitation, visual/tactile hallucinations, fever, dilated pupils.

Alcohol

INTOXICATION

Smells of alcohol (caused by other substances in drinks and not correlated with blood alcohol levels).

Effects vary greatly between persons but below are some typical effects with increasing Blood Alcohol Concentrations ($\leftrightarrow$ *by degree*):

Disinhibition, vivaciousness, flushing of skin/warmth, lessened judgment.
Slurred speech, lessened fine motor skills, perplexity, emotional lability, inappropriate laughter.
Very slurred speech, staggering, double vision, lethargy, falling, poor recall.
Stupor, briefly arousable with pain, deep snoring.
Coma, unarousable, incontinent, lowered blood pressure, irregular breathing.
Possible death from cessation of breathing, too low blood pressure, or vomiting into lungs without cough reflex.

WITHDRAWAL ("HANGOVER")

Fatigue, weakness, headache and muscle aches.
Thirst, nausea, vomiting, stomach pain.
Decreased sleep.
Vertigo and hypersensitivity to light and sound.
Decreased attention and concentration.
Depression, anxiety, irritability.
Tremor, sweating, increased pulse rate and systolic blood pressure, hyperreflexia.
Possible and variable Delirium Tremens.

Stimulants (Amphetamines and Variants, Cocaine, Nicotine, Caffeine)
See "MDMA," below.

INTOXICATION

Increased attention and decreased fatigue, increased activity and speech, decreased appetite.
Insomnia.
Euphoria, "rush" feelings of competence and power, grandiosity, exhilaration.
Increased respirations, hyperthermia, tachycardia, dilated pupils, fine tremor, sweating, delayed orgasm.
Muscle twitching, agitation, irritability.
Mild hallucinogenic effects (for MDMA).
Longer-term effects:
    Psychosis, paranoia, hallucinations, repetitive motor activity.
    Aggression, impulsiveness, stroke, weight loss.

WITHDRAWAL

Apathy, depression, irritability, agitation, anxiety.
Fatigue, increased appetite, prolonged sleep.
Suicidality, craving, bizarre dreams.

Opioids/Narcotics (Heroin, Morphine, Opium, Fentanyl, Oxycodone, Methadone, Codeine)

INTOXICATION

Euphoria. Pain relief.
Apathy, decreased concentration, decreased physical activity, slowed and slurred speech, staggering gait.
Alternating sleep and drowsiness ("on the nod").
Constricted ("pinpoint") pupils, drooling, itching.

WITHDRAWAL

Vomiting, sneezing, diarrhea, anorexia.
Watery eyes, runny nose, yawning, tremors, restlessness, increased respirations, chills, fever and sweating, fatigue, muscle twitching (kicks), aches and cramps (leg, abdominal).
Dilated pupils, piloerection ("goose bumps").
Insomnia.
Drug seeking behaviors, cravings.

Cannabis (Marijuana, Hashish)

INTOXICATION

Disinhibition (giggling, silliness).
Dreamy flowing consciousness, altered perceptions of time and sensory input.
Decreased communicative ability and coordination, slowed reaction time and thinking.
Increased appetite ("munchies"), dry mouth.

WITHDRAWAL

Hyperactivity, insomnia, decreased appetite.
Anxiety.

Hallucinogens (LSD, Mescaline, Psilocybin)

INTOXICATION (A "TRIP"—UP TO 12 HOURS)

Effects vary greatly with setting, personality, mood, expectations, amount, etc.

> Heightened sensitivity to color, texture, shapes, music, and internal stimuli; visual and depth distortion.
> Poor judgment, risky behavior.
> Mood changes, usually euphoric, sometimes depressive.
> Dilated pupils, sweating, anorexia, sleeplessness, dry mouth, tremors.

WITHDRAWAL

> No immediate effects.
> "Flashbacks," especially with use of another drug, for up to a year.
> Possible persistent psychotic state.

MDMA ("Ecstasy")

INTOXICATION

> Mental stimulation, emotional warmth, empathy toward others, a general sense of well-being, enhanced sensory perception, decreased anxiety.
> Memory loss, poor judgment.
> Dehydration.
> Rare hallucinations.

Dissociative Anesthetics (Phencyclidine or "PCP"/Ketamine/Dextromethorphan)

> Dissociative amnesia ("out of body," floating), impairment of recent and immediate memory (for "date rape"/robbery).
> Giddy euphoria, often followed by bursts of anxiety.
> Altered perception of time and space, paranoia, delusions, decreased concentration.
> Increased heart rate, sweating, nausea, numbness, slowed reflexes.
> Excessive salivation, rotatory and vertical nystagmus, ataxia, jerking.
> Anxiety and panic; withdrawal and catatonia.
> Prolonged psychotic state.

> Ketamine is much less potent and shorter-acting than PCP.

> Dextromethorphan, from cough medications, produces its effects in dose-dependent "plateaus."

Inhalants ("Huffing" Industrial Solvents/Gasoline/Nitriles or "Poppers," Glue Sniffing)

INTOXICATION

> Excitation, then drowsiness, disinhibition, lightheadedness, agitation.
> Anesthesia, a loss of sensation, unconsciousness.
> Dizziness, drowsiness, slurred speech, clumsiness, unsteady gait.
> Illusions, hallucinations, delusions, confusion, emotional lability, impaired thinking.
> Euphoric, dreamy "high," culminating in a short period of sleep.

Screening Questions about Effects

A large number of assessment instruments for alcohol abuse in all populations can be found online at *pubs.niaaa.nih.gov/publications/AssessingAlcohol/index.htm*).

"What happens to you when you drink/use drugs? Do you change a lot/act very differently/do strange things/have other parts of your personality come out?"

"Has drinking/drug use affected your school/work/job/career, caused you legal problems or in your friendships/family/marriage, health, or changed any other area of your life?"

"What problems has the use of alcohol/drugs caused in your life at any time? During the last month?"

"Which of these have you had: shakes, blackouts, visions or voices, aches and fevers, injuries from falls/fights/car accidents?"

"Are you or other people concerned/worried about your drinking/drug use? Have other people tried to get you to stop drinking/using?" *(If so:)* "How do you feel about them?"

History/Consumption Patterns

A detailed and individualized history is desirable, because an individual's patterns of use/overuse/ misuse/abuse may change with availability, resources, setting, choice, treatment, and aging, and may involve cross-addictions, temporary substitutions or preferences, and many other factors. However, such tailoring of questions is not possible in the format here. Therefore, follow your clinical intuition and the client's lead (or avoidances) in history taking to get all the relevant facts and experiences.

✓ It may be useful to construct a table like this as you obtain the history, especially if the history is complex.

Drug name/type	Age started	Amount	Frequency	Route	Last dose	Control efforts and outcome

Begin with this question: **"What is/are your drugs of choice/preference?"** Depending on the answer, go to "Alcohol" or to "Drugs," below.

Alcohol

Let us be clear about how much alcohol is dangerous. The National Institute on Alcohol Abuse and Alcoholism (2000, pp. 429–430) indicates that "safe" alcohol use is 2 drinks per day (1 drink if over age 65 years) for men and 1 drink per day for women; "at-risk" alcohol use is 14 drinks per week or 4 drinks per occasion for men and 7 drinks per week or 3 drinks per occasion for women; and "heavy" alcohol use is over 5–6 drinks per day for men and over 3–4 drinks per day for women. Any alcohol is dangerous at every stage of pregnancy.

"How much do you need to drink before you start to feel it?"
"How much does it take for you to get drunk?"
"When and where did you first drink any kind of alcohol?"
"When and where did you first drink to drunkenness/intoxication?"
"When did you first start drinking regularly?"
"How did you progress to the quantity you now drink?"

"What is your preferred drink? What else will you drink?"
"Do you ever drink substances such as shaving lotion, cough medicine, or mouthwash?"
"Where do you get your alcohol?" (From peers, stores, bartenders, steal it, sneak it from others?)
"Where do you drink?" (At work, home, parties, bars?)

"With whom do you drink?" (Alone, with buddies, friends, spouse?)

"Do you drink without eating anything?"

"Do you drink every day or every other day or only on weekends?"

"Do you stay drunk during the day? Most days? When?"

"When you drink, how much do you consume? Do you drink more than a case of beer/fifth of whiskey[7] in a day?"

"At what time of day do you start drinking?" (Upon awakening, all day long, no particular time, at lunch, after work, with dinner, late at night?)

"Do you ever feel you need a drink to get going/can't get through the day without a drink?"

"What are the usual situations or moods just before you start drinking?"

"Do you ever drink heavily after a fight or disappointment?" (Other possible precipitating emotions: angry, frustrated, lonely, bored, agitated.)

"Do you drink more when you feel under a great deal of pressure?"

"When you are drinking at a party or social occasion, do you sneak a few extra drinks?"[8]

"Have you ever gulped your drinks to get drunk quickly?"

"Have you ever concealed/lied about the amount of your drinking?"

Drugs

"What street drugs have you used?" (Marijuana, cocaine, crack, heroin, "ice," hallucinogens, LSD, "Ecstasy," "uppers," "speed," "downers," pain killers, "ludes," "Reds," "Black Beauties," tranquilizers, etc.?)

"Have you huffed/used inhalants, such as glue, gasoline, butane, naphtha, or thinners?"

"What drugs or medications have you used in the last month/6 months? How did you get them?"

"Have you ever used drugs prescribed for you (pain killers, sleeping pills, tranquilizers, barbiturates, etc.) in a way that the doctor didn't prescribe?"

"Have you ever taken medications prescribed for someone else?"

"When did you first use street drugs/misuse medications/sniff chemicals?"

"What effects did they have on you?"

"What did you use at first?"

"When did you first start using it/them regularly?"

"How did you progress to the quantity you now use?"

"What are the usual situations or moods just before you start using?"

"How often do you use? When do you start using? Do you ever feel you need to do some drug just to get going/get through the day or night?"

"Where do you use?" (At work, home, parties, friends' houses?)

"With whom do you use?" (Alone, with buddies, friends, spouse/partner?)

"How do you take each drug/chemical? What is the usual/maximum amount you take?"

Positive and Negative Effects

See the "Points in a Cost–Benefit Analysis Approach" heading under Section 12.39, "Substance Use, Abuse, and Dependence."

"What kind of person are you when you are drunk/high?"

"What are the effects of your drinking/drug use you like most?"

"What are the effects you like least?"

---

[7]Starting with a large amount may reduce defensiveness and inaccuracy.

[8]Janet L. Smigel, RN, CD, suggests adding: "Do you drink one or several drinks before the party because you fear that there won't be alcohol or enough alcohol at the social gathering, or that someone might think you drink too much if you have your usual amount?"

Control

"When was the first time you became concerned about your use of drugs or alcohol?"
"Do you think you need to drink to function normally/get through the day?"

"Once you start drinking/drugging/smoking, what stops you?" (Internal forces such as self-control/decisions, self-created rules as to location or time; external forces such as intoxication, unconsciousness, lack of money, other people, etc.)

"Have you ever tried to cut down or stop and couldn't? What thoughts/feelings/urges did you have when you tried to stop or refrain?"
"What means have you tried to control your drinking/drug use?" (Relocating, prayer/religion, switching to another form of alcohol/another drug, willpower, scheduling, detoxification, rehabilitation programs, Alcoholics Anonymous, new friends, isolation, etc.)
"Do you think you have lost control of your drinking/drug use? When?"
"What was the longest period of sobriety/staying clean you have had?"
"Have you ever attended an Alcoholics Anonymous/Narcotics Anonymous meeting?"

Emotional or Psychological Aspects

"Have you ever regretted what you have done or said when you were drunk/high?"
"Do you feel guilty/embarrassed/remorseful/apologetic about the way you drink/use drugs?"
"Do you ever lie about/conceal/justify/avoid discussion of your actual drinking/drug use?"

Health Consequences

"Did a doctor ever tell you to stop drinking/using drugs for your health?"
"Is your drinking/drug use worsening a health problem you have?"
"Has using drugs/alcohol ever changed your eating/weight? Your sleeping?" (Irregular patterns, day–night reversal, interruptions, staying up 24 hours or more when using?)
"Have you ever had any of these when you drank/used drugs or stopped doing so: cramps, sweats/fevers, runny nose/watery eyes, diarrhea, dry heaves, seizures/convulsions, tremors/shakes, Delirium Tremens, weight loss (without dieting), hearing voices, seeing things that others didn't, feeling things crawling on your skin?"
"Have you ever been diagnosed with cirrhosis, pancreatitis, jaundice, hepatitis, AIDS, or other drug-related diseases?"
"Have you ever had blackouts/times where you couldn't remember what you did or how you got to where you were?" *(If so:)* "When did these first happen and when most recently? How often?"
"Have you ever become very drunk when you had only one or two drinks?"

Family/Social Consequences/Impacts

"Have you ever gotten into a serious fight with/hit/beaten/been beaten by your spouse/children/relatives/friends when drunk/high?"
"Is your partner also a problem drinker/alcoholic/drug abuser?"
"Do any family members, like your brothers/sisters/parents/children, have a problem with alcohol or drugs?"
"Does or did drinking/drug use cause strained relations with your children or family/neglect/verbal/sexual/physical abuse?"
"Does drinking ever spoil family gatherings/create an atmosphere of tension/make your children afraid of you/cause others to talk about you?"
"Do you avoid your family when you are drinking/high?"

"Has drinking/drug use caused you any sexual problems?" (Erectile/arousal problems, high-risk behavior, etc.)

"How would you describe the overall effect of drinking/drugs on your marriage/children/family/friends?"

"How do you spend your leisure/free time and with whom?"

Vocational/Financial Consequences

"Did your drinking/drug use ever cause problems when you were in school?"

"How much work have you missed because you were drunk/high/hung over?"

"Did you ever get into arguments or problems at work because you were drunk/high/hung over?"

"Have you ever been disciplined/been fired/damaged anything/hurt anyone because of your drinking/drug use?"

"If you were in the military, did you drink there? Did your drinking cause problems there?"

"Did your work suffer because of your drinking/drug use, such as being less productive, losing out on a promotion or a raise, or other problems?"

"How did/do you get the money to buy drugs?"

Legal Consequences

"Have you been arrested for disorderly conduct, <u>D</u>riving <u>W</u>hile <u>I</u>ntoxicated/<u>D</u>riving <u>U</u>nder the <u>I</u>nfluence, assault, or destructive behavior when you were drunk/high?"

"Have you ever been arrested for possession, sale, or distribution of drugs?"

"How much dealing in drugs have you done?"

"Have you run up large debts/been evicted because of drinking or drug use?"

Spiritual Consequences

"Has your drinking/drug use caused you any spiritual problems?" *(See Section 19.9, "Religious and Spiritual Concerns.")*

Identity

"Would you say you engage in 'social drinking' or have a 'drinking problem'? Or how would you describe your use?"

"Do you think of yourself as alcoholic/addicted to drugs? Why or why not?"

Treatment[9]   *See also Section 25.5, "Treatment Plan Components for Clients with Substance Abuse."*

"Have you ever attended an <u>A</u>lcoholics <u>A</u>nonymous/<u>N</u>arcotics <u>A</u>nonymous meeting?" *(If so:)* "When was that? What was it like? Why did you stop going?"

"What treatments have you received for drug/alcohol use?"

✓ It may be clarifying to construct a table to record this information.

---

[9]I am grateful to Bryan Lindberg, of Portsmouth, RI, for ideas for this section.

Date	Kind of treatment[10]	Duration	Location/provider	Duration of abstinence	Relapse trigger	Client's comments[11]

"What brought you into (or back into) treatment?"

3.29. Substance Use: Tobacco and Caffeine

Tobacco

"Do you smoke cigarettes/cigars/a pipe? Do you chew/dip snuff/use smokeless tobacco?" *(If so:)*
   "How many/how much do you smoke/use each day?"
"When do you have your first smoke/tobacco use of the day?"
"Where and when do you always/never smoke/use tobacco?"
"What positive things does smoking/tobacco use do for you?"
"When did you start smoking/using tobacco?"
"Did you ever smoke/use more or less than you do now?"
"Have you changed the brand you smoke/use to cut down?"
"Have you tried to stop smoking/using tobacco?" *(If so:)* "How? How many times? For how long?
   What has and hasn't worked for you?"

Caffeine

"How much of each of these do you drink in an average week?"

   "Coffee (except decaffeinated coffee), iced coffee, latte, cappuccino, etc.?"
   "Tea (hot, iced, green, etc.)?"
   "Colas or other soft drinks with caffeine?"
   "Power drinks like Red Bull?"

"How often do you take caffeine tablets like No-Doz?"
"How often do you have chocolate in any form?"
(For all of the above:) "When do you drink/take/have it?"

---

[10]For example: inpatient, outpatient, detoxification, residential/"halfway house," medications (methadone, disulfiram [Antabuse], Campral, etc.), marital or couple therapy, motivational interviewing (Miller & Rollnick, 2002), harm reduction (Marlatt, 1998), etc.

[11]Here I would listen for attitude toward treatment (such as pessimism, distancing, frustrations, disappointments, or other barriers) and for expectations (both reasonable and distorted).

3.30. Suicide and Self-Destructive Behavior

See Section 12.40, "Suicide," for descriptors.

Initial Inquiry

Begin by saying to the client:

> "You have told me about some very painful experiences. They must have been hard to bear, and perhaps you sometimes thought of quitting the struggle/harming yourself/even ending your life. Is that true?"

If this idea is accepted by the client, ask about the following areas.

Death Wish

> "When was the last time you wished you would not wake up/were dead/thought you/others/the world would be better off if you were dead?"
> "Have you ever thought this way before?"

Ideation

Suicidal ideation is more common than many people realize. Drum et al. (2009) offer good data for college students.

> "Have you recently said to yourself or others words like 'Life is not worth living,' 'I can't take any more of this,' 'Who needs this crap/pain?', 'You won't have to worry about me much longer,' 'Soon it will all be over'?"
> "When was the first time you thought of/considered ending it all/harming/killing yourself?"
> "When was the last time you thought of/considered ending it all/harming/killing yourself?"
> "Have you recently/in the last month made any plans to harm or kill yourself?"
> "When you have suicidal thoughts, how long do they last?"
> "What brings on these thoughts?"
> "How do you feel about these thoughts?"
> "Do you feel you have control over these thoughts?"
> "What stops/ends these thoughts?"

Affects and Behaviors

> "How often have you felt lonely/fearful/sad/depressed/hopeless[12]?"
> "Are there more themes of despair in your writing/art work/what you are reading/music you listen to than there were before?"
> "Are you now feeling reenergized after coming out of a depression?"[13]
>
> "Have you lost someone close to you?" (Through moving away, breakup, divorce, death?)
> "Have you lost interest in/given up some of your interests/hobbies/activities or friends?"
> "Have your grades dropped/your work performance fallen off?"
> "Are you more careless with your grooming, eating, and sleeping?"
> "Are you taking more risks than you used to?"
>
> "Because of a bad mood, have you ever ...
>   eaten or slept poorly?"
>   run away?"

---

[12]Hopelessness seems to be the crucial factor in suicide, not depression.

[13]This may be a high-risk period.

gotten into a physical fight or trouble in/been kicked out of school?"
damaged property?"
gotten into trouble with the police or been arrested?"
been involved in physical or sexual abuse, or other actions you have regretted later?"
gotten pregnant/gotten someone pregnant?"
increased your use of alcohol or drugs?"

Motivation

"Why are/were you thinking of killing yourself?"
"Have you felt 'My life is a failure' or 'My situation is hopeless'?"
"What would happen to you after you were dead?"
"What effects would your suicide have on your family/friends/coworkers/others who care about you?"
"Has any relative or friend of yours ever tried to kill/succeeded in killing himself/herself?" [If any, determine number, age/time when tried, reasons, most recent attempt.]
"Under what conditions would you kill yourself?"

Deterrents/Demotivators

"What reasons do you have to continue to live?"
"What would prevent you from killing yourself?" (Lack of "nerve"/courage, thoughts about children/other relatives, religious convictions, shame, "I wouldn't give her/him the satisfaction," wish to live/enjoyment, hope for improvement?)
"Have you considered what would happen if you were unsuccessful?" (Pain and permanent injury, such as being in a wheelchair, loss of vision, hearing, or speech; poverty; dependency; being abandoned; deterioration; "being a vegetable"?)

Threats/Gestures/Attempts

"When was the first time you tried to harm or kill yourself?"
"Have you tried more than once?"
"When was the last time you tried to harm or kill yourself?"
  "What were you thinking at the time about death or dying?"
  "Did you intend to die then?"
  "If not, what was your goal/motivation?"
  "How did you try to do it?"
  "Were you alone?"
  "Were you using drugs or alcohol?"
"What happened before each attempt?" (An argument, conflicts with family, a humiliating experience, disappointments, school difficulties, incidents with police, a pregnancy, an assault, physical/sexual abuse, being told "I wish you would die"?)
"What happened afterward?" (Hospitalization [intensive care unit, psychiatric, general medical]; effects on family and friends, on self; counseling or therapy?)

Preparations

"Have you ...
  given away any (prized) possessions of yours?"
  written a will?"
  checked on your insurance?"
  made funeral arrangements?"

told anyone about your plans?"
written a suicide note?"

Plan/Means/Method

"Have you thought about how/where/when you might kill yourself?"
"Have you thought about how easy or difficult it would be to kill yourself?"
"Have you made any plans to harm or kill yourself?" [If so, assess the degree of practicality/ effort.]
"How would you do it? Do you have the means?" [If means are present, assess the availability, opportunity, and lethality.]
"What preparations have you made?" (Collecting pills, keeping a gun loaded, etc.)

A most interesting approach to the evaluation of suicidal intention is the Firestone Voice Scale for Self-Destructive Behavior (Firestone, 1991), which ranks thoughts on an 11-point scale from self-critical to cynical, vicious, urging substance abuse, withdrawal, self-injury, and suicide. Other practical resources for suicide assessment include Bongar (2002), Shea (2002), Jobes (2006), and Rudd et al. (2001).

3.31. Violence

See also Section 3.17, "Impulse Control," for questions, and Sections 12.5, "Battered-Woman Syndrome," and 12.41, "Violent Behaviors," for descriptors.

In addition to the following questions, see McCloskey and Grigsby (2005) for detailed procedures for evaluating perpetrators (as well as victims) of intimate partner violence.

"When you get really upset/lose your temper, what sets you off/leads up to your losing your temper?"
"What do you actually do when you get really angry/lose your temper?"

"How long does it take you to calm down?"

"Have you ever threatened to hurt someone, such as a family member/your partner/a relative/a child/a pet?"
"Have you ever raised your fist or otherwise threatened someone? Got up in someone's face/ invaded someone's personal space?"
"Have you ever threatened anyone in order to have sex with him/her?"

"Have you ever broken/thrown things when you were angry/frustrated/disappointed? Punched a wall or broken a door?"
"Have you ever grabbed/slapped/pushed/poked/pinched/kicked/spit on/bitten/pulled the hair of/choked anyone?"
"Have you ever hit anyone with your fists/with a bat/with anything else when you were angry?"
"Have you ever used a knife or other weapon?"

(In regard to a specific incident:) "How long did the fight last? Why did you stop fighting with the other person(s)?"
"How much were the other(s) hurt?" (Bruised, scratched, torn clothing, required first aid/medical care, went to the hospital, severe disability, etc.?)

"Have the police ever been called because you were involved in a fight? (*If so:*) Were you arrested? What were you changed with? What happened then?"

"Have you ever planned to hurt or to kill anyone? (*If so:*) How far ahead did you plan it?"

Part II

Standard Terms and Statements for Wording Psychological Reports

Part II of this book is grouped into four subdivisions—A, B, C, and D—that correspond to the format and sequence of a typical evaluation report. The first main component of every report (A) has to cover what was known to you—old information. Upon this base you present your findings (B and C) and go on to your conclusions and recommendations (D).

The section "A Functional Guide to Report Construction" in "Getting Oriented to the *Clinician's Thesaurus*" provides step-by-step assistance with using Part II of this book to generate a report format. If you have decided not to use the sequence offered by Part II, you can go to Chapter 26 to select a different format.

A. Introducing the Report

Every report should begin with orienting information about you, the client, and the examination or treatment. Chapter 4 offers a suggested structure for this information, standard phrasings, and some legal and ethical issues about which you should comment. Chapter 5 lists possible reasons the client was referred to you, and Chapter 6 suggests ways to present the client's histories (medical, social, educational, family, and adjustment).

4

Beginning the Report: Preliminary Information

This chapter covers the **basic information** with which you would **begin** any report. **Reasons for the referral** are covered in Chapter 5; more detailed **background information about the client** is covered in Chapter 6.

4.1. Heading and Dates for the Report

Use prepared stationery or include full identification of the evaluator by name, degree, and title; and, where appropriate, affiliation, supervisor, license number, agency, address, and phone number.

Use a title for the report that fits the report's contents and audience—for example, "Psychological Evaluation" or "Case Closing Summary." Most titles are combinations of the words provided below. Always choose those favored by your practice setting.

Choose a word describing the discipline or activity:

> Psychosocial, Social Work, Psychiatric, Psychological, Neuropsychological, Psychoeducational, Nursing, Multidisciplinary.
> Forensic, Rehabilitation, Habilitation, Diagnostic, Testing, Case, Mental Status, Intake, Progress, Discharge, Closing.
> Educational, Intellectual, Personality, Ecological, Individualized, Behavioral, Treatment, Management, Life Management.

And then choose a word describing the kind of document:

> Summary, Evaluation, Assessment, Report, Examination, History, Plan, Update, Note, Formulation.

Always date the report. In addition, give all dates and locations (e.g., in the hospital room, school's office, private office, home) of examination/evaluation/interview(s)/testing. Indicate time of day, total time of testing, duration of interview, etc., as relevant.

4.2. Sources of Information for the Report

Begin describing information sources with one or more of these statements, as appropriate:

> In preparation for/advance of the interview, I received and reviewed the following records...
> The records I received were without clear provenance/were from a source I could not establish.
> Records were illegible/unavailable/scant/irrelevant/adequate/pertinent/voluminous.

Sources of information may include the following:

> Review of documents furnished—treatment summaries and reports, school records, previous evaluations, etc.
> Observations of the client during a clinical interview.
> Collateral interviews with friend/spouse/parents/family/relatives/caregiver/interpreter/etc.
> Testing: List each test or questionnaire separately by its full name, and use abbreviations/acronyms in the body of the report. *(See Sections 11.10, "Intelligence, Development, and Cognition: Assessment," and 13.1, "Models of Personality Diagnosis," for tests' names.)* [If appropriate, add this statement: "All tests were administered, scored, and interpreted by this report's author without the use of assistants or supervisees."]
> Consultation with other professionals.
> Observation by other professionals of/interview with the client/child/family.

4.3. Identifying Information about the Client

The description should be so detailed as to enable the identification of the unique individual. *(See Chapter 7, "Behavioral Observations," for specific language.)*

Name

Always state the client's given name and surname. As appropriate, also specify family of origin/ maiden name, changes, aliases/<u>A</u>lso <u>K</u>nown <u>A</u>s.

> ***For a Child:*** Indicate preferred name/nickname(s) in quotes, or "Prefers to be called _____."

Other Identification

Give the client's address, phone number, case number (if any), and name of current therapist/physician/referrer/case manager (as appropriate).

Gender/Sex

Specify the client's gender or sex (the term "gender" is more accurate here).

Age

For adults, give age in years.

> ***For a Child:*** Use 9 years and 3 months, 9 3/12, 9:3, or 9'3", not the ambiguous 9.3 years.

For birth order: **Client is the third of a sibship of four/client is third of four children.**

Marital Status

Be consistent in reporting marital status for males and females. Give number and duration of marriages/common-law marriages, separations/divorces.

> Current: **Never married** [preferable to "single" because it is less ambiguous], **living with a {paramour}/partner/fiancé/fiancée, married/common-law marriage, separated/divorcing/ divorced, widow/widower, unknown.**
> **Childless/parent of ____ children.**
> (Insert numbers:) **____ children currently reside with the client/are in the client's care. Children have been adopted/placed in foster care, temporarily reside with their mother/ father/grandparent(s)/other relatives.**

Occupation

Specify whether the client is employed/unemployed/underemployed, working full- or part-time, a student, retired, etc. And describe other occupations, previous occupations, etc., not simply jobs held.

> ***For a Child:*** Give date of alleged industrial/other injury, date last worked.

Nationality/Ethnicity

✓ Report on this for all clients or none. In reporting nationality/ethnicity, note also place of birth and what language is used in the home.

Race

✓ Be consistent across reports in reporting race; do not report it only for minorities. Race does not equal skin color. If in doubt about a person's race or about currently, locally, or personally acceptable terms, ask. I personally see no value in the descriptors of "biracial," "multiracial," or "of mixed races," as the concept of race has no scientific basis in humans, and almost all of us are of mixed genetic backgrounds. However, such terms are used in medical and social research, and may in some situations convey meaningful, nongenetic information, although the likelihood of erroneous overgeneralization is as great.

> African American, "white"/European American/"Anglo," Asian/Asian American {Oriental},[1, 2] Hispanic/Latino/Latina,[2] Native American, Inuit {Eskimo}, Oceanic/Pacific islander, Caribbean, etc.

Residence/Living Circumstances   *See Section 14.8, "Living Situation/Level of Support Needed," for descriptors.*

Religion

Report on religion only as relevant.

> Parents' religion/born into, religion baptized into/raised in/converted to/recent if changed/current.
> No preference: Unimportant, unaffiliated, nonpracticing, rejected, agnostic, atheist.
> Preference (↔ *by degree*): Practicing, pious, devout, righteous, zealous, proselytizing, evangelizing, preoccupied, delusional.

Legal Mental Health Status

> Involuntary/voluntary admission/treatment/commitment. (Perhaps give the number or name of the applicable section of the local law.)

Referral Reason   *See Chapter 5, "Referral Reasons."*

4.4. Self-Sufficiency in Appearing for Examination

> Came to first (or second, etc.) appointment, late by _____ minutes/excessively early/appropriately early for examination/on schedule/exactly on time for examination.

---

[1]My thanks to Fay Murakawa, PhD, of Los Angeles, CA, for clarification and correction.

[2]Be wary of using any global term that can obscure the psychological/cultural diversity of large population groups.

Came alone/without escort, came with friend/spouse/children/escort/caseworker/etc. [If companion is present, specify role of companion in examination, if any.]
Had _____ degree of difficulty finding the office.
Drove/was driven/used other mode of transportation (specify).

4.5. Consent Statements

Consent to Assessment or Treatment

With regard to the information you should provide to your patients, the guideline is this: "What would a reasonable, prudent adult need to know to decide whether to agree to engage in this assessment or treatment or to refuse it?"

For assessments, the client has to be informed of who will see the report (e.g., the courts, managed care staff, the referrer, an adolescent client's parents, etc.); to be advised of what decisions these persons or organizations will be making based on it; and to be offered the opportunity to refuse to participate or discontinue participation at any time if the client decides that specific revelations would not be in her/his best interests.

As regards a course of treatment, you must discuss the risks and benefits that can reasonably be anticipated. You might couch your statements to the patient in terms like these, based on ones suggested by the Group for the Advancement of Psychiatry (1990):

"Although no completely satisfactory statistics are available, I believe that this combination of treatments offers the best chance of success."
"The success rate of this treatment is about 85%.[3] That is, about 85% of all patients receiving this treatment experience complete or substantial relief of their symptoms."

The discussions and handouts in Zuckerman (2008) can be very helpful in this regard.

Informed Consent

We discussed the evaluation/treatment procedures; what was expected of both the client and the evaluator/therapist; who else would be involved or affected; the treatment's risks and benefits; and alternative methods' sources, costs, risks, and benefits.
This client understands the risks and benefits of giving and withholding information.
The client understands the procedures that he/she is being asked to consent to and their likely consequences/effects, as well as alternative procedures and their consequences.
I have informed the client that the information he/she provides will be incorporated into my report, which I will send to _____, who referred him/her to me for evaluation.
I advised the client that I am not her/his treating psychologist, that we will not have a continuing professional relationship, and that no records will be kept at this/my office.
The client knows that the results of this evaluation will be sent to ... and used for ...
In a continuing dialogue, these have been explained in language appropriate to his/her education, intellect, and experience.

Voluntary Consent

This client understands and willingly agrees to participate fully.
The client understands that she/he may withdraw her/his consent at any time and discontinue the evaluation/treatment.

---

[3]Obviously this figure would differ with each proposed treatment.

Competency to Consent

Based on our interactions, I have no reason to suspect that this person is not competent to consent to the evaluations/procedures/treatments being considered.

The client is not a minor or mentally defective; nor does he/she have any limitation of communication, psychopathology, or any other aspect that would compromise his/her understanding and competency to consent.

4.6. Reliability/Validity Statements

Basis of Data

On the basis of the ...

observations of this person for ____ hours on ____ occasions in (specify settings) ...

internal consistency of the information and history ...

absence of omissions/deletions of negative information, contradictions ...

the character and cohesiveness of the client's responses, spontaneous comments, and behaviors ...

consistency of information from different sources ...

client's ability to report situations fully ...

the data/history are felt to be completely/quite/reasonably/rather/minimally/questionably reliable.

I consider her/him to be an adequately/inadequately reliable informant.

Disclaimers

Readers of this report are advised that it reflects only the information available at the time of its creation, and not information that may be received later/that may be pertinent but is currently unavailable. Any such information may change the findings or recommendations of the evaluator.

This report reflects this person's condition at the time of this consultation and may not reflect this person's condition at the time of discharge or final diagnosis, or at any later or earlier time period. I reserve the right to reappraise and revise my statements and conclusions about this individual made in this report if I receive additional information. Also, over time, the statements and conclusions in this report may come to be no longer accurate.

This report is based upon only the information sources noted in the report.

No independent corroboration of the factual or background information presented by the client was attempted.

I have relied on the client's report of his/her history and assumed that it was accurate (except as noted), and so I cannot assume any responsibility for any errors of fact in this report.

The diagnoses and opinions in this report are offered with a reasonable degree of psychological certainty.

The opinions offered in this report have not been influenced by the referrer/referring agency.

Representativeness/Validity

Results are believed to be a valid sample of/accurately represent this person's current level of functioning/be typical behavioral patterns/behaviors outside the examination setting.

Because this client refused no test items/questions, worked persistently/was most cooperative and helpful, and had no interfering emotions such as anxiety or depression, test findings/results of this evaluation are felt to be representative of her/his minimal/usual/optimal level of functioning.

The client's performance on the [name(s) of test(s)/structured interview(s)/task(s)] was not consistent with his/her clinical presentation, educational history, and employment history, and so is not likely to be a valid measure of his/her general intellectual/other ability.

Results obtained in this testing are plausible (i.e., within the range of that which I observed). Should information from a neutral third party become available, these results could be reevaluated.

Consistency

His/her appraisals tended to be supported/corroborated by my observations/others' records.

She/he presented personal history in a spontaneous fashion, organized in a chronological sequence and with sufficient detail, consistency, logic, and attention.

He/she was a poor/adequate/good/excellent historian.

(↔ *by degree*) Complete/quite organized presentation, accurate recall of details/names and sequences, sparse data/stingy with information/only sketchy history, disorganized/scattered/haphazard, nebulous/vague/ambiguous, illogical, contradictory, facetious.

Accuracy

The client's self-description was credible, forthright, and informed.

I believe he/she has been honest/truthful/factual/accurate.

Although somewhat dramatized, the core information appears to be accurate and valid for diagnostic/evaluative purposes.

The client tries hard to be accurate in recalling events, but ...

She/he is not an astute observer.

He/she tried to provide meaningful responses to my question, but ...

She/he had difficulty presenting historical material in a coherent and chronological manner.

Client was questioned extensively and creatively, but it was not possible to determine/get a clear picture of/obtain more information on _____/obtain any delineation of symptoms other than his/her informal description of "I lost it."

She/he becomes tangential when pressed for specifics.

The patient seemed convinced that she gave an accurate account of her personal situation, although she also seemed unaware of her many limitations and deficits.

He expresses himself with great confidence, apparently unaware of any mistakes or confusions.

Although the client seemed to present the information above in an honest manner, its accuracy must be questioned because of possible difficulties with accurate perception of social/consensual/chronological reality/the accepted meaning of behaviors/patterns in relationships/etc., or the very unusual nature of her/his accusations/reported experiences.

She/he gave a history that did not so much appear to describe symptoms as to describe a major characterologically disturbed style of living.

Trustworthiness/Honesty/Malingering

She seemed to be honest in her self-descriptions of her strengths and weaknesses.

He appeared to be a truthful witness and an accurate historian.

She did not appear to be fabricating any of her history.

His response to questions appeared to be free of any deliberate attempts to present a distorted picture.

She made no special efforts to convince me of the gravity or authenticity of her problems.
She gave no evidence of a deliberate distortion of her test-taking efforts.

The history offered should be taken with a grain of salt/was fabricated/grandiose.
Much of what he said sounded like it was what someone told him/sounded rehearsed.
Responded eagerly to leading questions, endorsing the presence of all symptoms or problems
    suggested.

Ganser's syndrome {hysterical pseudodementia}/{VORBEIREDEN}.

It should be noted that in each of these complaints her description was vague, self-contradictory,
    and not completely consistent with any recognized clinical pattern.
She is motivated only to obtain financial benefits.
Despite allegations of pain and deficiency, he is able to get up and down from a chair without
    difficulty and sit for long periods comfortably.
She offered an exaggerated/minimized description of her behaviors.
Client is deliberately deceptive/malingering/faking.
This examiner believes the client is very capable of claiming conditions and reporting experi-
    ences that will enhance his application for disability but that bear little relation to reality.
Client was a willfully poor historian.
She lies with panache.
He presented a staged/rehearsed performance.
He indicated a sense of righteous entitlement to his (alcoholism/violence/irresponsibility/
    etc.).

Client's attitude toward her illness/disability suggests indifference/tolerance/acceptance/tran-
    scendence.

✓ **Note:** In some medical settings, terms and concepts other than "reliability" or "validity" are used
for these headings (Coulehan & Block, 1987). "*Objectivity* is the removal of systematic biases due
to the observer's beliefs, prejudices, and preconceptions" (p. 5). "*Precision* is how widely observations are scattered around the 'real' value" (p. 9), due to random error. "The *sensitivity of a test*"
expresses its ability to "'pick up' real cases of the disease in question" (p. 11)—that is, the ability
to separate true positives from false ones. "*Specificity*, by contrast, refers to a test's ability to 'rule
out' disease in normal people" (p. 11)—that is, the ability to separate true negatives from false
ones.

4.7. Confidentiality Notices

Guidelines

In order to ensure confidentiality, it is *not* sufficient to stamp the pages of a report "Confidential" or
"For professional use only," because these are too general and vague. Instead, provide a notice (on
at least the first page) that makes the following points clear:

1. The contents of this report are considered a legally protected medical document.
2. The information in this report is to be used for a stated/specific purpose.
3. The report is to be used only by the authorized recipient.
4. The report is not to be disclosed to any other party, including the patient/client. [Any exceptions to this must be clearly and specifically stated.]
5. The report is to be destroyed after the specified use has been made/stated need has been
   met.

Since the advent of the Health Insurance Portability and Accountability Act of 1996, you must know what information can be released with the HIPAA Consent (signed at the beginning of your relationship with the client after he/she has read your Notice of Privacy Practices) and when a fuller authorization is required by your state's laws. For more on HIPAA, see Zuckerman (2006). *See Section 26.9, "Formats for Therapy Notes," on the content of routine Progress Notes and HIPAA-compliant Psychotherapy Notes.*

Examples

Any of these examples may be reworded as necessary to meet the requirements of your own setting and the specific communication.

This information has been disclosed to you from records protected by federal confidentiality rules (42 C.F.R. Part 2, P.L. 93-282) and state law (e.g., Pennsylvania Law 7100-111-4). These regulations prohibit you from making any further disclosure of this information unless further disclosure is expressly permitted by the written consent of the person to whom it pertains or as otherwise permitted by 42 C.F.R. Part 2. A general authorization for the release of information is **not** sufficient for this purpose. The federal rules restrict any use of the information to criminally investigate or prosecute any patient with alcohol or drug abuse.

This is privileged and confidential patient information. Any unauthorized disclosure is a federal offense. Not to be duplicated.

Persons or entities granted access to this record may discuss this information with the patient only insofar as necessary to represent the patient in legal proceedings or other matters for which this record has been legally released.

I have in my possession a signed and valid authorization to supply these records to you.

This information is not to be used against the interests of the subject of this report.

This is strictly **confidential** material and is for the information of only the person to whom it is addressed. No responsibility can be accepted if it is made available to any other person, including the subject of this report. Any duplication, transmittal, redisclosure, or retransfer of these records is expressly prohibited. Such redisclosure may subject you to civil or criminal liability.[4]

This report may contain client information. Release it only to professionals capable of ethically and professionally interpreting and understanding the information it contains.

This report is to be utilized only by professional personnel, because its information will require interpretation for others.

It is inappropriate to release the information contained herein directly to the client or other parties. If this information is released to interested individuals before they are afforded an opportunity to discuss its meaning with a trained mental health professional, it is likely that the content of the report may be misunderstood, leading to emotional distress on the part of the uninformed reader.

For a Child:

The contents of this report have/have not been shared with the child's parent(s)/guardian. She/he/they may review this report with the evaluator or his/her specific designee. Copies of this report may be released only by the evaluator or his/her departmental administrator, or in accord with the school district's policy.

---

[4]This is from *The Paper Office* (Zuckerman, 2008).

The information contained in this report is private, privileged, and confidential. It cannot be released outside the school system except by the examining psychologist/evaluator/creator of this report, upon receipt of written consent by the parent or guardian. Not to be duplicated or transmitted.

4.8. Ethical Considerations in Report Writing

Ethical concerns permeate all the clinician's activities. They are an inescapable part of the work—not to be added on, or to be addressed only occasionally. The following is only a short and simple list.

Respect the client.

- Clarify not only the way your report's information will be shared, but also the limits on confidentiality, since what the client reveals may require you by law to report abuse or other situations/conditions, or to issue warnings.

- Keep the client's long-term best interests in mind in shaping your work. Respect his/her confidentiality, and edit your report's content with this in mind.

- Inform the client of the implications, and discuss these with her/him, before asking for consent.

Understand and remember the limits of your competence.

- Competence depends on the fit between the demands of the tasks and your resources. Competence may vary with your understanding of the client's age, sex, gender identity, ethnicity, culture, national origin, religion, sexual orientation, language, socioeconomic status, locale, etc.

- Remind yourself of what you don't know or understand.

- The fact that you are legally allowed to do something does not mean that you are competent to do it or that you will do it at the accepted standard of practice.

Don't go beyond your data.

- Select measures appropriate for the goals of the evaluation, and interpret the results validly for the client.

- Tests and interviews are only a sample of the universe of behaviors the client is capable of performing, not the whole range. Don't draw extensive conclusions from selected data.

- Being interviewed by a mental health professional is a unique relationship, and your observations may not generalize to other settings and persons. Consider the context and demand characteristics of the evaluation's setting.

- Use currently valid instruments, and maintain their security.

Michaels (2006) offers a more comprehensive discussion of these and related issues.

5

Referral Reasons

This chapter covers **reasons for referral only.** Everything else that should be included in the introduction to a report is covered in Chapters 4 and 6.

After a suggested phrasing for a referral statement, this chapter concentrates on **referral reasons for children**. This has been done because adult referral reasons are thoroughly covered in Chapter 12, "Abnormal Signs, Symptoms, and Syndromes," and many other chapters.

5.1. Statement of Referral Reason

A statement of the reason for referral should cover the referral source, date, type of evaluation/ service, and purpose, as well as the referral reason itself.

> Client was referred by _____ (referral source/person and agency) on _____ (date of referral), for _____ (type of evaluation or other service), to _____ (rationale/purpose) in regard to _____ (referral reason).

The rest of this section gives descriptors that can be used to fill in the blanks for type of evaluation or other service and for rationale/purpose in this basic statement. As noted above, the remainder of the chapter gives descriptors that can be used as referral reasons for children.

Types of Evaluations/Services

Mental Status Evaluation.
Clinical interview.
Diagnostic clarification.
Competency evaluation.
Forensic evaluation.
Custody evaluation.
Pretreatment evaluation and recommendations.
Reevaluation.
Educational placement.
Vocational recommendations, rehabilitation potentials/needs.
Fitness for duty.

Purposes

Determine necessary levels of care/intensity of treatment.
Assist with placement/admissions/decisions.

Determine the nature and extent of psychiatric/psychological disabilities.
Assist with the development of a treatment/rehabilitation/education program.
Assist in hiring/promotion evaluations.
Evaluate suitability for entry into _____ program.
Assess extent of neuropsychological losses and coping abilities.
Determine benchmarks of current functioning.
Meet organizational needs for evaluation/state and federal regulations/Joint Commission on Accreditation of Healthcare Organizations guidelines.
Assist with legal/forensic decisions.

5.2. Common Referral Reasons for Children at Home

For problems at school, see Section 5.3, below. See also the adult symptoms listed in Chapter 12, "Abnormal Signs, Symptoms, and Syndromes."

These are presented in alphabetical order, as no theory provides an agreed-upon structure.

Abused, consequences of being: Suspected, reported being investigated, founded/confirmed/not founded, by whom/relationship, duration.

Attention-seeking behaviors: Tattling, baiting, provoking others, taunts, teases, overly demanding of attention from siblings/peers/adults, craves _____'s attention, disruptive noises, "clowning around," pranks, "daredevil," interrupts, compulsive talking, manipulates.

Autistic withdrawal: Lack of responsiveness to people, resistance to change in the environment.

Conflicts with parents over: Persistent rule breaking, spending money, doing chores, doing homework, school grades, choices in music/clothes/hair/friends.

Dawdles/lingers/procrastinates/wastes time/starts late in dressing/eating/bedtimes/homework.

Eating: Poor manners, refuses, appetite changes, odd combinations, pica.

Imaginary playmates/fantasy.

Legal difficulties: Truancy, loitering, panhandling, hangs out with delinquent peers, underage drinking, vandalism, fighting, drug sales, "joyriding"/auto theft, trespassing, burglary, extortion, steals, shoplifts.

Need for _____ degree of supervision at home over play/chores/schedule.

Oppositional/resists/noncompliant.

Parent's role as disciplinarian: Uses lectures/threats/guilt inductions/force/spankings/groundings/allowance reductions/privilege losses as a consequence irregularly/arbitrarily/regularly, with good/mixed/poor success at control.

Relationships with sibs/peers: (↔) Rivalry, competition, abuses, teases/provokes, bullies, tyrannizes, assaults.

Running away/wandering off (not "disappearing"), tardiness.

Shyness/avoidance/reticence/withdrawal.

Sleep problems: Parasomnias, refusing to go to bed, nightmares, night terrors, sleepwalking, excessive drowsiness, refusal to get out of bed.

Verbal abuse: Criticizes, berates, belittles, humiliates.

Violence: Abusing, aggressive, threatening, bullying.

5.3. Common Referral Reasons for Children at School

Academic Performance

Fails tests, difficulty with _____ (specify subject), subject matter appears too difficult, extracurricular activities interfere with academics.

Kept back/retained/repeated grade, social promotion.

Lacks order and system in work and method of study, disorganized, careless/sloppy, lacks neatness, is irregularly/rarely/never prepared.

Does not seek help when appropriate, copies from peers.

Cheating, lying, plagiarism.

Poor academic progress due to low attendance/dropping out.

Social Factors

With Peers

Loner, relates to few students, isolates self, "different," doesn't belong/fit in, relates to adults only on request.

Clique membership/exclusion.

Is easily influenced/led, suggestible, engages in risky activities.

Verbally criticizes/abuses/insults peers, name-calling, unprovoked attacks, fights with _____, bullies.

Does not respect rights and property of others.

Does not participate in group activities.

Interacts inappropriately with peers.

Sexual inappropriateness.

With Teachers

Noncompliant, resists, disobeys, refuses to complete work assignments, seldom prepared.

Unmotivated, reluctantly participates, requires 1:1 supervision.

Does not follow classroom rules and procedures, challenges, disrupts.

Attention-seeking behaviors: Tattling, baiting, lying, provoking others, overly demanding of attention from teachers/peers/adults, craves _____'s attention, tantrums, disruptive noises, "clowning around," pranks, "daredevil," "class clown."

Overly dependent on teacher.

Low respect for authority/confronts teachers/defiant, insults, defies, lies, troublemaker.

Conduct/Deportment/Behavior

Oral aggression/interrupts/talks out.

Disruptive: Agitates/disturbs/disrupts other kids.

Bullies/intimidates, teases, manipulates.

Overactive, inappropriate, out-of-seat behaviors/in-seat behaviors, restlessness, fidgety. *(See Section 12.3, "Attention-Deficit/Hyperactivity Disorder.")*

School's response to behavior problems: Expulsions/suspensions/disciplinary conferences, other (specify).

Motivation/Initiative

Does not try, makes little effort, content to "get by."

Has ability to do better work, but lacks interest to do so, shows no interest in subject matter/in learning.

Does not persevere, needs great encouragement, gives up too easily/at first sign of difficulty, low frustration tolerance/"That's too hard."

Doesn't pay attention, daydreams, preoccupied, stares out of window, slow to respond.

Does not complete homework/in-class assignments.

Does not make up missed assignments.

Turns in assignments late.
Careless work.
Does not spend enough time on work.
Copies assignments from others, does not do own work.
Comes to class without necessary work materials.
Forgetful.

Attendance: Misses excessive days, absenteeism, tardy, tardiness, cuts classes, truancy.

School "phobia"/avoidance. *(See Section 12.32, "School Refusal/Avoidance/'Phobia.'")*

Student's Perceptions

Accurate/distorted perceptions of: grades, source of problems, other problems, fairness of system, attitude of peers/teachers/administrators.
Low/high sense of identity, self-esteem, confidence.
Deflects/denies/rejects responsibility for actions.
Minimal acceptance/rejection/shunned/ignored.
Teased/insulted/humiliated/bullied.

Other Aspects

Behavior deteriorates when confronted by academic demands.
Inappropriate behavior in structured/unstructured situations.
Is too tired/hungry during the school day to put forth best effort.
Hearing/sight/coordination/medical/medication problem.
Behaviors inimical to other students' welfare or exercise of rights (specify).

5.4. Common Referral Reasons for Children at Both Home and School

Cognitive

Distractible, hyperactive, inattentive, handles new or exciting situations poorly, lacks foresight, low frustration tolerance, gets confused in group, does not finish his/her work, daydreams, low concentration. *(See Section 12.3, "Attention-Deficit/Hyperactivity Disorder.")*

Behavior

Alcohol/drug/substance abuse. *(See Section 12.39, "Substance Use, Abuse, and Dependence.")*
Encopresis, enuresis.
Fire setting, plays with matches/cooking equipment.
Hypochondriasis.
Overactive/restless.
Self-Injurious Behavior: Hits, bites/chews, head banging, cuts, crude or excessive tattooing/piercings/body modification, etc. *(See also Section 12.33, "Self-Injurious Behavior.")*
Sexual behaviors:
  Sexual preoccupation, public masturbation, inappropriate sexual behaviors, obscenity/swearing, sexualized gestures and remarks, exhibits genitals/disrobes/public nudity/provocative clothing, etc.
  Molests/molestation/molested, threatens, touches, fondles/rubs against, battery.
  Intercourse/entry: Oral/vaginal/anal/femoral.
  Repeated/single episode/recurrent.
  Assault/rape/force used/damage/threats.

Protective services/police/court/medical/school/family interventions.

Prostitution.

Movement: (↔ *by degree*) Slow-moving or responding, lethargic, hypoactive, <normal>, restless, fidgets, out of seat, impulsive, hyperactive/overactive.

Speech difficulties, stuttering. *(See Section 7.4, "Speech Behavior.")*

Thumb sucking/rocking, stereotyped movements.

Tics: Involuntary rapid movements, noise or word productions.

Violence/aggression. *(See below.)*

Social

Aggression/violence: Verbal aggression, intimidation, bullying, repeated threats, throwing things, destructiveness of own/others'/peers'/teacher's/school property, physical fights/attacking/violence, hits parents/caregivers. *(See Section 12.19, "Impulse-Control Disorders.")*

Noncompliance: Antagonistic, "smart-aleck," disobedience, negativism, resistive, oppositional, argues, "sasses/talks back/mouthy," ignores, defiant of authority, lying in regard to chores/homework/house rules, complies only when threatened, independent/autonomous/"stubborn."

Immaturity: Impaired judgment, does not take responsibility for own work/belongings, own words/actions, own behavior and consequences; does not demonstrate positive/resilient self-concept.

Mutism (elective/selective).

Prejudiced, bigoted, insults, vandalism, threats, hate crimes.

Lacks respect for authority, insults, dares, provokes, acts out.

Swearing/blasphemy/obscenities.

Temper tantrums: Falls to floor and bangs heels/head, breath-holding episodes, throws objects, screams, weeps, destructive. [Note duration, as well as how handled: time out, spanking, ignored, punished, mocked.]

Timid/shy/dependent/anxiety-prone.

Is not accepted/valued as friend, doesn't sustain friendships.

Is an object of scorn/ridicule/mockery/teasing/name calling/insults/threats/physical attacks, is scapegoated/picked on, does not defend self when attacked, ostracized.

Isolation, withdrawal.

Affects

Anxiety, fears, phobias; nervous habits (tics, tapping, restlessness, mannerisms, drumming); avoids certain things/actions/situations, "freezes" in these situations. *(See Section 10.3, "Anxiety/Fear.")*

Angry, irritable, outbursts/rage/tantrums/"meltdowns."

Cries easily, pouts, "thin-skinned," whines, feelings are easily hurt.

Depressed, sad, unhappy, cries, hurt, low energy, easy fatigue, apathy, withdrawn, suicidal. *(See Section 10.7, "Depression.")*

Emotional constriction: Has limited range of emotions, expresses only high-intensity feelings.

Emotional dilation: Dramatizes, overreacts.

Physical

Problems with fine motor coordination (cutting, drawing, writing, etc.), confuses right–left/ambidextrous.

Problems with gross motor coordination (walking, running, climbing, bicycling, etc.).

Many physical/medical complaints, accident-prone.

Dysgraphia, dyslexia, eye preference, hand preference.

6

Background Information and History

A primary reason to acquire and report background information and history is to explain the historical stressors the client has suffered, the coping methods employed, and the results experienced. Sequentially, the material might be described as predispositions, precipitants/provocations, and presenting problems, with some attention to preventers/protectors. This chapter covers the client's **history and adjustment** in many areas. **Referral reasons** are covered in Chapter 5; **other preliminary information** is covered in Chapter 4.

6.1. History/Course of the Present/Chief Complaint/Concern/Problem/Illness

This section covers the patient's view of the problem in his/her own words, and beliefs about the source(s) of the complaints. It can also cover the following:

For a Child: Parents'/teachers'/authority's perception of problem(s).

For a Disability Report: Claimant's view of the impairment created by the injury/complaint/disorder.

Onset, Circumstances, and Effects

Formal statement of presenting/Chief Complaint. Duration, progression, and severity of complaint.
Premorbid personality and functioning levels.
Circumstances/precipitating stresses/stressors/triggers/cues/situations/events, anniversary reactions.
Development of signs/symptoms/behavioral changes, longitudinal/chronological/biographical sequence, periods of/attempts to work/return to functioning since onset, current status.

Effects of the complaint on the functioning of the patient.
Effects of treatments on complaint.
Reasons and goals for seeking treatment at this time. (**Note:** This is the important "Why now?" question.)
Evaluator's clarification/reformulation/elaboration of complaint.

Summary Statements:

Reason for current admission is/Current admission is result of ...
This is the ____ (#) admission to (name of hospital) and the ____ (#) lifetime psychiatric hospitalization, rehabilitation, partial hospitalization, etc.

Course   *See also the "Course Descriptors" heading under Section 23.1, "General Prognostic Statement."*

First episode, or multiple episodes? If the latter, describe as:
   Recurrences, relapses, exacerbations, worsenings, flareups, fluctuating course.
Duration of each episode?
Remissions, if any:
   Therapeutic/spontaneous.
   Duration of each?
   Return to what level of function/symptomatology? Describe as ($\leftrightarrow$ *by degree*):
      Decompensation, damage, recompensation, recovery, adjustment, growth, overcompensation.

6.2. Medical History and Other Findings

Medical History

Current/recent illnesses.
Symptoms. [Consider using a checklist such as the Symptom CheckList–Revised 90 (Derogatis, 1994) for completeness.]
Diseases/disorders with known psychological aspects: e.g., thyroid disorders, mitral valve prolapse, AIDS, diabetes, cancer of the pancreas, alcohol abuse, hepatitis (interferon treatment), etc. *(See Chapter 29, "Psychiatric Masquerade of Medical Conditions.")*
Surgeries and treatments.

(For women:) Pregnancies (Gravida), Live births (Para), stillbirths, spontaneous/induced abortions (Abortus). Written as G (#), P (#), A (#). Sometimes A is dropped and P is expanded to include term births, preterm births, induced abortion or miscarriage, and living children. For example, $G5P_{3114}$ would mean 5 pregnancies with 3 term births, 1 preterm (early) birth, 1 induced abortion or miscarriage, and 4 living children. $G1P_{1002}$ would mean twins.

Injuries/accidents, especially Traumatic Brain Injury, Closed Head Injury, and all unconsciousness-producing incidents. *(See Section 12.26, "PostConcussive Syndrome.")*
Drug treatment, use, and abuse, especially street/illegal/illicit drug use. *(See Section 3.28, "Substance Abuse: Drugs and Alcohol," for questions, and Section 12.39, "Substance Use, Abuse and Dependence," for descriptors.)* Also, use/misuse of prescription drugs and Over-The-Counter medications (sleep and digestive aids, cough and cold remedies, vitamins, herbals, other supplements, etc.).
Exposure history: Toxins, duration and amount, type, source, treatments.

Psychiatric History

Psychological difficulties in the past, and treatment(s)/professional help sought.
Current and past medications/therapies/treatments received, effects of/response to/treatments, side effects, condition on discharge(s) from treatment, involvement with other agencies/treaters.
Hospitalizations: Date(s), name(s), location(s), condition on admission(s), therapies instituted and response to treatment(s), duration(s) of hospitalization(s), condition on discharge(s), time before next hospitalization(s), course *(see above).*

Previous psychotherapy or counseling: Dates, <u>C</u>hief <u>C</u>omplaints/problems, provider(s), services provided, outcomes.

After discharge: Follow-up treatments, referral, compliance, lost to follow-up?

Previous Testing or Evaluations

Evaluations: <u>H</u>istory <u>and</u> <u>P</u>hysical, neurological, intellectual, educational, vocational, neuropsychological, personality, projectives, organicity, other/specialized.

Results/findings: Availability, scores, comparisons with current results, omissions and contradictions, "rule-outs."

6.3. Personal, Family, and Social Histories, and Current Social Situation

✓ Construction of a genogram *(see Section 6.6)* may be useful to guide inquiries and to record findings as you interview.

Parents' Qualities

Ages or birth dates/dates of death; cause of death (if deceased); client's age and reaction to death and its consequences (if applicable).

General physical and mental health during client's childhood; present health; chronic or severe illnesses, disabilities.

Personality characteristics, manner of relating to client, disciplinary methods, client's perception of parents' influences.

Marriages/divorces/separations.

Qualities of the marital relationship:

Stormy, close, distant, warm, functional, abusive, demonic, etc. *(See also Chapter 16, "Couple and Family Relationships.")*

Other: Extended family, patterns, obligations, familial "debits and credits."

Occupation(s), effects of employment/career on client.

Parental history of substance abuse or misuse, physical or sexual abuse, traumas, losses.

Composition of family during patient's childhood and youth.

Family's response to patient's behavior/problems/illness.

Client's Development and Early Health/Medical History

Pregnancy:

Eagerly anticipated/planned, unplanned, unaccepted/accepted.

Full-term, premature/postmature by ____ weeks.

Uncomplicated/complicated (specify difficulties/illnesses before/during pregnancy).

Delivery:

Natural, prepared, unprepared, difficult, uneventful, easy.

Normal duration/prolonged (specify ____ hours' duration).

Uncomplicated/complicated (specify difficulties).

Birth weight, Apgar scores, birth defects.

Exposure to toxins, drugs, alcohol, diseases, other insults pre-, peri-, postnatally.

Development:

Postnatal difficulties, weight gain, eating, sleeping, daily routines.

Milestones: Timing of crawling, sitting up unaided, walking, toilet training, speech and language acquisition; delays in development, loss of previously acquired skills (specify); immature behavior patterns.

Growth: Charts for growth by weight, height, body mass, and head circumference for boys and for girls from birth to 3 years and from 2 to 20 years are available from the <u>C</u>enters for <u>D</u>isease <u>C</u>ontrol and Prevention *(www.cdc.gov/growthcharts)* at no cost.

Childhood illnesses, medication(s), disabling/handicapping conditions.

Siblings/Stepsiblings/Half-Siblings

Ages, genders, locations in birth order/sibline/sibship/confraternity/constellation of ____ children/sibs/siblings. Possible language: **The client has a brother age 18, and two sisters age 22 and 16; he is the second of the four children.** Or, more briefly: Client is second of four sibs: F22, M19 (client), M18, F16.

Relationships among sibs in past and at present.

General physical and mental health during client's childhood; present health; chronic illnesses, disabilities.

Social Context for a Child

Cultural/ethnic background and, as appropriate, country of birth and language spoken in the home.

Living arrangements: Specify applicable relationship/legal issues.

Lives with both parents/stepparent and remarried parent/blended family/single parent/ grandparents/other relatives (specify), is adopted, lives in foster home/institution, other (specify).

Location:

City/metropolitan/urban/inner-city, suburban, rural, institution, military base, other (specify).

Home supports:

Destitute/homeless, poverty, "welfare," <u>A</u>id to <u>D</u>ependent <u>C</u>hildren, <u>S</u>ocial <u>S</u>ecurity (<u>S</u>upplemental <u>S</u>ecurity <u>I</u>ncome, <u>SS</u> <u>D</u>isability <u>I</u>ncome), "working poor," one/both parents working part-time/full-time/several jobs, other (specify).

Stability:

Stable, separated/divorced when client was ____ (age), changing, unstable, multiple moves, placements, changing parental partners, tumultuous, chaotic.

Social relationships:

Organizational memberships, cultural interests, many/few/no friends, close/best friends, buddies/clique/peer group membership, isolation/exclusion/rejection/"loner." *(See also Chapter 15, "Social/Community Functioning.")*

Social History and Situation for an Adult

This can be integrated with Section 6.4, "Adjustment History."

Dating history.

Marriage(s): Age at/date of each marriage, termination reason (if applicable). *(See Chapter 16, "Couple and Family Relationships.")*

Number, age, gender of children. Possible language: **She has sons age 3 and 5, and a daughter age 6.**

Relationship with ex-spouse(s) (if applicable), spouse(s)/partner(s), children.

Adultery/extramarital relationships/satellite relationships, exclusivity/monogamy.

Living circumstances:

Lives independently, lives with family/relatives/friends/other persons, lives alone but with much family/social/community support.

Vocational/occupational factors:
>   History of sheltered/adapted employment, part- and full-time competitive employment.
>   Nature, demands, duration of previous jobs (if any).
>   Present occupation: Chosen/not chosen, duration, satisfaction, intellectual demands, social–behavioral requirements/demands, advancement, aspirations, frustrations.

Military service characteristics:
>   **None, rejected, alternate service, avoided, enlisted/volunteer, draftee.**
>   Branch of service, training, work performed, promotions/demotions.
>   Combat/combat zone/noncombat location.
>   Reenlistments, duration of service, final grade, kind of discharge.
>   Military adjustment: Article XVs, time spent in the stockade (Army)/brig (Navy), court(s)-martial.

Legal/criminal history: Warnings from police, charges as a minor, charges/indictments, arrests, prosecutions, convictions, incarceration/probation/parole, civil suits, current litigation/lawsuits, bankruptcy, violence directed against others (specify).

Other: Special skills, career goals, debts/burdens, adequacy of income to meet responsibilities/needs, religious/spiritual issues, substance use and abuse.

Recreational activities. *(See Chapter 18, "Recreational Functioning.")*

Sexual History and Situation   *See Section 3.25, "Sexual History," for questions.*

Educational Situation for a Child or Adult

Nature of enrollment:
>   **Day, full-time, part-time, other** (specify).

Type of school/study:
>   **Public, charter, private, parochial/religious/sectarian, alternative school** (state reasons for placement), **itinerant teacher, home schooling** (state reasons for placement), **cyberschool.**

Location of school:
>   **Rural, suburban, metropolitan/urban/inner-city.**

Name(s) of teacher(s), relationship(s) with teacher(s), teacher report/description of problems.

Class assignment/level (specify), age–grade differential (if any).

Educational supports/placement:
>   **Special education (life skills, learning support for learning/intellectual/pervasive developmental/social and emotional/visual/hearing/other disability/disorder), classroom aide/Therapeutic Support Staff, Section 504 and other accommodations, mainstreamed, regular classes, scholars' program, gifted/talented.**

Overall level of academic achievement/performance/grades, Quality/Grade Point Average, standing in class.

Major area of study and its relationship to present employment (if any).

Educational program:
>   **Academic, technical/vocational, General Equivalency Diploma, college preparatory, etc.**

Extracurricular activities:
>   **Athletics, social service, music, scholarly, religious, political, special interests** (specify), **other** (specify).

Other aspects: Favorite subjects, peer and teacher relationships, position in peer group, aspirations.

Level/highest grade completed:
>   **Preschool/kindergarten, elementary/middle/junior high/high school, technical school, 2- or**

4-year college, graduate school; _____ grades completed; dropped out of school in grade _____ at age _____ because of _____ *(specify reason).*

Summary Statements:

The client has received special services/educational support through his/her whole school history/since the _____ grade/in grades _____.

Her/his attainment of developmental milestones was within the normal range of expectation.

There are no remarkable factors to suggest the presence of unmeasured potential.

Referral Reason   *See Chapter 5, "Referral Reasons."*

Sexual History, Nonsymptomatic   *See Section 6.4, below; see also Section 3.25, "Sexual History."*

Substance Abuse History   *See Section 3.28, "Substance Abuse: Drugs and Alcohol."*

6.4. Adjustment History

Of concern here are the client's important life events and transitions.

Making a table or timeline of the client's significant life events may clarify and suggest connections. With rows for dates and the client's ages at these dates, the columns could be "Child Events/Transitions" and "Family and Environment Events." These could include moves, changes in schools, shifts in finances, parental separation/divorce, major illnesses, legal difficulties, and so on.

Sexual Adjustment   *See also Sections 3.4, 3.14, 3.25, and 3.26 for questions and issues.*

Dysfunctions/disturbed sexual performance:
Loss of desire, inhibited arousal, primary/secondary/occasional difficulty getting or keeping an erection/"impotence," fast/premature/delayed ejaculation, inhibited orgasm, dyspareunia, vaginismus.

History of sexual/emotional/physical abuse:
Involved/threatened exploited/being exploited, victimizing/victimization, violence, traumas, legal ramifications, other (specify).

(For sexual abuse:) Involved/threatened molestation/touching, penetration, other (specify). [Be aware that sexual abuse is very differently defined in the literature and may involve molestation/touching, obscene phone calls, harassment/insults, exhibitionism, etc. as well as penetration (oral, anal, vaginal, femoral, etc.).]

Orientation and object choice:
Celibate, "sexual addiction," heterosexual, homosexual, gay, lesbian, bisexual, asexual, etc.

Paraphilias/sexual minorities/variations/special interests:
Pedophilia, hebephilia, exhibitionism, voyeurism, pornography, prostitution, <u>S</u>adism <u>and</u> <u>M</u>asochism/<u>S</u>lave <u>and</u> <u>M</u>aster, zoophilia, frottage, <u>B</u>ondage <u>and</u> <u>D</u>omination/<u>D</u>iscipline/<u>D</u>omination <u>and</u> <u>S</u>ubmission, fetishism, Trans<u>V</u>estism, "water sports"/"golden showers"/"toilet service"/urolagnia, Greek (anal)/French (oral)/English (whipping) sex, transsexualism, etc.

Summary Statements:

The client reports no/some traumatic sexual/traumatizing experiences (if any, specify).
The patient was not questioned about sexual preferences/orientation, history, or interests.

Social Adjustment

Acquaintances, clique membership/exclusion, friends/buddies/best friends/confidants, relationship with sibs/other family members/friends/enemies.
Ability to adjust to marriages, childbirth/parenthood, losses, aging, illness, health care/services/treatments, transitions.
Ability to conform to social and vocational expectations; hold employment; advance in a career; adjust to superiors/bosses, peers/coworkers/fellow workers, schedules, work load, and task changes.

Summary Statements:

His/her history is remarkable only for ... (specify findings).
The client has no history of military service/drug or alcohol difficulties/special training/police involvement.

_____ (pathology) is present in the client's bloodline/consanguinity/relations/family tree.
The client has a history of having lived for ____ years in an agonizing/tormenting/abusive/sociopathic/criminal/tumultuous/chaotic/pathogenic family.
The family environment was unstable, unstimulating, and unstructured.
The client's early life situation was victimizing/traumatic/tragic/disastrous.

6.5. Social History for a Disability Examination

See also Chapter 17, "Vocational/Academic Skills."

Applicant's description of industrial/workplace stressors, onset of complaints, and (alleged) injuries or illness associated with onset.
Psychological response to (alleged) injury situation:
    History of mental health problems since (alleged) injury.
    History of treatment(s) since (alleged) injury.
    Current treatment and medication, including medication taken on day of examination.

For each of the following areas, distinguish baseline, periinjury, and postinjury events:

Educational level and training: professional, technical, etc.
Sequential description of occupations pursued (including military service):
    Training and skills required.
    Supervisory responsibilities.
    Career advancement: upward, downward, lateral, static.

Difficulties and/or accomplishments in each occupational setting.
Previous occupational injuries, time lost, and outcome.
Previous life changes (external stresses and losses) and responses to these.
Legal history, when applicable:
    Previous workers' compensation and other personal injury claims, with the circumstances and outcome.
    Criminal history if relevant to diagnosis and/or disability.
Substance use and abuse.
Applicant's description of a typical day.

6.6. Family Genogram/Family Tree/Pedigree

Constructing a genogram can guide you and the client during history taking and can encourage exploration and insight when parallels in family history are visualized. Make as many copies of the genogram as are necessary, and perhaps revisit it during treatment. The symbols and a few words can record demographics (family members' genders, names, dates of births and deaths, marriages, separations, divorces, remarriages, ethnic and religious qualities) and some relationships (e.g., triangulations and balances).

The figure below shows the conventions for recording a genogram.

Draw a line around members of the current household.

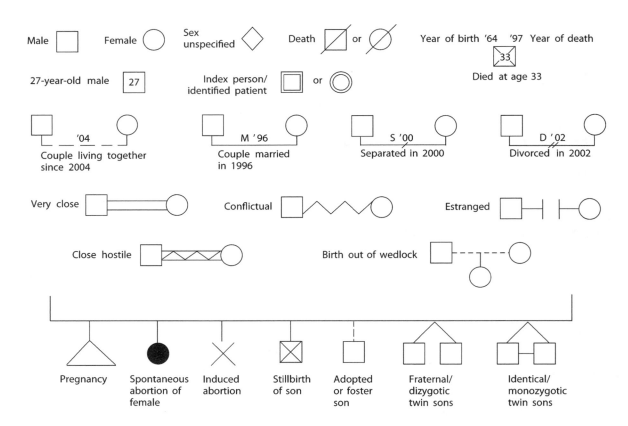

Other family information for evaluations can be found in Chapter 16, "Couple and Family Relationships." The design and use of genograms[1] in family therapy is explored in McGoldrick et al. (2008) and Kaslow (1995).

---

[1]If you do a lot of genograms or want to use them in family therapy, paper forms, checklists, and other quite useful materials are available from Genoware (*www.genogram.org*).

B. The Person in the Evaluation

7

Behavioral Observations

This chapter covers the following areas: **appearance**, including clothing; **movement** of all kinds; and **speech behaviors** (but not content).

How the client **responded to the evaluation interview**, and how he/she **presented him-/herself** in the examination, are covered in Chapters 8 and 9, respectively. **Speech behaviors** that reflect abnormal cognition are covered in Section 11.19, "Stream of Thought."

7.1. Appearance

✓ **Note**: Because physical beauty is so tightly associated in North American culture with goodness and health, and has such an impact on a person's life course, all clinicians should be fully informed about the distortions of judgment caused by socially supported prejudices (e.g., sexism, racism, ageism, beautyism) and cautiously circumspect of wordings supportive of these.

Overall Appearance: Summary Statements

The client seems to be well kept, well nourished, and in No Apparent Distress.
Hygiene is managed independently, effectively, and appropriately.
Clean, well groomed, and well dressed.
The client took good care of his/her appearance in regard to dress, hygiene, and grooming.

His/her appearance is not unusual.
No unusual visible features/deformities/dysmorphic features.
Nothing unusual/remarkable/noticeable about his/her posture, bearing, manner, or hygiene.
Her/his hygiene and grooming habits were adequate and normative for a socially conscious individual with an active self-interest and common social concerns.

This client showed some signs of self-neglect, specifically ...
Client appears about/older than/younger than chronological/stated age.
Haggard, weak, pale and wan, frail, sickly, sleepy/tired. [Note time of day; ask about sleep.]
Disfigured, disabled/"handicapped," "maimed" by ... (specify).
Shows the ravages of drug/alcohol/illness/stress/overwork/age/disease, dissipated, ill-looking, wasted-looking, out of shape.

Client shows evidence of current alcohol or drug use/physical dependence. [Note presence of recent needle marks, thrombosed veins, etc.] *(See Section 3.28, "Substance Abuse: Drugs and Alcohol," for signs.)*

For a Child:

Appears to be well cared for/assisted/supervised/trained in self-care, ignored/neglected.

For a Vocational Evaluation:

The client has a suitable appearance for work involving contact with the public.
He/she would not be identified as unusual in a group on the basis of physical appearance alone.

Build (↔ by degree)

emaciated	thin	average	stocky	formidable
sickly	lean	well developed/built	chubby	hulking
malnourished	wiry	weight proportionate	heavy-set	enormous
undernourished	slender	to height	husky	
underweight	lanky	well nourished	heavy	multiple chins
cachectic	skinny	within usual range	pudgy	jowly
frail	bony	"healthy"	barrel-chested	"beer belly"
gaunt			chunky	pot-bellied
	petite	large-boned	portly	flabby
	small-boned	rangy	fleshy	fat [See note on
	diminutive	large-framed	burly	obesity below]
		robust	beefy	rotund
		full-framed		
		rugged		

Height

✓ It is preferable to state height objectively (i.e., to give measurement) rather than to use relative terms ("short/average/tall"), unless you also include your own height.

Weight

Ask: "What do you now weigh?" and "Is this your usual weight?"

✓ **Note:** "Obesity" and "hardly/mildly/moderately/extremely/massively/morbidly obese" are all misleadingly subjective and subject to changing tastes and styles. It is far preferable to report measured height, weight, and general "build." Remember, obesity is *not* a psychiatric diagnosis.

Body types: Android/abdominal/"apples," truncal obesity, or gynoid/femoral/"pears."

For a Child:

Stature in relation to age is short/normal/tall.
Child is at the _____ percentile of the standard table for height, weight, and head circumference for children. [Tables for these are available online (*www.cdc.gov/growthcharts*).]
Child is at Tanner stage _____ of sexual development. *(See Section 19.7, "Puberty," for a description of the Tanner stages.)*

Complexion

Ruddy, tanned, sunburned, jaundiced, sickly, pale, wan, washed out, sallow, pallid/pallorous, leathery, pimply, warty, mottled, shows negligence, birthmarks/port-wine marks, scars, acne vulgaris.

BEHAVIORAL OBSERVATIONS

Face

General: Pinched, puffy/swollen, washed out, emaciated, old-/young-looking for chronological/ true age, baby-faced, long-faced, moon-faced.

Movement: Tics, twitches, drooping, mobility during interview/over topics.

Chewed gum/toothpick/other items.

Head: Odd-shaped, microcephalic/macrocephalic, dolichocephalic/mesocephalic/brachycephalic, normal, cretinous, damaged.

Teeth: Unremarkable hygiene, dentures, gaps and missing teeth, over-/underbite, carious, edentulous, unusual dentistry, bad breath/breath odor/"halitosis."

Facial hair: *See "Beard" under "Hair," below.*

Makeup: None, minimal, lipstick only, eye makeup, brows removed, <customary>, excessive, odd, outrageous.

Notable features: Ears, nose, cheeks, mouth, lips, teeth, chin, neck. (Examples: Dark circles under eyes, bulbous/red/richly veined nose, large/small features, toothy grin.)

For a Child:

Sucked thumb, used pacifier, etc. *(See Section 12.15, "Fetal Alcohol Syndrome.")*

Facial Expressions   *See also Chapter 10, "Emotional/Affective Symptoms and Disorders."*

Attentive, alert, interested, focused.

Tense, worried, indrawn, frightened, alarmed.

Sad, frowns, downcast, in pain, grimaces, forlorn, drawn.

Tearful, watered/tears up, tears falling, open crying/sobbing.

($\leftrightarrow$ *by degree*) Dramatic, expressive, changes with topic, apathetic, preoccupied, inattentive, unspontaneous, withdrawn, vacuous, vacant, absent, detached, mask-like, did not smile/ change expression during the long interview, lacks spontaneous/appropriate/expected facial expression, hypomania, flat, expressionless, lifeless, frozen, rigid.

Calm, composed, relaxed, dreamy, head bobbed as if nodding off.

Smiling, cheerful, happy, delighted, silly/sheepish grin, beaming.

Angry, disgusted, distrust, contempt, defiance, sneering, scowling, grim, dour, tight-lipped, hatch marks between his/her eyes, a chronic sour look.

Eyes   *See also "Eye Contact/Gaze" under Section 7.3, "Movement/Activity."*

Size, shape, etc.: Large, small, close-set, wide-set, almond-shaped, sunken, bloodshot, reddened, bleary-eyed, bulging, hooded, wide-eyed, cross-eyed, "wall-eyed"/disconjugate gaze.

Expression: Staring, unblinking, glassy-eyed, vacant, penetrating, piercing, vigilant, nervous/ frequent blinking, darting, squinting, tired, "eyes twinkled," limpid, unusual.

Brows: Beetling brows, heavy, massive, raised, pulled together, pulled down, shaven, plucked.

Glasses: Regular corrective lenses, half-lenses, bifocals, reading glasses, contact lenses, sunglasses, needed but not worn, broken/poorly repaired.

Hair

Hairstyle: Unremarkable, fashionable length and style, long, ponytail, "pigtails," plaits, cornrows, braided, crew/brush cut, natural/"Afro," frizzy, curly, finger curls, dreadlocks, wavy, straight, uncombed, tousled, "punk," "Mohawk," "mullet," shaven, currently popular haircut, stylish, unusual hair cut/style/treatment, moussed, permed, "relaxed," unbarbered, simple/easy-to-care-for cut, short, pageboy.

Color: Bleached, colored/dyed, frosted, streaks of color, different-colored roots, flecked with gray, salt-and-pepper, gray, white, faded color, albino, platinum/blonde/fair-haired, red-haired/carrot/coppery/rust/auburn, chestnut, brunette, brown, black, raven.

Hair loss: Thinning, receding hairline, high forehead, widow's peak, male-pattern baldness, balding, bald spot, bald, head shaven, alopecia.

Artificial hair: Wig, toupee, hairpiece, "a rug," implants, transplants, an obvious hairpiece.

Other: Clean, dirty, unkempt, greasy/oily, matted.

Beard: Clean-shaven, unshaven/needs a shave, several days' growth, had the beginnings of a beard/ wispy/scraggly, stubble, cultivated/deliberate stubble, poorly/well maintained/groomed, stylish, neatly trimmed, full, closely trimmed, mutton chops, goatee, chin beard/chin strap, unbarbered, Van Dyke, Santa Claus style, wore his facial hair in a _____ .

Moustache: Wore/sported/maintained a moustache/moustached/moustachioed, handlebars, pencil-thin, mandarin, colonel, neat, drooping, scraggly, just starting/light.

Other Aspects of Appearance/"Body Habitus"

Grooming/hygiene/cleanliness: Excellent/good/unremarkable/fair/marginal/poor, scruffy/ bedraggled, neglected, indicating indifference, acceptable but not optimal, unremarkable/ as expected, neat, tidy, meticulous.

Grooming reflective of: Impoverishment/very limited resources, cultural background, identification with subpopulations/celebrities/ideal, physical limitations, cognitive limitations, pride in appearance.

Odor (body or clothing): Musty, noticeable, offensive, ineffective deodorant, lack of bathing, excess perfume, smells of alcohol/tobacco/smoke.

Nails: Clean, tobacco-stained, dirty, grimy, bitten down to the quick, overlong, broken, painted/ colored, polished, manicured, artificial/extensions.

Skin: Bruises, cuts, abrasions, scabs, sores, scars, damage, tattoos, piercings, acne, acne vulgaris scars, birthmarks.

Breathing: Noisy, wheezed, <u>S</u>hortness <u>O</u>f <u>B</u>reath, used oxygen.

Notable aspects: Shoulders, chest, belly, back, pelvis, legs, feet, ankles, hands, fingers.

Jewelry (rings, earrings, bracelets, pins, piercings, etc.), makeup.

Other: Hearing aid, prosthesis, colostomy bag, catheter, other device, bags carried.

7.2. Clothing/Attire

✓ The relevant perspectives are not fashion, cost, or newness, but what clothing means about the client's ability to care for her-/himself and her/his judgment of appropriateness.

Appropriateness

Appropriate for situation/occasion/weather, nothing unusual for a visit to a professional appointment/office.

Presentable, acceptable, suitable, appearance and dress appropriate for age and occupation, businesslike, professional appearance, nothing was attention-drawing, modestly attired.

Client's idea of suitable, not suitable for age/suitable for a younger person, not suitable for his/her station in life, too casual to be acceptable, care of person and clothing was only fair.

Other: Institutional, odd/unusual/eccentric/peculiar, unique combinations, carefully disordered, dressed to offend, un/conventional, attention-seeking/-drawing, outlandish, garish, bizarre.

Qualities of Clothing (↔ *by degree*)

filthy	rumpled	needing	plain	**neat**	**stylish**
grimy	disheveled	repair	out of date	careful	fashionable
dirty	neglected	threadbare	old-fash-	dresser	elegant
smelly	wrong size	seedy	ioned	clothes-	dandified
dusty	ill-fitting	clean but		conscious	natty
musty	unkempt	worn	regional/	in good taste	dapper
		worn	foreign		
food-spotted	messy	shabby	designs	overdressed	meticulous
greasy	slovenly	tattered	eccentric	seductive	immaculate
oily	sloppy	torn	"grunge"	revealing	
	baggy		prim	flashy	
	bedraggled	shows	somber	too tight-	
	raggedy	unilateral		fitting	
		neglect		tasteless	
		unzipped		design	
		unbuttoned			

Other

Dressed in a manner typical of today's youth/of an earlier decade (specify), attired in the style of her/his contemporaries.

Clothes were loosely fitting/quite tight suggesting a recent change in weight.

7.3. Movement/Activity

Speed/Activity Level

(↔ *by degree*) Frozen, almost motionless, little animation, mask-like facies, psychomotor retardation, slowed, showed great economy of movement, slowed reaction time/latency to questions, <normal>, normokinetic, restless, squirming, fidgety, fretful, constant hand movements, continual flexing of _____, hyperactive, overactive, agitated, frenetic.

For a Child:

High activity level, motorically active, fidgets, difficulty remaining in his/her chair/seat, many out-of-seats, restless and distractible, rambunctious, difficult to redirect, redirectable, investigated all the contents of the room/desk/testing materials, intrusive, overactive/hyperactive/aggressive, a darter. *(See Section 12.3, "Attention-Deficit/Hyperactivity Disorder.")*

Coordinated–Uncoordinated

(↔ *by degree*) Awkward, clumsy, "klutzy," often injures self, "accident-prone," inaccurate/ineffective movements, jerky, uncoordinated, <normal>, purposeful, smooth, dextrous, graceful, agile, nimble.

✓ Note degree of body awareness, body ego, body confidence.

Noticeably poor manual dexterity, held objects such as pencils and scissors awkwardly, difficulty coordinating hands and fingers when asked to copy designs, hands shaky on tasks, problems in drawing lines (specify).

For a Child:

Coordination delayed by _____ months/years, <normal>, good/poor gross and fine motor coordination.

✓ Note handedness/preference/dominance, presence of astereognosis.

Dominance: Right/left/mixed, as seen in hopping on a foot, preferred use of one eye, able to use only one hand to flip a coin/catch a thrown object.

Praxis

Grip: Held pencil in the usual grip/atypical/awkward/in a fist-like grip, in a palmar grasp, perpendicular to the table, down by the graphite/with fingers too close to the point, thumb overlapping the forefinger/forefinger overlapping the thumb, with two fingers and the thumb, with three fingers and thumb, between the forefinger/index/pointer and third/middle finger, tensely.

Handwriting (↔ *by degree*): Elegant, precise, stylized, legible, sloppy, prints, primitive, scrawls, illegible, no recognizable letters.

Handshake (↔ *by degree*): Avoided, "fishy," moist/sweaty/nervous, limp, tentative, weak, delayed, <normal>, firm, exaggerated, painfully hard.

✓ Ask client to walk, write a sentence, and/or tie shoes/tie, and observe skill/difficulties.

Mannerisms/Oddities

This subsection covers peculiarities of motor behavior, automatisms, unusual uses of hands/body. *(See also "Symptomatic Movements," below.)* If a client exhibits no such peculiarities, use this statement:

There were no mannerisms, tics, or gestures indicative of any psychopathology or physical distress.

Stereotyped movements: Twirling, rocking, self-stimulation, hand flapping, aimless/repetitious/unproductive/counterproductive movements, head bobbing, wriggling, hand or finger movements, bounces leg, posturing, picks/pulls at clothing, blinking.

Perseverations: Pauses and repeats movements at choice points (as when leaving the room/in doorway), makes same response to different/changed/new stimulus.

Manneristic mouth movements: Tongue chewing, lip smacking, whistling, made odd/animal/grunting sounds, belching, pulls lips into mouth.

Squints, made faces/grimaced.

Childlike facial expressions/speech (e.g., "Gol-lee"), giggles, snickers.

Sniffles repeatedly/loudly, uses/needs but does not use tissues/handkerchief, freely and frequently picks his/her nose, repetitively "cleans" ears with fingers.

Yawned excessively/regularly/elaborately, rubbed eyes.

Made audible breathing sounds.

Smoked incessantly/carelessly/dangerously/compulsively/selfishly.

Deliberately dropped items so she/he could retrieve them.

For a Child:

Kept thumb in mouth for _____ minutes of the _____ hour session, sucked fingers.
Covered face with hands and peeked out.
Walked on toes/heels/ankles.

Symptomatic Movements

Waxy flexibility (CEREA FLEXIBILITAS), tardive dyskinesia, dysdiadochokinesia, Parkinsonian/ ExtraPyramidal Symptoms/movements, athetosis, hemiballismus, ataxia, choreiform, akinesia, "pill rolling," "chewing," "restless leg syndrome," opened and closed legs repeatedly, paced, hyper/hypotonic, hyper/hypokinetic, echopraxia, cataplexy, denudative behavior. *(See also Section 12.36, "Side Effects of Psychotropic Medications/Adverse Drug Reactions.")*

Tremor: None/mild/at rest/essential/familial, intentional/hovering, quivers, shivers, twitches, tics, shakes.

Autonomic hyperactivity. *(See Section 10.3, "Anxiety/Fear.")*

Mobility

(↔ *by degree*) Confined to bed/bedfast, uses wheelchair/adaptive equipment, requires support/ assistance/supervision, uses a gait aid (cane, leg/back brace, walker, crutches/Canadian crutch), walks, slow, careful, avoids obstacles, runs, athletic.

Stood up frequently, roamed the room, stretched/walked around periodically, attempted to leave.

Gait, Carriage, and Station

(↔ *by degree*) Astasia/abasia, ataxic, steppage, waddling, awry, shuffles, desultory, effortful, dilatory, stiff, limps, drags/favors one leg, awkward, walks with slight posturing, lumbering, leans, rolling, lurching, collides with objects/persons, broad-based, knock-kneed, bow-legged, <normal>, ambled, no visible problem/no abnormality of gait or station, fully mobile (including stairs), springy, graceful, glides, brisk/energetic, limber.

Mincing, exaggerated, strides, dramatic/thespian/for effect, unusual.

For a Child:

Difficulty climbing stairs, brushed ankles against each other, unsteady forward gait, stumbled at intervals. [**Note:** Observe the wear patterns on shoes.]

Balance (↔ *by degree*)

Dizzy, vertigo, staggers, sways, fearful of falling/unsure, unsteady, positive Romberg sign, complains of light-headedness, <normal>, no danger of falling, steady.

Posture/Bearing

"Hunkered down," hunched over, slumped, slouched, stooped, round-shouldered, limp, hangs head, cataplexy, relaxed, <normal>, dignified, stiff, tense, guarded, rigid, erect, "military," upright, sat on edge of chair, leans, peculiar posturing/atypical/inappropriate (sat sideways in the chair, reversed chair to sit down).

Suggests chronic illness, appeared weak/frail, low stamina/endurance/easily winded, listless, labored, burdened.

Eye Contact/Gaze (↔ *by degree*)   *See also "Eyes" in Section 7.1, "Appearance."*

None, avoided, stared into space, kept eyes downcast, broken off as soon as made/passing/intermittent, wary, alert, looked only to one side, brief, flashes, fleeting, furtive, evasive, appropriate, <normal>, expected, modulated, lingering, staring, steady, glared, penetrating, piercing, confrontative, challenging, stared without bodily movements or other expressions.

Other   *If any movement or posture indicates pain, see Section 12.23, "Pain Disorder/Chronic Pain Syndrome." For anxious behaviors, see Section 10.3, "Anxiety/Fear." For depressed behaviors, see Section 10.7, "Depression."*

7.4. Speech Behavior

Give quotes/verbatim examples. *(See also Section 11.19, "Stream of Thought.")*

✓ Difficulties noted in at least the first two areas below should be followed up with an assessment by a speech therapist (a <u>S</u>peech–<u>L</u>anguage <u>P</u>athologist with a <u>C</u>ertificate of <u>C</u>linical <u>C</u>ompetence.)

Articulation

Unintelligible, stammer/stutter, stumbles over words, mumbles, whispers to self, mutters under breath, lisp, sibilance, slurred, "juicy," garbled, understandable, clear, precise, clipped, choppy and mechanical, poor diction, poor enunciation, misarticulated, unclear, dysfluencies, dysarthrias (spastic, flaccid, ataxic), aphasias.
Pace/cadence/rate: Too slow/fast, _____ rhythm.
Accent: Noticeable, mild, strong, foreign, regional, odd, intense, confusing, drawl, burr.

For a Child:

Immature, simpler sentences/formation than expected, expected/age-appropriate/inappropriate articulation errors, difficulty in speech articulation (especially sounds such as /r/, /sh/, /th/, /z/, or /ch/), slid over some consonant sounds.

Voice's Qualities

Loud/noisy/almost screaming, strident, brassy, harsh, gravelly/hoarse/raspy, throaty, nasal, screechy, squeaky, shrill, staccato, mellifluous, quiet, soft, weak, frail, thin, "small" voice, barely audible, whispered/aphonic, affected, tremulous/quavery, low-/high-pitched, singsong, whiny, odd inflection/intonation, monotonous pitch/tone, sad/low tone of voice, muffled, bass/baritone/alto/soprano.

Phraseology: Summary Statements

Consider these as they apply to writing where relevant, as well as to speaking.

Client spoke in "baby talk"/infantile/childish/immature style.
He mispronounced words, used uneducated vocabulary/uncultured language/vocabulary reflective of limited education/cultural deprivation, used slang words, made grammatical mistakes, used nonstandard English.
She used dialect, regionalisms, colloquialisms, provincialisms, foreign words/idioms.
Speech was notable for cliches, habitual expressions, repetition of catch phrases, much use of "You know"/"like."
Client's vocabulary was pedantic, pseudointellectual, stilted, excessively formal, jargon.
Inappropriately familiar terms were used (e.g., "dear," "honey").
Client engaged in punning, rhyming, contrived language.
Speech included casual and familiar swear words, epithets, hostile cursing, racial/ethnic/religious slurs.
Aphasias: Expressive/nonfluent, receptive/fluent, global/total, transcortical (intact repetition

BEHAVIORAL OBSERVATIONS

with fluent or nonfluent aphasia), anomic, amnestic, auditory/word deafness, visual/word blindness, etc.).

Alexia, alexithymia, agrammatism, syntactical errors.

Misspoke; confused words (e.g., "wall" for "while"), requiring repetition and inquiry for clarification.

For a Child:

Child has underdeveloped vocabulary for his/her age.

Conversation consisted of three- or four-word phrases rather than sentences.

Speech Amount/Productivity/Energy/Rate (↔ by degree)

halting	**slowed**	**normal**	**pressured**	**verbose**
hesitant	minimal	initiates	loquacious	overproductive
delays/ed	response	alert	garrulous	long-winded
inhibited	unspontaneous	productive	excessively	bombastic
blocked	reticent	animated	wordy	nonstop
lags	terse	talkative	voluble	vociferous
slowed/long	sluggish	fluent	expansive	overabundant
response time	paucity	easy	blurts out	copious
	sparse	spontaneous	run-together	overresponsive
mute	impoverished	smooth	raucous	excessive detail
selective mutism	laconic	chatty		voluminous
only nods	economical	even	rapid	hyperverbal
unresponsive	taciturn		fast	
	single-word		rushed	flight of ideas
word-finding	answers		hurried	
difficulties				
word searching				
difficulty generating responses				

Speech Manner (↔ by degree)

distant	**normal**	candid	empathic
hurried	responsive	open	touching
pedantic		frank	insightful
somber	well modulated	guileless	wise
inarticulate	articulate	free	charming
whiny	gets ideas across well	untroubled	witty
	good-natured	easy	jovial
expressionless	engaging	warm	
mechanical	well spoken	sincere	
	eloquent	self-disclosing	
dramatic	realistic	in touch with	
	measured	own feelings	
naive	thoughtful		

Summary Statements for Normal Communication/Speech Behaviors

I noted no impairments in language functioning reflecting disordered mentation.

The client could comprehend and carry out the test/evaluation instructions and tasks, and didn't misinterpret or misunderstand the test materials or questions.

He/she displayed no language impairment, either receptively or expressively.
Communication was not impeded in any way; satisfactory/adequate/normal expressiveness.

Auditory comprehension was adequate, and oral delivery was effective.

The client's speech was without articulatory deficit.

The client's comprehension of English/spoken words was normal/defective/abnormal.
Her/his ability to understand the spoken word was adequate within the context of this examination, but might not be in other situations, such as ... (specify).
Client did not have to have the questions/instructions rephrased/simplified/repeated.

Summary Statements for Conversational Style

She is a reciprocal conversationalist/dialogued spontaneously/is able to carry on a conversation.
He is able to initiate topics appropriately.
She follows the conventions/social rules of communication (including appropriate phrasing and turn taking), and understood the suppositions and expectations of native speakers of American English.
Client participated/did not participate in appropriate social dialogue.
She exchanged the expected social amenities of offering and expressing gratitude.
He engaged in little/normal/expected/excessive small talk.
She did not initiate conversation or develop spontaneous themes.
The client's speech was sophisticated, with considerable emphasis on intellectual/personal/medical/historical/family matters.

Client assumed that I, the listener, knew more than I did about her history/ideas/the subject of the conversation.
Speech was excessively colloquial for our relationship.

Speech was slow, deliberate, and at times evasive.
All of the client's speech was defensive/designed to emphasize his degree of disability.
Her answers were not to be relied upon, but were pertinent and to the point. *(See also Sections 4.6, "Reliability/Validity Statements," and 8.5, "Relationship with the Examiner.")*

Client uses vulgarity/blasphemy/scatology/sexuality to shock.
Speech reflects preoccupations. *(See Section 11.19, "Stream of Thought.")*
Client engaged in rote retelling of an often-told story.
Uses psychiatric language sophisticated enough to suggest a person who is system-wise.
His language choices were, in reality, more odd than I am able to reproduce here.

She was reluctant to expand on/denies her complaints/problems/symptoms.
Client offered little information but responded readily to direct questions.
He was very verbal but not articulate.
Where one word would suffice/answer the question asked, she produced a paragraph.
He was an excessively verbal person who needed more braking than prompting.
Client attempted to be helpful by trying to tell a great deal, and so created pressured speech.

For a Child:

The child was perseverative/was echolalic/mimicked examiner's speech.
Delayed language acquisition is evident.
Child had difficulty in comprehending or expressing/oral language/speech.

BEHAVIORAL
OBSERVATIONS

7.5. Other Behavioral Observations

Brought items to the examination: Possessions, cigarettes, presents, papers, briefcase, coffee/refreshments/candy/food, pets, children.
Belched, etc., without apology.

✓ If a client's responses seem odd, consider unacknowledged hearing loss as a factor. It is more common in the older population (from 25% of females over age 65 to 40% of over-65 males; more than 80% of those over 85), but it is not uncommon in younger people. Unacknowledged hearing loss is a common cause of believing that others are against one (Holt et al., 1994).

For a Child:

Tantrum: Assaultive, destructive to property, aggressive to others, not redirectable, duration of ____ minutes.

8

Responses to Aspects of the Examination

This chapter describes **face-to-face**, one-on-one, **interpersonal behaviors** reflecting the client's **responses to aspects of the examination**, including responses to the procedures of evaluation, rapport with the examiner, response to the methods of evaluation, concentration, motivation, response to failure, and approach to the tasks of the examination. Chapter 9 covers **self-presentation** of the client to the evaluator.

8.1. Reaction to the Context of the Evaluation

See also Sections 8.2 and 8.5, below.

($\leftrightarrow$ *by degree*) The following five paragraphs are sequenced by increasing degree of responsiveness.

Unable to recognize the purposes of the interview/the report to be made, unaware of the social conventions, did not understand or adapt to the testing situation, did not understand give and take of question-and-answer format, did not grasp nature of questions, gave inappropriate responses, not relevant, not logical, not goal-directed, was not able to comprehend or respond to questions designed to elicit _____ symptoms of _____, low attending skills, just able to meet the minimum requirements for appropriate social interaction, misconstrued what was said to him/her, unaware, withdrawn, unresponsive, echolalic, preoccupied, estranged, didn't grasp essence or goal, autistic.

Indifferent, bland, detached, distant, uninvolved, uncaring, lackadaisical, no effort, did not try, no interest in doing anything but playing out her/his time, haphazard responding, insensitive, bored, showed the presence of an interfering emotion, overcautious, related obliquely.

Dependent, sought/required much support/reassurance/guidance/encouragement from the examiner, desperate for assistance, self-doubting, ill at ease.

Tense, anxiety appropriate/proportionate to the interview situation, initially responded only to questions but later became more spontaneous, began interview with an elevated level of anxiety that decreased as the evaluation progressed, needed assistance to get started.

Understood the social graces/norms/expectations/conventions/demand characteristics of the examination situation, comfortable, confident, relaxed, interested, curious, eager, intense, carefully monitored the testing situation, oriented, aware, alert, cooperative, no abnormalities, attended, responded, reciprocated, continued, participated, initiated, communicated effectively, clear and efficient, high quality of interaction, with depth.

For a Child: Summary Statements

✓ Note that "parent" in these statements should be taken to mean biological/custodial parent/ grandparent, foster parent, or any other caregiver/major attachment figure.

Parental Interaction with Examiner

Parent's manner of relating to examiner was arrogant/threatening, suspicious, impatient, cooperative/trusting, controlling/manipulative, seductive, dependent, plaintive, grudging, etc.
Parent's attitude did/did not change during interview.
Parent took _____ role and assigned _____ role to examiner during interview (specify).

Behavior When with Parent

Child played easily/unwillingly/not at all in the waiting room, did/did not put away the toys used.
Child exhibited _____ level of play, with playthings appropriate for _____ age.
Parent used control in the following ways (specify degree, kind/methods/means, timing), over issues of ... (specify).
Parent's relationship to child was supportive/unsupportive, negotiated/unilaterally controlling.
Parents showed agreement/disagreement/conflict over discipline, rewards, language, attention given, etc.

Separation from Parent

Upon separation, child showed excessive/expected/limited/no anxiety, expressed as ... (specify).
Child used appropriate/a few/no coping mechanisms upon separation (if any, specify).
Child separated easily/poorly/reluctantly from the parent/examiner.
Child's reaction upon rejoining parent was ... (specify).

Child/parent described symptoms of separation anxiety: Worry over possible harm to parent/ parent deserting child/disaster keeping child away from parent, school refusal in order to stay with parent, refusal to sleep without parent, "clinging" or "shadowing" behaviors, nightmares about separation, physical complaints when separated, tantrums/pleading not to separate, excessive homesickness, not easily redirected/distracted from parent, need for much reassurance, discomfort with other adults, inability to master own anxiety.

Playing Observed

Child played eagerly/willingly/unenthusiastically/not at all with same-age/younger/older peers.
Child showed eager/expected/limited/no approach to and interest in toys/materials.
Toys/materials actually used were ... (specify).
Mode of play was incorporative/extrusive/intrusive/other (specify).
Manner of play was constructive/disorganized/mutual/parallel/distractible/disruptive/other (specify).
Child was tractable/intractable to discipline, such as ... (specify).

Child's Attitudes and Feelings

Child did/did not grasp purpose of clinic visit(s).
Child did/did not seem aware of own difficulties.
He showed excessive/expected/limited/no reaction to own symptoms.
She showed positive/negative/no feelings about returning to clinic.

Child showed positive/negative/no feelings/attitudes about/toward ... (specify aspects of self, as appropriate:) behavior, appearance, body, gender/sex, intellect.

Child showed positive/negative/no feelings/attitudes about/toward parents/siblings/school/peers/authorities/others (specify).

Feelings Aroused in Examiner by Child

Child aroused feelings of irritation, anger, dislike, sympathy/protectiveness, concern, pity, admiration, curiosity, etc. (specify) in examiner.

For an Adolescent:

✓ Attend to any limited spontaneity that is excessive but not inappropriate/abnormal for the adolescent's age and the evaluation/evaluator.

8.2. Attention/Concentration/Effort

See also Sections 8.3, "Response ...," 8.4, "Persistence/Motivation ...," 11.3, "Attention," and 11.4, "Concentration/Task Persistence."

apathetic	**sluggish**	**distractible**	**normal energy**	**eager**
dull	worked slowly	low attending	cooperative	animated
uninvolved	in slow motion	skills	interested	fascinated
uninvested	slow reactions	easily distracted	adequate	initiates
passive	slowed	from task	good effort	inquisitive
anergic		lost concentration	spontaneous	enthusiastic
shunned effort	**flat**	did not stick	attentive	
bored	no originality	with task	alert	
uninterested	unchanging	had great difficulty	responsive	
inattentive	expressionless	following		
indifferent	uncreative	directions		
	paucity of	nonpersistent		
tired	worthwhile ideas			
listless	skimpy responses			
exhausted				
resigned				
inconsistent				
sporadic efforts				
varied with task				

Summary Statements

The client showed adequate attention span/concentration, with little distractibility, anxiety, or frustration.

The source of distractions were ... and the client was successfully able to resist distraction by ... (specify).

I observed no significant anxiety that would have interfered with the interview or distorted the client's responses.

8.3. Response to the Methods of Evaluation/Tests/Questions

Comprehension of Instructions/Questions

See also Section 8.4, "Persistence/Motivation," and Section 8.1, "Reaction to the Context of the Evaluation."

($\leftrightarrow$ *by degree*) The following two groupings are sequenced by increasing degree of comprehension.

Rarely understood instructions, required much repetition/elaboration, needed to have instructions repeated often, became confused, required restructuring of my questions in a manner to make them more concrete and simplistic, required elaboration of the standard instructions before comprehending the nature of the tasks, required excessive time and repetition to understand what was required of him/her.

Attentive, understood, good comprehension, quickly grasped problem/demands/goals/point of situation, anticipated the response expected/desired, responded well to the interview's implicit rules of conversation and procedures, was respectful and cooperative.

Approach/Attack Strategy ($\leftrightarrow$ *by degree*)

random	**indifferent**	**scattered**	**organized**	**rigid**
haphazard		inconsistent	coordinated	compulsive
distracted	flippant	careless	controlled	ritualistic
guessed at	giggled	disorganized	goal-oriented	perseverative
answers		sloppy	active	perfectionistic
	acted without	uncoordinated	diligent	manneristic
distrusted own	instructions		caught on fast	
ability		**baffled**	well ordered	tense
self-doubting	thought aloud	nonplussed	thought through	
second-guessed	absent-minded		before acting	plodding
self	used trial-and-	**perplexed**	noted details	excessively
insecure	error approach	bewildered	orderly	careful
unsure		confused	methodical	
refused to guess/		uninformed	deliberate	
take chances			persistent	
underestimated		**hurried**	neat	
own abilities		fast	contemplative	
		rapid	thoughtful	
		speedy	efficient	
		rushed	reflective	
		hasty	self-examining	
		impulsive		
		agitated		

Summary Statements

The client waited/did not wait for full instructions.

He listened attentively to the interviewer's questions.
No problems with test directions or instructions.
Directions/instructions did not have to be repeated or rephrased/simplified.
Only repetition/slowed presentation, not simplification, of test directions was required.
She was able to follow multistep directions.
He responded fully to all tasks' demands.

The client was consistent and organized.
He organized his ideas before responding to test questions.
She stepped back and reviewed behavior when she failed; did not stick with an obviously ineffective approach.

The client worked quickly, with little deliberation.
She took a marginal approach to the evaluation, reflective of ...
mildly/moderately/severely reduced intellectual capacity.
poorly developed cognitive/problem attack/problem-solving skills/strategies.
generalized undisciplined mental processing.
lack of self-evaluation/little concern for the quality of her responses.

The client used a random approach on most tasks, showed little comprehension/visualization/analysis of the overall tasks, little learning from attempts, low planning skills.
Client perseverated, in that he had difficulty adjusting and responding appropriately to the next task's demands/instructions.
There was no change in her approach toward the more difficult items.
She used avoidance techniques in the examination, such as dropping test materials, starting conversations between tasks/subtests, attending to sounds in the hallway, asking repeated questions regarding the test materials and procedures, wandering off task, etc.
He gave impulsive responses with poor organization and planning skills, without forethought, minimal reflection/consideration before answering, before the instructions were completed.
She was apparently satisfied with/unaware of poor-quality performance/failure.

8.4. Persistence/Motivation

($\leftrightarrow$ *by degree*) The following groupings are sequenced by increasing degree of involvement in tasks.

Refused test items/subtests/questions, withdrew, showed irritation/anger, complained.

Only brief responses, had to be prompted to elaborate, gave up on easy items, sought to terminate interview, quit quickly, gave up easily, "defeatist," terminated responding after minimal effort, performed halfheartedly, showed minimal compliance, responded slowly/gave purposefully erroneous responses as a form of resistance.

Variable level of interest/motivation, slowed/varying reaction time to questions, hesitant, sustained effort only for _____ time period, often discouraged, low frustration tolerance, preferred only easy tasks, little tolerance for ambiguity, initially refused to attempt tasks but upon re-presentation later was cooperative, no motivation to succeed with difficult tasks/perform well for the examiner, became frustrated and wanted to give up when the test materials became necessarily too difficult, took breaks and recovered willingness to continue, began to lose interest in the evaluation tasks and in conversing with the examiner after _____ time, offered only perfunctory cooperation.

Average perseverance and effort were demonstrated, only rarely discouraged or inattentive, completed all tasks fully and competently, work-oriented, applied her-/

himself to the tasks presented, was cooperative and put forth best effort on each evaluation task administered, willingly/eagerly attempted each task presented, participated well and fully in the evaluation process, demonstrated serious efforts to respond to tasks' demands, became quite involved in the tasks, changed tasks appropriately.

Eager to continue, challenged by difficult tasks, concentrated on one task for a long time, finished every task, distracted only by extreme circumstances, sustained effort, persisted, diligent, systematic, conscientious, wanted to do well, evaluation seemed to be challenging to him/her.

8.5. Relationship with the Examiner

Cooperation/Positive Behaviors (↔ *by degree*)

pleasant	cooperative	dependent	indifferent	seductive
affable	helpful	institutionalized	noncommittal	plaintive
friendly	easy to	agreeableness	nonchalant	help-seeking
familiar	interview	docile	blasé	bartered
	eager		neutral	affection
chummy	enjoyed	deferential	minimal	wanted to please
outgoing	interview	ingratiating	cooperation	practical joker
socially graceful	responded with-	trying to please	careless	clowned around
amiable	out hesitation	eager to please		
	responsive	accommodating	submissive	exhibitionistic
	answered readily		passive	
tactful	obliging	effusive		spooky
cordial	agreeable	obsequious		
solicitous	amicable	pleading		curt
warm	conciliatory	oversolicitous		monosyllabic
		compliant		legalistic
genial	civil	obedient		passive–
joked around	polite			aggressive
breezy	courteous	oily		"sassy"
playful	well-mannered	fawning		flippant
easy		flattering		
"upbeat"	spontaneous			
	engageable	eulogistic		
inoffensive	available	apple-polishing		
"laid-back"	open	deferential		
low-key		humble		
"mellow"	frank	overpolite		
placid	forthright	overapologetic		
	candid	mealy-mouthed		
	confiding			

Resistance/Negative Behaviors (↔ *by degree*)   *See also Section 10.2, "Anger."*

guarded	surly	resentful	demanding	hostile	argumentative	belligerent
reserved	sulky	subtle	imposing	irritating	territorial	insulting
reticent	petulant	hostility	insistent	instigating	possessive	defiant
recalcitrant	balky	uncoop-	indignant	obnoxious	antagonistic	obstreper-
resistive	touchy	erative	confrontative	tested limits	contentious	ous

reluctant	pouty	"sick and	presump-	rebellious	oppositional	scolding
	peevish	tired"	tuous	had an		
inaccessible	sullen	defensive		"attitude"	manipulative	name-
distant	brooding	noncom-	frustrated	bristled when	provocative	calling
remote	crabby	pliant	complaining	questioned	quibbled	vilifying
evasive	testy	refused	domineering		questioned	slandering
wary	gruff		rude	**superior**	hypercritical	menacing
withdraws	snappish		nagging	condescend-	irascible	intimidating
withholding				ing	quarrelsome	venomous
avoidant	grouchy		**stubborn**	pitying	challenging	threatening
not forth-	irritated		mulish			nasty
coming	bored		intractable	aloof	**abusive**	malicious
tight-lipped	scowled		unbending	disdainful	derisive	caustic
	"snippy"		unyielding	egocentric	scornful	loathing
suspicious			unadaptable	entitled	overbearing	
cagey	**childish**		rigid	cocky	arrogant	
sneaky	immature		adamant	contemp-	sarcastic	
			obtuse	tuous	carping	
overcon-			inflexible	supercilious	berating	
trolled			negativistic	toyed with	derogatory	
businesslike			abrasive	examiner	mocking	
stiff			opinionated	"know-it-all"	taunting	
unfriendly			willful	smart-alecky	sneering	
desultory			contrary	cantankerous	facetious	
habit-bound			pushy	"chutzpah"	teasing	
only perfunctory/				"brassy"	sarcastic	
superficial				smug	quips	
cooperation					demeaning	

For a Child:

"Mouthy," "mouthed off," "sassed," talked back, mimicked examiner's speech, noncompliant, threw things, hit.

Summary Statements about Rapport   *See also Chapter 9, "Presentation of Self," and Section 4.6, "Reliability/Validity Statements."*

Client appeared relaxed and comfortable with the interview process/shared thoughts without hesitation/gave responses that appeared genuine and thoughtful.

Rapport was easily/intermittently/never established and maintained.

Response to authority was cooperative/respectful/appropriate/productive/indifferent/hostile/ challenging/undermining/unproductive/noncompliant/contemptuous.

The client required/allowed another to answer none/some/all of the questions posed.

She seemed to enjoy the attention received.

I could easily understand his/her meanings.

I found it hard to like/feel for this person.

Summary Statements about Cooperation

The client made every effort to be cooperative and maintained a cordial attitude toward the examiner.

She put forth good effort to collaborate in the evaluation.

He was aware of the social norms and was able to conform to them.

Client was cooperative within limits; she refused some test items/tests/topics.
He was fully cooperative with the examination only after determining my credentials.

Client would not accept direction from people in authority.
She repeatedly/irrelevantly/provocatively interrupted the interviewer.
He talked over me/interrupted, made efforts to control the interview.
She was equally unresponsive to an empathic tone, matter-of-fact interviewing style, confrontation about her hostility/lack of cooperation/self-defeating behaviors, etc.

Client showed inappropriate forwardness toward male/female staff.

The testing/questions/history taking/examination was particularly trying for this client.

Eye Contact   *See "Eye Contact/Gaze" under Section 7.3, "Movement/Activity."*

8.6. Response to Success/Failure/Feedback

The items in this section describe the client's responses to his/her performance and to the evaluator's reaction; they also describe self-awareness/self-monitoring/self-criticism. *(See also Section 8.5, "Relationship with the Examiner.")*

($\leftrightarrow$ *by degree*) The following groupings are sequenced by increasing degree of responsiveness.

Oblivious to failure, no response to either success or failure, unaware of/unconcerned about/ failed to recognize errors, unaware of the low level at which he/she performed, low self-monitoring/error correction skills, accepted own inferior performance, satisfied with inadequate work, minimal concern and care about doing well on evaluations, indifferent, hypocritical, inappropriately overconfident, examiner's questions/suggestions/hints didn't improve performance, gave up easily.

Flustered, embarrassed, ashamed, chagrined, apologetic, self-reproached, self-derogated, feelings easily hurt, reluctant to expose weaknesses, rationalized failures, extremely critical of own work/hypercritical, disparaged own performance, not satisfied with less than perfection, vulnerable to humiliation, loath to say he/she didn't know so clammed up instead, discouraged/dejected/very angry at failure, attempted to cheat or compromise.

Tensed, grimaced, tense breathing, nervous cough, bit nails, cleared throat, looked around, asked to go to the bathroom/to go home/if the session were over.

Normal responsiveness and coping with failure, tried his/her best, surprised at failure, accepted mistakes with regret, accepted need to go on despite failure/mistake/incorrect answers, confident, calm, understood easily, adapted, modulated, good balance of self-criticism and self-confidence, self-sufficient, learned from errors/experience, accepted own limitations so failure had little effect.

Self-congratulatory, sought help appropriately, proud, took pride in accomplishments, delighted with success, persisted, worked harder, self-monitored, sought errors in own work and self-corrected, gave up only on items clearly beyond ability, refused to concede defeat, wasn't discouraged by errors, was easily motivated by "Try again," redoubled efforts when faced with increased difficulty/ challenged.

Summary Statements

The client required/did well with/ignored no/usual/copious praise.
Needed frequent/constant reinforcement/encouragement/reassurance/praise/commendation for continued performance.

Responded to help with distrust/indifference/gratitude, rejected it with indignation/thanks/ learned and altered own approach.

The client was not so skillful as he thought.
Her perception of her status and abilities was somewhat inflated.
Efforts at compensation through _____ (e.g., a pedantic style) created a negative impression of which he was apparently unaware.

The evaluation setting, which was generally empathic, reinforcing, and accepting of the client's behavior, proved to be ... (specify).

9

Presentation of Self

This chapter covers the **client's self-presentation to the evaluator,** as seen by the evaluator. These behaviors can also be seen as **interpersonal skill and impression management.**

Many of the descriptors in this chapter are inferences and judgments about a client, and not objective assessments. They should be used sparingly and only when well supported by information from multiple sources and repetitions over time and places.

9.1. Dependency–Surgency

See also Section 9.3 below, as well as Sections 13.13, "Dependent Personality," and 13.17, "Narcissistic Personality."

($\leftrightarrow$ *by degree*) "Spineless," meek, a follower, servile, dependent, clinging, whining/whiny, tentative, docile, defers/deferential, inoffensive, passive, yielding, acquiescent, amenable, "wishy-washy," lacking in self-sufficiency, socially immature, compliant, assenting, consenting, cooperative, <normal>, self-confident, spunky, forceful, overbearing, pushy, self-centered, demanding, dominant, masterful, high-handed, autocratic, dictatorial, blustery, pugnacious.

9.2. Presence/Style ($\leftrightarrow$ *by degree*)

See also Section 8.5, "Relationship with the Examiner."

withdrawn	**threatened**	**shy**	**friendly**	autonomous
isolating	distrustful	timid	inviting	direct
estranged	fearful	bashful	jocular	self-assured
distant	anxious	demure	warm	dominant
suspicious	distraught	passive	outgoing	surgent
guarded		reserved	jolly	businesslike
asocial	**vulnerable**	retiring	extraverted	assertive
introverted	weak	humble	chipper	
solitary	delicate	subdued	animated	stubborn
seclusive	would crumble	reticent	engaging	insistent
detached	fragile	introverted	charming	
aloof	low resilience	restrained		eccentric
dejected	threat-sensitive	composed		bizarre
		placid		dramatic
		mild-mannered		
		unassuming		
		plaintive		

9.3. Self-Image/Self-Esteem

The concepts of self-image/self-esteem include components/functions relating to the interior self and ones relating to the social self. Aspects of the interior self include the following:

> Self-concept, identity, ego boundaries.
> Self-perception, self-consciousness, self-assessment, self-evaluation, self-monitoring, self-disclosure.
> Self-determination, self-management, self-control, self-direction, self-efficacy, self-reinforcement.
> Self-differentiation, self-discovery, self-knowledge, self-realization, self-actualization.

And aspects of the social self include the following:

> Age and gender roles, gender identity, sexual identity.
> Body image, appearance, body ego, boundaries, personal space, personal property.
> Other aspects of the self in relation to others (self as child, parent, spouse/partner, friend, worker, etc.).

Be alert for the client's manifestations of these aspects. In particular, watch for evidence of self-defeating/self-destructive behaviors, such as suicidal ideation/attempts *(see Section 12.40, "Suicide")*, self-injury *(see Section 12.33, "Self-Injurious Behavior")*, and high-risk activities (specific coverage of these is provided in many other sections of this book). The following are descriptors that apply to a few particular components of self-image/self-esteem.

Confidence Levels

> Expressed an exaggerated opinion of him-/herself, believes he/she is exceptionally capable despite evidence to the contrary, grandiose, self-exalting, boastful, vain, has "chutzpah," cocky, pompous, conceited.
> (↔ *by degree*) Confident, accepting, congruent, self-respecting, modest, unassuming, humble, self-doubting, unrealistic, inadequate, pessimistic, self-deprecatory, self-accusing, self-abasing, described self as "a loser"/untalented/failure/misfit/unworthy.

Goals for Self

> Hopeful, optimistic, eager, anticipates improvement, proactive, high aspirations, future orientation.
> Has plans, plans are clear/comprehensive/realistic, has alternative approaches/backups.
> Plans are vague/unrealistic/poorly thought out, below reasonable expectations, pessimistic.
> (↔ *by degree*) Describes life as stagnant/unraveling, presents self as a victim of her/his life, has no apparent interest in improving/motivation to improve her/his lot in life, is at least aware that improvements could be made, is willing to try to work on problems, is strongly motivated for change.

Pride (↔ *by degree*)

> Dignity, good self-respect/esteem/regard/image, confidence, self-righteousness, vanity, ego, puts on airs, arrogance, conceit, condescension, narcissism, paints the consequences of his/her actions in a very rosy color.

9.4. Social Sophistication/Manners

Sophistication

(↔ *by degree*) The following groupings are arranged by increasing degree of sophistication.

Naive, unsophisticated, gullible, overly trusting, wide-eyed, suggestible, "Pollyanna"-like, unschooled, backward, inept, culturally unsophisticated, medically/psychologically naive, naive attempts at manipulation, guileless, overused "Yes, Ma'am/Sir" and "No, Ma'am/Sir."

>**Immature,** socially inept/unskilled, awkward, graceless, limited ability to interact, "nerdy," simple, simplistic, self-conscious, giddy, flighty.

>>**Sophisticated,** socially skilled, cultured, articulate, able to lobby/defend her/his interests, "street-smart."

>>>Opportunistic, callous, predatory, indignant, righteous, "innocent"/blames others, denies, irresponsible, "finesses," seductive, manipulative, Machiavellian, sociopathic.

Manners ($\leftrightarrow$ *by degree*)

Polite, well-behaved, mannerly, graceful, poised, tactful, gracious, knows etiquette's rules, careless, thoughtless, blunt, pointed, tactless, offered outspoken criticisms, provocative, abrasive, offensive, vulgar, rude.

9.5. Warmth–Coldness

>*See Section 8.5, "Relationship with the Examiner."*

($\leftrightarrow$ *by degree*) The following groupings are arranged by degree of decreasing warmth.

Overindulgent, soft-hearted, doting, overly affectionate, sweet, saccharine, oily, phony.

>Responsive, warm-hearted, sympathetic, considerate, compassionate, intimate, gentle, tender, yielding, solicitous, thoughtful, fond, loving, benevolent, charitable, humane, forgiving, merciful, tolerant, devoted.

>>Friendly, affable, kindly, genteel, outgoing, convivial, companionable.

>>>Reticent, taciturn, subdued, shy, inhibited, restrained, reluctant, aloof, uninterested, tough, remote, distant, cold, detached, indifferent, unresponsive.

>>>>Uncharitable, unfeeling, cold, callous, harsh, rough, severe, forbidding.

9.6. Other Aspects of Self-Presentation

Self-Containment/Rigidity   *See Section 13.8, "Authoritarian Personality."*

Self-contained and in good charge of him-/herself, reserved, collected, matter of fact, static, mechanical, stereotyped, compulsive about neatness/order/planning, rigid, expressionless, stoic toward his/her illness/limitations.

Prim and proper, straight-laced, prudish, dour, austere, prissy, "stuffed shirt," self-righteous, puritanical, pious, sanctimonious, overreligious.

Childishness

Childish, immature, juvenile, silly, excessively attention-seeking, needy, pleading, begging, coaxing, manner suggestive of a much younger person/suggestive of a person much younger emotionally than physically, preoccupied with irrelevancies, feelings are easily hurt, easily upset.

The client seems to be suggestible to the whims and commands of his peers, who victimize him/expose him to ridicule.

She tempts peers to take her money/books/possessions so that an adult/another will intervene on her behalf.

He is often teased/taunted/bullied/harassed/insulted/humiliated/tortured.

Dullness/Inattention

Dull, "airhead," vapid, bland, insipid, inattentive, forgetful, wistful, preoccupied, mind elsewhere, "space cadet," "spacey," "zombie-like," "burned out."

Worry/Anxiety　*See "Cognitive Facets" in Section 10.3, "Anxiety/Fear."*

Worrisome, a "worry wart" or excessive worrier, easily threatened, feels inept, manifested anxiety throughout the interview around every topic.

Flamboyance/Histrionics　*See also Section 13.15, "Histrionic Personality."*

Flamboyant, exaggerated, dramatic, melodramatic, theatrical, overdone, affected, artificial, thespian, histrionic, vivacious, bubbly, volatile, labile.

Seductive, oversexualized, saucy, coy, titillating, suggestive, flirtatious, excessively girlish/boyish.

Responds to the interviewer's innocuous questions with dramatized surprise/as if they had high emotional import.

A "character," individualistic, idiosyncratic, "marches to her/his own drummer," unusual ways of perceiving/behaving, eccentric, "oddball," does not fit in, outlandish, strange, odd, peculiar, bizarre, weird.

Antisocial Features　*See also Section 13.7, "Antisocial Personality."*

Arrogant, bragging, cocky, disdainful, tended to praise self excessively, cavalier, limited empathy, assumed/maintained an attitude of tolerant amusement, has a rapid-fire/smooth-talking style.

Swaggering in order to impress interviewer with youthfulness/energy/toughness, "has a chip on his/her shoulder," uses embellishments to appear as a "bad actor" or powerful and dangerous person (e.g., uses vulgarity to shock, presents as a "tough cookie") or as possessing a high potential/many friends/social power/etc.

Menacing, frightening, imposing, intimidating, manipulating, "spooky," vaguely but intensely frightening, enjoys sadistic humor/is prankish.

Intellectualization

Intellectualizes all experiences, provides psychological jargon/"psychobabble"/labels when asked for descriptions of behaviors/symptoms, "reports" feelings.

Sense of Victimization

A "victim," recites life as a series of mishaps, melodramatically enumerates life's misfortunes, made a saga of his/her life in the telling, offered a woeful tirade/jeremiad of woes/baleful stories/"Oliver Twist"-like story, presented self as a "born loser"/perpetual victim/outcast.

Presented self as frail and inadequate person of whom one should not expect much.

Guilt/Shame　*See also Section 10.8, "Guilt/Shame."*

Apologetic, described failures/mistakes/harm, apologized indirectly/simply/fully/appropriately/effusively.

Embarrassed, ashamed, self-blaming, self-reproaching, guilty, "worthless," became apprehensive when talking of behavior she/he now realizes was inappropriate.

Off-Task Behaviors

Clock-watched.

Repeatedly asked when we would be finished.

Offered/desired inappropriate bodily contacts.

Focused on examiner's office/speech/clothing/manner/role/appearance rather than the content of his/her/examiner's speech or the point of the interview.

Other Statements

There are no obvious behavioral stigmata that would set this client apart from other individuals of his age, social, or cultural group.

Her responses reflect wishful thinking rather than realistic plans.

He is dependent on institutional support and content to be hospitalized/taken care of.

Client put up a good front to cover ... (specify).

She made sure to tell me what she thought I should hear and know, and then it seemed that she felt satisfied.

He had his story to tell and went on without any assistance from me.

Client describes _____ (symptoms) that she labels as _____ (behaviors).

For a Child:

Child is pseudomature, uncommonly independent.

Child exhibits primitive, socially inappropriate, nonaggressive behavior.

Speech and Verbal Interactions

See Sections 7.4, "Speech Behavior," and 8.5, "Relationship with the Examiner."

PRESENTATION OF SELF

10

Emotional/Affective Symptoms and Disorders

10.1. General Aspects of Mood and Affects

See Section 3.5, "Affect/Mood," for questions.

"Mood" refers to pervasive and sustained emotional coloring of one's experience, a persistent emotional trend (like the climate). It is usually self-reported (but is sometimes inferred). "Affect" is of shorter duration, such as what the clinician observes during the interview, and is more variable and reactive (like the weather) to the subjects discussed. Note and document any differences between the two during the interview.

Give quotes/self-reports/verbatim descriptions of mood/affect/emotion. In addition, note or report the following:

> **Behavior** reflecting emotional state: See sections on individual emotions below. In general, note tears, flushing, movements (tremor, etc.), respiratory changes and irregularities, voice changes, facial expression and coloring, wording, somatic expression of affects through ... (specify).
> **Nature/source:** Is the emotion reactive, endogenous, exogenous, characterological, lifelong?
> **Degree:** Is the client mildly, moderately, severely, or profoundly depressed (for example)?

Amount/Responsiveness/Range of Affect (↔ *by degree*)[1]

flat	blunted	constricted	normal	broad
affectless	apathetic	contained	**usual**	deep
bland	inexpressive	low-intensity	**average**	intense
unresponsive	unspontaneous	shallow	responsive	generalized
vacant stare	dispassionate	muted	normal range	pervasive
absent	detached	subdued	supple	
remote	unattached	"low-key"	adequate levels of	
passive-appearing	uninvolved	restricted	emotional energy	
expressionless	uncomplaining	uninflected	no/some/great difficulty in	
			initiating, sustaining, or	
unvarying			terminating emotional	
unchanging			expression	

[1]Consider the possible effects of medications. (*See Chapter 29, "Psychiatric Masquerade of Medical Conditions," especially Sections 29.4 and 29.5.*)

Duration of Mood or Affect Changes (↔ *by degree*)

Mercurial/quicksilver, volatile, affective incontinence, dramatic, transient, unstable, fickle, rapid mood fluctuation, labile, turbulent, plastic, changeable, mood swings, excitable, flexible, diurnal/seasonal mood cycles, short cycles (days), long cycles, shifts in tension, mobility of emotional state, appropriate, consistent, showed little/normal/much variation in emotions, frozen, permanent.

Appropriateness/Congruence of Affect or Mood and Behavior

(↔ *by degree*) The following groupings are sequenced by degree of increasing appropriateness/congruence.

Inappropriate, incongruent, inconsistency of reported/observed feelings and those expected in the circumstances described.

Indifferent to problems, floated over his/her real problems and limitations, LA BELLE INDIF-FÉRENCE, showed no/very minimal/much less than expected affect when discussing experiences that would normally be accompanied by intense feelings, treated own intense experiences too lightly.

Affect variable but unpredictable from the topic of conversation, modulations/shifts inconsistent and unrelated to content or affective significance of statements.

A range of emotions/feelings, appropriate emotions for the ideational content and circumstances, emotional reactions relevant to the thought content and situation, emotions seemed appropriate during the interview/examination, although depressed he was able to smile at the comic elements of his history.

Emotions highly appropriate to/congruent with situation and thought content/subject of discussion, face reflects emotions reported, all thoughts colored by emotional state.

Episodes of Mood Disorder

Is this an initial/single episode? Or are episodes repetitive, recurrent, irregular, cyclothymic, cyclical, seasonal, annual, anniversary reactions?

Is the disorder presently exacerbated, chronic, in full/partial remission?

Do recurrent episodes appear to be worsening over time?

Does the client have longer/shorter symptom-free periods?

Do periods of improvement not produce as much improvement as before? And does medication produce slower/less improvement?

Consider drawing a time-by-mood timeline for diagnostic accuracy (see, e.g., the mood charts at *www.manicdepressive.org/tools_clinical.html*).

10.2. Anger

See also Section 8.5, "Relationship with the Examiner," for more behavioral aspects.

General Aspects

Look for the following:

Sources of anger.
Intensity and variability.
Direction, target.
Handling/coping methods, impulse control, anger out/in.

Situational/state or personality/trait nature of anger.
Guilt over anger.

Hostility/Verbal Hostility (↔ *by degree*)

irritated	**temperamental**	**hostile**	**furious**
annoyed	whining	provoked	enraged
disgruntled	piqued	embittered	incensed
cranky	"pissed off"	exasperated	choleric
miffed	"burned up"	indignant	
displeased	"bugged"	simmering	threatens
"snippy"	smoldering	seething	shouts
"bothered"	ill-tempered	infuriated	yells
restive	bad-tempered		
bristled	bellicose	insults	combative
grudging	irascible	swears	assaultive
resentful	abrasive	curses	violent
sarcastic	chronically angry	foul-mouthed	
complaining	pugnacious		

Violence/Aggressive Behaviors

See Sections 12.19, "Impulse-Control Disorders," and 3.31, "Violence."

10.3. Anxiety/Fear

See Section 3.6, "Anxiety," for questions; see also Section 10.10, "Panic."

✓ Depression coexists (is "comorbid") with anxiety in more than half of all cases, and is more common than either alone in primary care settings (Rivas-Vasquez et al., 2004), so consider both diagnoses.

Autonomic Nervous System/Somatic Hyperactivity/Overarousal Facets

pallor or flushing	**Shortness Of Breath**	**dizziness**	**clamminess**
heart palpitations	difficulty breathing	vertigo	sweaty palms
racing heartbeat/	chest pain/tightness	room spinning	cold sweats/chills
tachycardia	choking/smothering	light-headedness	excessive perspiration
	fast and deep	faintness	sweaty forehead
diarrhea	respiration	syncope	dry mouth
urgent urination	air hunger	"wobbly"	
stomach	hyperventilation	"wobbly knees"	piloerection/
"butterflies"	sneezing		"goose bumps"
stomach churned	yawning	overall weakness	
queasiness	sighing	unsteadiness	hot flashes
nausea			
dry heaves	tingling	**paresthesias**	
"lump in throat"			
	numbness		

Fight-or-flight response/arousal: Any of the above, plus more acute hearing, spleen contracts, peripheral blood vessels dilate, bronchioles widen, pupils dilate, more coagulates and lymphocytes in blood, adrenaline secreted, stomach acid production decreases, loss of bladder/anal sphincter control, decreased salivation, etc.

Behavioral Facets

Motor Tension

Agitation, trembling, tightness, twitching, fidgets, feeling shaky, tremulous, body swaying, rigid posture, stiff neck/back/muscles, muscle aches, sits on edge of chair, inhibited movements, restlessness, easy fatigability.

"Nervous Habits" (↔ by degree)

self-grooming	**can't sit still**	hair twirling	**panicked**
scratching	leg/arm swinging	combing fingers	rushed out
nail biting	rocking	through hair	vomited
	pacing	hair pulling	fainted
repetitive move-	stretching		
ments	body swaying	facial expressions	
fretful	tapping	of fear	
muscle tension	fidgeting	worried look	
wringing hands		tense face	
clutching hands	hands restrained/	flashes of smiles	
yawning/sighing	in pockets	tears/crying	
self-hugging	rigid arms	wide-eyed	
	shuffles feet	brow grooves	
moistens lips	"deadpan"		
coughing	avoids eye contact		
swallowing			
clears throat			
heavy breathing			

Speech/Voice   *See also Section 7.4, "Speech Behavior."*

Strained, quavery, tremor, stuttering, voice cracks, uncompleted/disconnected sentences. Inappropriate/"nervous" laughter/smiling, titters, giggles.

Vigilance and Scanning

Easily startled, jumpy, oversensitive to stimuli, overreactive.
Lessened concentration, erratic, mind goes blank, unable to proceed, unable to function, immobilized, freezes.
Difficulty falling asleep or staying asleep, mind racing.

Affective Facets (↔ by degree)

imperturbable	**calm**	**"nervous"**	**fearful**	**terrified**
stolid	phlegmatic	uneasy	apprehensive	horrified
inhibited	steady	harried	frightened	rigid
	unemotional	irritable	alarmed	frozen
	stable	vulnerable	distraught	petrified
	composed	fragile		paralyzed
	nonchalant	tense	"on edge"	
	"cool"	edgy	frazzled	panicky
	confident	unable to relax	flighty	panic attacks
	SANGFROID	"uptight"	distressed	
		jittery		

Cognitive Facets

"A worrier," "a worry wart," apprehensive, worrisome, fretful, ruminates, thoughts of impend-
ing doom, exaggeration of the objective danger, anticipates dreadful occurrences/doom/
catastrophe, "my world is caving in"/"getting out of hand," feels threatened by people or
events commonly seen as of little or no concern, upset by fantasies/imagined scenarios/crit-
icisms/attacks/hurts, dread, desire to escape, fear of losing control/dying/being attacked/
losing consciousness/going crazy/being rejected or abandoned.

Baffled, confused, jumbled thoughts, blurred thoughts, perplexed, lessened concentration,
unable to recall/indecisive, forgetful, preoccupied, many errors, diminished initiative/pro-
ductivity/creativity.

Depersonalization, derealization, preoccupied with bodily sensations, "fluttery," "quavery."
(See Section 12.12, "Depersonalization and Derealization," for descriptors.)

Overwhelmed/can't manage/can't get control/can't control thoughts, high internal tension,
feels inept/nervous, can't handle stress/pressure/demands, "feels like I'll explode/my heart
will burst through my chest," vulnerable, low self-confidence/efficacy, insecure.

No depth of feeling when recounting events, erratic, guardedness, rigidity, confuses self, self-
induced pressures, jumps from one subject/topic to another, low frustration tolerance, low
stress tolerance, low tolerance for ambiguity.

For a Child:

Fears of animals, ghosts, demons, "the bogeyman," darkness, getting lost, parental illness/dis-
ability/death/loss, punishment, being embarrassed/humiliated, separation anxiety.

Interpersonal Facets   *See also Chapter 9, "Presentation of Self."*

Thin-skinned, easily threatened/aroused to anxiousness, insecure, vulnerable, oversensitive,
self-conscious, timid, timorous, uncertain what to say/how to act, dependent, clinging.

Avoids eye contact, withdraws, reduced involvement.

Hypercritical, self-deprecation.

Blames others, impulsive/acts out.

Ill at ease, uneasy, social anxiety.

10.4. Bipolar I Disorder

The ICD-9-CM and DSM-IV-TR codes for Bipolar I Disorder are various 296.xx codes. *(See Section
21.5, "Mood Disorders.")*

> *Because of the presence of both depressive and manic components in different intensities, mixtures,
> and sequences, see Sections 10.7, "Depression," and 10.9, "Mania," for descriptors.*

10.5. Bipolar II Disorder

The DSM-IV-TR code for Bipolar II Disorder is 296.89. The same code is used for Other and
unspecified bipolar disorders: Other (which includes Bipolar II as a "Note") in ICD-9-CM.

The cardinal features are chronic mood instability and at least one major depressive episode with
at least one episode of hypomania (but not full mania, as in Bipolar I). Hypomanic episodes may
be missed without a complete family and individual history, which also helps to distinguish Bipolar
II from personality disorders, anxiety disorders, unipolar depression, and Bipolar I. The diagnosis

EMOTIONS/
AFFECTS

may be hidden by substance abuse (60% of individuals with Bipolar II have substance use disorders as well), and the suicide risk may be higher in Bipolar II than in Bipolar I.

10.6. Cyclothymia

In both ICD-9-CM and DSM-IV-TR, Cyclothymic Disorder is coded as 301.13. (In ICD-9-CM, however, it is classified as a personality disorder rather than a mood disorder.)
    See also Sections 10.4 and 10.5, above, and Section 10.9, below.

Cyclothymia runs a biphasic course, milder than Bipolar I or II Disorder, alternating between hypomanic and depressive symptom patterns.

10.7. Depression

    See Section 3.11, "Depression," for questions. See also Sections 10.11, "Seasonal Affective Disorder," and 12.28, "PreMenstrual Dysphoric Disorder."

Affective Facets

Anhedonia   *See also Section 10.1, "General Aspects of Mood and Affects."*

    Absence of pleasure, loss of pleasure in living, "nothing tastes good any more," joylessness, lack of satisfaction in previously valued activities/hobbies, loss of interests, no desire/motivation/energy to do anything, no fun in his/her life, indifference, "couldn't care less," apathy, boredom, lowered/no desires, nothing good to look forward to in life, indifference to praise/reward, emotional impoverishment, drabness, colorless, coldness, emptiness, "life is a chore," "just marking time."

Dysphoria (↔ *by degree*)

wretched	**melancholy**	**sad**	moody
inconsolable	despondent	blue	plaintive
anguished	dejected	somber	pessimistic
suffering	sorrowful	gloomy	
miserable	forlorn	beaten down	
desperate	bitter	glum	
pathetic	dysphoric	tearful	
in pain	morose	distraught	
	funereal	cheerless	
suicidal	despairing	dour	
self-destructive	grave	disconsolate	
	profoundly sad	dismayed	
	woeful	downcast	
	profoundly unhappy	down in the dumps	
	morbid	"down"	
	doleful	"wiped out"	
	sour	troubled	
	cynical	dispirited	
		"bummed out"	
		downhearted	

Thoughts of Suicide   *See Section 3.30, "Suicide and Self-Destructive Behavior," for questions; see Section 12.40, "Suicide," for descriptors.*

Behavioral Facets

Included here are the vegetative signs/physical malfunctioning.

Sleep Patterns   *See Section 12.37, "Sleep Disturbances," for descriptors.*

Eating

Appetite/hunger increase or decrease, anorexia, fewer/more frequent meals, fasting, selective hungers, "comfort foods," binges, weight increase/decrease.

Energy

Anergic, lowered energy, slowed down, listless, sluggish, "needs to be pushed to get things done," "everything is an effort," easy fatigue, tired, feels "run down," mopes, muddles through, weakened, lethargic, deenergized, torpid, lassitude, "can't shake off the blues," "can't get out of bed," energy is just adequate for life's tasks, inability to cope with routine responsibilities, weary, drained, exhausted.

Psychomotor Retardation/Acceleration   *See also Section 7.3, "Movement/Activity."*

Absence of/lessened spontaneous verbal/motor/emotional expressiveness, long response time to questions [indicate number of seconds], thoughts slowing/laborious/impoverished/racing.

Libido   *See Section 10.12, "Sexuality," for descriptors.*

✓ Remember that libido is sexual interest, not activity.

Lessened/no interest, indifferent, passive, "I'd like to but it is too much trouble," "I can take it or leave it," "My partner wants to but I don't care."

Bowel/Bladder Habit Changes

Increased frequency of urination, diarrhea/constipation, overconcern with elimination, chronic use or abuse of laxatives, sensations of abdominal distention or incomplete evacuation of bowels.

Substance Use

Overuse of prescription and over-the-counter medications (analgesics, laxatives, sleeping aids, vitamins), alcohol, caffeine, stimulant drugs.

Appearance/Presentation   *See also Section 7.1, "Appearance."*

Sad/fixed/expressionless/unsmiling/downcast face, scowl, downward gaze, distracted look, glum, blank stare, furrowed brow, smiled without warmth, "smiling depression."
($\leftrightarrow$ *by degree*) Close to tears/tearful/teary, tears well up, weepy/weeps, cries, cries openly/fully, blubbers, sobs.
Dissipated, worn, drained, "a shell of a person," haphazard self-care, self-neglect.
Wrings hands, rubs forehead, shuffling gait.
Little inflection, flat/expressionless/monotonous voice.
Audible sighs, moans.

Summary Statements

All appetites are muted.

Client has persistent physical symptoms that do not respond to medical treatment. [Note especially headaches, digestive disorders, and chronic and migratory pains.]

Cognitive Facets

Caring/Energy Investment (↔ *by degree*)

hopeless	**pessimistic**	cold	**bored**
helpless	suspicious	unconcerned	indifferent
unchangeable	disappointed	stoic	unspontaneous
drained	disillusioned	phlegmatic	apathetic
defeated	cynical	ennui	matter-of-fact
futile	discouraged	weary	
negative	demoralized	humorless	
bleak	disenchanted	malaise	
feeling lost	defeatist	{WELTSCHMERZ}	
dreary	repetition/urging		
nihilistic	needed		
meaninglessness	exhausted		

No plans for self, no future, nothing to look forward to in life, only an empty repetition of meaningless actions, loss of ambition, no goals/plans, resigned, futureless, no anticipation.

Mental Dullness

Inadequate, unable to cope, empty, exhausted.

Slowed, ruminative, mulls over, indecisive, decreased concentration, trouble mobilizing thoughts, abulia.

Confused, perplexed, "I'm not mentally here," worsened memory, spotty memory, vague, unclear.

Excessive worrying, worrisome, frustrated.

Self-Criticalness/Brooding (↔ *by degree*)   *See also Section 10.8, "Guilt/Shame."*

self-doubting	sorry	self-pitying
self-distrusting	regretful	"poor me"
self-deprecating	chagrined	"ruined/wasted life"
low self-esteem	embarrassed	"my life is over"
	ashamed	bitter
self-blaming	humiliated	sarcastic/ironic
self-critical		suppressed rage
self-reproaching	vulnerable	self-condemning
fault-finding	threat-sensitive	self-hating
	criticism-sensitive	self-abusing
"inept"	rejection-sensitive	caustic
"ineffectual"	overawed	"a misfit"
"unproductive"	cowed	"of no value"
"inadequate"	intimidated	"a failure"
"inferior"	overwhelmed	"a loser"
		"a piece of shit"

Dysfunctional Cognitions

Clinicians such as Beck et al. (1979), Burns (1999), and Ellis and Dryden (1997) have described the following types of dysfunctional cognitions in the depressed:

Arbitrary inference: Drawing a negative conclusion not supported by the evidence.

Dichotomous thinking: Oversimplifying; black or white, good or bad, right or wrong, all or nothing.

Mind reading: Assuming one knows the other's thoughts (usually negative).

Magnification or minimization: Loss of proportion; exaggerating or minimizing the importance of an event.

Overgeneralizing: Basing a general conclusion on too few data or one incident; jumping to conclusions, "always" or "never."

Personalization: Relating negative events to oneself without an empirical or rational basis.

Selective abstraction: Attending to only the negative aspect(s) of a situation and ignoring the other (positive) ones; mental filter; selective attention; disqualifying the positive.

Catastrophizing: Automatically assuming that the worst-case scenario will occur.

Telescoping of time and options so that a single, final, negative outcome is seen as inevitable.

Emotional reasoning: "Because I feel afraid, there must be danger."

"Fortune teller" error: Overprediction; the future will be repetitions of the past.

"Shoulding" on oneself or others; "should" statements. "Musterbation."

Summary Statements

Client demonstrated Aaron Beck's (Beck et al., 1979) depressive triad of negative views of the self, world, and future.

Cyclic negative thought processes/dysfunctional cognitions were revealed.

Client's attributions are negative, stable/unstable, global/specific/situational, internal/external.

She/he dwelled on past failures, lost opportunities, what could never be, roads not taken, etc.

Alexithymia was evident.

He/she appeared to be feigning good spirits.

Social Facets

Interpersonal

reclusive	**avoidant**	envious	irritable	strained
inaccessible	distances	resentful	low frustration	relationships
asocial	self-absorbed	argumentative	tolerance	dependent
	withdraws		bitter	passive
barricades self	low social	feels scorned	demanding	unassertive
away	interest	feels abandoned	crabby	
isolates	subdued		easily irritated	wary
hermit-like	painfully shy		easily annoyed	distrustful
secludes	separates from life/others		petulant	suspicious
	only watches		self-righteous	
	less interactive			

Support-Seeking   *See also Section 9.1, "Dependency–Surgency."*

Complains of life's unfairness, gossips, gripes, futilely indignant, sympathy-seeking, whiny, self-pitying, manipulative, emotionally hungry, seeks support only when in crisis, finds others always inadequately supportive or sympathetic.

Other Facets of Depression

Bear the following possibilities in mind:

Is client depressed because forced into dependency by disability/losses/injury?
Does client interpret deaths as desertions, yet is simply alone because she/he has outlived others?
Is depression worse during winter? *(See Section 10.11, "Seasonal Affective Disorder.")*
Is client self-defeating, self-victimizing? *(See Section 13.26, "Self-Defeating Personality.")*
Are there diurnal mood variations? Are depression's symptoms worse in the morning and lessen as day wears on?
Is there day–night reversal of activities?

Depression in Children (5–15 Years)

✓ **Note:** Children under 7 are usually unable to characterize internal mood states. Most symptoms are similar in children and adults, but some listed below are slightly different or in addition to adult ones. Scales for depression in children include the Children's Depression Inventory (Kovacs, 1992) for ages 7–17 years, and the Children's Depression Rating Scale–Revised for ages 6–12 years.

Cognitions: Catastrophizing, assumption of personal responsibility for negative outcomes.
Lack of interest in playing/favorite activities, isolation, agitation, despair, hypersensibility, insecurity, boredom, temper tantrums, fugues, feelings of inferiority, nihilistic thoughts, suicidal impulses, obsessive thoughts, loneliness.
Irritability, difficulty getting out of bed in morning.
School problems: Learning difficulties, school refusal/"phobia," dyslexia, concentration difficulties.
Vegetative symptoms: Fatigue, anergia, sleep disorders/terrors, appetite changes *(very common at different ages)*, weeping, abdominal pains, alopecia aureata, tics, eczema, allergies, anorexia, bulimia.
Other: Fears of parents' dying, clinging, isolation in room, aggression, substance abuse.

Grief/Bereavement

Normal Grief

Distress, sorrow, anguish, despair, heartache, pain, woe, suffering, affliction, troubles.
Preoccupied with loss/loved one/consequences/memories, poignant.
Easily made/becomes tearful, slowed thinking and responding with long latencies of response, stares into space.
Feels helpless/vulnerable/useless/lowered self-esteem.

Kübler-Ross (1969) identified five stages of the normal reaction to loss: denial, anger, bargaining, depression, and acceptance.

Unresolved/Morbid/Pathological Grief

Partial denial of death, absence of grieving, pathological identification, hypochondriasis, chronic depression, bitterness, chronic grieving, avoidance of cues to the deceased, isolation, reattachment.
Decreased immune system functioning, increased use of drugs and alcohol, depression, over-/misuse of medical care for grief.

Suicide

See Sections 3.30, "Suicide and Self-Destructive Behavior," for questions, and 12.40, "Suicide," for descriptors.

EMOTIONS/ AFFECTS

Embarrassment   *See Section 10.8, "Guilt/Shame," just below.*

10.8. Guilt/Shame

See also Kohlberg's stages of moral development in Section 19.3, "Developmental Stages."

General Descriptors

Apologetic, penitent, begging, pleading, repentant, sorry, chagrined, contrite, remorseful, burdened.

Guilty, responsible, guilt proneness, mortified, self-condemning, self-reproaching, has a punitive superego, transgressed superego boundaries, unacceptable impulses, fears of annihilation.

Embarrassed, humiliated, disgraced, reproached, depreciated, devalued, humbled, wishes to disappear/become invisible, avoids disclosure of flaws, hides inadequacies.
Ashamed, feels inferior, fears rejection/abandonment, fails to attain goal/measure up.

Guiltless, cold, hardened, cynical, unrepentant, conscienceless, shameless, unscrupulous, parasitic, incorrigible, predatory.

Distinctions between Shame and Guilt

The following distinctions are adapted by permission from Potter-Effron (1989).

Central trait	Shame	Guilt
Failure	Of being, of meeting goals, of whole self.	Of doing, of moral self.
Primary feelings	Inadequate, deficient, worthless, exposed, disgust, disgrace.	Bad, wicked, evil, remorseful.
Precipitating event	Unexpected, possibly trivial event.	Actual or contemplated violation of values.
Involvement of self	Total self-image involvement: "How could *I* have done that?"	Partial self-image involvement: "How could I have done *that?*"
Central fear	Of abandonment.	Of punishment.
Origins	Positive identification with parents.	Need to control aggressive impulse.
Primary defenses	Desire to hide (withdrawal), denial, perfectionism, grandiosity, shamelessness.	Obsessive thinking, paranoid, intellectualization, seeking excessive punishment.
Positive functions	Awareness of limits of human condition, discovery of separate self, sense of modesty, identification with community, mastery, autonomy.	Sublimation, moral behavior, initiative, reparation.

Assessment

Tests have been developed by Mosher (1988), Tangney and Dearing (2002), Harder and Greenwald (1999), O'Connor et al. (1997), Rüsch et al. (2007), and others.

EMOTIONS/ AFFECTS

10.9. Mania

See Section 3.18, "Mania," for questions; see also Sections 10.4, "Bipolar I Disorder," 10.5, "Bipolar II Disorder," and 10.6, "Cyclothymia."

Affective Facets (↔ *by degree*)

cheerful	**high**	**hypomanic**	**exuberant**	**manic**	**ecstatic**
light-hearted	gay	happy	elated	laughing	exalted
positive	laughing	silly	ebullient	binges	rapturous
bright	buoyant	giddy		euphoric	
vivid	jovial	excessively	irritability	false joy	panics
intense	elevated	boisterous	anger	false elation	
		effervescent	rages		
labile	optimistic	rapid		accelerating	
unstable	self-confident	fluctuations		course	

Behavioral Facets

(↔ *by degree*) Unkempt, disheveled, poorly groomed, overdressed, decorated, garish.

(↔ *by degree*) Pressured speech, fast/rapid speaking, rapid-fire speech, hyperverbal, overtalkative, overabundant, loud, verbose, rhyming, punning, word play, hyperbole, overproductive, garrulous, tirades, singing.

(↔ *by degree*) Animated periods of hyperactivity/overactivity, paces, gesticulates, restless, speeded up, accelerated, quickened, fast, going fast, cannot be calmed, dancing, racing, frenzied, frenetic, manic, anger, rages, assaultive.

Overconfident, exaggerated view of own abilities, starts many activities but does not finish or follow through with most, makes grandiose plans.

Insomnia, decreased total sleep time, decreased need for sleep, no acknowledgment of fatigue.

Incautious, frivolous, poor social judgment, fearless, engaging in reckless activities (e.g., dangerous driving, foolish business investments or impulsive spending), disinhibited activities, increased smoking, telephoning.

Cognitive Facets (↔ *by degree*)   *See also the speech descriptors under "Behavioral Facets," above.*

expansive	overproductive	**flight of ideas**	loosened	delusions
exaggeration		illogical	associations	incoherent
grandiosity	idiosyncratic	racing thoughts	disjointed	bizarre
	associations	thought bom-	disorganized	
little or no	ideas of ref-	bardment	disoriented	hallucinatory
insight	erence		disconnected	experiences
		sexual/religious	thoughts	echolalic
limited concen-		preoccupa-	abrupt topic	
tration		tions	changes	
brief attention			rhyming	
span				
distractible				

Social/Interpersonal Facets

(↔ *by degree*) Impatient, intolerant, irritable, annoyed, oversensitive, touchy, insulting, uncooperative, resistive, negativistic, critical, sarcastic, provocative, angry, easy/inappropriate anger, nasty, loud, abusive, crude, foul language, swears, curses, blasphemes, vulgar, bathroom language, obscene.

Suspicious, guarded, distrustful, believes that others collude against him/her, asserts that he/she was tricked into ... (specify), denies validity or reality of all criticisms.

(↔ *by degree*) Gregarious, likeable, dramatic, entertaining, pleasant, vivacious, seductive, cracks jokes, prankish, naive, infantile, silly, {WITZELSUCHT}.

Sexual indiscretions or acting out, sexualize all interactions, greatly increased need for sexual activities, increased sexual drive/interests, hypersexual.

Entitled, self-important, grandiose, cocksure, self-confident, "chutzpah."

Dominating, controlling, boastful, challenging, surgent, conflicts with authority figures, threatens.

Hypomania

Hypomania is a less severe set of symptoms than mania proper, but it is different from joy or normal happiness because of sudden onset, lapses in judgment, and the fact that it is out of proportion to the situation causing the high mood. It and the bipolar disorders of which it is a component are occasional consequences of treating depression with antidepressants.

Delusions   *See Section 12.10, "Delusions."*

10.10. Panic

See also Section 10.3, "Anxiety/Fear."

The DSM-IV-TR and ICD-9-CM codes for Panic Disorder With and Without Agoraphobia are 300.21 and 300.01, respectively.

Fear of fear, rapid escalation of anxiety, loss of control over anxiety, intense fear/discomfort.

Feelings of impending/near "doom."

Unexpected/unpredictable/"out of the blue" onset.

Fears of loss of control/dying/going crazy/embarrassing oneself/doing something uncontrolled (loss of bladder control, falling down).

A cascade of physical symptoms, especially autonomic.

10.11. Seasonal Affective Disorder

Seasonal Affective Disorder can be given the ICD-9-CM code 296.90 (Unspecified episodic mood disorder) or 296.99 (Other specified episodic mood disorder). No particular DSM-IV-TR code applies, but the "With Seasonal Pattern" specifier can be added to the appropriate mood disorder diagnosis.

SAD can be bipolar or manic, but it presents primarily as depression. A milder form is called "winter blues" (Rosenthal, 2005).

The symptoms are worse or occur only in the fall/winter. The rate increases from south (1.4%) to north (9.7%) of the United States, but is affected by cloud cover and storms. SAD usually begins in a person's 30s; 75–80% of people with SAD are female. Light treatment to the eyes controls serotonin levels (10,000 lux for 30 minutes per day, starting before 8 A.M. and in the fall, is common). Symptoms include the following:

Lethargy, easy fatigue (especially in the mornings), nonrestorative although prolonged sleep (hypersomnia).

Ravenous appetite/weight gain/carbohydrate cravings.

Withdrawal from relationships, decreased libido.
Inability to concentrate, problems at work, inefficiency.
Anxiety and despair.

10.12. Sexuality

See Section 3.25, "Sexual History," for questions; see also "Sexual Adjustment" in Section 6.4, "Adjustment History."

(↔ *by degree*) Asexual, celibate, abstinent, apathetic, inhibited, disgusted, ashamed, puritanical, prudish, prim, restrained, passive, hesitant, permissive, romantic, amorous, erotic, sensual, assertive, passionate, seductive, overactive, soliciting, compulsive, demanding, lustful, lewd, wanton, aggressive, assaultive.

Increased or decreased libido/desire, arousal, activity/relations, satisfaction, hypo-/hypersexuality.
Reluctance to initiate, slowness to respond.
Previously inhibited interests.

Shame   *See Section 10.8, "Guilt/Shame."*

10.13. Other Affects/Emotional Reactions

Sense of Humor

(↔ *by degree*) Spontaneously humorous, excellent/normal/adequate/diminished/absent sense of humor, humorless, "stuffed shirt," takes self too seriously.
Mirth response is brief/flashes, "grim little smile," capable of responding to but not initiating humor.
Gentle, mirthful, playful, jovial, jesting, impish, funny, entertaining, tells stories/jokes, flip, puns, wisecracks, mocks, silly, slapstick.
Cosmic/existential/absurdist sense of humor, wry, deadpan, dry, ironic, cynical, sophisticated, witty.
Sarcastic, tendentious, teasing, hostile, offensive "humor," off-color jokes, inappropriate remarks excused as "just kidding."

Ambivalence

Mixed feelings, conflicted, at cross-purposes, approach–avoidance conflicts, "left hand doesn't know what right hand is doing," alternates, "I want and don't want it at the same time," indecisive, can't decide/make up mind, repetitive weighing of alternatives, seeking of other options, stuck, abulia.

11

Cognition and Mental Status

This chapter contains descriptors for all the aspects of cognitive functioning assessed in a Mental Status Examination; the questions to elicit these behaviors and functions are provided in Chapter 2.

11.1. No Pathological Findings: Summary Statements

The relevant ICD-9-CM and DSM-IV-TR code is V71.09, No Diagnosis or Condition on Axis I/No Diagnosis on Axis II.

Based on behavior observed during the interview, I believe . . .
In my professional judgment . . .

Examination is entirely normal/benign.
Examination was entirely Within Normal Limits.
The client seems average/unremarkable/intact.
Nothing unusual was found.
No limitations in any of the domains assessed by these instruments/this examination.

No evidence/signs of a thought disorder or a major affective/cognitive/behavioral disorder was/
    were elicited.
No abnormalities of thought, affect, or behavior/no gross abnormalities/nothing bizarre.
I did not find any unusual kinds of logic or strange associations.
No obvious indications of psychosis or organicity, no hallucinations in any field.
He/she experiences thoughts in a spontaneous and normal manner, and is lucid and coherent.
No indication of disordered mentation in the form of incoherent or incomprehensible speech.
Speech is relevant as to content and spontaneous as to delivery.

He/she is in full/partial/marginal/recent/fragile remission.
I failed to elicit any symptomatic behaviors/indications of previously described symptoms or
    disorders.
Based on current observations, there is no decompensation, deterioration, or exacerbation of
    past conditions.
I find no indication of notable decline of intellectual abilities.

No evidence of drug or alcohol abuse/legal record/psychiatric history of diagnosis or treat-
    ment.

11.2. Arithmetic

See also Section 17.4, "Math Ability"; see Section 2.16, "Calculation Abilities," for questions.

Overall (↔ *by degree*)

Anumerate, lacks practical/everyday/survival/basic mathematical skills, dyscalculia, skills approximately equivalent to those mastered in school grade ____ .

Financial   *See Section 14.6, "Financial Skills."*

11.3. Attention

See Section 2.6, "Attention," for questions. See also Section 12.3, "Attention-Deficit/Hyperactivity Disorder."

(↔ *by degree*) The following groupings are sequenced by degree of increasing attentiveness.

Unaware, unable to attend, unengaged, daydreams, autistic reverie, muses, pensive, "wool-gathering," ignored questions, attention could not be gained or held, attention limited by extraneous sounds/concurrent activities/fantasies/affects/memories.

Distractible, inattentive, attention wandered, redirectable, attentive only to irrelevancies, responses were irrelevant, unable to reject interfering stimuli from environment/viscera/affects, guided by internal rather than external stimuli, easily overloaded by stimulation, needed much repetition, could not repeat familiar lists/phrases, attended only for brief intervals, fleeting attention, can't absorb details needed for responsible judgments beyond the routine.

Low attending skills, preoccupied, had difficulty with tasks requiring vigilance, selective attention/inattention, showed lapses of attention.

Attends, could focus on/select the relevant from among the irrelevant aspects of a situation, could maintain the focus/resist distraction, attention is sufficient for question responding/interview/psychotherapy/effective life management, showed freedom from distractibility, capable of prolonged attention but occasionally distracted, vigilant.

11.4. Concentration/Task Persistence

See Section 2.7, "Concentration," for questions. See also Section 12.3, "Attention-Deficit/Hyperactivity Disorder."

General Descriptors

Unable to maintain concentration for more than several minutes/duration of the examination, defective when compared with peers, could not follow a three-stage command/written directions, cannot attend to coping/adaptive/purposeful tasks, could not spell words forward and backward.

For a Child:

Daydreams, has strong/weak subjects, doesn't complete assignments in class/homework, materials are disorganized/messy, forgets teacher's instructions, has to be reminded to sit still/

pay attention, loses needed supplies and materials. *(See also Section 8.3, "Response to the Methods of Evaluation . . . ")*

Interfering Factors

Concentration intact to direct questioning, but subtle recall deficits are evident when certain topics (e.g., symptoms or denied behaviors) are inquired into.

Performance anxiety, fear of failure, fear of being found wanting/inadequate, general anxiety, preoccupations with self or others.

Performance on Serial Sevens

Was able to subtract 7 from 100 _____ times/fully/down to 2 accurately.

Did serial sevens down to _____ in _____ seconds with _____ errors, at which point I stopped her/ him.

Was able to do serial sevens _____ times before making an error.

Self-corrected errors in the sequence.

Performed serial sevens with _____ errors, but subsequent subtractions were accurate based on the prior numbers.

Could sustain concentration only to the _____ plateau/on _____ trials, even with sincere effort.

Demonstrated adequate numerical reasoning, but made incorrect computations because of interfering anxiety.

11.5. Consciousness Levels

> *See also Sections 2.3, "Rancho Los Amigos Cognitive Scale," and 2.4, "Glasgow Coma Scale."*

($\leftrightarrow$ *by degree*) The following groupings are sequenced by degree of increasing consciousness.

Coma, comatose, coma vigil, unarousable, unresponsive, obtunded.

> **Stuporous,** delirious, responsive only to persistent noxious stimulation, postictal, twilight/ dreamy state, drifts off, fluctuates, arousable/rousable, semicoma.

>> **Lethargic,** reduced wakefulness, somnolent, only briefly responsive with a return to unconsciousness.

>>> **Clouded consciousness,** drowsy, falls asleep, responding requires special effort, lessened ability to perform tasks, frequent hesitations, starting/startles, disoriented, groggy, "drugged," under the influence of medications that . . . (specify), in a daze.

>>>> **Alert,** responds to questions, attentive, makes eye contact, interacts, asks questions, converses, lucid, intact, was spontaneously verbal.

11.6. Decision Making

> *See also Section 11.13, "Moral/Social Judgment . . . "; see Section 2.21, "Decision Making," for questions.*

($\leftrightarrow$ *by degree*) The following groupings are sequenced by degree of increasing decision-making ability.

Easily confused, easily overwhelmed in choice situations, lacks understanding of options, fails to evaluate choices.

> Indecisive, flounders, dithers, procrastinates, ponders endlessly, avoids decision situations, reverses decisions, wishy-washy, vacillates, ambivalent, seeks/requires others to decide.

Unable to carry out choices verbalized, deficient in carrying out instructions/in finishing tasks started, can make only simple/work-related decisions.

Decisive, effective, follows through, tolerates frustration/ambiguity/delay/errors/peers/setbacks/changes/ambivalence.

11.7. Dementia

See also Sections 11.12, "Memory," 11.17, "Reasoning ...," and 11.13, "Moral/Social Judgment ... "; see Section 2.10, "Memory," for screening questions.

Types of Dementia

Alzheimer's dementia (most common type), multi-infarct dementia/vascular dementia (second most common), dementia with Lewy bodies, FrontoTemporal Dementia/Pick's dementia.

Treatable dementias due to hypothyroidism, cardiovascular disease, vitamin B1 deficiency, folate deficiency, hypoglycemia, hypercalcemia, etc.

Rarer dementias: neurosyphilis, AIDS dementia complex, dementia pugilistica, porphyria-related dementia.

Reminders

✓ First, do not use "senility" to mean "dementia," because aging doesn't cause dementia. Aging is not a disease. At no age is dementia a normal state, and in many cases dementia is reversible while age isn't. "In the absence of disease there is no dementia." Differential diagnoses include depression, the "mindlessness" created by routine and passivity (Langer, 1989), diabetes, alcohol abuse, infections, trauma, tumors, vascular disease, sensory restrictions, normal-pressure hydrocephalus, metabolic disturbances, poor nutrition, drug interactions/toxicity, sleep deprivation, and a variety of Central Nervous System conditions. *(See Sections 12.36, "Side Effects of Psychotropic Medications/Adverse Drug Reactions," and 29.6, "Organic Brain Syndrome/Dementia.")*

✓ Second, be alert to the possibility of AIDS Dementia Complex, whose onset is insidious. *(See Section 12.2, which covers this topic.)*

✓ Third, consider whether dementia-like symptoms may be caused by another psychiatric disorder—most commonly depression (in which case the symptoms are called "the dementia syndrome of depression"), but sometimes schizophrenia or somatoform disorders. This condition was formerly called "pseudodementia," but it is not functionally a "pseudo-." Differentiating the dementia syndrome from depression can be difficult, but a website (*neuro.psyc.memphis.edu/NeuroPsyc/np-dx-demen.htm*) provides guidance.

Phases of Decline in Alzheimer's Disease: Global Deterioration Scale

A commonly accepted and detailed seven-stage model can be found online (*www.alzinfo.org/clinical-stages-of-alzheimers-disease.asp*).

11.8. Information

See Section 2.11, "Fund of Information," for questions.

Impoverished/deficient fund of information/general knowledge, unaware of current/practical/general information, doesn't know facts regarding his/her culture, fund of factual knowledge is low/spotty, unaware of many basic factual/measurement/historical/geographical concepts.

Summary Statements:

Limited education was apparent/demonstrated in low levels of the information typically acquired in elementary school.

Considering his/her cultural background, level of formal education, and self-education, this client's information was ... (specify).

11.9. Insight

See Section 2.23, "Insight into Disorder," for questions.

Nil or Little

No insight, blindly uncritical of own behavior, denies presence of psychological problems/illness/symptoms, aware of problem but blames others/circumstances/physical factors/something unknown or mysterious for problems, rebuts psychological or motivational interpretations of behavior, fights the system and does little or nothing to help self, fatalistic resignation.

Denies (despite the evidence) that current symptoms are important or that he/she needs help, feels no need to change attitude/behavior/feelings in some specific way, minimizes/denies/obfuscates/evades staff evaluations/findings during discussion.

Confused, perplexed, befuddled. Does not know what to make of his/her situation.

Superficial, shallow, platitudinous, difficulty in acknowledging the presence of psychological problems, self-deceiving, unable to focus on issues, lacks objectivity.

Some

Understanding is more peripheral than central or visceral.

Unable to make use of correct insights, only flashes of insight, doesn't understand self too well.

Is aware of not functioning up to capacity/potential.

Seems to recognize some symptomatology but not to have any understanding of its mechanisms or processes.

Insight is emerging/coalescing/accumulating.

Continues trying to make sense of own psychotic thinking.

Has some insight into behavior, but apparently is not able to respond appropriately or perceive satisfactory solutions to life situation.

Full

Believes/accepts that he/she is ill, recognizes need for treatment, came to treatment voluntarily, labels own illness, takes medicines, attends therapy sessions, works in therapy, acknowledges psychological/physical/historical limitations present.

Accepts that her/his symptoms/problematic behaviors/failures in adaptation are at least in part due to irrational thoughts/feelings/internal states/defenses/personal history, can identify the emotional/cognitive antecedents and consequents of symptomatic behaviors, recognizes relation of symptomatic behavior (e.g., alcohol abuse) to emotional states, acknowledges its impact on life's duration/quality/satisfaction.

Open to new ideas/perspectives on self and others, self-aware, psychologically minded, accepts explanations offered by caregivers, can apply understanding to change actions/direction of his/her life, understands causes/dynamics/treatments/implications of illness.

Understands outcomes of behavior and is influenced by this awareness, is able to identify/distinguish/comprehend behaviors contrary to social values/socially nonacceptable/personally counterproductive.

For a Disability Report: Note applicant's perception of relationship between injury/illness and psychological conditions.

11.10. Intelligence, Development, and Cognition: Assessment

For assessment of <u>Activities of Daily Living</u>, see Section 14.1. For personality assessment, see Section 13.2. For assessment of <u>Attention-Deficit/Hyperactivity Disorder</u>, see Section 12.3. For memory assessment, see Section 11.12. For vocational assessment, see Section 17.1.

Keep in mind that there are more kinds of "intelligence" than are assessed by widely available tests. Gardner (2006) has suggested at least eight.

✓ If you suspect the presence of a learning disability, information-processing disorder, mental retardation, or any physical condition that would affect school performance, consultation with or referral to a school psychologist or educational specialist who can utilize the many specialized instruments for evaluation and remediation is usually appropriate.

There are thousands of published instruments for evaluating almost any aspect of mental functioning, and hundreds of these have good reliability and validity. Inclusion in the listing below does not indicate endorsement of the named purpose or validity of any test by the present author or publisher. Inclusion is based on the presumed likelihood of encountering the test in clinical practice. Each entry offers the title of the current edition or version of each test (with acronym, abbreviation, or common name indicated as usual by underlining); its copyright date if available; its current publisher or distributor; and the applicable age range.

Child Development

<u>Battelle</u> Developmental Inventory–2 (2004), Riverside, birth–8 years.
<u>Bayley</u> Scales of Infant and Toddler Development–III (2005), Pearson Assessments, 1–42 months.
<u>Brigance</u> Early Childhood Complete Assessment Kit (2009), Curriculum Associates, 0–5 years.
<u>Denver</u> Developmental Screening Test–<u>II</u>, Denver Developmental Materials, birth–6 years.
<u>D</u>evelopmental <u>A</u>ctivities <u>S</u>creening <u>I</u>nventory–<u>II</u>, PRO-ED, birth–60 months.
<u>Hawaii</u> <u>E</u>arly <u>L</u>earning <u>P</u>rofile, Vort, birth–6 years.
<u>L</u>earning <u>A</u>ccomplishment <u>P</u>rofile–<u>III</u>, Kaplan Early Learning, 3–6 years.

Intelligence (Screening Tests)

<u>Slosson</u> Intelligence <u>T</u>est–Revised–<u>3</u>rd ed., Slosson, 4–65 years.
<u>Kaufman</u> <u>B</u>rief Intelligence <u>T</u>est–<u>2</u>, Pearson Assessments, 4–90 years.
<u>R</u>eynolds <u>I</u>ntellectual <u>S</u>creening <u>T</u>est (2003), <u>P</u>sychological <u>A</u>ssessment <u>R</u>esources, 3–94 years.

Intelligence (Individualized Administration for More Precise Evaluations)

<u>B</u>racken <u>B</u>asic <u>C</u>oncept Scale–<u>3</u> (2006), Pearson Assessment, 3:0–6:11 years.
<u>D</u>as–<u>N</u>aglieri <u>C</u>ognitive <u>A</u>ssessment <u>S</u>ystem (1997), Riverside, 5–17:11 years.
<u>K</u>aufman <u>A</u>dolescent and <u>A</u>dult Intelligence <u>T</u>est, Pearson Assessments, 11–85+ years.
<u>K</u>aufman <u>A</u>ssessment <u>B</u>attery for <u>C</u>hildren–<u>II</u>, Pearson Assessments, 3–18 years.
<u>Stanford</u>–<u>Binet</u> Intelligence Scales, <u>5</u>th ed. (2003), Riverside, 2 years–adult.
<u>W</u>echsler <u>A</u>bbreviated <u>S</u>cale of <u>I</u>ntelligence (1999), Pearson Assessments, 6–89 years.
<u>W</u>echsler <u>A</u>dult <u>I</u>ntelligence <u>S</u>cale–<u>IV</u> (2008), Pearson Assessments, 16–90 years.
<u>W</u>echsler Intelligence Scale for <u>C</u>hildren–<u>IV</u> (2003), Pearson Assessment, 6–16:11 years.

Wechsler <u>P</u>reschool and <u>P</u>rimary <u>S</u>cale of <u>I</u>ntelligence–<u>III</u> (2002), Pearson Assessments, 2:6–7:3 years.

<u>W</u>ide <u>R</u>ange Intelligence <u>T</u>est (2000), <u>P</u>sychological <u>A</u>ssessment <u>R</u>esources, 4–85 years.

Nonverbal Scales of Intellectual Functioning

Test <u>O</u>f <u>N</u>onverbal <u>I</u>ntelligence–<u>3</u> (1997), PRO-ED, 6–90 years.

<u>C</u>omprehensive <u>T</u>est <u>O</u>f <u>N</u>onverbal <u>I</u>ntelligence–<u>2</u> (2009), PRO-ED, 6–91 years.

<u>L</u>eiter International Performance Scale–<u>R</u>evised, Western Psychological Services, 2–20 years.

<u>M</u>errill–<u>P</u>almer Revised Scales of Development (2004), Western Psychological Services, 1 month–6:6 years.

<u>N</u>aglieri <u>N</u>onverbal <u>A</u>bility <u>T</u>est–Individual Administration (2003), Pearson Assessments, 5–17:11 years.

<u>R</u>aven's Progressive Matrices (1986), Pearson Assessments, 5 years–adult (three levels for different age and ability groups).

<u>U</u>niversal <u>N</u>onverbal <u>I</u>ntelligence <u>T</u>est (1998), Riverside, 5–17:11 years.

Educational Achievements

<u>P</u>eabody <u>I</u>ndividual <u>A</u>chievement <u>T</u>est–<u>R</u>evised/<u>N</u>ormative <u>U</u>pdate (2001), Pearson Assessments, 5–22 years.

Wechsler <u>I</u>ndividual <u>A</u>chievement <u>T</u>est–<u>III</u> (2009), Pearson Assessments, 4–20 years.

<u>W</u>ide <u>R</u>ange <u>A</u>chievement <u>T</u>est, 4th ed. (2006), PAR, 5–94 years.

<u>W</u>oodcock–<u>J</u>ohnson <u>III</u> (2001), Riverside, 2–90+ years.

11.11. Intelligence Scores: Classifications

See Chapter 21, "Diagnostic Statement/Impression," for DSM-IV-TR/ICD-9-CM diagnoses and codes for Mental Retardation (and DSM-IV-TR Borderline Intellectual Functioning).

IQ Categories for Adults

Category	IQ score range	% of population included in each
Gifted	130 and above	2.27
Above average	115–129	13.59
High average	100–114	34.13
(Average)	(85–115)	(68.26)
Low average	85–99	34.13
Borderline	71–84	13.59
Mild mental retardation	50–55 to 70	2.14
Moderate mental retardation	35–40 to 50–55	0.13

This table is based on Wechsler (2003, 2008) and DSM-IV-TR (American Psychiatric Association, 2000).

Validity of Scores: Summary Statements

The obtained test scores are believed to be valid indicators of/significantly underestimate current intellectual functioning.

The scores are consistent with developmental history and degree of functional loss but not with potential, because … (specify).

Notes

✓ Weigh the levels of adaptive behavior (<u>A</u>ctivities of <u>D</u>aily <u>L</u>iving, needs for assistance), as well as the results of intelligence testing (and the standard errors of these scores), into your diagnosis.

✓ Consider the potential effects of education, depression, dementia, distracting anxiety, relationship with the examiner, intercurrent medical illnesses, etc., on intellectual functioning.

✓ After 3 years from the date of the evaluation, test data and findings (especially on a child) should be treated with caution.

✓ Generally, IQ scores below 40 (or near the floor of scores available on a test) are not meaningful discriminators.

✓ Consider the possibility that current functioning represents a decline; if so, offer an estimate of premorbid intelligence based on current subtest results, earlier testing, changed levels of adaptive behavior, etc.

11.12. Memory

See Section 2.10, "Memory," for questions. See also Section 11.7, "Dementia."

Indications of Defect (↔ *by degree*)

Forgetful, "spotty memory," "absent-minded," uncertain/expresses doubts, perplexed, foggy, hesitating, dreamy presentation, "spaced out," detached, confused, befuddled, confabulates, falsifies, perseverates, contaminations, diffusions.

Confuses time frames/sequences, nonsequential, overfocused on externals/situational issues, vague, guesses/estimates/approximates, Ganser's syndrome, disjointed, gaps, skips over, skimpy/superficial history, contradictions, a poor historian/reporter of past events.

Can only recognize, sluggish recall, recalls only with much prompting/cueing, reproduces/reconstructs with much difficulty/inaccuracy.

Amnesias

Anterograde, retrograde, <u>T</u>otal <u>G</u>lobal <u>A</u>mnesia, "infantile," fugue, amnestic/amnesic disorder, Korsakoff's syndrome, Wernicke's syndrome.

Paramnesias

FAUSSE RECONNAISSANCE, retrospective falsification, confabulation, preknowledge of events/others' speech, DÉJÀ VU, DÉJÀ ENTENDU, DÉJÀ PENSÉ, JAMAIS VU, hypermnesia, anomia, agnosia, prosopagnosia, <u>T</u>ip-<u>O</u>f-the-<u>T</u>ongue phenomenon.

Impact of Memory Defect on Patient (↔ *by degree*)

Maximal/effective/poor/no use of compensatory mechanisms/coping skills, constricts lifestyle, ignores, denies.

Summary Statements about Memory Performance

Normal Memory

All components of memory are grossly intact.
The client is able to recount personal history normally/at all time stages.

His/her remote, recent, and immediate memories appear to be intact, as far as I can determine without independent verification of the historical facts.

Normal forgetfulness/age-related memory loss/age-consistent memory decline/<u>A</u>ge-<u>A</u>ssociated <u>M</u>emory <u>I</u>mpairment/<u>A</u>ge-<u>R</u>elated <u>C</u>ognitive <u>D</u>ecline is present.

AAMI is the term most often used by the <u>N</u>ational <u>I</u>nstitute of <u>M</u>ental <u>H</u>ealth, and ARCD is the term used in DSM-IV-TR (the code is 780.9).

As Historian

The client was un/able to give an account of his/her activities/life events in a chronological order.

Memory, as reflected in her/his ability to provide an intact, substantial, sequential, detailed, and logical history/narrative, was defective/quite poor/poor/adequate/normal/exceptional/ unusual because ... (specify).

Memory for events in temporal sequence was vague/incomplete/contradictory/chaotic.

He/she could not recall the time frames of school/work/family development/treatments.

Defective Memory

The client was able to recall no/one/two/three objects/words after 5/10 minutes of different/ unrelated activities.

Memory was limited/deficient/defective/a problem in all time frames.

Memory is organically intact, but anxiety/depression interfere.

She seems defective/normal/exceptional in immediate/short-term retention/recent/recent past/ remote memory.

Client shows the pattern of memory deficits typical of those with/with a history of _____ (specify diagnosis).

_____ memory is not affected/normal, but _____ memory is defective/exceptional.

Remote and recent memories appeared to be intact, but there was an emptiness and lack of color in client's descriptions of critical events.

Client did not offer a rich description of important events from personal history.

Client's recall appeared deliberately vague/evasive/distorted by distrust/self-protectively edited.

Other Aspects of Memory

Types of Memory

Storage:

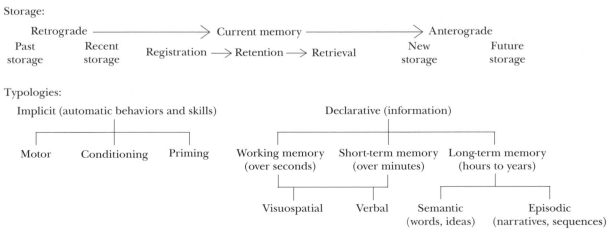

Typologies:

Clinical: Recognition ("identify, select, pick, or find"), reproduction ("say, repeat, or copy"), recall (remember without cueing).

Types: Immediate, short-term/active/working, long-term, generic, eidetic, narrative, declarative/explicit vs. procedural/implicit, automatic vs. effortful, semantic vs. episodic, verbal (words, phrases, stories, associated word pairs), visual (colors, designs, pictures), spatial (positions of objects), episodic (contexts, situations, components, details, sequences, themes), practical/praxis (ability to demonstrate/pantomime how to open a can, brush one's teeth, butter bread, etc.).

Functions or processes: Acquisition, registration, encoding, recoding, chunking, consolidation, rehearsal, transfer, storage, retention, decay, retrieval, recall, reconstruction.[1]

Possible causes of forgetting: Decay, displacement, interference, retroactive and proactive inhibition, consolidation block theory, retrieval failure theory, explicit memory defect.

Factors affecting recall: Primacy, recency, vividness, frequency.

Methods for enhancing recall: Method of loci, mnemonics, elaborative rehearsal, priming, spatiotemporal markers, Tip-Of-the-Tongue phenomenon.

Characteristics of Senescent Forgetfulness

The following table is adapted from Kral (1978).

Malignant	*Age-Associated Memory Impairment {Benign Senescent Forgetfulness}*
Shortened retention time.	Failures to recall are limited to relatively unimportant parts of an experience (e.g., a name or date).
Inability to recall an event of the recent past, including not only unimportant facts but the experience itself.	Details forgotten on one occasion may be recalled at another time.
Failure to recall accompanied by disorientation to place and time and, gradually, to person.	"Forgotten" data belong to remote as opposed to recent past.
Absent self-awareness of deficiencies.	Subjects are aware of shortcomings and may apologize or compensate.
	No language or praxis impairments.

Assessment Instruments for Memory

As in the listing of tests in Section 11.10, each entry here gives the title of the current edition or version of each test (with acronym, abbreviation, or common name indicated as usual by underlining); its copyright date if available; its publisher or distributor; and the applicable age range.

Wechsler Memory Scale—IV (2009), Pearson Assessments, 16–90 years.
Benton Visual Retention Test, 5th ed. (1991), Pearson Assessments, 8–adult.
Wide Range Assessment of Memory and Learning 2 (2003), PAR, 5–90 years.
Rey Complex Figure Test and Recognition Trial (1995), Pearson Assessments, 6–89 years.
Rivermead Behavioural Memory Test—3, Pearson Assessments, adult.

---

[1]I am indebted to Mustaq Khan, PhD, of London, Ontario, Canada, for several corrections in this section.

11.13. Moral/Social Judgment and Knowledge

See also Sections 11.6, 11.9, 11.16, 11.17, and 11.18. See Section 2.20, "Social Judgment," for questions.

Defective Understanding/Lack of "Common Sense"

Substantial defects in capacity to appreciate common/consensual reality.

Impaired ability to make reasonable and realistic life decisions.

Makes major decisions without sufficient information/impulsively/depending on hearsay/so as not to refuse a friend, impulsive.

Makes decisional errors under even the mildest stress.

Seems guided by false beliefs.

Heedless/reckless/feckless/careless, irresponsible.

For a Child:

Excessive imagination, confuses wishes/fears/impulses with objective/consensual reality.

Normal Judgment/"Common Sense"

Has common-sense understandings, common-sensical, is "street-smart," realistic.

Subscribes to usual explanations of people's motivations.

Has sought treatment for medical/psychological problems.

Learned from experience/feedback/others' mistakes/correction/instruction.

Understands/anticipates the likely outcome of behavior and thinks/plans ahead effectively.

Responsible, understands/anticipates the likely consequences of his/her behavior/actions.

Has strong/weak executive functions (decision making, social perception, flexibility of thinking/judgment), generates good/poor alternatives/solutions/positions.

Shows discernment, discretion, wisdom.

Propriety/Impropriety

Distinguishes socially acceptable from unacceptable behaviors and acts on this understanding.

Able to identify and control behaviors harmful to self and others/contrary to acceptable rules/beyond the limits of the community.

Does not display outlandish or bizarre behaviors inappropriate to social interactions.

Acts contrary to acceptable behavior.

Judgment intact in terms of understanding (e.g., the demand characteristics of social settings), but not in terms of the social acceptability of the behaviors.

Does not comprehend/anticipate/defer to the expected/usual consequences of his/her behaviors or the impact/impression upon others.

Inadequately cognizant/aware of basic social conventions.

Victimization

Engages in actions harmful to self.

Has been taken advantage of repeatedly.

Easily misled and swindled/misused/taken advantage of.

Not discriminating in choice of companions.

Makes blatantly defective and self-damaging choices.

Might unwittingly enter a situation of jeopardy or be unable to extricate self from one.
Requires close support/monitoring to avoid loss/harm/exploitation.
Judgment insufficient for independent living/assisted living.
Has a lifelong history of ineffective coping.

Other Statements

The client has difficulty with performing the tasks supportive of/related to carrying out the decisions made.
Given the defective quality of her/his thinking/understanding, judgment has to be impaired.
Evaluation of client's judgment, as based on a comparison with premorbid state or with expected ability based on intellect/age/education/social experience, is ... (specify).

11.14. Motivation for Change: Summary Statements

See also Chapter 23, "Prognostic Statements"; Section 11.9, "Insight"; the "Responses to Treatment" heading in Section 12.39, "Substance Use, Abuse, and Dependence"; and "The Stages-of-Change Model" heading in Section 25.3, "Various Formats for Treatment Plans.

Motivation is limited by low frustration tolerance/dependency/ambivalence/low initiative.
Increased motivation is needed for change/therapy/habilitation/rehabilitation/self-improvement.
Client is aware of problems but is not yet sufficiently motivated to take action.
Client is powerfully motivated for change, as seen in ... (specify).

11.15. Orientation (↔ *by degree*)

See Section 2.5, "Orientation," for questions.

Incorrectly/inadequately identified self by name, mistook/confused present location/correct time/objects/others, mistook/confused dates/persons/places, was off the mark by _____ years/months/days.

> Appeared to be oriented only in the most simple sense/on basic measures, oriented to _____ but not to _____.

> Fully oriented times three/to time, place, and person; times four/to time, place, person, and common things.

11.16. Reality Testing

See also Section 11.13, "Moral/Social Judgment ... "

Intact, functional, not distorted by psychodynamics/defenses/psychopathology, perceives the social world as most people do, understands cause–effect links as other people do, shares common attributions of causality, functional/adequate/good/extensive fund of knowledge/awareness of the external world, shows maturity.
Defective reality testing, repeatedly makes poor judgments, easily misled and taken advantage of, misinterprets common-sense reality, cannot anticipate others' reactions to her/his behaviors, overresponds to stimuli/others' behavior, distorted/idiosyncratic interpretations of events and their meanings, acts as if the world was as she/he would like it to be, lives in a fantasy world.

11.17. Reasoning/Abstract Thinking/Concept Formation

See also Section 11.13, "Moral/Social Judgment ... "; see Sections 2.12–2.15 and 2.17–2.18 for questions.

Level of Interpretation (↔ *by degree*)

Greatly defective, failed to grasp nature of question, it was not possible to find proverbs simple enough for him/her to interpret, no evidence of abstract thinking or even extended thought processes, "I've heard that one before" (without elaboration).

Distorted by thought disorder, showing personification/bizarre features/delusions.

Concrete (noted only surface features or appearance aspects of stimuli), offered only very specific examples, paraphrases, reasoned in a concrete manner, stimulus-bound associations.

Simplistic, difficulty with concept formation/judgment, abstraction, opposites/similarities/differences, comparative analogies, absurdities, proverbs.

Couldn't use appropriate/expected levels of abstraction in dealing with test materials, mixed up categories in hierarchies, poor abstract thinking and concept-handling ability, degree of generalization was overly broad/narrow, some difficulty with reasoning at an easy/moderately difficult/difficult level, offered unusual/idiosyncratic/antisocial interpretations.

Functional levels of interpretation, responded only in terms of the uses for the stimulus item or literal meanings.

Offered **popular** interpretations of proverbs, adequate reasoning skills, common sense.

Abstracted common properties of the stimuli (noted the verbal or logical relationships between the stimuli), used principles, reasoned abstractly, offered similar proverbs/spontaneous rephrasings, comprehensive level of reasoning.

Overly abstract, attended only to selected/irrelevant aspects of stimuli, stylized, overly philosophical/obscure/arcane references, highly theoretical, Byzantine reasoning.

Summary Statements

Normal Abstraction

The client had a common-sense/functional understanding of everyday objects.
She was able to respond with an abstract relationship between pairs of terms/items I presented to her.
He was able to form concepts well and without concreteness.
She was able to identify opposites, similarities, differences, and absurdities.

Client was able to analyze the meaning of simple proverbs, all at appropriate levels of abstraction.
He could give me the deep meanings of the proverbs I offered.

Faulty Reasoning

The client engaged in faulty inductive/deductive inference/reasoning.
She reached conclusions based on false/faulty premises.
He made errors of logic and judgment/came to incorrect conclusions.

She was unable to relevantly support answers given.

His reasoning appears autistic/dereistic/idiosyncratic.

NON SEQUITURS/PARS PRO TOTO/trance logic/AD HOMINEM/POST HOC ERGO PROPTER HOC/other errors were evident.

> *See also "Dysfunctional Cognitions" in Section 10.7, "Depression."*

11.18. Social Maturity

> *See also Section 11.13, "Moral/Social Judgment . . . "*

Irresponsibility   *See also Section 13.7, "Antisocial Personality."*

Denies/distorts responsibilities, steals/destroys others' property, refuses to pay debts/for property destroyed, cheats, blames innocents, shows no guilt or remorse, offers no explanations, fakes guilt, offers only empty/"phony" apologies, falsely begs/pleads, "crocodile tears."

On the job he/she resists/doesn't cooperate with/ignores/defies rules/directions/deadlines, starts many tasks but does not complete any, manipulates coworkers into doing his/her work, "cons," needs close/continuous supervision, absent without excuse/slips away, tardy/takes too many/overlong rest periods/breaks/leaves early, intoxicated at work, conducts own business during work hours.

Self-Centeredness   *See also Section 13.17, "Narcissistic Personality."*

Manipulates, lacks/has unrealistic/has only immediate goals, selfish, uncaring, resents limits, self-indulgent, impulsive, arousal-seeking, acts out, immature, infantile.

Financial Behavior   *See Section 14.6, "Financial Skills."*

Social Interaction   *See also Chapters 15, "Social/Community Functioning," and 16, "Couple and Family Relationships."*

Resistant to authorities (parents, supervisor, police, human service professionals), chooses/imitates inappropriate or pathological models.

Touches others without consent, touches self inappropriately.

Threatens vaguely to leave/take revenge/destroy property/commit violence, threatens when confronted with own irresponsible behaviors, bullies/intimidates, harasses.

Has only limited contact with others, so little opportunity to behave inappropriately.

Client never/rarely/often/usually plays/socializes with/relates to persons of her own age group.

He prefers to relate to things/paper/numbers/ideas/people.

Summary Statements

Child is as mature as same-age peers/is only pseudomature/has been "parentified" by his family/is overly mature.

When/as compared with others of same age/culture/education, she demonstrated _____ degree of maturity.

11.19. Stream of Thought

> *This section covers speech as a reflection of cognition. See also Section 7.4, "Speech Behavior," and Section 11.17, "Reasoning . . . "*

MENTAL STATUS

Amount/Productivity (↔ *by degree*)

impoverished	laconic	**normal**	rapid	**flight of ideas**
paucity	slowed	spontaneous	overabundant	
restricted	hesitant	average	"logorrhea"	
decreased		abundant	copious	
unelaborated				
underproductive				
blocked				
slowed speed of				
cognitive process-				
ing				

Continuity/Coherence (↔ *by degree*)

incoherent	**loose**	**idiosyncratic**	disconnected	**clear**
incomprehensible	circumstantial	unusual	topic changes	realistic
clang associations	irrelevancies	associations	difficult to	rational
neologisms	tangential	personalized	follow	lucid
word salad	vague	meanings	fragmented	consistent
confabulations	derailed		flighty	coherent
{verbigerations}	rambling	conjectural	confusing	relevant
perseverative	garbled		disjointed	integrated
chaotic	confused	preoccupied		goal-directed
jabbers	sidetracked		baffling	logical
babbles	evasive		Byzantine	pertinent
prattles	distracted		perplexing	easy to
"rattles on"	digressive			follow
silly conclusions	drifting		irrelevant	intact
	circumlocutions			sequential
	paraphrases		incorrect	not pre-
	word substitutions		conclusions	occupied
	nonsequential		unclear	articulate
	jumbled		imprecise	linear
	illogical		indefinite	
	repetitive		poorly defined	

Coherence

(↔ *by degree*) The following groupings are sequenced by increasing degree of coherence:

No stepwise progressions, no logical sequences, lacking internal logic/structure.

    Loosening of associations, connected associations by small and/or unusual similarities, needed to be refocused/redirected, failed to answer the questions asked.

        Clear cause-and-effect thinking, responses cohered with/addressed the questions asked, common/realistic associations, coherent, to the point, linear.

Qualities of Thought Content

Personalized, idiosyncratic, carefully chosen, eccentric, odd, monothematic, overvalued ideas.
Sexual, earthy, erotic, scatological, pornographic, obscene, profane, blasphemous, vulgarities.
Bizarre themes, magical thinking, fabulized.
Trivial, platitudes, sentimental, oversimple, empty.

Preoccupations   *See above; see also Sections 12.10, "Delusions," 12.21, "Obsessions," and 12.24, "Paranoia."*

mental health
obsessions
compulsions
fears/phobias
symptoms

death
suicide
homicide
dying
morbid thoughts
losses
tragedies

religion
piety
excessive prayer
blasphemous ideas
denigrating activities
irreligious practices/acts
fears/delusions about
    clergy/theology

his/her plight
life situation
stressors
frustrations
disappointments
shame/embarrassment
regrets
ambivalences

sexuality

**somatic/hypochondriacal
    concerns**
current physical illness
mortal illnesses
popular diseases

escape
running away

Other Problems with Stream of Thought

Loss of goal, spontaneous but unproductive speech, condensations, overinclusive thinking, autoecholalia, interpenetration of themes, loss of segmental set, cognitive slippage.

Paraphrastic errors/dysnomias/unusual word and sentence formations/errors of syntax/constructional dyspraxia/malapropisms/alexia/alexithymia.

Summary Statements for Normal Thought Content

The client showed an average number of thoughts, which were neither speeded nor slowed/moved at a normal pace/normal flow of ideas.

His/her thinking seems normal from the perspective of productivity, relevance, and coherence.

The client answered questions appropriately.

She presented her thoughts in an appropriately paced, understandable, and relevant fashion.

His thoughts were coherent, well organized, and relevant to the subject at hand.

She reached the goal of her thought processes without introducing any irrelevant material.

His train of thought was goal-directed, relevant, logical, coherent, focused, without digressions, irrelevancies, disturbances of logic, or bizarreness.

There was no tangentiality, circumstantiality, or distractibility.

Speech was relevant, appropriate, and without evidence of unusual ideation.

Speech showed good grammatical complexity.

The client showed no obsessions or phobias, ideas of reference, hallucinations, delusions, faulty perceptions, perceptual disturbance, misinterpretations of consensual reality, or psychotic distortions.

Her logic was easy to follow, although the responses were superficial.

He is very concerned about his health, but understandably and appropriately so.

Her thoughts about _____ (e.g., health problems) dominate her thinking but are not exclusive or preoccupying.

Summary Statements for Problematic Stream of Thought

The client will refer to topics in a symbolic or associational manner, which requires deciphering by the listener.

The client apparently does little analytic or discriminatory thinking.

He conversed in response to questions rather than speaking spontaneously.
    Self-sufficient in providing responses, but volunteered little additional information.
    Would not enlarge/expand/elaborate on topics of interest or responses to my questions.

She showed word retrieval deficits/reported "forgetting"/had difficulty finding words/groped
    for words, would stop suddenly in middle of a sentence/speech.
He had great difficulty gathering thoughts rather than in finding words.
She substituted related words approximating the definitive/appropriate term.
When interrupted, he became confused and rambled.
She shows a tendency toward anecdotal thinking that could, if unchecked, become tangential.

11.20. Test Judgment: Summary Statements

The client gave reasonable responses to hypothetical judgment questions.

He/she responded appropriately to imaginary/contrived situations requiring social judgment/
    knowledge of the norms/usual rules/customs and expectations of society.

Performance on the judgment questions asked/tests used was poor/adequate/good/normal/
    expected/excellent, which suggests that in the external/social/"real" world this client would
    ... (specify).

11.21. Other Summary Statements for Mental Status

This client appears to have impaired mental control functions.
He/she seems unable to shift cognitive sets/rigid/inflexible/unable to learn or plan ahead.

Cognitive functioning seems limited rather than faulty.
He/she showed a good balance of self-esteem/confidence and self-criticism.
Cognitive functioning is intact, according to my casual office-based testing.

This client is precocious/very learned/brilliant.

Problem-solving ability is lacking/defective/distorted/limited by intelligence/disorder.

Considering this client's age and education ...

Critical judgment was fine, given his/her viable responses to standard hypothetical situations.

For a Child:

This child showed evidence of incoordination, poor balance, poor speech, delayed develop-
    ment, etc.

Disclaimer

Assessments and conclusions in this report about cognitive processes, including _____, are
based primarily on verbal expressions and secondarily on behavioral expressions representing those
processes. They are inferences about and not signs of such processes. As such, other conditions (such
as receptive–expressive language disorders, medications and other substances used, individual history,
etc.) may have affected these expressions and made inferences based on them inaccurate.[2]

---

[2]This disclaimer is courtesy of Joe Elwart, PsyD, of Royal Oak, MI.

12

Abnormal Signs, Symptoms, and Syndromes

In this chapter you will find ways to report areas of **psychopathology** that are not purely **emotional/ affective symptoms and disorders** (for those, see Chapter 10) or purely **cognitive dysfunctions** (for those, see Chapter 11). It is a somewhat heterogeneous collection containing some actual diagnoses (such as conduct disorder and schizophrenia), as well as many symptoms (such as compulsions, denial, hallucinations, and paranoia).

You are likely to be asked to evaluate conditions that are not yet formal diagnoses but are more than isolated symptoms. Some of these conditions are included here: battered-woman syndrome, Chronic Fatigue Syndrome, chronic pain syndrome, PreMenstrual Dysphoric Disorder, and Rape Trauma Syndrome. Other sections in this chapter address topics of similar concern, such as the risk factors for homicide and suicide, the commonly encountered and confusing side effects of psychotropic medications, sexual "addiction," and malingering.

The topics are presented in simple alphabetical order.

12.1. Abuse

> *See also Sections 12.5, "Battered-Woman Syndrome," 12.19, "Impulse-Control Disorders," 12.34, "Sexual Abuse, Child," 12.41, "Violent Behaviors," and 13.6, "Aggressive Personality."*

The relevant ICD-9-CM and DSM-IV-TR codes are complex. *(See Section 21.21, "V Codes, Etc.")*

Since often there are several kinds of abuse, you can use this format: "P(hysical)/V(erbal)/ E(motional)/M(ental/S(exual) abuse." Be aware that each of these terms is quite inclusive and should be described more fully and less ambiguously.

Consider the following risk factors for abusing families (described by Nietzel and Himelein, 1987):

Parents' histories: Experienced abuse/neglect, lack of parental affection, large families, started family early.

Current family status: Socially isolated/lack of social support, marital discord/conflict, impulsivity of parents, parental illiteracy, parental mental retardation, stressful situation (poverty, generational conflict, incarceration, absence of a parent, etc.).

Parental child-rearing practices: Rarely praising children, strict demands, ignorance of development/unrealistic expectations, low level of supervision of children, early toilet training, dislike of caretaking, caregivers' disagreement over child-rearing practices.

Depending on the work you do, you should keep a list of contacts and phone numbers for the local police, women's shelters, programs for both victims and perpetrators of abuse, supportive social and legal agencies, and so on.

Addictions   *See Sections 12.16, "Gambling," 12.35, "Sexual Impulsivity . . . ," and 12.39, "Substance Use, Abuse, and Dependence."*

Adult Children Of Alcoholic Parents   *See Section 13.11, "Codependent Personality."*

Affects   *See Chapter 10, "Emotional/Affective Symptoms and Disorders."*

Aggression   *See Section 12.19, "Impulse-Control Disorders."*

12.2. AIDS Dementia Complex

The relevant DSM-IV-TR code is 294.1x, Dementia Due to HIV Disease. The relevant ICD-9-CM code is 294.8, Other persisting mental disorder due to conditions classified elsewhere (specify HIV disease).

Other names include HIV-1 mild neurocognitive disorder, HIV-1-associated cognitive/motor disorder, and HIV-1-associated dementia. Although now rarer (under 10%) in People Living With AIDS, this complex is insidious and still seen in untreated individuals. Kalichman (2003) offers information in an accessible format, and Grant and Atkinson's (1995) textbook chapter is psychiatrically complete. A comprehensive website is provided by the National Institutes of Health (*www.aidsinfo. nih.gov*). The following material is adapted from Greenwood (1991) with permission.

Cognitive Changes (↔ *by degree*)

Loss of memories, inability to concentrate, loses train of thought in midsentence, mild confusion, absentmindedness, verbal deficits across intellectual/memory/language tests, mental slowness, forgets to practice safer sex, agitation, inability to speak, loss of self-care functions, unaware of degree of illness/losses, seizures, indifference to surroundings, hypersomnolence, coma.

Motor Dysfunctions (↔ *by degree*)

Leg weaknesses, unsteady gait, poor coordination, handwriting difficulties, tremor, paraplegia, incontinence.

Other Changes

Headache, lethargy, reduced sexual drive, apathy, indifference, suicide risk, withdrawal *(especially in previously gregarious personalities)*, cerebral atrophy/edema/areas of demyelination.

12.3. Attention-Deficit/Hyperactivity Disorder
See Sections 2.6, "Attention," and 2.7, "Concentration," for questions; see Sections 11.3, "Attention," and 11.4, "Concentration/Task Persistence," for additional descriptors.

The relevant DSM-IV-TR codes are 314.00, ADHD, Predominantly Inattentive Type; 314.01, ADHD,

Predominantly Hyperactive–Impulsive Type or Combined Type. The diagnostic criteria in DSM-IV-TR are the same for adults as for children.

The most relevant ICD-9-CM codes are as follows: 314.00, <u>A</u>ttention <u>D</u>eficit <u>D</u>isorder: Without mention of hyperactivity; Predominantly inattentive type; 314.01, ADD: With hyperactivity; ADD combined type; Simple disturbance of attention with overactivity; 314.1, Hyperkinesis of childhood with developmental delay; and 314.2, Hyperkinetic conduct disorder of childhood, without developmental delay.

ADHD can be seen as a concentration disorder. Also consider high lead levels, heavy metal poisoning, maternal drug/alcohol use, etc., as causes of impulsivity, distractibility, low frustration tolerance, etc. Barkley (2005) is the standard reference. Although ADHD may present differently with maturation, it is not outgrown, as two-thirds of children diagnosed with ADHD still meet the criteria as adults (Resnick, 2000). High rates of comorbidity exist with oppositional defiant disorder, conduct disorder, anxiety, depression, learning disorders, and cognitive processing disorders.

Behavior

Restless, fidgets, wriggles, twists, squirms, "antsy," much out-of-seat/off-task behavior, does not sit through an interview or meal, always "on the go," prefers to run rather than walk, climbs on furniture, hops/skips/jumps rather than walking, fiddles with objects, taps/hits and makes noises, moves unnecessarily, disrupts shopping and family visits, acts "wild" in crowded settings, babysitters complain about his/her behavior.

Shifts from one incomplete task to another, does not finish what she/he starts, play is frenetic/nomadic, rushes/jumps from one topic of conversation to another, avoids conversing at any length.

Noncompliant, does not obey instructions, does not sit when told to, breaks school/game's rules, unable to follow a routine, resistant, "sassy"/"talks back," argumentative [and these are not due to oppositional patterns or failure to understand the instructions, so child should not be called defiant].

Does not play quietly, talks excessively, does everything in the noisiest way, makes odd noises.

Needs constant/continual/one-to-one supervision/monitoring/redirection, needs closeness and eye contact to understand instructions, fails to attend to details in schoolwork or other activities, disregards instructions.

Impulsive, blurts out answers, reacts without considering, acts before thinking, limited self-regulatory functions, is disorganized/forgetful and careless with possessions.

Senseless/repetitive/eccentric behaviors, darts around aimlessly, destroys toys and property.

Ignores consequences of own behaviors and so engages in physically dangerous activities.

Adapts to changes in situation/routine/personnel poorly.

Poor fine motor skills, clumsy, low concern for accuracy/neatness/quality of work.

Has difficulty only at specific times, behavior/mood deteriorates during course of day.

Cognitive Features

Attention

Easily distracted, self-distracting, lessened ability to sustain attention/concentration on school task/work/play, low attending skills, often stares into space, reports daydreaming.

Needs/asks for repetitions of instructions, gets confused, doesn't "listen" although hears normally, inattentive to significant details, misses announcements, needs excessive individual supervision.

Low short-term memory skills (two- or three-step instructions), fails to remember sequences, loses place when reading, poor self-monitoring, makes careless mistakes.

Academic Difficulties

Problems with counting/telling time/recognizing letters, adds/substitutes/reverses letters/ words/sounds, copies letters and words poorly, word-finding difficulties, stops in middle of a sentence or thought, confuses/reverses word order in sentences, mistakes similar-sounding words.

Performs below ability level, refractory to usual instructional approaches, may seem unresponsive to punishment or rewards.

Disorganized Work Habits

Difficulty organizing schoolwork, does not study/prepare/organize/protect own work/do problem's steps in sequence, does not complete assignments on time, starts work before receiving full instructions, has great difficulty organizing goal-directed activities, poor at gathering materials and sequencing activities toward a goal, fails to finish tasks, is destructive of materials, loses things necessary for an activity (such as toys, pencils, keys, assignments, books, equipment), unprepared for school assignments, does not use study times.

Affects

Unpredictable and unrelated mood changes, often sad/pessimistic/gloomy, has low self-esteem/image, feels worthless, feelings are easily hurt/offended, cries easily or frequently, easily angered/upset, gets overexcited, irritable/touchy, easily frustrated/low frustration tolerance, no patience, impulsive, excitable, explosive, temper outbursts, unpredictable behavior.

Social Characteristics

Interrupts/intrudes/"butts in," talks out in class, talks out of turn, shouts/blurts out answers/ comments, makes disruptive noises, does not wait turn in group situations, grabs others' possessions, breaks school behavior rules/norms, continually argues.

Fights with sibs/peers/teachers, violent, aggressive, destructive, plays "tough guy/girl," often involved in physically dangerous activities without considering possible risks/dangerous consequences, hits/punches/strikes/kicks/bites, cries/withdraws, verbal conflict/insults/ harasses/threatens, coerces/intimidates/manipulates/"bosses," provokes/disrupts other children's activities, betrays friends, peers avoid/reject him/her, has great difficulty keeping friends, blames others for own mistakes/misbehaviors, takes anger out on others, tries to get even, is avoided/rejected by peers.

Tolerates only a minimum of questions about mood/behavior, reacts adversely if pressed, avoids talking about own problems.

Developmental Pattern of People with ADHD

Infancy: Very frequent crying, sleep difficulties, restless sleep, overactivity, difficult to soothe.

Preschool: Inattentiveness, overactivity, temperamental/emotional, misconduct/aggression, rejection by peers.

Elementary school: Overactivity, impulsivity, inattention, fidgeting, poor school achievement, low self-esteem, slightly below-average IQ, much subtest scatter/variability, clumsiness, disorganization.

High school: Restlessness, poor grades, rebelliousness, difficulty studying, lying, defiance, alcohol/drug use, failure to graduate.

Post-high school: Restlessness, poor concentration, impulsivity, motor vehicle accidents, alcohol/drug abuse, antisocial personality patterns, low self-esteem, emotional/behavioral problems. *(See "Characteristics of Adult ADHD," below.)*

Assessment

For accuracy, multiple informants and multiple measures of the traits are essential (DuPaul, 2003). These can include teacher and parent ratings based on observations at school and in the home; computerized measurement of inattention and impulsivity; and medical, educational, and intellectual evaluations. Some commonly used rating scales include the following:

ADHD Comprehensive Teacher Rating Scale (1991, 2nd ed.) (ACTeRS; available at *www. metritech.com/Metritech*).

ADHD scales from the parent report form of the Achenbach Child Behavior CheckList (CBCL/6–18 and CBCL/1½–5) and the Teacher's Report Form of the CBCL for ages 6–18 (all available at *www.aseba.org*).

Barkley Home Situations Questionnaire and School Situations Questionnaire (available in Barkley & Murphy, 2005).

Brown Attention Deficit Disorder Scales (2001), for ages 3 years–adult (available at *pearsonassessments.com*).

Conners 3 (2008), with forms for child, parent, and teacher, for ages 6–18 (available at *www.mhs. com* or *www.pearsonassessments.com*).

These are timed computerized tests:

Conners Continuous Performance Test–II (available at *www.mhs.com*).

Intermediate Visual and Auditory +Plus Continuous Performance Test for ages 6 years–adult, and IVA Advanced Edition Continuous Performance Test for adults (available at *www.brain-train.com*).

Tests Of Variables of Attention (available at *www.tovatest.com*).

The following tests are specifically designed to assess characteristics of ADHD in adults (see below):

Amen's Adult ADHD Checklist (available at *w3addresources.org/?9=node/43*).

Conners Adult ADHD Rating Scales (available at *www.pearsonassessments.com*).

Possible Adverse Effects of Stimulant Medications

Irritability, sad/weepy, anxious, "spaced-out"/blank stares.
Withdrawn, isolates self, overly quiet.
Unusually cheerful, talkative.
Decreased appetite, difficulty falling asleep.
Headaches, upset stomach, dizziness.
Tics, twitches, nail biting, unusual limb movements.

Characteristics of Adult ADHD

Inattentive Type

Difficulty initiating tasks, procrastination, indecision, avoiding tasks or jobs that require sustained attention.

Chronic forgetfulness, poor time management, losing track of time, tardiness, taking on more tasks than he/she can complete, relying on a spouse or sibling for reminders of commitments and obligations.

Difficulty recalling and organizing details required for a task, difficulty shifting attention from one task to another, difficulty multitasking.

Hyperactive–Impulsive Type

Prefers more active/stimulating jobs, avoids low-physical-activity or sedentary work.
Frequent job changes, may work long hours or two jobs, underachievement despite ability.

Seeks constant activity, easily bored, intense interest followed by boredom (even after substantial investments), inability to stick with long-term projects.

Impatient, low frustration tolerance, easily irritated, loses temper easily/angers quickly, poor self-control.

Interrupts others' conversations, heedless of the effects of statements on others.

Impulsive, poor-quality/snap decisions without appropriate planning, irresponsible behaviors.

Resources

Tuckman (2007) and Resnick (2000) have written comprehensive books on ADHD in adults.

Work

Underachievement compared to peers or sibs (despite intelligence), intense interest followed by boredom (even after substantial financial commitment), inability to stick with long-term projects.

12.4. Autism Spectrum Disorders

The major relevant DSM-IV-TR codes are 299.00, Autistic Disorder; 299.80, Asperger's Disorder; and 299.80, Pervasive Developmental Disorder Not Otherwise Specified.

The major relevant ICD-9-CM codes are 299.0, Autistic disorder; 299.8, Other specified PDD (which includes Asperger's disorder); and 299.9, Unspecified PDD.

In addition to these disorders, the PDDs or ASDs include Rett's, and Childhood Disintegrative Disorders. They share many elements, some of which are listed below and may present with different severity.

Aloneness

Fails to develop attachment, no social smile, does not seek comforting from others or seeks it in strange ways when distressed/upset/frightened, ignores people, avoids eye contact and gaze monitoring, looks "through" people.

Emotionally distant, no affection or interest when held, going limp/stiff when held, preoccupied so is neither receptive to nor defensive of touch, does not need caregiver, unaware of caregiver's absence.

Lacks social give and take/reciprocity/turn taking/modulation/resonance/mutuality, marked lack of awareness of the existence of feelings in others (lacks a "theory of mind"), lacks imitation/pretend play, lacks parallel/social play, plays alone, ignores/withdraws from/does not return affection, uses others in mechanical way, no friendships, lacks understanding of social rules, little imagination.

Relates to inanimate objects, carries objects, ritual behaviors *(see below).*

Communication

Delayed speech or muteness, lack of verbal spontaneity/sparse expressive speech, does not imitate or does it strangely/mechanically, echolalia (immediate or delayed).

Affirmation by repetition *(repetition of the question asked as agreement),* pronoun reversal *(referring to self in second and third persons and by name),* neologisms, extreme literalness or "metaphorical language" *(e.g., using a specific "No" situation to mean all other "No" situations),* part–whole confusion *(e.g., "ketchup" to mean dinner).*

Rituals and Compulsions

Preservation of sameness: *Change in any aspect of daily routine or surroundings leads to persistent crying or temper tantrum.*

Stereotypic behaviors: Manipulating things, rocking, hand flapping, tiptoe walking, spinning, twirling, staring at spinning things like fans.

Unpredictable/bizarre behaviors: Lunging, darting, sudden stops, swaying, head rolling.

12.5. Battered-Woman Syndrome

See Sections 3.2 and 3.4 for questions about physical and sexual abuse, 3.31 for questioning perpetrators, and 12.1 for physical abuse risk factors. See also Section 12.27, "PostTraumatic Stress Disorder."

The relevant DSM-IV-TR codes are V61.12, Physical Abuse of Adult/Sexual Abuse of Adult when abuse is by partner and focus is on the perpetrator); 995.81, Physical Abuse of Adult (when focus is on the victim); and 995.83, Sexual Abuse of Adult (when focus is on the victim).

The relevant ICD-9-CM codes are V61.12, Counseling for perpetrator of spousal and partner abuse, and V61.11, Counseling for victim of spousal and partner abuse.

Battered-woman syndrome is a result of Intimate Partner Violence and a form of PTSD. IPV is common across all demographics; it should be routinely screened for and, when found, fully assessed. McCloskey and Grigsby (2005) offer detailed questions and procedures for evaluations of batterer, victim, lethality, and safety factors, as well as other relevant materials.

✓ Because 92% of a sample of battered women reported blows to the head, 40% reported loss of consciousness, and 77% reported some signs of PostConcussive Syndrome, Jackson et al. (2002) recommend that **all** cases should be evaluated for mild Traumatic Brain Injury and PCS. *(See Section 12.26 on PCS.)*

Characteristics of Victims

Denial or minimization of the details of the abuse. [Paralleling the perpetrator's sense of entitlement and his denial—of responsibility, of the fact that it is "abuse," of its severity/consequences, etc.]

Fear of accusations of being crazy/exaggerating/making it up, if she seeks help.

Caught up in cycles of violence: violence, fear, placating, more violence or leaving, promises to change by the perpetrator, return to the relationship, etc.

Low self-esteem (especially efficacy).

Putting the perpetrator's needs first even at great cost to herself, remaining in a psychologically and physically harmful situation, passive and dependent behavior.

Types of Partner Abuse

Nonviolent: Overly calm talking, sulked, withdrew/isolated/ignored/shunned, yelled/swore, insulted, called names, threatened abandonment of children/support/obligations.

Intimidation: Prevented movement/restrained freedom/denial of privacy, interrupted activities, financial control.

Threats of violence: Driving dangerously, with weapons, toward children/pets/spouse/relatives.

Violence: Threw items, pushed, painful restraint, wrestled.

Assault/battery: Slapped, kicked, bit, punched, choked, raped.

Attempted murder: Severe beating, out of control, used weapon.

Ten Risk Factors

Presence of two of these factors doubles the rate of families with no factors; with seven of these factors, the rate is 40 times greater. However, remember that abuse occurs in all kinds of relationships, so **always ask every client**. *(See Sections 3.2 and 3.4.)*

The following list is based on Geller (1992).

1. Male is unemployed.
2. If employed, male has blue-collar occupation.
3. Male uses illicit drugs at least once a year.
4. He saw his father hit his mother.
5. He did not graduate from high school.
6. He is age 18–30.
7. Male and female have different religious backgrounds.
8. They cohabit and are not married.
9. They use severe violence toward the children in home.
10. Total family income is below poverty line.

Bipolar I and II Disorders   *See Sections 10.4 and 10.5; see also Sections 10.7, "Depression," and 10.9, "Mania."*

Bulimia Nervosa   *See Sections 3.13, "Eating Disorders," for questions, and 12.14, "Eating Disorders," for descriptors.*

12.6. Body Dysmorphic Disorder

See Section 3.7, "Body Dysmorphic Disorder," for questions.

The relevant DSM-IV-TR code is 300.7, Body Dysmorphic Disorder (a somatoform disorder). The code in ICD-9-CM is the same, but BDD is categorized there as a type of hypochondriasis.

BDD is also known as "dysmorphophobia," "body dysmorphia," or "dysmorphic syndrome." It affects men and women equally. It is often comorbid with depression and social phobia; associated suicide risk is high. The best, most accessible, and most thorough resources are by Phillips (2004, 2009).

Beliefs

Preoccupied by a perceived defect in one or more physical features or general appearance, ugliness.
Defect is believed to be easily noticeable by others as well.

Emotions

Embarrassed, ashamed, self-conscious, low self-esteem, fear of ridicule.
Depression, social anxiety.
Suicidal ideation.

Behaviors

Checking in mirrors/reflective surfaces, or refusal to be photographed/avoidance of mirrors.
Repetitive, compulsive behaviors of examining, improving, or hiding the "defect."
Excessive/elaborate grooming rituals, shaving, plucking, combing, skin picking.

Camouflaging with one's hand, postures, clothing, hats, or excessive makeup.
Distracting with extravagant clothing or jewelry.
Consulting dermatologists or plastic surgeons, undertaking painful or risky procedures.
Critical comparisons with others, obsessive viewing of favorite celebrities or models.
Excessive information seeking about the "defect."
Repeatedly measuring or touching the "defective" part.

Effects on Social Interactions

Limited friendships, impaired occupational and/or social functioning.
Social withdrawal/isolation, avoidance, dependency.
Repeated requests for reassurance about the "defect."
Avoiding social situations where the "defect" might be seen by others.
Anxiety when with other people.
Ruminations about appearance limit productivity.

Muscle Dysmorphia

This is seen primarily in males.

Belief that body is puny, musculature inadequate/small. Compulsive working out, abuse of anabolic steroids and supplements.
"Bigorexia," "Adonis complex."

12.7. Chronic Fatigue Syndrome

The emphasis in CFS is on the fatigue, and that in fibromyalgia is on the pain, but many symptoms overlap.

Persistent/interfering/debilitating fatigue, 50% or more decrease from premorbid activity level, easily and persistently fatigued after little exercise, abrupt onset of fatigue, not relieved by rest.
Mild/low-grade fever, tender/palpable lymph nodes, inflammation of mucous membranes, sore throat, cough, chronic headaches, joint pain/muscle pain, diffuse pains, weakness.
Irritability, confusion, poor concentration, depression, photophobia, sleep disturbances.

A fine starting point for resources and learning about CFS is a page on the Centers for Disease Control and Prevention site (*www.cdc.gov/CFS/cfssymptomsHCP.htm*).

Chronic Pain Syndrome   *See Section 12.23, "Pain Disorder/Chronic Pain Syndrome."*

12.8. Compulsions

See Sections 3.9, "Compulsions," and 3.19, "Obsessions," for questions; see also Section 12.21, "Obsessions," for descriptors.

The relevant DSM-IV-TR codes are 301.4, Obsessive–Compulsive Personality Disorder, and 300.3, Obsessive–Compulsive Disorder, whereas ICD-9-CM offers 301.4, Compulsive personality disorder, and 300.3, Obsessive–compulsive disorders.

The Goodman et al. (1989) measure, the Yale–Brown Obsessive Compulsive Scale, is available at many sites on the Internet.

Greist et al. (1986) suggest this classification for rituals:

Cleaning of real or imagined contamination by dirt or germs (e.g., handwashing).
Avoiding of contamination by rituals (to make unnecessary the need to clean).
Repeating a ritual behavior a certain number of times.
Completing a sequence of actions correctly. Restarting from beginning if interrupted.
Checking and rechecking, especially locks, items of potential danger (e.g., knives, stove).
Meticulousness about the exact and proper location of objects for balance or symmetry.
Hoarding, collecting, or sorting or stacking of nonuseful objects (see below).

Hoarding

Hoarding is a compulsive disorder of collecting what appears worthless to others and adding to the collection until it is unmanageable, becomes dangerous, and interferes with normal life. People with this compulsion are usually perfectionistic and broadly indecisive, but they are often articulate and offer rationalizations. They may be embarrassed and promise to change, but cannot part with accumulations without treatment. (*See www.ocfoundation.org/hoarding.*)

People who hoard animals typically start with a few pets that they can manage; they then collect or breed more until the situation is unmanageable, abusive, and horrendous, but they cannot stop by themselves. Recidivism is almost 100%. (*See www.paws.org/help/report/hoarding.php.*)

Summary Statements

Client denied problems with common compulsions.
Client engages in rituals for meals/sleep/dressing, house cleaning/washing/defecation, school or work tasks/other mental tasks, etc.
Client feels compelled to repeatedly check the house/kitchen/windows/doors/locks/dangerous objects/children, etc.
Client feels compelled to repeatedly touch/rub, count, order, arrange/rearrange objects.

12.9. Conduct Disorder

See also Sections 12.22, "Oppositional Defiant Disorder," and 13.7, "Antisocial Personality."

The relevant DSM-IV-TR codes are 312.81, Conduct Disorder, Childhood-Onset Type; and 312.82, Conduct Disorder, Adolescent-Onset Type.

The relevant ICD-9-CM codes are 312.0, Undersocialized conduct disorder, aggressive type; 312.1, Undersocialized conduct disorder, unaggressive type; 312.2, Socialized conduct disorder; 312.81, Conduct disorder, childhood onset type; and 312.82, Conduct disorder, adolescent onset type.

In both DSM-IV-TR and ICD-9-CM, very similar symptoms are diagnosed as Antisocial Personality Disorder in adults.

Aspects

Will cheat/lie in order to win/be seen as the winner, believes others are against him/her or that he/she is being treated unfairly, makes an effort on a task or toward others only if it serves his/her interests, selfishly accepts favors without any desire to return them.
Aggressive, violent, dangerous, assaults, fights with anyone, threatens, intimidates, bullies, lies/ cheats/breaks any rules, steals, denies truth/blames others, swears offensively/vulgarisms.
Violence toward property: Vandalism, deliberate destruction of property known to belong to others, firesetting, stealing, shoplifting, burglary, theft/auto theft, joyriding, purse snatching, armed robbery.

Violence toward people: Extortion/blackmail, physical cruelty to animals or people, mugging, assault, initiating physical fights, using a weapon.

Running away, truancy, trading sex for money/goods/drugs, coerced sexual activities, substance use before age 13 and recurrent use after 13.

Callousness, toughness, low frustration tolerance, temper, recklessness.

Occasionally/often self-injuring without suicidal intent, self-mutilating.

Occasional/single/repeated suicidal ideation/preoccupation/threats/gesture/attempt with/without clear expectation of death.

✓ Prognosis is worsened by ADHD, parental rejection, harsh discipline, absence of a father, delinquent friends, and parental substance abuse.

Cyclothymia   *See Section 10.6, "Cyclothymia," for descriptors.*

12.10. Delusions

See Section 3.10, "Delusions," for questions; see also Sections 12.24, "Paranoia," and 12.31, "Schizophrenia," for descriptors.

Degree of Confidence/Organization/Expression

(↔ *by degree*) Faint/occasional suspiciousness, distrust, allusions to others' trickery or deceit, personalized meanings, ideas of reference, magical thinking, believes in _____ but not in _____, pervasive distortions, convinced of the truth of _____, formed delusions/deluded, lives in a fantasy world.

(↔ *by degree*) Fragmented, clustered, poorly organized, well organized, integrated, systematized.

The delusions are . . .

denied, rejected, doubted, trusted, fixed.

encapsulated, isolated, circumscribed, spreading, reinforced, extensive, comprehensive.

expressed only with exceptionally trusted others/rarely/often/continually expressed.

shared with family members. [Shared delusions are described as *folie á deux* or *á trois*; DSM-IV-TR and ICD-9-CM offer Shared Psychotic Disorder, 297.3.]

Contents of Delusions

grandiosity	**persecution**	poverty	suicide	**somatic disease**
megalomania	ideas of		homicide	hypochondriasis
omniscience	reference	**erotomania**[1]	approaching	infection[2]
omnipotence	being followed	sexual identity	death	distorted body
extraordinary	being	alleged lover		image
abilities	influenced	infidelity	nihilistic fears	foul odors[3]
self-importance	misidentification	jealousy	self-deprecation	disfigurement[4]

---

[1]DeClérambault–Kadinsky complex.

[2]For example, parasitosis.

[3]Bromosis.

[4]Dysmorphophobia. Distinguished from dissatisfaction with appearance.

special relation-ship with famous person or deity special mission for goverment/religion	special identity alien control thoughts known to others being ridiculed being watched	"lovesickness" zooanthropic	self-accusation guilt derogation shame sin blamelessness innocence neglect of an urgent responsibility caused harm to befall another contaminated others accidentally	voodoo occult communication with dead mind reading mental telepathy foreknowledge psychokinesis ExtraSensory Perception

✓ Distinguish delusions (demonstrably false, unshakeable, and idiosyncratic beliefs, not supported by the social reality of the client's culture or subculture; for examples, see above) from "overvalued ideas" (idiosyncratic or shared beliefs that greatly influence the person's actions and seem exaggerated to the observer—e.g., morbid jealousy, racial superiority); from "illusions" (false but reasonable interpretations of perceptions—e.g., perceiving someone lurking in a shadow); from "*pseudologica fantastica*" (storytelling where the true and false, imaginary and real are mixed); and from "hallucinations" (perceptions without sensations or without an objective stimulus for the perception) *(see Section 12.17, "Hallucinations," for examples).*

12.11. Denial

Denial can be either adaptive or maladaptive. Breznitz (1988) identified several kinds of denial, which are listed below and illustrated with sample client statements.

Type	*Example*
Denial of provided information	"I never knew that." "No one ever told me about it."
Denial of information about a threat	"No one ever told me there was anything to worry about." "I never saw the risk involved."
Denial of personal relevance (externalization)	"That doesn't apply to me, only others." "I have nothing to worry about."
Denial of vulnerability	"Nothing bad will happen to me."
Denial of urgency	"There is no rush." "I can think about that later."
Denial of emotion	"I'm not afraid/angry/hurt/upset by it."
Denial of the emotion's relevance	"Yes, I'm scared, but there is no reason to feel that way."

Other types of denial: of a problem's importance; of one's ability to change; of the problem's persistence; of the rationality or necessity of change.

12.12. Depersonalization and Derealization

See Section 3.12, "Dissociative Experiences," for questions.

The major relevant DSM-IV-TR and ICD-9-CM code is 300.6, Depersonalization Disorder. DSM-IV-TR also offers 300.15, Dissociative Disorder NOS. ICD-9-CM offers 3.15 as Dissociative disorder or reaction, unspecified.

✓ **Note:** Most symptoms of depersonalization and derealization can also be symptoms of temporal lobe epilepsy.[5]

Reports observing self from a distance/corner of the room, feels as if outside one's body, body appears altered.

Self-estrangement, extreme feelings of unreality/detachment from self/environment/surroundings, floating in the sky, "dreaming"/living a dream, feels as if the world were not real, sometimes not part of the world, feels mechanical/robot-like.

Experienced thoughts as not his/her own, felt as if body and mind were not linked.

(↔ by degree) Daydreaming, fanciful story, trance, hysterical attack/episode, amnesia, fugue, somnambulism, automatic writing, out-of-body experience, dying and coming back, extraterrestrial travel, previous lives lived.

✓ **Note:** Episodes are pathological if they are more frequent and of longer duration; occur with other symptoms; and are *not* related to single/severe psychological trauma, fatigue, sleep times, drug and alcohol use, medical illness, etc.

Depression
See Section 3.5, "Affect/Mood," for questions; see Sections 10.7, "Depression," and 12.40, "Suicide," for descriptors.

Dissociative Identity Disorder
See Section 13.14, "Dissociative Identity Disorder."

12.13. Dual Diagnoses

See Section 12.39, "Substance Use, Abuse, and Dependence," for descriptors.

Those with both a major Axis I disorder and substance abuse or dependence are said to have a "dual diagnosis." Synonyms include Mental Illness with Substance Abuse; Mental Illness with Chemical Abuse and Addiction; and Co-Occurring Disorder. (Less commonly, this term is used to refer to those with mental retardation and substance abuse or dependence.)

12.14. Eating Disorders

See Section 3.13, "Eating Disorders," for questions.

Anorexia Nervosa

The relevant ICD-9-CM and DSM-IV-TR code is 307.1, Anorexia Nervosa. (307.50, Eating Disorder NOS [DSM-IV-TR] or Eating disorder, unspecified [ICD-9-CM], is used for cases that do not meet the full Anorexia Nervosa criteria.)

---

[5]I am grateful to Frank O. Volle, PhD, of Darien, CT, for this insight.

Physical Presentation

Cachexia/cachectic, emaciated, amenorrhea, bradycardia, hypothermia, edema, weight loss of at least 15% without disease.

Cognitive Aspects

"Food phobia," morbid fear of gaining weight/becoming fat, distorted and implacable attitudes toward food, avoidance of "fattening" foods, overvalued ideas of/dread of fatness, obsessional, preoccupied with food, obsession with thinness.

Dissatisfaction with bodily appearance, distorted body image (believes she/he is always too fat), denial of exhaustion/hunger/illness, fear of pubertal changes.

"Positive" view of family, denial of family conflict, enmeshment with a parent.

Perfectionism, self-disciplined, overly controlled, pride in weight management/self-inflicted starvation, overly critical of others, does not reveal feelings.

Behavioral Aspects

Laxative/diuretic misuse/abuse, fasting/starvation/restricted food intake, overexercising.

Ritualized food habits (cutting food into very small pieces, chewing for long periods), eating only low- and no-fat/calorie foods.

Social Aspects

Shy, compliant, dependent.

Sexual immaturity/inexperience.

Less antisocial behavior than in Bulimia Nervosa.

Mistrusting of professionals.

Bulimia Nervosa

The relevant ICD-9-CM and DSM-IV-TR codes are 307.51, Bulimia Nervosa; 307.50, Eating Disorder NOS (DSM-IV-TR) or Eating disorder, unspecified (ICD-9-CM).

Physical Presentation

Insomnia, constipation, lanugo, premature aging, hair loss, dental erosion due to acid vomitus, amenorrhea, dehydration, weight fluctuations, cardiovascular disorders, electrolyte imbalances, irregular menstrual periods.

Near-normal weights (sometimes obese), great body weight fluctuations ($\geq$20 lbs. $\geq$5 times).

Cognitive Aspects

Distorted/irrational body image, overconcern with body appearance/shape/weight, dissatisfaction with bodily appearance, fear of obesity [and this does not decrease as weight drops].

Inability to think clearly, dichotomous thinking, overpersonalization, perfectionism, rationalization of eating/symptoms.

Low self-esteem; weight central to self-evaluation, feels powerlessness about weight, lifelong dieting, self-loathing, disgust over body size.

Awareness that eating pattern is abnormal, preoccupation with food, craving/urges/hungers.

Behavioral Aspects

Purchases large quantities of food that suddenly "disappear," makes such purchases/eating "on the spur of the moment," other people's food "disappears," many takeout meals.

Frequently eats large quantities/high-calorie foods yet does not gain weight.

Hyperactivity, overexercising.
Frequent weighing, attendance at weight control clinics.
Overuse of laxatives/diuretics/cathartic/thyroid preparations/appetite suppressants.
Junk food consumption, binge eating, vomiting, sneaking binges, severely restrictive diets/fasting.
Shoplifting, sexual acting out, suicide attempts.

Social Aspects

Eating alone due to embarrassment over amount eaten, frequent trips to bathroom (for purging).
High achievement, academic success.
Oversensitivity to criticism, fragility, vulnerability.

Affective Aspects

Mood swings, impulsivity, depression, masked anger, specific affective precipitants of binge.
Feeling disgusted with self/self-deprecation, depressed/guilty/distressed over binge eating/vomiting.

Other Aspects

These factors may or may not matter:

Diet's composition (various foods or only some such as sweets, salty, snacks, etc.).
Dissociative qualities ("numb," "spaced out").
Higher-than-usual levels of various psychopathologies and medical conditions.

Binge-Eating Disorder

DSM-IV-TR offers Binge-Eating Disorder as a diagnosis for further study. It is not in ICD-9-CM.

Eats larger quantity than normal, eats rapidly, eats alone, irritation or self-disgust after overeating, doesn't purge.

Obesity   *See "Weight" in Section 7.1, "Appearance."*

Pica

Eats nonfood items: dirt, worms/insects, feces, etc.

Additional Note

✓ People with eating disorders may and do present as morbidly obese, overweight, average-weight, underweight, maintaining periodic control, or unable to control compulsive eating. They may present with only obsession over body size, weight, and shape; grazing, bingeing, compulsive dieting, or starving; overexercising, vomiting, and/or laxative/diuretic abuse; use of food as reward or for comfort; use of diet pills, quick-loss schemes, and/or medical/surgical interventions; etc. A full investigation is therefore necessary. They are all very likely to have disordered eating habits and distorted beliefs about body image, effects of food on mood, and dietary rules. Conditions that do not meet all of the DSM criteria for any of the eating disorders are very common and should be diagnosed as Eating Disorder NOS.

Explosive Disorder   *See Section 12.19, "Impulse-Control Disorders."*

Extra**P**yramidal **S**ymptoms   *See Section 12.36, "Side Effects of Psychotropic Medications/Adverse Drug Reactions."*

12.15. **F**etal **A**lcohol **S**yndrome

Typical diagnostic features of FAS are (1) thin upper lip, (2) absent or indistinct philtrum (the vertical depression under the nose), and (3) short palpebral fissures (the horizontal length of the eyes' openings between the lids). Height and weight are typically below the 10th percentile from birth. Also commonly found are a flat midface with flat nasal bridge and upturned nose tip, underdeveloped upper ears, narrow forehead, microcephaly, deformities of the fingers, toes, and brain.

Common psychological phenomena include mental retardation, developmental delays, poor speech, impulsiveness, incoordination, and ADHD.

FAS is the most common cause of mental retardation and the leading preventable cause of birth defects in the United States. Consuming any amount of alcohol during any part of pregnancy is considered likely to result in a defect diagnosed as a **F**etal **A**lcohol **S**pectrum **D**isorder.

A short but comprehensive article can be found at *www.aafp.org/afp/20050715/279.html*, and a large resource website is that of the U.S. government's FASD Center (*www.fasdcenter.samhsa.gov*).

12.16. **G**ambling

The relevant ICD-9-CM and DSM-IV-TR code is 312.31, Pathological Gambling. Gambling that warrants professional attention may also be called "addictive," "compulsive," or "problem" gambling.

The genders are equally affected, although their courses may differ; in addition, men generally gamble for the excitement and action, while women gamble to cope with stressors. High rates of comorbid substance abuse and suicidality are found. Recreational gambling is very common among teens and students, and may progress after a big win to pathological gambling.

Summary Statements

His thoughts and speech are filled with stories of and plans for gambling.

Her gambling is compulsive—anxiety-controlling, depression-reducing, showing habituation, felt as an irresistible impulse, chronic and repetitive, concealed, demonstrating superstitions/special techniques/rituals, etc.

He shows the typical cognitive distortions of gamblers: Overconfidence in his ability to predict the outcomes, irrational expectations of a "big win" to compensate for losses/start over fresh, feeling "lucky," superstitions, illusions of control or prediction of the outcome of a bet, poor sense of probabilities, selective recall, minimization of losses.

Her emotional reactions include remorse, lessened ambition, motivation, or efficiency.

Gambling has been used to compensate for frustration or disappointment, to escape worry or troubles, to celebrate good fortune.

His gambling has been harmful to his family/career/reputation. She has missed work to gamble.

He/she has borrowed money to gamble, sold items for money to gamble, gambled for money to pay debts, gambled until the money ran out, considered/committed a crime for money to gamble.

The **S**outh **O**aks **G**ambling **S**creen (Lesieur & Blume, 1987) is a reliable assessment device of 20 items and is available at several sites on the Internet. DSM-IV-TR offers 10 criteria to distinguish recreational from pathological gambling.

12.17. Hallucinations

See Section 3.15, "Hallucinations," for questions, and 12.31, "Schizophrenia," for more descriptors.

✓ Hallucinatory experiences are common before sleep (hypnagogic) and on partial awakening (hypnopompic), and also in temporal lobe epilepsy.[6]

Sensory Modalities

Modalities are listed here in rough order of prevalence.

Auditory: Noises or voices, whistling/ringing, familiar sounds, whispering, one's name being called.

Visual: Unformed/lights/flashes, formed/people/things/animals. (One variant is **micropsia/Lilliputian hallucinations**—the perception of objects' being much smaller but retaining all detail. Seen in delirium tremens.)

Olfactory: Disgusting/repulsive/objectionable odors (e.g., of death or disease).[7]

Kinesthetic: Twisting, churning, pains, phantom limb.

Gustatory: Poisons, acids, metallic tastes, foul tastes.

Visceral/somatic: "Hollow insides," "rotting insides," "made of glass."

Vestibular: Falling, flying, lightness.

Much less commonly seen are these:

Synesthesia: Blending of sense impressions (e.g., "It smells red").

Extracampine: Impossible visual sensations, such as seeing someone behind oneself (Most common in Lewy body dementia.)

There are dozens more.

✓ In the case of voices, note whose they are (if this can be identified), what their sex and age seem to be, and whether they are clear or muffled. Note also the content of utterances (disconnected words, client's own thoughts, remarks addressed to client, etc.); Schneider (1959) noted that audible thoughts, voices arguing, and voices commenting are diagnostically most important.

Nature

Informative, friendly, benign, comforting, helpful, socially focused.

Arguing, dialoguing/conversing among themselves, commenting on thoughts/behavior/motives.

Condemning, malevolent, accusatory, persecutory, harassing, hateful, spiteful, berating, threatening, menacing, terrorizing.

Seductive, premonitory, hortatory/imperative/commanding/compelling/controlling, consuming.

Attitudes toward Hallucinations

($\leftrightarrow$ *by degree*) Ego-alien, frightening, terrifying, "bizarre," resisted/struggled against, engages in conversations/dialogue with imaginary interlocutor, comforting, familiar, ego-syntonic, accepted.

($\leftrightarrow$ *by degree*) Convinced of their reality, vivid fantasy, "altered state," impossibility, "only a fantasy," doubting its reality/own perceptions, making various efforts to control/cope with it, "rare."

---

[6] I am grateful to Frank O. Volle, PhD, of Darien, CT, for this perspective.

[7] Olfactory hallucinations are common in temporal lobe epilepsy as auras.

Circumstances of Occurrence

Hypnagogic, hypnopompic, with delirium, in substance withdrawal, flashbacks, spontaneously, unbidden, cultural/situational/external stimuli influence the hallucinatory experience, having an undiscoverable relationship to circumstances.

Comparison of Organically and Psychogenically Based Hallucinations

Organically based	*Psychologically based*
Sharply demarcated in time.	Fleeting and transient.
Vivid and well formed.	Vague, shadowy, misty.
Polychromic and/or polysonic.	Usually in shades of gray.
Hypermobility (e.g., bugs creep).	Usually static.
Accompanied by terror, apprehension.	Other emotions.
Perseverative quality.	Changeable.
Patient *acts* as though he/she really sees/hears/feels.	Patient has an idea that he/she sees, feels, etc., but then does not act consistently.
	May be associated with his/her psychodynamics.

Summary Statements

Hallucinations are denied by the patient, but she/he seems to be responding to internal/unseen stimuli.
They involve small/moderate/great distortion of consensual reality.
The hallucinations are suspected/undoubted/denied.

Hyperactivity   *See Section 12.3, "Attention-Deficit/Hyperactivity Disorder."*

Identity   *See Section 9.3, "Self-Image/Self-Esteem."*

12.18. Illusions

See Section 3.16, "Illusions," for questions.

Sense deceptions, deceptive sensations, visual/auditory/tactile distortions, speeded-up or slowed passage of time, macropsia, micropsia, Lilliputianism, gigantism.

Intermittent Explosive Disorder   *See Section 12.19, below.*

12.19. Impulse-Control Disorders

See Sections 3.17, "Impulse Control," and 3.31, "Violence," for questions. For descriptors, see also Sections 10.2, "Anger," 12.40, "Suicide," 13.6, "Aggressive Personality," 13.7, "Antisocial Personality," 13.8, "Authoritarian Personality," and 13.23, "Sadistic Personality."

Types of Impulse-Control Disorders

Impulse-control disorders as described here include, but go beyond, those covered in the Impulse-Control Disorders Not Otherwise Classified section of DSM-IV-TR. Those discussed here include the following:

Intermittent Explosive Disorder (ICD-9-CM and DSM-IV-TR code, 312.34).
Kleptomania (ICD-9-CM and DSM-IV-TR code, 312.32).
Pathological Gambling (ICD-9-CM and DSM-IV-TR code, 312.31). *(See Section 12.16, "Gambling.")*
Pyromania (firesetting) (ICD-9-CM and DSM-IV-TR code, 312.33).
Self-damaging/self-mutilating behaviors. *(See Section 12.33, "Self-Injurious Behavior.")*
Sexual impulsivity, "nymphomania," "satyriasis," "sexual addiction." *(See Section 12.35, "Sexual Impulsivity/'Addiction'/'Compulsion'").*
Trichotillomania (DSM-IV-TR code, 312.39; same code in ICD-9-CM, but classified under Disorders of impulse control, not elsewhere classified: Other).

Degree of Control (↔ *by degree*)

overcontrolled	patient	volatile	impulsive	violent
armored	tolerant	loses temper	may attack	explosive
inhibited	controlled	"short fuse"	"blows his/	aggressive
denied	thoughtful	low frustration	her top"	combative
overcautious	deliberate	tolerance	impetuous	assaultive
rigid		quicksilver	hot-headed	dangerous
staid	cool-headed	quick-tempered	flares up	
	restrained	"flies off the	lashes out	
	self-possessed	handle"	abrupt	
		"gets riled up"	precipitous	
		easily offended	unpredictable	
		excitable	incontinent	
		irritable	reckless	
		easily irritated	outbursts	
			leaves situation	
			hasty	
			rash	

What Person Fears Doing

Embarrassing self, losing control, "wetting pants"/losing bladder control, fainting, harming self or others, homicidal ideation, unable to resist impulses to commit delinquent or illegal acts.

Reason's Influence

Acts without weighing alternatives/with little hesitation, unreflective, acts without examination, unmediated, "acts on spur of the moment," easily agitated, off-handed/ill-considered actions, self-centered actions, seeks immediate gratification of urges, heedless, willful, limited intellectual control over expression of impulses, poor planning.

Antisocial Behavior   *See also Section 13.7, "Antisocial Personality."*

Obstructiveness, irresponsibility, cheating, lying, stealing, crimes, arrests, fighting, forceful aggression.

Insight   *See Section 11.9, "Insight," for descriptors.*

Late Luteal Phase Dysphoric Disorder   *See Section 12.28, "PreMenstrual Dysphoric Disorder."*

12.20. Malingering

See also Section 13.16, "Hypochondriacal Personality."

The relevant ICD-9-CM and DSM-IV-TR code is V65.2; ICD-9-CM uses the label Person feigning illness instead of Malingering.

According to Rogers (2008), this condition is not rare, not easy to detect, and not a global response style; is not significantly correlated with psychopathy or criminality, or with the presence of other valid psychiatric symptoms; and is not easily detected on psychological testing.

Some criteria for suspicion of malingering of mental disorders include the following:

1. Highly atypical symptom presentation (rare, blatant, absurd, contradictory, indiscriminate, rapidly changing). Rogers (1984) offers these: Client recounts symptoms of extreme severity, endorses a large number of symptoms, describes symptoms inconsistent with clinical formulations and diagnostic impressions, exhibits a "heightened" recall of psychological stressors.
2. Noncorroboration of this presentation by interviews with collaterals, or by psychological or medical tests.
3. Exclusion of patients with diagnoses of borderline personality or factitious motivations.

Adams (1991) adds the following as markers of possible malingering:

4. Patient's being directly referred by an attorney.
5. Marked discrepancy between claimed disability and objective findings.
6. Lack of cooperation with either evaluation or recommendations.
7. Antisocial personality disorder or traits.

Other aspects include identifiable incentives for malingering; poor cooperation with diagnosis or treatment, despite assertions of wanting to find a cause or to return to work; invariable relapse after improvement; self-induced worsening of condition; resistance to communications with prior treaters; overly dramatic or exaggerated symptom presentation; and logical inconsistencies between statements or between statements and behaviors. Be aware that the security of many psychological tests has been breached by publicly available Internet sites (Ruiz et al., 2002), and do not rely solely on the results of such tests in making any diagnosis. Ken Pope, PhD, has generously collected the literature on published tests of malingering and similar research on his website (*www.kspope.com/assess/malinger.php*).

The following criteria for differential diagnosis of symptoms presenting as physical illness are suggested by Hyler and Spitzer (1978); the footnotes have been added.

Diagnosis	Can a known physical mechanism explain the symptom?	Are the symptoms linked to psychological causes?	Is the symptom under voluntary/ conscious control?	Is there an obvious goal?
Conversion	Never	Always	Never	Sometimes
Malingering	Sometimes	Sometimes	Always	Always*
Psychosomatic disorders	Always	Always	Never	Sometimes
Factitious disorders	Sometimes	Always**	Always	Never (other than medical attention)***
Undiagnosed physical illness	Sometimes	Sometimes	Never	Never

*Such as money, obtaining drugs, avoiding responsibility and prosecution, controlling others.
**Symptom amplification for unconscious needs.
***Or being seen as ill or injured and assuming the role of patient.

Terms for similar presentations: Simulation, exaggeration, symptom amplification, magnification of pain and disability, overevaluation, functional overlay, supratectorial factors, conscious embellishment.

Munchausen Syndrome

The relevant ICD-9-CM code is 301.51, Chronic factitious illness with physical symptoms (classified as a form of Histrionic personality disorder). Munchausen syndrome is described in DSM-IV-TR as a variant of Factitious Disorder (300.16 or 300.19), in which the patient mimics symptoms of disease or induces medical illness for some psychological gain. It should therefore be distinguished from malingering. The name comes from Baron Karl Friedrich Hieronymus von Munchausen, a German nobleman who lived in the 18th century and told fantastic stories.

Identifying features:

> Peregrination: Moving from one caregiver to another. Use of aliases.
> *Pseudologia fantastica*: Telling extravagant and fantastic falsehoods about one's self and experiences.
> An initial story that is quite plausible but not consistent upon probing.
> Creation of one or more medical illnesses by self-infection, modifying lab test procedures or results, interfering with wound healing, etc.
> Strong denial of any falsehood if the client is confronted. Unconscious motivations.
> Done only during periods of great stress.

Treatment requires these difficult steps: Keeping the client from moving on to other treaters when discovered, confronting him/her, and overcoming the resistance. Marc Feldman, MD, has a rich website (*www.munchausen.com*).

Mania   *See Section 10.9, "Mania," for descriptors.*

Mild Traumatic Brain Injury   *See Section 12.26, "PostConcussive Syndrome."*

Multiple Personality   *See Section 13.14, "Dissociative Identity Disorder," for descriptors.*

12.21. Obsessions

> *See Section 3.19, "Obsessions," for questions. See also Sections 13.20, "Obsessive Personality," 3.9, "Compulsions," 12.8, "Compulsions," and 11.19, "Stream of Thought."*

The relevant ICD-9-CM and DSM-IV-TR code is 300.3, Obsessive–Compulsive Disorder(s) (ICD-9 -CM uses the plural).

> Monomania, monothematic thought trains, repetitive themes, egomania, megalomania, overvalued ideas (e.g., dysmorphophobia).
> Contamination/cleaning: Touching or being touched, bodily excretions, germs, clothing, dirt/trash/contaminants, animals, resulting illness of self or other.
> *Sexual:* Erotomania, children/incest, homosexuality in heterosexuals, aggressive sexuality, "perversities."
> *Religious:* Sacrilege, blasphemy, morality, right/wrong, scrupulosity, guilt.
> *Somatic:* Illness or disease, body parts, somatic "symptoms."
> *Other:* Colors, sounds, music, names, titles, numbers, phrases, memories, unpleasant images, impulses to hurt/blurt/harm/steal/cause disaster, not saying certain things, not losing things, needing to remember, etc.

12.22. Oppositional Defiant Disorder

See also Sections 10.2, "Anger," 12.9, "Conduct Disorder," 12.19, "Impulse-Control Disorders," and 13.7, "Antisocial Personality."

The relevant ICD-9-CM and DSM-IV-TR code is 313.81, Oppositional Defiant Disorder.

Persistently resists others' ways of doing things, independent, stubborn, noncompliant.
Argumentativeness, talks back, "sasses," insubordinate, challenges, disputes.
Irritability, resentfulness, negativism, provokes others, mean, spiteful, rude, temper outbursts or tantrums, obstructive.
Always places blame on others/denies all responsibility.

12.23. Pain Disorder/Chronic Pain Syndrome

See Section 3.21, "Pain, Chronic," for questions.

The relevant ICD-9-CM codes are 307.8, Pain disorders related to psychological factors; 307.80, Psychogenic pain, site unspecified; 307.89, Pain disorders related to psychological factors; Other.

The relevant DSM-IV-TR codes are 307.80, Pain Disorder Associated with Psychological Factors; 307.89, Pain Disorder Associated with Both Psychological Factors and a General Medical Condition.

A useful mnemonic for taking a pain history is SOCRATES: Site; Onset; Character; Radiation (spreading to other area); Alleviating factors/Associated symptoms; Timing (duration, frequency); Exacerbating factors; and Severity, or, alternatively, Signs and Symptoms.

Pain Behaviors

Groans, flinches, winces, grimaces, grits teeth, lengthy/loud sighs.
Slow and careful movements/body placements, assumes/maintains odd positions, needs to shift position/stand/walk/stretch frequently.
Takes multiple/ineffective medications.
Increased resting ("down"/"horizontal"/bed) time and decreased active ("up/vertical") time, appears fatigued, decreased sleep effectiveness.
Decreased or absent sexual activity/duration/frequency/interest.
Interference with appetite, and associated weight change.
Lessened concentration.

Mood

Restricted range and intensity of expression.
Irritability, "cranky," anger, threatening, low frustration tolerance.
Depressed, demoralized, pessimistic, critical, expressions of hopelessness re: change/improvement/return to work, intermittent depressions as reaction to pain's exacerbation.
Grieving over losses: Health, autonomy, ability to travel freely/earn a living/care for family, etc.

Thought Content

Preoccupied with losses/forced accommodations/new roles/somatic sensations/treatments/pains/symptoms/health status and its implications, focus on small signs of progress.
May create illusory correlations of pain/limitations/depression/symptoms with progress/change/bodily processes.
Ruminations concerning "Why me?"/causation/revenge/financial concerns.

Feels "like a cripple," "worthless," helpless, optimistically reports "learning to live with it/the pain" but without change, loss of self-esteem because of loss of old roles.

Desperate for the situation to change but doubting the effectiveness of any intervention.

Inward focus on physical self that is not hypochondriacal but a reaction to chronic pain.

Suicidal ideation in the form of passive death wishes.

Has a sense of entitlement, focuses on the unfairness of the situation.

Feels/believes self harassed/unappreciated by current or former employer(s) or by Workers' Compensation boards/insurance companies/Social Security Disability, resentful of unfair way treated by helpgivers/insurance carriers.

Reports being "sick and tired" of pursuing insurance claims/being medically evaluated/filling out forms/"jumping through hoops" to obtain only what is rightly his/hers.

Social Aspects

Decreased social activities, withdrawal/isolation, decreased/absent recreation.

Adopts role of "patient": Dependency, passivity, helplessness, avoidance/displacement of responsibility, medical/biological model of pain and recovery, seeks a "miracle cure" vs. accepts limitations and "tries another way," etc.

Wants to be believed more than relieved, concerned that her/his symptoms be accepted as authentic.

12.24. Paranoia

See Section 3.22, "Paranoia," for questions; see also Sections 12.10, "Delusions," and 13.21, "Paranoid Personality."

The relevant ICD-9-CM and DSM-IV-TR codes are 295.30, Schizophrenia, Paranoid Type; 297.1, Delusional Disorder; and 301.0, Paranoid Personality Disorder.

The following groupings are sequenced by degree (↔) of increasing paranoia:

Not paranoid, denies any special powers or missions, feels that she/he is quite well treated by individuals and the community.

Believes self to be exceedingly virtuous, denies that he/she distrusts others, persistently naive about other's motives, believes self to be especially sensitive, overvalues own subjective knowledge.

Alert watchfulness, demonstrations of suspiciousness, distrust, belief that everything is not as it should be, paranoid trends, persecutory ideas, reports inappropriate suspiciousness, feels scrutinized, systematized delusions, protective thinking (selective attention to confirm suspicions and blaming of others for own failures), paranoid illumination ("Now everything makes sense").

Pervasive suspiciousness about everyone/everyone's actions, expects people to seek retribution, views people as vindictive, sees self as victim of others/enemies/vendetta, partially supported delusions, likely story of persecution/evidence of persecution, on guard, hyperalert, vigilant, wary, spied on, plotted against, attempts made to harm, attacks, attacks foiled, demonstrates Cameron's (Cameron & Rychlak, 1968) "pseudocommunity" of all those united in a plot against him/her.

12.25. Phobias

See Section 3.23, "Phobias," for questions, and Section 10.3, "Anxiety/Fear," for descriptors.

The relevant ICD-9-CM codes are 300.21, Agoraphobia with panic disorder; 300.22, Agoraphobia without mention of panic attacks; 300.23, Social phobia; and 300.29, Other isolated or specific phobias.

The relevant DSM-IV-TR codes are 300.29, Specific Phobia; 300.23, Social Phobia; 300.22, Agoraphobia Without History of Panic Disorder; and 300.21, Panic Disorder with Agoraphobia.

Phobias involve persistent, recognized-as-unrealistic fears; high levels of circumscribed anxiety; and avoidance of the anxiety-arousing situations/animals/social settings/persons.

Types of phobias include traumatically learned phobia, animal phobias, "school phobia," social phobia, agoraphobia, acrophobia, algophobia, claustrophobia, xenophobia, and zoophobia. About 375 named phobias are listed in an appendix to the *Blakiston's Gould Medical Dictionary* (1972). "Homophobia" is more likely a part of a personality disorder. *(See Sections 13.8, "Authoritarian Personality," and 13.21, "Paranoid Personality.")*

12.26. Post<u>C</u>oncussive <u>S</u>yndrome

The relevant ICD-9-CM code is 310.2 Postconcussion syndrome. Related diagnoses for these conditions are found under 310.x. Postconcussional Disorder is listed in DSM-IV-TR as a disgnosis for further study.

PCS is a set of physical, affective, cognitive, and interpersonal symptoms due to an interaction between mild <u>T</u>raumatic <u>B</u>rain <u>I</u>njury and stress or environmental demands. Mild TBI, also called "minor head injury" or "concussion," results from blows to the head and may be transient or permanent and cumulative. Symptoms may begin immediately after the trauma or may be delayed up to 10 days or so.

Jackson et al. (2002) suggest that three or more of the following are needed for a diagnosis of PCS: easy distraction; trouble concentrating, remembering, paying attention to more than one thing, doing more than one thing at a time, or attending in a distracting environment; forgetting appointments; headaches; difficulty finding the right words; losing things; dizziness; trouble following directions; and increasing difficulty with work. Sensitivity to light and/or noise, loss of hearing, stress intolerance, and/or alcohol intolerance may also be seen.

The suggested DSM-IV-TR criteria for Postconcussional Disorder include the following:

Loss of consciousness (for more than 5 minutes after the head injury).
Amnesia (for more than 12 hours after the injury).
Onset or worsening of seizures (within 6 months of the injury).
Deficits in memory or attention (concentration, shifting the focus of attention).
Three or more of the following if they persist for at least 3 months after the injury: easy fatigue, sleep disorder, headaches, dizziness, irritability or aggression, anxiety, depression or affective lability, lack of spontaneity, changes in social or sexual behavior.

12.27. Post<u>T</u>raumatic <u>S</u>tress <u>D</u>isorder

The relevant ICD-9-CM and DSM-IV-TR code is 309.81.

Components and Symptom Clusters for Evaluation

Affective Symptoms

Emotional numbing, deadening, lack of emotional responsiveness to usual experiences, estrangement, detachment.

Cognitive Symptoms

Decreased concentration and memory functioning.
"Flashbacks," reexperiencing/reliving of the traumatic situation, intrusive memories.
Foreshortened future, believes will not have a family/career/normal lifespan.

Behavioral Symptoms

Avoidance of stimuli similar to or elements of the original traumatic situation because these cause experiences of recall.
Worsening of symptoms when in situations like the original.
Symptoms of increased arousal, such as easy startling, hypervigilance, and sleep disturbance.
Impulsive behaviors.

Social Symptoms

Fear of intimacy, general alienation, family discord.
Intolerance of authority.
"Survivor guilt," integrity problems (feelings of betrayal, responsibility for acts of omission/commission, personalized responsibility and guilt).

Considerations for Veterans

ICD-9-CM offers V codes (V61.01 and V61.02) about the effects of military deployment on a soldier and family.

Stressors/traumatic events could include receiving incoming fire, receiving sniper fire, having a unit on patrol ambushed, having a unit engage in a firefight, bomb blasts, etc. Integrity problems may include feeling betrayed by the government or by how the war was fought. Recent approaches to trauma include emphasizing the normality of guilt resulting from killing or other war acts, as well as fear of the dangers of combat. Consideration should be given to Gulf War syndrome, combination of medical and psychological disorders. Veterans of the Iraq/Afghanistan wars are likely to be older, married, and/or parents.

A very complete review of Gulf War syndrome is available (*www.pbs.org/wgbh/pages/frontline/shows/syndrome*). The National Center for PTSD (*www.ncptsd.va.gov*) offers superb resources for care providers and researchers on PTSD assessment and treatment.

Key Features of PTSD

Pies (1993) offers the TRAUMA acronym as a way of summarizing PTSD's key features:

Trauma or actual harm outside normal range.
Recurrent disturbing dreams, recollections.
Avoidance of troubling memories, Amnesia for key events of trauma.
Unwanted images, "flashbacks."
Markedly diminished interest.
Autonomic overactivity, Anger outbursts.

Related Conditions

Acute Stress Disorder has similar but fewer symptoms, which last from 2 days to 4 weeks.

Complicated PTSD is more likely with prolonged or repeated exposure and with escalating trauma, and is likely to involve the following symptoms (Courtois, 2004):

Problems with the regulation of affective impulses.
Disturbances in attention and consciousness.
Altered self-perception.
Altered perception of the perpetrator.
Changes in relationships with others.
Shifts in systems of meaning.
Somatization and/or medical problems.

Related symptoms of C-PTSD include these:

Emotions of helplessness, shame, guilt.
Emotional dyscontrol resulting in suicidal ideation, rages, passive–aggressive behaviors.
Making huge life changes.
Loss of faith.
Amnesia for the trauma, derealization/depersonalization, other dissociative symptoms.
Preoccupation with revenge.
Attributing omnipotence to the perpetrator.

12.28. PreMenstrual Dysphoric Disorder

DSM-IV-TR offers PMDD as a diagnosis for further study. Be careful in using this diagnosis, as its rationale has mixed research support and is obviously pejorative and gender-specific.

PMDD is a more severe form of PreMenstrual Syndrome. Disabling symptoms of PMS, occurring in the week or two before menses, are summarized below. The somatic symptoms are usually much less severe than the psychological ones.

Vegetative Aspects

Appetite/eating changes, anorexia, craves specific foods.
Sleep changes/hypersomnia/hyposomnia/insomnia, lethargy/fatigue, stays in bed/naps.

Affective Aspects

Depression, hopelessness, despair, out-of-control self-deprecation.
Mood swings, feeling overwhelmed/stressed, sadness, suicidal ideation, crying.
Anxiety, tension, "on edge," restlessness, persistent anger/irritability, lability.
Decreased interest in activities.
In some cases, affectionate, need for closeness.
Excitement, well-being, burst of energy/activity.

Pains

Cramps, headache, mastalgia, joint/muscle pain, general aches and pain, muscle stiffness, backache.

Autonomic Nervous System Aspects

Nausea/vomiting, palpitations, sweating/cold sweats, "hot flashes/flushes," dizziness, fuzzy vision, numbness/tingling, heart pounding, chest pain, ringing in ears, feeling of suffocation.

Fluid Balance

Weight gain, "bloating," edema, breast tenderness/swelling.

Cognitive Aspects

Lessened concentration/distractibility, forgetfulness, confusion, lowered judgment, indecision.
Decreased efficiency, lowered school or work performance, accidents, motor incoordination, decreased orderliness.
Impulsivity.

Interpersonal Aspects

Irritability, increased conflicts, distrust, oversensitivity to rejection, isolation, avoidance, loneliness.

12.29. Rape Trauma Syndrome

The following is largely based on Burgess and Holmstrom (1974), who first described RTS as occurring in three stages.

The Acute Phase

This occurs within days or weeks.

Response Patterns

Expressed: Agitated, crying, anxiety.
Controlled: Without emotion, "nothing really happened."
Shock/disbelief: Disorientation, poor concentration, difficulty making decisions or doing ADLs, possible poor recall of the assault.

Cognitive Changes

Less alert, poor memory, disorganized thoughts, confused, bewildered.
Self-blame.

Somatic Reactions

Gynecological trauma (bruising, bleeding, etc.).
Headaches, fatigue, sleep changes, nightmares.
Startle overreactions.
Gastrointestinal: Nausea, vomiting, stomach pains, appetite changes, inner tremor.
Genitourinary: Discharge, itching, burning, pain, rectal pain/bleeding.

Affective Reactions

Anger, anxiety, tension, restlessness.
Numbing, paralyzing anxiety, crying.
Fears of death, dying, attack.
Humiliation, embarrassment.

Lifestyle Changes

Changing residence, taking trips, visiting family/friends for support.
Changing phone number.
Disruption of routines.
Obsessive cleansing.
Oversensitivity to others' reactions.

Not all survivors show their emotions outwardly. Some may appear calm and unaffected by the assault, and their reactions may blend into the next phase.

The Outward Adjustment–Inner Turmoil Phase

The victim may appear to have resumed previous life patterns, but experiences intense internal turmoil and symptoms.

Symptoms

Anxiety, helplessness, fears, depression, mood swings, sleep disturbances, flashbacks, dissociation, panic attacks, etc.

Coping Mechanisms

Family and friend support.
Substance abuse.
Minimization: "Everything is fine," refusal to discuss it.
Dramatization: Continual talking about the assault.
Explanation: Trying to understand what happened.
Flight to a new home or city.
Changes in appearance.

Cognitive and Behavioral Changes

Loss of sense of personal security, constriction of activities.
Avoidance of new relationships.
Disturbed sexual relationships—flashbacks, avoidance, hypersexuality for control.

Somatic Reactions

Tension headaches, fatigue, soreness or localized pain in the chest/throat/arms/legs.
Symptoms related to the body area assaulted (e.g., mouth and throat complaints after oral rape).
Nausea/vomiting, developing Anorexia Nervosa and/or Bulimia Nervosa.

Phobias Specific to the Rape's Circumstances (Traumatophobia)

Being in crowds, being approached from the rear or side, being left alone anywhere, leaving the house.
Men in general.
Characteristics of the assailant (e.g., mustache, curly hair, the smell of alcohol or cigarettes, type of clothing or car).
Suspicions, paranoid feelings about strangers.

The Resolution/Reorganization/Renormalization Phase

Insight into own adjustment, ending of denial, giving up coping mechanisms that are no longer needed and/or are harmful.
The rape is no longer central to the victim's life.
Guilt, shame, and self-blame come to an end.

12.30. Reactive Attachment Disorder

The DSM-IV-TR code is 313.89, Reactive Attachment Disorder of Infancy or Early Childhood. The code is the same in ICD-9-CM, but the disorder is classified under Other or Mixed emotional disturbances of childhood or adolescence: Other.

Cardinal Features

Severely inappropriate social relating by a child in either of two forms:

- The disinhibited form, with indiscriminate familiarity and excessive efforts to get comfort or affection from any available adult (including strangers), or peers if the child is older.

- The inhibited form, showing failure or great reluctance to initiate or accept comfort and affection, even from familiar adults, especially when distressed.

Other Features

No identifiable, preferred attachment figure.
Poor relating to peers.
Aggression toward self and others.
Misery.
Growth failure (in some cases of the inhibited form only).
Onset before 5 years of age (Infants to 18–24 months may show nonorganic failure to thrive and abnormal responsiveness to stimuli.)
A history of significant neglect and possible abuse.
Some normal social relating with appropriately responsive, nondeviant adults (disinhibited form only).

12.31. Schizophrenia

See also Sections 11.19, "Stream of Thought," 12.10, "Delusions," and 12.17, "Hallucinations."

The relevant ICD-9-CM and DSM-IV-TR codes are as follows: 295.10, Schizophrenia, Disorganized Type; 295.20, Schizophrenia, Catatonic Type; 295.30, Schizophrenia, Paranoid Type; 295.60, Schizophrenia, Residual Type; 295.90, Schizophrenia, Undifferentiated Type (DSM-IV-TR) or Unspecified type (ICD-9-CM).

"Schizophrenia" is so called because it is a split between thoughts and feelings. Note that it does not mean "split personality." It includes what Eugen Bleuler (1911/1968) referred to as the "four A's": disorders of <u>A</u>ssociation, <u>A</u>ffect, <u>A</u>mbivalence, and <u>A</u>utism.

Schneiderian or First-Rank Symptoms

The following list is based on Schneider (1959).

Primary delusional perception (a common perception that takes on special significance and is elaborated in a delusional way).
Passive reception of a somatic sensation imposed from an outside agency.
Thought diffusion, broadcasting, thought insertion, withdrawal, or interference.
Clouding of consciousness.
"Made" (externally directed) impulses (delusions of somatic passivity).
"Made" volitional acts.
"Made" feelings or sensations.
Voices arguing with the client in the third person, calling his/her name.
Voices making a continuous commentary on the subject's actions.
Audible thoughts: Speaking the client's thoughts aloud (ÉCHO DE PENSÉES).

✓ **Note:** These symptoms have not been found to be pathognomonic to (unique to, confirming the diagnosis of) schizophrenia, although they are more common in it and rarer in other conditions.

Positive versus Negative Symptom Patterns

Factor	Type I: Positive subtype (behaviors not usually found in normal persons)	Type II: Negative subtype (absence of behaviors usually found in normal persons)
Diagnosis	Paranoid, Undifferentiated, Disorganized, Catatonic, Residual.	"Simple."
Symptoms	Positive: Behavioral excesses. Hallucinations, delusions (q.v.). Thought disorder, incoherence. Bizarre or disorganized behavior. Thought disorder.	Negative: Behavioral deficits. Alogia: Poverty of speech and thought processes, vagueness, blocking, great latency. Flattened affect, anhedonia. Asociality, withdrawal. Avolition, apathy. Attentional impairment. Psychomotor retardation, monotone.
Brain abnormalities	Overactivity of dopamine in limbic system; normal CT scans.	Underactivity of dopamine in frontal cortex. Enlarged ventricles.
Intellectual impairment	Minimal.	Significant.
Premorbid functioning	Better.	Worse.
Onset	Acute.	Insidious.
Gender	More women.	More men.
Course	Episodic, exacerbations, and remissions.	Chronic.
Response to treatment	Favorable response to older neuroleptics.	Poor response to older neuroleptics.
Prognosis	More likely to return to previous level of functioning.	Less likely to return to previous level of functioning.
Social functioning	Normal social functioning between remissions and exacerbations.	Poor social functioning in social, vocational, educational, relationship areas.

✓ **Note:** A factor analysis of symptoms suggests five types (not just two): (1) positive/psychotic symptoms/disorganized thoughts, (2) negative symptoms (as described above), (3) excited/activation/motor symptoms, (4) dysphoric mood/anxiety–depression, and (5) autistic preoccupation (White et al., 1997).

Schneiderian Symptoms   *See Section 12.31, "Schizophrenia," for descriptors.*

12.32. School Refusal/Avoidance/"Phobia"

School refusal is not truly a "phobia," as it may not be a fear and avoidance of school, but a fear of the consequences of absence from the home.

Summary Statements

Child is fearful of leaving home because of fears that he/she must guard against some danger to the caregiver/death of parent/abandonment by parent/own failure to fulfill obligations/ separation anxiety.

Child wishes to avoid school because of bullying/harassment/abuse/scapegoating/threats/exclusion from cliques/poor social skills/inappropriate disciplinary methods/shaming/demands beyond child's abilities/very poor teaching methods.

Compeled attendance caused rifts between the parents and the child/further loss of self-confidence/more abuse/panics/increased symptoms of depression/psychosomatic symptoms, because it was implemented without examination of the child's experiences in school/best setting to meet the child's educational needs/family issues.

Seasonal Affective Disorder   *See Section 10.11, "Seasonal Affective Disorder," for descriptors.*

12.33. Self-Injurious Behavior

SIB is "the deliberate, direct destruction or alteration of body tissue without conscious suicidal intent, but resulting in injury severe enough for tissue damage (e.g., scarring) to occur" (Gratz, 2003, p. 193). Klonsky and Glenn (2009, p. 147) add "for purposes not socially sanctioned." SIB includes skin cutting, carving, burning, severe scratching, needle sticking, and interference with wound healing. It excludes decorative tattooing, scarification, piercing, and insertion of objects into the body. Another common term for SIB is NonSuicidal Self-Injury. SIB or NSSI is seen in many diagnoses, and so does not imply the presence of any particular disorder or even any disorder; it is equally common in both sexes (Klonsky & Glenn, 2009).

✓ The terms "self-abusive," "-harming," "-mutilation," "-violence," "-destructive," and "masochistic" embody assumptions about the motives and goals (e.g., self-hate, suicide) of the activity, but most often these assumptions are inaccurate. SIB is mainly used to manage overwhelmingly intense emotions because of emotion regulation skills that are not well developed. Gratz (2003), after a thorough review of the literature, has identified these possible functions: "(1) to relieve anxiety; (2) to release anger; (3) to relieve unpleasant thoughts and feelings; (4) to release tension; (5) to relieve feelings of guilt, loneliness, alienation, self-hatred, and depression; (6) to externalize and concretize emotional pain; (7) to provide an escape from emotional pain; (8) to provide a sense of security; (9) to provide a sense of control; (10) to self-punish; (11) to set boundaries with others; (12) to terminate depersonalization and derealization; (13) to end flashbacks; and (14) to stop racing thoughts" (p. 199). Clients may be inarticulate about these motives.

Clients often report experiencing aspects of dissociation during SIB. These may include depersonalization, poor recall, distance from one's body, confusion about who did what, anesthesia, or the perception that it is happening to an alter *(see Section 13.14, "Dissociative Identity Disorder")*.

After sufficient rapport is established, inquire about behaviors (frequency, location, and cutting implements); antecedent situations (social aspects, thoughts, and then feelings); consequences; and, last, motives and expectations.

Risk factors include childhood sexual and physical abuse, neglect, separation and loss, and insecure attachment.

12.34. Sexual Abuse, Child

See Section 3.4, "Abuse (Sexual) of Child or Adult," for questions.

The relevant DSM-IV-TR code is V61.21, Sexual Abuse of Child, or 995.53 if the focus of clinical attention is on the victim. The same code numbers are used in ICD-9-CM, but V61.21 signifies Counseling for victim of child abuse, and it is used *with* 995.53, Child sexual abuse.

Almost all of the phenomena listed below occur fairly often in nonabused children. Be extremely judicious in interviewing, hypothesizing, and making statements. Operating in this area requires specialty training.

Physical Aspects

Genital or anal area pain/swelling/itching/bleeding, bruises, torn/stained/bloody underwear, frequent urinary tract infections, painful urination, vaginal or penile discharge, symptoms of <u>S</u>exually <u>T</u>ransmitted <u>D</u>iseases, pregnancy.

Behavioral Aspects

Unexplained changes in eating habits, sleeping habits (nightmares and insomnia), difficulties in sitting or walking, inappropriate/public or unusual masturbation, indiscriminate hugging/kissing/seductive behaviors with children and adults.

Affective Aspects

Excessive, and especially sudden, fearfulness about particular persons or places.

Social Aspects

At home/play: Clinging, withdrawal, regression, poor peer relations.
At school: Refusal to attend, absences, drop in grades, refusal to attend or participate in physical education, arriving early or leaving late.

Cognitive Aspects

Premature knowledge of sexual behaviors, changes in fantasy play to themes of sexuality or harm.

✓ Sexual or physical abuse of a child must be reported according to your state's rules, which you *must* know. If in doubt, call and ask a "hypothetical" question.

12.35. Sexual Impulsivity/"Addiction"/"Compulsion"

At this writing, no criteria for sexual addiction have been accepted by the American Psychiatric Association. However, criteria have been generated by drawing analogies with substance dependence (Goodman, 2005).

In general, sexual addiction is a pattern of sexual behavior without reliable control that leads to significant impairment or distress. "Significantly, no form of sexual behavior in itself constitutes sexual addiction. Whether a pattern of sexual behavior qualifies as sexual addiction is determined not by the type of behavior, its object, its frequency, or its social acceptability, but by how the behavior relates to and affects a person's life" (Goodman, 2009).

Symptoms

Pornography/erotica dependence.
Compulsive masturbation.
Protracted promiscuity.

12.36. Side Effects of Psychotropic Medications/Adverse Drug Reactions

Common Side Effects

Anticholinergic effects: Dry mouth, blurred vision, constipation, urinary retention.

Extrapyramidal effects (caused by dopamine blockade in basal ganglia):

> Parkinson-like effects: Reduced accessory movements, cogwheel rigidity, shuffling gait, resting tremor, mask-like facies (not flat affect), "woodenness," hypomimia, bradykinesia.
>
> Dystonias: Spasms in neck (torticollis), oculogyric crises, etc. *(See "Acute Dystonic Reaction," below.)*
>
> Involuntary movements: Lip smacking, tongue rolling/thrusting, jaw clenching, drooling, tics/jerky movements, writhing.
>
> Akathisia *(uncomfortable sense of inner restlessness)*.
>
> Tardive dyskinesia *(See "Tardive Dyskinesia," below.)*

Autonomic effects: Orthostatic hypotension (which can cause dizziness and imbalance).

Sedation: Drowsiness, excessive or daytime sedation, oversleeping, insomnia, nightmares. *(See Section 12.37, "Sleep Disturbances.")* Also, lethargy, easy fatigue, weakness, anergia.

Cognitive effects: Impaired concentration or reaction time, memory impairment, confusional states.

Sexual effects: Decreased libido/desire, difficulty getting or sustaining an erection/lubrication, anorgasmia, irregular menstruation.

Other effects: Weight gain, reduction of seizure threshold, liver problems, photosensitivity, pallor/flushing, impaired temperature regulation and risk of heatstroke, blurred vision, cardiac rhythm changes, itching/uticaria.

The following are also side effects of psychotropic medications, but there are idiosyncratic side effects and illusory correlations as well, so attend carefully to what the client reports.

Neuroleptic Malignant Syndrome

The ICD-9-CM and DSM-IV-TR code is 333.92.

NMS is a potentially life-threatening but rare reaction to just about any neuroleptic medication (it affects 1% or fewer of those taking such drugs). Pelonero et al. (1998) provide a comprehensive review on diagnosis and treatment.

> Severe Parkinsonian rigidity with high fever, Autonomic Nervous System instability (flushing/pallor, unstable blood pressure, diaphoresis, tachycardia).

Tardive Dyskinesia

The DSM-IV-TR code is 333.82, Neuroleptic-Induced TD. The corresponding ICD-9-CM code is likely to be 333.85, Subacute dyskinesia due to drugs.

TD can be a serious adverse effect of psychotropic medications. It is assessed with the Abnormal Involuntary Movement Scale, available from many sites on the Internet. TD usually occurs after 3–6 months, but it can begin after up to 6 years of treatment. Although it is often irreversible, many recover.

> Irregular/spastic/choreiform or slow/writhing/athetoid movements, chewing, swallowing, licking, sucking, tongue movements, blinking, grimaces *(usually involving mouth and sometimes fingers)*.

Acute Dystonic Reaction

The DSM-IV-TR code is 333.7, Neuroleptic-Induced Acute Dystonia. The corresponding ICD-9-CM code is 333.72, Acute dystonia due to drugs.

> Spasms of the neck/trunk/muscles of the eyes *(usually occurring within the first few days of neuroleptic medication)*, torticollis, retrocollis, hip rocking, oculogyric crisis, laryngeal spasm.

Serotonin Syndrome

Due to drug interactions involving Selective Serotonin Reuptake Inhibitors, an excess of serotonin may accumulate and cause significant effects:

> Confusion, agitation, anxiety, hypomania, insomnia, hallucinations, headache.
> Hyperreflexia, myoclonus, restlessness, tremor, incoordination, rigidity, clonus, teeth chattering, trismus, seizures.
> Diaphoresis, hyperthermia, hypertension, tachycardia, pupillary dilatation, nausea, diarrhea, shivering.

Immediate medical care is essential.

SSRI Discontinuation Reaction

If an SSRI is not tapered off over a few weeks, the following symptoms often result. A useful mnemonic is FINISH:

> Flu-like symptoms: Headache, lethargy/fatigue, achiness/myalgia, sweating, sinus congestion.
> Insomnia, vivid dreams, nightmares.
> Nausea.
> Imbalance, lightheadedness, dizziness, vertigo.
> Sensory disturbances: "Burning," "tingling," "electric-like," tinnitus, feeling abnormal.
> Hyperarousal: Anxiety, irritability, agitation/restlessness, jerkiness.

This discontinuation reaction occurs in about 20% of all those who stop taking any serotonin-affecting medication. This reaction is more likely when drugs with short half-lives are used or when adherence to medication regimens is poor. It may be confused with absence of improvement, or even with worsening of the depression or anxiety.

12.37. Sleep Disturbances

See Section 3.27, "Sleep," for questions.

In ICD-9-CM, sleep disorders are coded 327.xx and 307.xx. The DSM-IV-TR code for the majority of sleep disturbances is 307.4x.

✓ Avoid the use of the term "insomnia" alone, as it has multiple meanings and so is vague.

Continuous sleep of 5–9 hours is typical but not universal. Awakening, engaging in nonstrenuous activity for an hour or two in the "middle of the night," and then entering a "second sleep" constitute a normal variant (Brown, 2006).

Sleep and arousal disorders are classified in DSM-IV-TR and ICD-9-CM as Dysomnias (disturbances in the amount, timing, or quality of sleep) and Parasomnias (dysfunctions of arousal and sleep stage transitions). However, the most complete diagnoses are provided in the *International Classification of Sleep Disorders* (American Academy of Sleep Medicine, 2005).

Dysomnias

<u>D</u>ifficulty <u>F</u>alling <u>A</u>sleep: Initial insomnia, sleep latency.
<u>S</u>leep <u>C</u>ontinuity <u>D</u>isturbance: Interrupted/broken/fragmented sleep, middle insomnia.
<u>E</u>arly <u>M</u>orning <u>A</u>wakening: Terminal insomnia (frequent in depression).

Parasomnias

Night Terrors

Pavor nocturnus in children, expression of terror with distorted features (reported by others and not recalled by client in morning), sitting up or jumping from bed, profuse sweating, sudden screaming/thrashing/calling out, sleep not interrupted *(or if awakened client cannot recall scream or reason for scream)*, still asleep/cannot be awakened or have terror shortened by others, if awakens does not recognize others/location, hallucinates dream objects, terror may last up to 20 minutes, peaceful sleep upon end of terror.

Nightmares

Frightening/often paranoid quality, awakening follows, only moaning or small movements, no sweating, no hallucinations, is awake when others arrive and can recall dream, can recognize others and surroundings, may stay awake and review dream, maximum duration 1–2 minutes, fairly well recalled in morning.

Vivid Dreams

"Almost real," well-organized contents, of neutral mood, felt as very different from usual dreaming, concerning persons and events from dreamer's remote past.

Sleep Paralysis

Besides inability to move, reports intense fear/terror/joy/anger, thoughts of imminent death, false belief of having awoken, sensed presence.

Clients may also report many kinds of vivid hallucinations, often involving supernatural assaults, near-death experiences, or other paranormal experiences (Cheyne et al., 1999).

Other Parasomnias

Somnambulism, somnirexia, somniloquy, nocturnal vocalizations.
Hypnagogic/hypnopompic hallucinations.

Other Patterns

Apnea: Central, upper airway, mixed, obstructive.
Nocturnal jerking/myoclonus/"restless leg syndrome."
Itching/crawling symptoms.
Bruxism/clenching/grinding teeth.
Incontinence, bedwetting/enuresis, urinary urgency.
Day–night reversal.

Other Aspects of Sleep Disturbance

Poor sleep architecture: Extended time to fall asleep, wakes with headache, choking, etc.
Sleep deprivation/debt, daytime sleepiness/drowsiness, tiredness/fatigue, repeated or extensive daytime napping, wakes unrefreshed.

Total sleep time decreased/increased/unaffected/normal/underestimated.
"Lark" pattern *(morning alertness with evening ineffectiveness)* or "owl" pattern *(the opposite).*

Etiological Considerations

Disorders: Depression, chronic illness, pain, drug/alcohol use to sleep.
Poor sleep hygiene: Irregular bedtimes/locations, consumption of meals/stimulants/alcohol/tobacco/medications/strenuous exercise too near bedtime, disruptive noise or light, effortful attempts to go to sleep, television/phone/computer in bedroom, media violence.
Disruptions due to bed partner/small children/need to use the bathroom, transmeridianal travel, being away from home, changed family demands.

Somatization Disorder   *See Section 13.16, "Hypochondriacal Personality."*

The relevant ICD-9-CM and DSM-IV-TR code is 300.81, Somatization Disorder. (This disorder used to be called "Briquet's syndrome.")

12.38. Stalking

See Sections 12.29, "Rape Trauma Syndrome," and 12.41, "Violent Behaviors."

Common Actions

Spying, following, notes sent/left, calls/visits at work, property damage, thefts.
Asks others about victim, verbal harassment, threats of harm to victim/family/pets, describes sexual activities.
Ignores hints/requests/refusals of contact, spreads false rumors, takes photographs, confronts victim in public, argues/swears/apologizes, etc.

The Victim

Relationship to perpetrator: Personal (usually ex-spouse or ex-partner), professional, employment-related, through the mass media, through the Internet ("cyberstalking"), casually acquainted, other (specify).
Consequences: Life restriction by job change or abandonment, limiting social relationships, isolation, sleep disorders, substance abuse, depression, anxiety symptoms.

The Perpetrator

Mullen et al. (1999) have classified individuals who stalk others as follows:

Rejected individuals, who seek reconciliation, reparation, or both.
Those seeking intimacy, who mistakenly believe they are or will be loved by their victims.
Incompetent individuals, who are ignorant or indifferent to courting rituals and use means that terrify.
Resentful persons, who stalk as vengeance for perceived injury or insult.
Predatory individuals, who seek sexual gratification and control (stalking is a rehearsal of violent fantasies).

12.39. Substance Use, Abuse, and Dependence

See Sections 3.28, "Substance Abuse: Drugs and Alcohol," and 3.29, "Substance Use: Tobacco and Caffeine," for questions. See also Section 13.11, "Codependent Personality."

ICD-9-CM and DSM-IV-TR offer about 100 codes for substance-related disorders. *(See Chapter 21, "Diagnostic Statement/Impression.")* Many terms with different implications are used in different settings: "Alcohol and Other Drugs," "Drugs & Alcohol," "Chemical/Substance/Polysubstance Abuse/ Dependence," "alcohol addiction," and "cross-addiction," as well as the generic "alcoholism." *(For signs of intoxication and withdrawal, see Section 3.28.)*

Symptoms of Problem Drinking/Drug Use

Tolerance/habituation/increased consumption needed for same effect.

Withdrawal symptoms (substance-specific syndromes).

Use to control withdrawal symptoms, "hair of the dog," morning drinking/use.

Preoccupation with drinking/use, spends time buying/selling/taking/talking about drugs/alcohol.

Continued use despite physical/medical disorder or social problem made worse by use.

Consumption pattern: Impulsive, gulping, in inappropriate circumstances, solitary, secret/hidden supply, use of drugs and alcohol together.

Guilt over drinking/use.

Rationalizations: "My medicine"/self-medicating, health benefits, relaxation, social ease, etc.

Periodic attempts at abstinence/cutting down.

Social avoidance/isolation, frequent intoxication/impairment when expected to fulfill social or occupational obligations.

Missing appointments/work/recreation/etc. in order to drink/use.

Use to point of intoxication/unconsciousness, loss of control.

Arrests for: Driving While Intoxicated/Driving Under the Influence, public intoxication, violence.

Stages in the Progression of Alcoholism

Jellinek (1960) and others have described a disease model reflecting a sequence/"pathological pattern of use," which is widely accepted but often does not fit the individual's history.

Prodromal phase: Periodic excessive drinking, drinking to reduce tension/forget stressors, increased tolerance, furtive drinking, guilt, urgency, blackouts.

Crucial phase: Loss of control over drinking, repeated efforts at control (promises, geographical escapes, scheduling, change to "only beer"), excuses for drinking, remorse, use of alibis/ rationalizations, grandiose/aggressive behavior, avoidance of family/friends, work/financial difficulties, loss of interests, tremors, morning drinking, decreased tolerance, deterioration and illness, can stop for days, "benders"/episodic heavy consumption.

Chronic/compulsive phase: Defeat, impaired thinking, drinking with inferiors, obsession with drinking, inability to initiate actions, neglect, drinking despite serious consequences, Delirium Tremens, hospitalizations, consumption of nonbeverage alcohol.

Rehabilitation phase: Learns of disease model, meets formerly addicted individuals, stops drinking, medical aspects attended to, does personal stock taking, group therapy, improved appearance, appreciates possibilities of different future, regular habits, realistic thinking/ recognition of rationalizations, return of self-esteem, new interests, new friends, contentment in sobriety, economic stability.

Stages-of-Change Model   *See Section 25.3, "Various Formats for Treatment Plans."*

Temperamental Risk Factors   *See Section 13.5, "'Addictive' Personality."*

High activity level, disinhibition, impulsivity, short attention span, lack of persistence, high emotionality, low soothability, high sociability.

Sex Differences in Drinking

Most of the following is based on work by Lawson et al. (2001). Note that females of lower Socio-Economic Status may have patterns more like males; females of middle and upper SES may show patterns like those below. Middle- and upper-SES women have traditionally been more protected against public disgrace, but more punished within the family, than those of lower SES have been.

> Less likely than men to get into trouble with the law.
> Risk factors: Difficulty participating in traditional female sex roles, frustrations in the family and with children.
> More likely than men to suffer physical illness from drinking and at an earlier stage in the disorder, and to die of cirrhosis.
> Blood alcohol levels from the same intake vary with menstrual cycle times.
> Begin drinking and having problems later than men do.
> Move more rapidly through stages of abusive drinking than do men.
> More likely than men to cite a specific stressor or traumatic event that led to abusive drinking.
> More solitary drinking/more at home, due to greater social disapproval of female drinking.
> More depressions/guilt/anxieties and fewer sociopathic behaviors than men.
> More consequences in the family (men have more consequences in the workplace).
> More likely than men to have a model of abusive drinking in the family (e.g., spouse).

A good quick summary can be found online (*pubs.niaaa.nih.gov/publications/brochurewomen/women.htm*).

Points in a Cost–Benefit Analysis Approach

The following table is adapted by permission from Horvath (1993). See Miller and Rollnick (2002) for use of this material in "motivational interviewing."

Benefits/motivators	*Costs/demotivators*
Reduction of negative emotions (anxiety, guilt, depression, helplessness, worthlessness).	Reduced productivity
Submission to social pressure of friends to consume/not be abandoned or criticized.	Impaired relationships.
Ability to ignore irresolvable interpersonal conflict.	Impaired health.
Enhancement of positive emotional states.	Diminished self-respect.
Prevention of painful withdrawal symptoms.	Unstable moods and emotions.
Avoidance of pain, pressures, problems.	Legal risks.
Hope to improve sexual performance.	Financial costs.
Elimination or reduction of cravings so as not to "go crazy."	Diminished sexual enjoyment.
Opportunity to test self-control.	Impaired cognitive functioning.
Pleasures of taste, novelty, locations.	Impaired sleep and rest.
Improved socializing.	Impaired response to obligations.
Elimination or reduction of sense of separateness because will always have this habit: "the bottle."	Guilt.
Belonging to a social group.	Uncomfortable cravings.
Need to feel normal, not "a wreck" or "falling apart."	Dishonesty (or temptation thereto).
Time filling, pastimes.	Association with dealers, other addicted individuals.
A way to get going.	Diminished sense of self-control.
Expansion of consciousness.	Reduced energy, endurance, ability.
	Reduced available time.
	Unhealthy appearance.
	Impaired driving.

Factors Indicating Poor Prognosis

Person has no sobriety support system, lives in a high-use area, has low self-esteem/efficacy expectations, has a history of physical/sexual/emotional abuse.

Responses to Treatment

See Section 25.5, "Treatment Plan Components for Clients with Substance Abuse."

Identification as Having Alcoholism/Addiction

(↔ *by degree*) The following groupings are sequenced by degree of increasing identification.

Denial: Does not admit to any intemperate use/drinking problem/bingeing/alcoholism, brags about sprees, "not addicted," does not appreciate the need for treatment, grandiose/superior/ arrogant, seeks/exaggerates/manufactures differences between self and other addicts, complacent about own patterns of use, hostile to "accusations" of addiction, only external motivators.

Minimizes consequences of drinking/use, too easily/glibly admits his/her alcoholism/addiction, self-medicates with ... (specify substances), acknowledges the negative consequences of his/her use but fails to recognize using as self-defeating, verbally identifies as having alcoholism/addiction but shows no changed behaviors such as improved social skills, resists/denies alternative problem solutions that would support freedom from addiction, is unconcerned/too little concerned with failure of previous treatments for substance abuse, hopeless of change, seeks only to avoid problems from addiction/use or to please other people and not to change own symptomatic behaviors, fearful of facing the outside world, verbalizes motivation but seems insincere, "just going through the motions," "treatment-wise," uses defensive anger/blaming/projecting.

Identifies self as "an alcoholic"/"in recovery," has made sobriety her/his first priority, demonstrates insightful identification as having addiction/cross-addiction through change in identification/lifestyle/relationships/behaviors, is open and receptive to/ understands the concepts presented, shares honestly her/his complete chemical history, is dealing with the issues from a dysfunctional childhood, knows she/he is powerless over alcoholism/addiction and cannot recover without help and support from others, explains progress of the disease and the impact on her/his life, grieves over her/ his losses, expresses regret/anger, feels cheated/abandoned, has released a lot of emotion/cried, reports hope, demonstrates hope through new behaviors, has prepared an aftercare plan including a daily plan/home group meetings, plans to attend ____ meetings per week for a total of ____ meetings/weeks/days, understands A̲dult C̲hild O̲f Alcoholic Parent concepts.

Able to offer support/be appropriately confrontative, is keeping abstinence as his/ her top priority, willing to/does whatever is necessary, has a positive and optimistic attitude toward the future, spiritual commitment is an asset in a continued struggle, understands and practices relapse prevention techniques, has resisted/avoided high-temptation situations, recognizes and has plans for preventing H̲ungry, A̲ngry, L̲onely, and T̲ired cues to drinking, has dealt with the central issues of addiction/ anger/denial/grief, has a functioning and non-substance-centered support network/ role models, has stable life in terms of finances/relationships/legal aspects, appreciates the need for and uses meetings/sponsor, leads a recovering lifestyle.

Spouse's/Partner's Response   *See also Section 13.11, "Codependent Personality."*

(↔ *by degree*) Willing to examine self, becoming involved in her/his own recovery, supportive, participates, blaming/angry/resentful, untrusting, needing to be convinced, uncooperative, codependent.

Alcoholics Anonymous and Other Treatments: Summary Statements

This client has a history of previous chemical dependency treatments, going back to
(specify date). The longest period of sobriety afterward was _____.

Client denies need for/denigrates/rejects/grudgingly admits need for/is proud of membership
in AA/NA/other Twelve-Step group (specify).

Client attends Twelve-Step meetings never/occasionally/regularly/daily; he knows name of/is
a sponsor.

She attended rehabilitation programs with only short-term/time-limited/progressively greater/
excellent success at abstinence/control.

He has been exposed to/learned about/understood/applied/changed because of disease concept
of addiction/identity as having alcoholism/cross-addiction/codependency/etc.

Client has benefited from non-disease-oriented model/non-Twelve-Step program such as Rational Recovery.

Other Summary Statements

Concerning her insight, she treats her alcoholism with indifference and resignation; she feels
so hopeless and defeated that she continues to abuse alcohol as a lifestyle.

He rationalized about his drinking in an illogical manner suggesting its value to him. For example, he uses it to sleep, control the "shakes," and loosen up, or reports that being drunk
saved his life in an auto accident.

This clinically frustrating patient has been approached, encouraged, or lectured by most of the
staff to little effect.

12.40. Suicide

See Section 3.30, "Suicide and Self-Destructive Behavior," for questions; see also Section 12.19,
"Impulse-Control Disorders," and 12.33, "Self-Injurious Behavior."

Degree of Suicidal Ideation and Behavior

(↔ *by degree*) The following groupings are sequenced by degree of increasing suicidality.

"Impossible," highly unlikely, improbable, against strongly held religious beliefs or philosophy
of life, "never" considered, rejected, wishes to live, reasons for living exceed reasons for dying,
no thoughts of giving up or harming self, suicidal ideas are convincingly denied.

Passive death wishes/escape wishes, "subintentioned/subintended death" (Shneidman,
1980), "chronic suicide" (Menninger, 1967), "wish to die," would leave life/death to chance,
wishes without plan, tired of living.

Considered and abandoned, only flimsy rationales for refusing suicide, not currently
considered, fleeting thoughts of suicide, passive suicide attempt, would not take steps
necessary to save or maintain life, suicidal "flashes," whims.

Thoughts/ideation/wishes to end life, expressed ambivalence, debating, inclina-
tion, smoldering ideation, wonders if he/she will make it through this, raises questions of life after death, reunion wishes/fantasies.

Verbalizations, recollections of others' suicides, makes plans, discusses meth-
ods/means, states intent, used as a threat, thoughts of self-mutilation, asks others to help kill her/him.

Behaviors, gestures, rehearsals, nonlethal/low-lethality/nondangerous
method, acts of self-mutilation, symbolic/ineffective/harmless attempts,
command hallucinations with suicidal intent.

Attempt(s), deliberateness, action planning, method/means selected/ acquired, high-lethality method, gives away possessions, arranges affairs, wrote note, told others of intent, made "good-bye" calls.

Persistent/continuous/continual efforts, unrelenting preoccupation.

Risk Factors for Suicide

Listed below are most of the factors that increase the likelihood for suicide. These can be seen as warning signs. A useful mnemonic for them is SAD PERSONS:

S̲ex: Male.
A̲ge: Young, elderly.
D̲epression.
P̲revious suicide attempts.
E̲thanol and other drugs.
R̲eality testing/R̲ational thought (loss of).
S̲ocial support lacking or lost.
O̲rganized suicide plan.
N̲o significant other.
S̲ickness/Stated future intent.

A fuller explanation of these items can be found online (*www.capefearpsych.org/documents/SADPERSONS-suiciderisk.pdf*). A fine article, "Responding to suicide risk," is on the website of one of its authors (*www.kspope.com/suicide*).

Thorough reviews of the risk factors for subpopulations are valuable and have been done for adults (Maris et al., 1992), adolescents (Lewinsohn et al., 1996), elderly persons (McIntosh, 1995), and those with major depression (Peruzzi & Bongar, 1999).

Psychiatric Status

Having a psychiatric disorder/diagnosis raises the risk 8–10 times, and having depression raises the risk 80–100 times (and severe depression raises it 500 times), all for males. Prior hospitalization raises risk more than outpatient treatment. Risk-increasing diagnoses include psychotic disorders (especially when hallucinated commands to commit suicide are present), alcohol abuse/dependence, and Cluster B personality disorder diagnoses. More recent onset of these is riskier.

Among psychiatric patients, the rates of suicide for males and females are about equal, because the rate for females rises greatly.

Psychological Symptoms

Depressive symptoms, such as vegetative symptoms, hopelessness[8]/helplessness, anhedonia, sense of lessened worth/guilt over fault, increased irritability.
Cycling of mood within an episode of depression.
Extreme anxiety or panic, continual worry.
Psychosis, psychotic symptoms acute rather than chronic, remission of psychotic episode but continuing depression.
Severe sleep disturbances are highly correlated with suicide.
Confusion and disorganization of thoughts, no sense of control over ideations/etc.
Acceptance that painful situation is inalterable/final/irresolvable/incurable/permanent.

---

[8]Hopelessness is a much better predictor of suicide than is depression.

ABNORMAL
SYMPTOMS

Consistent pattern of leaving life crises rather than facing them.
Recent angry/enraged/violent behavior.
Morbid preoccupation with death/suicide.
Incomplete resolution of depression, with increased energy or activation.

Demographics

European American: Three times (3 ×) more adult and 2 × more adolescent completers than African Americans and other minorities, but rates are more nearly equal in urban centers.[9] Most completers are white, U.S.-born men ages 45–60.

Sex: 3–4 × as many male attempters, 70% male completers, 30% female completers. This difference is due mainly to the lethality of the means selected.

Lowest-SES groups have highest rates.

Age: Young adult (15–24; 50% of attempters are under 30) or geriatric (twice average rate for those 75–84, 4 × for white males age 85).

Medical/dental/mental health professionals, lawyers, etc., seem to have higher rates.

Protestants higher than Jews or Catholics.

Divorced status (4–5 × greater). Divorced people are also more likely to make repeated attempts or to have made an attempt shortly before present one (within 6 months).

Never-married or widowed status ("single" is 2 × greater). Married people with children have lowest rates.

History of suicide in the family.

Feasible Plan of Action

Availability of means/method/opportunity/resources (e.g., weapons).

Highly lethal method selected.

Specific/detailed plan, has made preparations (means, privacy, time, location), with little imminence of rescue.

Has made final arrangements (a will/funeral/burial), put life's affairs in order, given away favorite possessions, written a suicide note.

Feels capable/competent/courageous of taking action.

Concealed/denied ideation to interviewer.

Prior Suicidal Behaviors

✓ **Note:** Although 50–60% of those who complete suicide have one previous attempt, only 10–20% of those who attempt suicide complete it.

Current ideation of longer duration, higher frequency, greater acceptance.

Multiple attempts, multiple threats/statements/gestures, recent attempts.

High-lethality/painful/violent/medically severe method in past attempt.

Attempts with little chance of discovery.

Intended to die in earlier attempts.

Attempts on anniversaries of significant events.

Social Isolation

No friends nearby, living alone or with other than family members, few or no family members available.

Highly dependent personality.

---

[9] I am grateful to Robert W. Moffie, PhD, of Los Angeles, CA, for correction and clarification of this issue.

Family instability/early rejection, loved ones all rejecting/punitive/unsupportive, no warm/close/interdependent relationships.

Loss of sense of continuity with past or present.

Partner also suicidal, partner self-absorbed/competitive.

No therapeutic alliance with therapist.

Stressors/Precipitants

Sudden onset of stress.

Irrevocable losses: Serious medical illness or disability, chronic illness, failing health (especially in the previously robust).

Failure to perform major life role behavior (unemployment, failing grades, etc.) resulting in humiliations, shame at loss of social status.

Self-evaluation excessively based upon performance in standard gender roles.

Recent loss of persons/positions/possessions, without replacement.

Anniversary of death or loss.

Sexual assault, violence in a relationship.

Other Risk-Increasing Variables

High level of psychological pain, absence of "secondary gain" (e.g., message sending), beginning of recovery from depression, recent psychiatric hospital discharge, lack of plans for the future, few or weak deterrents, refusal or inability to cooperate with treatment.

Impulsiveness, agitation, history of criminal behavior, considering homicide as well as suicide, motivation based on revenge/attention getting, history of life-risking "accidents"/accident proneness.

Discussing own funeral/how friends will feel later, suicide attempt modeled on one reported in the media, suicide of friends/coworkers/colleagues.

Hypochondriasis, severe physical illness, schizophrenia, or organic brain syndrome.

Alcoholism: Current alcohol intoxication, or long history of alcohol abuse without current drinking.

Depression with low CerebroSpinal Fluid level of 5-HydroxyIndoleAcetic Acid/high level of cortisol/high ratio of adrenaline to noradrenaline.

Death of mother, especially within last 3 years.

For a Child or Adolescent: Causes of suicide and rationales differ with developmental age. Risk factors include the following:

Girls make 3 × more attempts; boys are more likely to complete suicide.

Older adolescents/young adults (15–24) are more at risk.

Greater risk in rural areas.

Native Americans are at highest risk; African Americans and European Americans are about equal.

Earlier attempts.

Strained family relationships (in 75% of attempters).

Substance abuse in family of adolescent.

Stressors such as loss of a significant other, recent suicide of peer or family member ("social contagion"), legal difficulties, unwanted pregnancy, recent changes of school, withdrawal, birth of a sibling.

Protective Factors

The absence or a low level of any of the risk factors above is protective. The factors listed below reduce but do not eliminate suicide risk.

Abilities/resources for coping with stressors.
Some religious beliefs (merciful God, only God decides on life, suicide as unforgivable sin, etc.).
Frustration tolerance.
A hopeful orientation toward the future.
Desire to finish big project (schooling, seeing a child married, etc.).
Sense of responsibility to care for family/children/beloved pets.
Unwillingness to hurt/disappoint partner/family/friends/others.
Social supports and connections, group membership/leadership.
Positive relationship with therapists.

Coping with the Aftermath of Suicide

"Suicide survivors" (friends and relatives of those who die by suicide) commonly experience shock, confusion, grief, anger, and despair. According to Lukas and Seiden (2007), they dwell on the cause, their role, and the ways it might have been prevented. Common coping methods include the following:

The long good-bye: Unending mourning and fixation.
Scapegoating: Blaming a few others, displacing rage from the suicider.
Guilt as punishment: Assumption of responsibility and self-blame.
Cutting off: Strangling all feelings, including pleasure.
Physical problems: Somatizing and focusing on these.
Running: Endless moves and changes.
Suicide: Following the suicider in death.

Psychological Autopsy

To determine the legal cause of death (a useful mnemonic is NASH: <u>N</u>atural cause, <u>A</u>ccident, <u>S</u>uicide, or <u>H</u>omicide), a thorough investigation of the psychosocial context—a psychological autopsy—may be necessary. See Shneidman and Collins (2004) and Ebert (1987) for guidance.

Ways of Classifying Suicidal Behavior

Anomic, egoistic, altruistic suicides (Durkheim, 1897/1966).
<u>I</u>ndirect <u>S</u>elf-<u>D</u>estructive <u>B</u>ehavior (Farberow, 1980), "parasuicide" (Farberow, 1980), "sub-intended death" (Shneidman, 1980).
Death seeker, death initiator, death ignorer, death darer, courts death (Shneidman, 1980).

Assessment of Suicidality

Two outstanding books address this complicated effort: Jobes (2006) and Shea (2002).

Thought Continuity, Content, and Other Aspects

See Section 11.19, "Stream of Thought," for descriptors.

<u>T</u>raumatic <u>B</u>rain Injury   *See Section 12.26, "<u>PostC</u>oncussive <u>S</u>yndrome."*

12.41. Violent Behaviors

See Sections 3.17, "Impulse Control," and 3.31, "Violence," for questions; see Sections 12.9, "Conduct Disorder," and 12.19, "Impulse-Control Disorders," for additional descriptors.

Targets of Violence

Objects, property, self, family, strangers, women, children, animals, authority figures, peers, elderly/weaker persons, any available target, inside/outside the home.

Correlates of Serious Aggression

Tortures animals.
Commits hidden aggressive acts.
Fights with weaker opponents.
Pride in history of aggression.
Profitless damaging of property (especially one's own).
Apparently purposeless aggressive actions.
Careless of risk of self-harm when acting aggressively.
"Out of control" when aggressive.
Plans aggressive actions.

Other Variables to Be Evaluated for Assessment of Violence

This list is based on work by Beck (1990).

History of violence before mental health diagnosis/treatment.
Mental status: Defective judgment, high arousal level, psychosis, impaired consciousness.
Impulsiveness, as seen in history of driving violations, spending money, sexual/social relationships, risk-taking behavior, work history.
Use of intoxicants, history of drug/alcohol abuse.
Availability of weapons/victims.
Childhood exposure to violence/abuse/neglect, chaotic family, violent subculture.
Instability: Frequent moves, firings, evictions, new partners.
Ability to vent frustration/anger nonviolently: Verbal skills, intellect, coping mechanisms, use of support system.
Need for external controls when internal ones are lacking/defective/easily overcome.

Characteristics of the violent behaviors:
　　Location, time, frequency, others present or alone, method, relationship with object of violence, lethality of method.
　　Motives/benefits/perceptions, threats, precipitants.

Other behaviors: Postural tension (on chair's edge, gripping edge), voice (loud, strident), motor activity (restlessness, pacing, leaving), startle response (easily, full).

Factors Associated with Violence Recidivism

This list is based on work by Monahan (1981).

Criminal history: Recidivism increases with each prior criminal act. Risk of recidivism exceeds 50% with more than five prior offenses.
Age: Youth is highly associated with crime. Greater risk if a juvenile at first offense.
Gender: Males are much more violent.
Race: African Americans are at higher risk.

S̲o̲cioE̲conomic S̲tatus: Lower status and job instability.

Drug and alcohol abuse history.

Nonstable, nonsupportive family environment.

"Bad company" peers and associates.

Greater availability of victims: Either a broad range of victims, or repeated assaults on a narrow class of victims who remain available (e.g., girlfriends).

Access to weapons.

Access to alcohol.

Homicide Risk Factors

✓ Consider your *Tarasoff* duty (the duty to warn/protect possible targets of a client's violence) and take appropriate steps. For more guidance, see Zuckerman (2008, Section 3.11).

Intense wish to kill, specified or named victim, command hallucinations, ambivalent wish to kill, nonspecific hostility.

Violent/destructive/antisocial behaviors, violent acts in unrelated settings, unpredictable destruction of objects, arrest/assault repeatedly in the same setting, carrying of weapons, chronic problems with the authorities, criminal record.

Attempted to kill by stabbing/strangling/shooting, severe physical abuse causing harm.

Young male, little education, patient with psychotic delusions, substance abuse history, character disorder diagnosis.

No home/family/friends, no institutional support or involvement, has home but no one can observe the patient, family not interested in patient.

Workaholism   *See Section 13.4, "A and B Personality Types."*

13

Personality Patterns

The descriptive words and phrases in this chapter's sections are organized into clusters. No validity claims are made for the clusters or their contents; these are simply descriptors that are commonly used in reports and in research studies. Because the clusters and concepts overlap, do review similar types as cross-referenced. The chapter begins with sections on models of personality diagnosis, assessment methods, and cognitive styles. Subsequent topics are presented in alphabetical order.

13.1. Models of Personality Diagnosis

Millon's Model

In Millon's model (see Millon et al., 2004) the focus is on reinforcement: What **types** of reinforcement (positive or enhancing/pursuit of pleasure vs. negative or relieving/avoidance of pain) does an individual of a certain personality type typically seek? What are the usual **sources** of this reinforcement (self/independent vs. others/dependent vs. vacillating/ambivalent vs. no one/detached)? And what instrumental processes or **strategies** (active/modifies environment vs. passive/accommodates to environment) does the person employ?

These three dimensions result in eight categories of **normal** personalities (defined as those of individuals who seek positive types of reinforcement) and eight categories of **abnormal** personalities (those of individuals who seek negative types of reinforcement):

	Source of reinforcement				
Strategy	*Self*	*Others*	*Vacillating*	*Detached*	*Type*
Active	Forceful	Sociable	Sensitive	Inhibited	Normal, positive reinforcement
Passive	Confident	Cooperative	Respectful	Introversive	
Active	Antisocial	Histrionic	Passive–aggressive	Avoidant	Abnormal, negative reinforcement
Passive	Narcissistic	Dependent	Obsessive–compulsive	Schizoid	

The Five-Factor Model of Personality

Costa and Widiger (2002) have given the five robust factors of personality the names listed below, and provided the dichotomous descriptors that follow (each factor is thought of as a continuum). Listed below these descriptors are applicable subscales from the well-validated <u>NEO</u> Personality

209

Inventory–Revised (Costa & McCrae, 1995), and terms from other sources that apply to one pole or the other of the continuum.

Neuroticism: Worrying–calm, nervous–at ease, high-strung–relaxed, insecure–secure, vulnerable–hardy.

Subscales: Anxiety, Anger–Hostility, Depression, Self-Consciousness, Vulnerability, Impulsiveness.

Other terms: Emotionality, temperamental, negative affectivity, hypochondriacal. Opposites: Ego strength, steady, cool, poised, self-confident.

Extraversion: Sociable–retiring, fun-loving–sober, affectionate–reserved, talkative–quiet, joiner–loner.

Subscales: Warmth, Gregariousness, Assertiveness, Activity, Excitement Seeking, Positive Emotions.

Other terms: Sociability, surgency, leader-like, dominance, capacity for status, social prescience, need for power, not withdrawn, frank and open, adventurous, sociable. Opposites: Reserved, not outgoing, secretive, cautious, reclusive.

Openness: Original–conventional, creative–uncreative, independent–conforming, untraditional–traditional.

Subscales: Fantasy, Aesthetics, Feelings, Actions, Values, Ideas.

Other terms: Open to new experiences, interested in experience for its own sake, eager for variety, daring, imaginative, intellectance, culturedness, unusual ideas, highly tolerant of uncertainty and what others think/do/say, broad-mindedness. Opposites: Concrete, practical, narrow interests.

Agreeableness: Good-natured–irritable, courteous–rude, lenient–critical, flexible–stubborn, sympathetic–callous.

Subscales: Trust, Straightforwardness, Altruism, Compliance, Modesty, Tendermindedness.

Other terms: Cooperative, interpersonally supportive, need for affiliation, need for love, friendly compliance, not jealous, mild and gentle, cooperative. Extreme forms: Dependent and self-effacing. Opposites: Grumpy, unpleasant, disagreeable, headstrong, negativistic.

Conscientiousness: Reliable–undependable, careful–careless, hard-working–lazy, punctual–late, persevering–quitting.

Subscales: Competence, Order, Dutifulness, Achievement Striving, Self-Disciplined, Deliberative.

Other terms: Thorough, ambitious, achievement-oriented, responsible, prudent, will to achieve, constrained, work ethic, fussy and tidy, scrupulous. Opposites: Undirected, lazy, fickle, unscrupulous, undependable.

A sixth personality factor may be intelligence.

Goldberg (1992) offers 50 bipolar rating scales (10 for each factor), or 100 well-established human traits that are subsumed under the five factors.

Clusters of Personality Types from DSM-IV-TR

Cluster	Diagnoses	Informal name	Mnemonics	
A	Paranoid, Schizoid, Schizotypal	Odd/eccentric	Weird	Atypical
B	Antisocial, Borderline, Histrionic, Narcissistic	Dramatic/erratic	Wild	Beast
C	Avoidant, Obsessive–Compulsive, Dependent	Anxious/fearful	Worried	Coward/Clingy

Interpersonal Diagnoses of Personality

The DSM's categories are rather insensitive to the social context in which an individual's maladaptive behavior occurs. A number of models for making interpersonal diagnoses of personality have been developed:

1. The Structural Analysis of Social Behavior (Benjamin, 1996) incorporates the most relevant interpersonal dimensions: friendliness–hostility (affiliation) and control–autonomy giving (interdependence). The SASB is designed not only to categorize interactions in psychotherapy, but to chart changes in a patient's intrapsychic functioning.
2. Transactional Analysis, as formulated by Eric Berne (1964) and others, is a well-worked-out paradigm. *(See Section 26.6, "Transactional Analysis.")*
3. Schutz's Fundamental Interpersonal Relations Orientation–Behavior describes relationships and personality (see *www.cpp.com/products/fir-b/index.aspx*).
4. Leary (1957/2004) developed an interpersonal model that deserves more attention than it has received.

For other aspects of the evaluation of personality, see Chapter 26.

Prototype Approach

Personality disorder diagnoses are notoriously overlapping. The DSM's approach bases diagnostic decisions on the presence or absence of individual criteria, the counting of these symptoms, and the imposition of a cutoff score to assert the diagnosis. In contrast, the prototype approach simultaneously examines clusters of several types of information (symptoms, adaptive functioning, treatment response, etiology) to generate clusters that are more reliable, are easier to use, and have more clinical utility. For more on this very promising alternative approach, see, for example, Westen and Schedler (2007) and Westen et al. (2006).

13.2. Assessment Methods

In the lists below, each entry offers the following information: the title of the current edition or version of each test (with acronym, abbreviation, or common name indicated by underlining); its copyright date if known; its current publisher or distributor; and the applicable age range.

Objectively Scored Tests

FOR CLINICAL POPULATIONS

Millon Adolescent Personality Inventory, Pearson Assessments, 13–19 years.
Minnesota Multiphasic Personality Inventory–2 (2001) and MMPI-2—Restructured Form (2008), Pearson Assessments, 17–64 years.
Minnesota Multiphasic Personality Inventory–Adolescent, Pearson Assessments, 14–18 years.
Personality Inventory for Youth, Western Psychological Services, 9–19 years.

FOR NONCLINICAL POPULATIONS

NEO Personality Inventory–Revised (1995), Psychological Assessment Resources, 17 years and older.
Personality Inventory for Children–2nd ed., Western Psychological Services, 3–16 years.
16 Personality Factor Test, 5th ed., Pearson Assessments, 16 years and older.
California Personality Inventory (CPI), Consulting Psychologists Press, 16 years and older.

Projective Tests

Children's Apperception Test and CAT-H (1974), Pearson Assessments, 3–10 years.
Drawings (House–Tree–Person, Draw-A-Person), Riverside, 5–17 years.
Piers–Harris Children's Self-Concept Scale–2nd ed., WPS, 7–18 years.
Thematic Apperception Test (1973), Pearson Assessments, children–adults.
Rotter Incomplete Sentences Blank, 2nd ed. (1982), Pearson Assessments, high school to adult.
Rorschach or Holtzman Inkblots, Pearson Assessments, 5 years and older.

Behavior Rating Scales

Burks Behavior Rating Scales–2, WPS, 3–6 years, grades K–12.
Behavior Assessment System for Children–2, Pearson Assessments, 2:0–21:11 years.
Achenbach System of Empirically Based Assessment (Child Behavior CheckList, Teacher's Report Form, Youth Self-Report, Direct Observation Form, Adult Behavior CheckList, Older Adult Behavior CheckList, ASEBA, 1½–90+ years.
Devereaux Behavior Rating Scale—School Form (1993), Pearson Assessments, 5–18 years.
Devereaux Scales of Mental Disorders (1994), Pearson Assessments, 5–18 years.
Revised Behavior Problem Checklist, Pearson Assessments, grades K–12.

13.3. Cognitive or Thinking Styles

The well-researched personality variables of cognitive or thinking styles have received less attention recently, but are still very powerful in understanding the interactions of personality and cognition: how someone processes information, draws conclusions, and chooses actions in school, on the job, and in relationships. For more information, see Sternberg and Grigorenko (1997).

Field-dependent vs. field-independent (psychological differentiation) (Herman Witkin).
Impulsive vs. reflective (or cognitive tempo) (Jerome Kagan).
Cognitively complex vs. fewer dimensions of a stimulus used (George Kelly).
Internal vs. external locus of control (Julian Rotter).
Global vs. analytical or scanning vs. focusing.
Sharpeners vs. levelers or splitters vs. levelers.
Abstract vs. concrete.
Constricted vs. flexible control.

13.4. A and B Personality Types

Not in ICD-9-CM or DSM-IV-TR.

Type A

Time Urgency

Impatient, hurries, under pressure, prompt and often early for appointments, watches clock, walks/talks/eats rapidly, does multiple activities simultaneously (multitasks), lives in the future/always planning, feels that "there's never enough time."
Hates delays, irritable/restless with others' pace, high impatience at having to wait for someone, rage at having to wait in line, detests wasting time, drives over the speed limit, evades red lights, is "hard on equipment," always underestimates the time a job will take.

Hostility/Struggle for Control

Competitive, "must win," makes bets, finds competitive aspect of all activities, plays as hard as works, detests losing, plays to win even against children/friends, sets higher goals for self, challenging, hard-driving.

Constant struggle for control/avoiding helplessness, helplessness is feared/denied, sees the world as threatening, cycles of desperate efforts to control environment, followed by profound abandonment of efforts, reluctant to share power/control/delegate.

Dominates conversations, emphasizes words when speaking, finishes others' statements, interrupts speakers, dislikes small talk.

Aggressive, high, but inhibited need for power.

Self-Injurious Behaviors

Gorging on high-fat foods, overuse of stimulants, low levels of exercise, high alcohol intake/smoking, no time for self-care.

Works during vacations, overplans vacation's activities, works in bed, inability to relax/be unproductive, fails to notice beauty/scenery/"smell the flowers," overschedules self, overcommitted, guilt over relaxing, always works more than 8 hours a day.

Sits on edge of chairs, makes fists, clenches jaws, taps fingers, jiggles legs, rapid blinks, never still.

Continual emergency reaction.

Cognitions

Measures everything in numbers/dollars, attributes success to own speed, concerned with getting and having rather than being.

Perfectionistic, demands continual self-improvement, demands excellence in every area, always seeking to improve efficiency, underestimates own achievements, underestimates time and effort needed, disappointment/self-doubt.

Negative, cynical, critical, ruthless in self-reproach/self-examining.

"Workaholic" Traits

Ambitious, gets higher grades/income.

Overworking, takes on more and more work, pursues more challenging tasks, recreation only with friends from work, better communication at work than at home, organized hobbies, work as substitute for intimate contacts, reading is all work-related, works late more than peers do, when awakened thoughts go to work, lives by deadlines and quotas, creates unnecessary deadlines.

Type B

Relaxes readily, focuses on quality of life, paces self, easy-going, "one day at a time."
Less ambitious, lower incomes/grades.
Less irritable.

Abusive Personality   *See Section 13.7, "Antisocial Personality." (See also Dutton, 2007.)*

There are many lists of "warning signs" of an abuser on the Internet (see, e.g., *www.sylviasplace.com/signs.html* or *www.hiddenhurt.co.uk/Abuser/signs.htm*).

Adult Children Of Alcoholic/Addicted Parents

See Section 13.11, "Codependent Personality."

Despite the popularity of the ACOA concept and the multiple publications about it, there has been little empirical support for the validity for a pattern of characteristics in ACOAs or in grandchildren of alcoholic/addicted parents. *(See, e.g., Logue et al., 1992, and Sher, 1991.)*

13.5. "Addictive" Personality

Not in ICD-90-CM or DSM-IV-TR.

There has been little research support for the concept of an "addictive" personality, perhaps because a particular substance's use creates the traits seen. Some general traits include the following:

Dissatisfaction with life.
Extreme dependence, resentment of authority, flagrant selfishness, insistence on immediate gratification.

13.6. Aggressive Personality

See also Sections 12.19, "Impulse-Control Disorders," 13.7, "Antisocial Personality," 13.8, "Authoritarian Personality," and 13.23, "Sadistic Personality."

Not in ICD-9-CM or DSM-IV-TR.

Cardinal Features

Aggression, low self-restraint.

Behaviors

Vicious, brutal, pugnacious, temperamental.
Reckless, unflinching, fearless, undeterred by pain/danger/punishment.

Interpersonal Aspects

Intimidating, dominating, surgent, obstinate, controlling.
Humiliating, abusive, derisive, cold-blooded, persecutes, malicious.

Cognitions

Opinionated, close-minded, prejudiced, bigoted, "authoritarian."

Self-Image

Proud of independence, hard-headed, tough, power-oriented, powerful.

13.7. Antisocial Personality

See also Sections 12.1, "Abuse," 12.9, "Conduct Disorder," 12.19, "Impulse-Control Disorders," 13.6, "Aggressive Personality," 13.8, "Authoritarian Personality," and 13.23, "Sadistic Personality."

The relevant ICD-9-CM and DSM-IV-TR codes are as follows:

For those over age 18: 301.7, Antisocial Personality Disorder.

For those under age 18: 312.81, Conduct Disorder, Childhood-Onset Type; 312.82, Conduct Disorder, Adolescent-Onset Type. (*See Section 12.9 for additional ICD-9-CM codes.*)

Those over age 18 who engage in criminal behavior without "psychological" motivation should be diagnosed as showing Adult Antisocial Behavior (DSM-IV-TR and ICD-9-CM code V71.01).

Cardinal Features

Classic criteria can be found in Cleckley's famous book *The Mask of Sanity* (1976), as well as in Hare (1999) and Lykken (1995).

Predatory attitude and behavior toward others, long-standing indifference to and repetitive violation of others' rights, parasitic lifestyle, repetitive socially destructive behaviors.

Absence of delusions or other signs of irrational thinking, of anxiety or other neurotic symptoms, of suicide attempts, or of a life plan or ordered way of living.

Social Aspects

Irresponsibility

Untrustworthy, evades responsibility, unreliable, rejects obligations, ruthless.

Told a lot of lies, used an alias, in trouble because failed to pay her/his bills, multiple financial irresponsibilities.

Multiple marriages/divorces, marital instability, frequent marriages, suddenly left/hit/unfaithful to spouse, irresponsible parenting, seriously hurt/neglected a child.

Cavalier, acting wild, slept around with people he/she didn't know very well, earned money by pimping/prostitution.

Selfishness

Unique and self-serving ideas of "right and wrong," lies easily, frequent lying not just to avoid negative consequences, does not believe her/his behaviors/crimes will be or should be punished, uses guilt inductions on others, externalizes all responsibility, blames others, takes no responsibility for unfavorable outcomes.

Feels or believes self to be harassed/misused/victimized/persecuted, resents, revengeful, distrusts, suspicious, justifies behavior with lies and manipulation, argues about "who's in charge," petty, superficial relationships.

A chronic pattern of infringement on the rights of others, violates social codes by lies or deceits, chronic speeder and drunk driver, reckless, indifferent to the rights of others, breaks rules, rebellious, unprincipled and deceitful in dealing with others who have something he/she wants.

Ingratitude, arrogance, sees aggressive persons as strong and prosocial persons as weak.

Unethical, unprincipled, unscrupulous, cavalier, showy acts of devotion, disloyal, untrustworthy, unfaithful.

Behaviors

General

Impulsivity, impetuous, spur-of-the-moment, short-sighted, incautious, imprudent, lack of long-term plans.

History of drug/alcohol/etc. overuse/abuse (but this is not the cause of antisocial behaviors).

Often likable, attractive, engaging, center of attention, socially skilled/capable/effective, charming/graceful, tells tall tales, brags of unlikely resources/relationships/experiences, flip, glib, fast, overabundant ideas, witty, word plays/puns.

Illegal or Immoral Activities

Lying, stealing, swindling, cheating, commission of/involvement in minor or serious illegal/delinquent acts.

Has conned/manipulated/cheated people out of their money/possessions, predatory, often victimizes the easiest/weakest members of society, "white-collar" criminal.

From an early age: Criminal arrests/convictions, served time, poor probation/parole risk, many types of offenses (including felonies) diagnosed as having antisocial personality.

Initiates physical fights, used a weapon in a fight, tortured animals, physically cruel to other people.

Has deliberately destroyed others' property, steals/vandalizes/"messes up" property, fire-setting.

Has forced someone into sexual activity with him/her, promiscuity.

For a Child: See also Section 12.9, "Conduct Disorder."

Starting fights, vandalism, tortured/abused ("played tricks on") animals/pets, early and extensive drug/alcohol use, behavior difficulties, theft, incorrigibility, running away overnight, bad associates, impulsivity, recklessness/irresponsibility, slovenly appearance, lack of guilt, pathological lying.

Trouble with the police/juvenile or school authorities, truancy/plays a lot of hooky, has been a discipline problem/expelled/suspended from school.

Cognitions

See especially Samenow (2004).

Does not believe she/he will be blamed/caught/punished, low planning of escape, no consideration of alternatives or consequences, projects blame, rationalizes, Machiavellianism, ends justify any means, does not profit from experience of punishment, low insight.

Average or above-average intelligence.

Affects

Lacking in remorse/guilt/regret/victim empathy, insensitive, lacks compassion, hardened, callous, cold-blooded, emotionally detached, low motivation to change, shallow affects, no deep or lasting emotions.

Irritability, aggressiveness, short-tempered, "bottled-up" anger, intolerance of delayed gratifications, easily provoked to violence, low frustration tolerance.

Deficient emotional arousal, stimulation/thrill seeking, easily bored.

Vocational Aspects

Unstable employment: Fired, ran away, quit a job impulsively/without another to start, didn't work because he/she "just didn't want to," court-martialed/demoted, missed a lot of work.

Lack of career or other long-term plans.

Anxious Personality   *See Section 13.18, "'Nervous' Personality."*

13.8. Authoritarian Personality

For descriptors, see also Sections 12.19, "Impulse-Control Disorders," 13.7, "Antisocial Personality," and 13.23, "Sadistic Personality," for contrast.

Not in ICD-9-CM or DSM-IV-TR.

See Adorno et al. (1950/1993), Milgram (1974), and Stone et al. (1993) for detailed discussions of the authoritarian personality.

Cognitions

Rigid adherence to middle-class/bourgeois/conventional values.
Commitment to severe punishment for deviation from conventional values.
Reactionary/ultraconservative, moral ideology overrides all other concerns.
Prejudiced against minorities, etc., outsiders seen as dangerous/dehumanized ("subhuman," "animals," "undeserving").

Social Aspects

Blind obedience, conformity, no questioning or criticism of authority, exaggerated need to submit to those above, harshness to those below.
Uses official/"clean" vocabulary.
Power and dominance are the most central dimensions of relationships, views people as either weak or strong, glorifies toughness/denies tenderness, values stern discipline.
Idealizes parents, father seen as stern/harshly punitive/demanding of absolute obedience.

13.9. Avoidant Personality

The relevant ICD-9-CM and DSM-IV-TR code is 301.82, Avoidant Personality Disorder.

Cardinal Features

Oversensitive and vacillating, discomfort in all social situations, watchful for any hint of disapproval.

Cognitions

Belief that others know of his/her anxiety and are constantly watching for his/her mistakes.

Interpersonal Aspects

Yearns for closeness/warmth/affection/acceptance but fears rejection/humiliation/disapproval in relationships.
Fears "goofing up"/gaffes/social errors/GAUCHERIES/FAUX PAS and so "making a fool of myself," fears crying/blushing/embarrassment.
Wary, distrustful, vigilant for offenses/threats/ridicule/abuse/humiliation, hypersensitive/keen sensitivity to potential for rejection or humiliation by others, expects not to be loved, needs constant reassurance/guarantee of uncritical affection.
Withdrawing, guarded, private, lonely, shy/reticent/timid, compliant.

Affects

Anguished, intensely ambivalent, anxious, "bored."

Self-Image

Devalues own accomplishments, angry and depressed at self for social difficulties, sees self as basically defective/flawed/odd/inadequate.

Other

Vicious cycle as follows: Low self-esteem, fear of rejection, shallow or awkward attempts at social relating, hypersensitivity to lack of enthusiasm/disapproval that confirms sense of low worth, feels rejection, withdraws, fears of relationships, loneliness, yearning, trying again, rejection, etc.

Extensive reliance on fantasizing for gratification of needs for contact and anger discharge.

13.10. Borderline Personality

The relevant ICD-9-CM and DSM-IV-TR code is 301.83, Borderline Personality Disorder.

These people often present a mixed picture, with elements of other personality disorders present; they often also have mood disorder diagnoses.

Cardinal Features

Instability in all aspects of living/personality functioning/mood/social relating, lack of personality consistency/cohesiveness, abrupt shifts of affect/tone of relationships.

Interpersonal Aspects

Close/demanding/dependent/intense relationships, disillusionment when intensity is not reciprocated, terror of abandonment.

Unstable intimate relationships, rare stable but not intimate relationships, inexplicable changes in attitude/feelings toward others, capricious, "ups and downs," vacillating reactions, dependence–independence struggles, intense dislike of isolation and loneliness so engages in a series of transient/stormy/brief relationships, superficiality of relationships based on alternating idealization and deflation.

Affects

Labile, mercurial, brittle, erratic, unpredictable, rapid/short-lived but intense mood swings, low tolerance for affects, lacks internalized soothing/holding function so relies on others.

Anger barely hidden/under the surface, pessimism, argumentativeness, irritable, easily annoyed, sarcastic, intense and sudden rages or depressions, sudden dramatic and unexpected outbursts, rage over failure of others to provide soothing, rage at intimates.

Spells of emptiness/boredom/dejection/apathy, numbness.

Areas of seemingly unalterable and crushing negativity, worthlessness/badness/blame/guilt/shame/fault assumption, feelings of unlovability.

Identity

Lack of individuation, identity diffusion/shakiness, shifts of identity/gender identity/career choices/long-term goals, frequent "Who am I?" questions, instability of self-esteem/self-image, uncertain values/loyalties, "incompetence," "imposter."

Fragmentation of self, splitting, nebulous/multiple identities/personalities, "parts"/"voices"/nicknames, threats to right to survive from parts of self. *(See Section 13.14, "Dissociative Identity Disorder.")*

Behaviors

Impulsivity/poor judgment, lapses of judgment.

Suicide threats/gestures or attempts/overdosing.

Self-destructive/mutilating/damaging behaviors.
Running up huge bills/shoplifting, gambling sprees, eating binges, sexual acting out.
Addictive traits and patterns, drug misuse/abuse, reckless driving.
Ambivalence, indecision, procrastination.

Treatment Aspects

Expect frequent crises, demands for special arrangements, misinterpretations of the therapist's words and motives, intense ambivalences, rapid shifts from idealization to denigration, intolerance of contact of any kind, overreactions to changes of arrangements, confusion of intimacy and sexuality, and possible brief periods of psychotic symptoms.

✓ Miller (1994) offers a brief but powerful description of borderline personality from a patient's perspective.

13.11. Codependent Personality

See also Section 10.3, "Anxiety/Fear," Section 10.7, "Depression," and the sections in this chapter on many other personality patterns (especially borderline personality).

The relevant ICD-9-CM and DSM-IV-TR code is likely to be 301.6, Dependent Personality Disorder, but dependent and codependent personality are not identical. Codependency as a syndrome has been largely shaped by addiction concepts.

Interpersonal Aspects

General Descriptors

Overresponsible.
Self-sacrificing, unassertive, does not pursue own rights, adapts rather than changing a bad situation.
Submission to others for predictability/security.
Oversensitive to others' difficulties.
Puts up a front, hides "true self."

Features

Caretaking: Undeserved loyalty, unappreciated/excessive devotion, excessive caretaking, over-reliable/overresponsible (to compensate for the addicted person's irresponsibility), anticipates and participates in satisfying the addicted person's needs ("enabling"), need to control people and situations, rigidity.
Dependency: Longing for love/approval, tolerates abuse, always meeting others' needs before one's own, especially when stressed.
Denial: Ignores/rationalizes/minimizes problem, denies increased substance abuse/dysfunction.
Loss of daily structure: Missing appointments, having meals at irregular times, not getting to bed or up on time.
Fails to complete tasks/follow through/make plans, easily overwhelmed with tasks, reactive rather than proactive.
Crisis orientation, not long-term: Good in crisis situation/beginnings and endings, but not in middles.

Roles Adopted

Rescuer: Protecting/covering for the addicted underfunctioning person by making excuses for absences or social mistakes.

Caretaker: Minimizing negative consequences of addicted person's negligence through over-responsibility and overfunctioning.

Joiner: Rationalizing or participating/assisting in addicted person's using.

Hero: Protecting the family's public image, drawing attention away from the addiction with enormous/"superhuman"/self-sacrificing efforts.

Complainer: Blaming all the family's problems on the addicted person with no hope of change.

Adjuster: Avoiding discussion of the addiction in hopes it will disappear, hiding concern and confusion with apathy.

Family Characteristics

Extreme family loyalty, but only superficial relationships, no intimate ones.

Family rules: "Don't talk, don't trust, don't feel."

Distorted family image: Happy, no problems, see only the good.

Overdeveloped sense of responsibility and concern for others.

Control is valued, lack of control is terrifying; order, stability, routine, regularity, peace, not chaos.

Self-Image

Low self-esteem, self-blame for any problems/other's substance use, guilt, extreme/unproductive self-criticism/flagellation, assumption of blame due to inconsistency of parental behaviors, insecurity, fear/belief in one's unlovability/insanity/badness/dirtiness, rejects compliments.

Sense of powerlessness.

Shame at addiction, secretive, very reluctant to ask for help.

Acts the way he/she believes is "normal," doesn't know what are normal behaviors/emotional responses, anxious over not feeling/acting sufficiently "normal" or feeling different from anyone else.

Adopts extreme role models and standards acceptable to a group with low self-esteem.

Affects

Depression, negativity, uncontrollable mood swings, no fun in life, dulled feeling, anhedonia, enjoyment only at someone else's expense/vicariously.

Seriousness, life as series of problems and crises to be solved, "worry is normal."

Frequent resentments and anger, "got a raw deal from life."

Numerous fears/anxieties, fear of anger (own and addicted person's) because it will end the relationship, indecision, fears of being hurt/abandoned/rejected.

Cognitions

Obsessive thinking, overreliance on analytical thinking, perfectionism.

Delusions/irrational beliefs (especially that love conquers all–or at least substance abuse).

Dishonest/lies/denial, unaware of dishonesty, "(The addicted person's behavior) is not the 'real' person."

Low memory of childhood.

Behaviors

Abused, neglected physically/sexually/psychologically.
"Addictive" behaviors (eating disorders, substance abuse) to cope with own frustrations/pain.
Compulsions as attempts to control.
Acting out to get attention or approval.

Other

Health problems: Stress-related disorders, lack of personal care.
Lack of attention in childhood ("stroke-starved") leads to denial of own needs.

For a Child:

Premature adulthood and responsibilities, struggle with adult problems as child, loss of childhood.
Impact of addiction varies with developmental stage of child living in addictive household:
    Bonding stage: World is not safe.
    Exploratory/separation stage: Sense of being either engulfed or abandoned; passivity; no right to say "No."
    Latency stage: Failure to learn rules, what is normal, problem-solving skills; living with lies, denial, and anxiety.

Overachieving: Trying to give the family something to be proud of.
Entertaining: Never taking anything seriously in order to relieve tension, "class clown."
Withdrawing: Escaping to friends' homes or spending time alone.
Rebelling: Acting out anger, causing trouble to draw attention away from family problems.

Characteristics of Codependent Individuals

Schaef (1986) describes the following:

External referencing: Distrusts own perceptions, lacks boundaries, believes one cannot survive without a relationship/addicted to relationships, fears abandonment, believes in the perfect union.
Caretaking: Becomes indispensable, becomes a martyr.
Self-centeredness: Personalizes all events, assumes responsibility for others' behaviors.
Overcontrolling: Increases control efforts when chaos increases, attempts to control everything and everyone, controls without caring for those controlled, believes that with more effort she/he can fix the addict/family.
Feelings: Unaware of feelings, distorts emotional experiences/accepts only "nice" feelings, fearfulness.
Dishonesty: Manages all impressions made, omits/lies about the truth, rigidity.
Gullibility: Is a bad judge of character, unwilling to confront, overtrusting, accepts what fits the way he/she wishes things were.

A critical review of the codependency concept can be found in Babcock and McKay (1995).

13.12. Compulsive Personality

See also Section 13.20, "Obsessive Personality."

The relevant ICD-9-CM and DSM-IV-TR codes are 300.3, Obsessive–Compulsive Disorder(s), and 301.4, Obsessive–Compulsive Personality Disorder.

✓ **Note:** DSM-IV-TR and ICD-9-CM do not differentiate between Obsessive and Compulsive Personality Disorders. But because the writer of reports is dealing with the unique individual, "obsessive" and "compulsive" *are* separated here, to allow emphasis on aspects of the presentation.

Cardinal Feature

Repetitive behaviors/routines/rituals, or else intense anxiety.

Behaviors

Highly regulated/organized lifestyle, orderliness.

Cognitions

See Shapiro (1965).

Rumination prevents task completion, hypercareful, doubting, indecisive, poor decision making/follow-through, poor time management.

Excessively moralistic concerns, scrupulousness, intense self-evaluation/scrutiny, "black or white" judgments, need for immediate closure.

Perfectionistic approach, overattention to detail and avoidance of error, neatness, meticulous, a "stickler for details."

Officious; concern with form over content, procedures/regulations more than the goals, letter of the law not the spirit, orderly task procedures rather than the outcome; sees the world in terms of schedule/rules/regulations, work as yet undone/burden.

Affects

Satisfaction in elaborate planning and arranging, only mild/brief pleasure with the completion of projects, a "work, not pleasure" orientation.

Joyless, solemn, controls most emotions, unrelaxed, occasional intense righteous indignation, perceived lack of control of environment leads to intense depression, great need/effort to control tension/anxiety.

Self-Image

Industrious, reliable, efficient, loyal, prudent/careful.

Interpersonal Aspects

Demands that others do things his/her way.

Is seen as somber/formal/cold/grim, a "stuffed shirt."

Respectful, conventional, follows the proprieties, polite, correct.

Shows reaction formation in positive/socially acceptable presentation of self.

13.13. Dependent Personality

See also Section 13.26, "Self-Defeating Personality," and 13.11, "Codependent Personality."

The relevant ICD-9-CM and DSM-IV-TR code is 301.6, Dependent Personality Disorder.

✓ **Note:** Be sensitive to gender bias in using this diagnosis. Many studies (e.g., Broverman et al., 1970) have demonstrated gender bias in diagnosing various personality disorders: Clinicians of all stripes equate healthy males with healthy adults, but see females as dependent, self-dramatizing, vain, demanding, and overreacting to minor events–all of which resemble society's view of "normal" women. A final caution: Do not assume sexual masochism in those with dependent traits, or confuse such masochism with dependent personality.

Bornstein (1997), who has written extensively on this pattern, finds (1) that the DSM symptoms of difficulty expressing disagreement and difficulty initiating projects are contradicted by research; and (2) that two of the others (seeking a new relationship as soon as one ends, and needing others to assume responsibility for his/her life) have not been tested empirically.

Cardinal Feature

A weak and helpless identity, with a resulting search for nurturant and protective relationships.

Interpersonal Aspects

Conciliatory, placates, deferring, uncompetitive, "niceifier," unwilling to make critical comments.

Dependent, allows others to assume responsibility for self, childlike, immature, reliance on others to solve problems or achieve goals, to decide on employment/friendships/child management/vacations/clothing/purchases, absence of independent decision making, avoids external demands and responsibilities, low self-reliance, low autonomy, exaggerated and unnecessary help-seeking behaviors.

Submissive, dominated, secondary status, self-defeating, abused, unable to make demands on others, passive, docile, compliant, supplicating.

Abused, neglected, insulted, belittled, berated, "imprisoned," exploited, tolerates partner's abusive affairs/beatings/drunkenness/irresponsibility.

Self-sacrificing, subordinates own needs so as to maintain protective relationships/fulfill core role/identity, anxiously watchful and agitated.

Overdevoted, superloyal, attached, overloving, "love slob" sacrificing anything for "love," willing to tolerate more negatives in a relationship than the evaluator would.

Gullible, too trusting, easily persuaded, naive, unsuspicious, "Pollyanna," overhopeful of change.

Vicious cycle of dependency, abuse, separation/desertion, proof of helplessness and worthlessness, emotional devastation, terror of being unable to care for self/needs, avoidance of taking self-respecting or independent actions, lessened self-esteem, greater dependency.

Behaviors

General ineffectiveness in autonomy but not incompetence (may demonstrate exceptional skill in some areas).

Lacking in skills/motivation for independent life, ill equipped to assume mature roles.

Mood

Hidden depression and angers, whiny/tantrums/complains.

Tries to keep emotions under tight control.

Separation leads to depression/terror of abandonment.

Cognitions

Believes in magical solutions to problems, belief in salvation through love [AMOR OMNIA VINCIT].

Unimaginative/cognitively constricted.

Guilt proneness, assumes blame.
Unwilling to take risks for satisfaction.
Preoccupied with fears of desertion/inability to cope on own.
Reluctant to make decisions.
Fails to identify own needs.

Self-Image

Weak/helpless, self-derogating, belittling, martyr-like, self-sacrificing, low self-confidence, "inferiority complex," "stupid," untalented, unworthy, humble, self-effacing, self-deprecating, inadequate, inept, fragile.
Hidden strengths, denies/undervalues own skills, needs great encouragement.

13.14. Dissociative Identity Disorder

See also Sections 12.12, "Depersonalization and Derealization," and 13.10, "Borderline Personality."

The relevant ICD-9-CM and DSM-IV-TR code is 300.14, DID. Its previous name was Multiple Personality Disorder.

✓ **Note:** Most studies have found extensive overlap with the symptoms of borderline personality. Ross et al. (1990) have suggested that the crucial differentiator is some form of amnesia or blank spell in DID or MPD. Good references are Ross (1997) and Putnam (1989, 1991, 1997).

Characteristics of Separate Selves

One central self/primary/host personality: Depressed, anxious, compulsively good, "masochistic," moralistic, seeks treatment.
Other personalities/alters: Semiautonomous, numerous [3 to 100, mean = 15], some good and some bad, some believe that the host cannot handle memories/pain, some convinced that host must be punished/should die, may have mutual or unidirectional amnesias for one another and for host (odd names/characterological titles).
Common "roles" of alters: Child, protector, persecutor, an opposite-sex person, a perfect person.
Transitions: Sudden/unexpected, precipitated by stress or some regular pattern of social/environmental cues, often accompanied by headaches/feelings of weakness/amnesia/blackouts.

Presenting Symptoms

Coons and Milstein (1986) mention the following symptoms of DID/MPD, listed here in descending order of frequency:

Amnesia, depression, history of childhood sexual abuse, fugue, suicide attempts, auditory hallucinations, history of drug abuse, history of childhood physical abuse, sexual dysfunction, headaches, child personalities, history of alcohol abuse, history of any type of conversion disorder, history of rape.

These are also common:

Problems with showing anger/frustration/defiance, problems with trust/safety/betrayal/suspicion, assumes that she/he will be disbelieved.
Confusion about location/time/person, responding to more than one name, marked and rapid

shifts in personality, forgetting recent events, losing track of time, intense and sincere denial of responsibility when confronted, hearing of voices.

Extreme or odd variations in skills (e.g., handwriting), food preferences, artistic abilities, responses to discipline.

Self-injurious behaviors, somatic complaints or "conversion" symptoms such as sleepwalking, sudden blindness, loss of sensation.

The following characteristics of a history of sexual and/or physical abuse are frequently seen:

Believes self responsible for abuse suffered, believes deserved abuse because of badness/anger/imperfection, believes abuse will/does continue although impossible, DID/MPD as a form of coping with victimization.

13.15. Histrionic Personality

The relevant ICD-9-CM and DSM-IV-TR code is 301.50, Histrionic Personality Disorder.

✓ Current usage does not support "hysteric," and individuals with histrionic personality are not all females. *(See also the caution concerning sexism in Section 13.13, "Dependent Personality.")*

Cardinal Feature

Attention seeking through self-dramatization and exaggerated emotion.

Affects

Exaggerated, labile/vivid/shallow affect, easily "overcome" with emotions, easily enthused/disappointed/angered, excitable, theatrical/flamboyant/intensely expressed reactions, overly dramatic behaviors, creates dramatic effects/seems to be acting out a role, exaggerated and unconvincing emotionality, weepy sentimentalism.

Behaviors

Overreacts to minor annoyances, inappropriate.
Affectations/affected, overdetermined, facades.
Repeated/impulsive/dramatic/manipulative suicide gestures/attempts or similar threats.
Creative/imaginative/artistic, stylish, sensitive.
Stylized/caricatured "femininity"/"masculinity."

Cognitions

See Shapiro (1965).

Forgetting, repression, unreflective, self-distracting/distractible.
Lives in a nonfactual world of experience/impressionistic perception/recollection, global/diffuse, lacking in sharpness, nonanalytical.
Impressionable, susceptible to the vivid/striking or forcefully presented.
Magical solutions to problematical situations, hunches, "intuition," childlike, does not adapt to change well.
Superficial and stereotyped insights, "psychobabble."

Interpersonal Aspects

Exhibitionistic, dominates conversation, trivializes topics, lengthy dramatic stories, self-dramatizing, bragging, "life of the party"/center of attention, fickle, wants to please, excessive needs for attention/praise/approval/gratification.

Romantic outlook: Fantasies of rescue and victory; nostalgia, sentimentalism, idealization of partner; world of "villains and heroes"; makes poor social relationship choices and decisions, poor judgments about partners/friends/spouses; stormy relationships with little real or durable enjoyment, involvement in melodramatic situations.

Vain, initially seen by others as warm and affectionate, guileless, vivid. Later seen as selfish, narcissistic, shallow/superficial and insincere, ungenuine, inconsiderate, self-pitying, shows astonishment at little understanding of the implications of her/his behavior or its consequences/effects on others/destructiveness.

Oppressively demanding, taking without giving, egocentric, vain, petulant, easily bored, requires excessive external stimulation, attention-seeking, help seeking, manipulates for reassurances, manipulative, asserts "a woman's right to change her mind"/"masculine prerogatives."

Helpless, dependent, suggestible, uncritical, unassertive, sees assertion as rude or nasty, seen as fragile.

Impetuous, period of wild acting out, irresponsibility, chemical abuse/"bar hopping," "bed hopping"/sexual promiscuity/casual sexuality, low/poor impulse control/judgment/insight, thoughtless judgments.

Self-centered, feels hurt/deserted/betrayed in all relationships, brief and superficial contrition, sees self as sensitive and vulnerable, unsubstantial sense of self, absence of political or other convictions.

Coy, seductive, flirtatious, sexually provocative, blushes, easily embarrassed, giggles, naive, lacking in accurate sexual knowledge, seductive but for help rather than sex, seems preoccupied with sex, immature, self-dramatizing/sexy/flamboyant/dramatic clothing/hairstyle/ makeup, looks/dresses like a teenager/prostitute/"slut"/"tramp"/"boy toy"/"macho man."

Self-Image

Charming, gregarious, stimulating, playful, sensitive to others/feelings, selective incompetencies in areas of low importance (e.g., numbers, specifics).

Somatic Complaints

Vague, changeable, movable, "women's problems," complains of aging/appearance changes/loss of sexual skills or performances, "faints" at the sight of blood, swoons, "the vapors," feigns illness, always wrong weight, LA BELLE INDIFFÉRENCE (infrequent—about 30%).

13.16. Hypochondriacal Personality

See also Section 12.20, "Malingering."

The relevant ICD-9-CM and DSM-IV-TR codes are 300.7, Hypochondriasis; 300.81, Somatization Disorder.

General Characteristics

Data do not suggest a more frequent presentation of hypochondriacal personality in elderly persons or in females. Tyrer et al. (1990) have described the following characteristics:

Preoccupation with maintenance of health through dietary restriction/"healthy" or "natural" medications/vitamins/herbal products.

Distorted perception of minor symptoms so that they are elevated to major and life-threatening diseases. Never feels completely well.

Demands medical consultations for investigation/treatment/reassurance, seeks alternative health care providers when these are unproductive.

Rigid and persistent beliefs about health and lifestyles.

"Familiar face," "crock" (treated by a "quack"), "frequent flier," "thick-chart patient."

Dependent hostility (expecting both care and failure).

Multiple and changing complaints, unusual/singular somatic complaints that are described in affect-laden terms, strange aches and pains, chronic/unvarying fatigue.

Hypersensitivity to all medications, many foods, etc.

Joyless/unfulfilling lifestyle/overresponsible.

Multiple Personality Disorder   *See Section 13.14, "Dissociative Identity Disorder."*

13.17. Narcissistic Personality

The relevant ICD-9-CM and DSM-IV-TR code is 301.81, Narcissistic Personality Disorder.

Cardinal Feature

Self-centeredness.

Associated Features

Exhibitionism, craves adoration.

Self-Image

Grandiose self, fantasies of self-importance/uniqueness/entitlement/"specialness," easy loss of self-esteem, "a fraud/fake," times of intense self-doubt/self-consciousness.

Fantasies of continuous conquests/successes/power/admiration/beauty/love, brags of his/her talents and achievements, predicts great success for self, believes self entitled to/deserving of a high salary/honors/etc., overvalues all of his/her own achievements.

Interpersonal Aspects

Entitled, confident, self-assured, expects to be treated as a sterling success/gifted person or at least better than others, feels special and preeminent, hides behind a mask of intellectual or other superiority, exaggerated self-esteem easily reinforced by small evidences of accomplishment and easily damaged by tiny slights and oversights.

Compliment hunger, demanding of affection/sympathy/flattery/favors, insatiably requires acclaim for momentary good feelings, attention-getting behaviors.

Fragile self-esteem, loss of self-esteem when disapproved, crushed/inflamed by life's wounds, responds to criticism with rage/despair/apparent cool nonchalance, compulsive checking on others' regard, may ruminate for a long time over nonthreatening social situations and interactions, extensive brooding.

Relationships seen entirely in terms of what others can give rather than as exchanges, exploitative, lack of objectivity, arrogant, socially insensitive, resents any failure to immediately and totally gratify her/his needs, shallow relationships, finds it easy to revoke commitments she's/he's made, no deep or abiding relationships, flouts social rules, alternates between idealization of and arrogant contempt for friends, long history of erratic relationships, takes others for granted, drives people away, conversations so self-centered that others lose interest, understanding of social conventions is distorted by egocentrism.

Striking lack of empathy, indifferent to rights of others, neglectful, thoughtless, tactless, selfish, ungrateful, unappreciative.

Oppositional/argues with authorities/instructions/examiner/supervisor, insistence on having his/her own way, little attention paid to work tasks, lies to protect ego/privileges/position, rationalizes, self-deceives, distorts facts.

Grandiose, cocky, intimidating, belligerent, resentful, pretentious, sarcastic, cavalier, boorish, bumptious, obnoxious, self-indulgent.

Affects

Nonchalant/imperturbable/insouciant/optimistic unless ego threats/damage occur, chronic unfocused depression, absence of expressions of warmth.

Cognitions

Envy, solipsism, preoccupation with own performance's value.

Approval-Seeking Styles

The following table is put together by permission with statements from Goleman (1988).

Normal self-interest	*Self-defeating narcissism*
Appreciates praise but does not require it to maintain self-esteem.	Insatiable cravings for adulation; praise leads to momentary good feelings about self.
May be hurt temporarily by criticism.	Is inflamed or crushed by criticism, broods at length.
After a failure, feels unhappy but not worthless.	Failure sets off feelings of shame, enduring mortification and worthlessness.
Feels "special" or especially talented, but only to a degree or in some areas.	Feels far superior to everyone and superior in many ways, demands recognition for that superiority.
Feels good about self despite criticism.	Requires continual bolstering from others to have a sense of well-being.
Takes life's setbacks in stride, although upset temporarily.	Reacts with hurt, depression, or rage over prolonged periods.
Self-esteem is fairly steady in face of rejection, disapproval, and attacks.	Reacts to rejection, etc., with keen rage or deep depression and severe loss of self-esteem.
Does not feel hurt if no special treatment is received.	Feels entitled to special treatment; rules do not apply to him/her as to ordinary others.
Is sensitive to the feelings of others.	Is insensitive to others' feelings and needs, exploits others.

13.18. "Nervous" Personality

See Section 10.3, "Anxiety/Fear."

The most relevant ICD-9-CM and DSM-IV-TR code is 300.02, Generalized Anxiety Disorder.

"High-strung," worrier, "worry-wart," anxiety-ridden, "bad nerves," excitable, easily upset, unstable, moody, skittish, temperamental, low stress/frustration tolerance, "cracks up," "falls apart."

Picky, chronically dissatisfied, carping, fault finding.

Avoids/dislikes crowds, socially anxious, shy, sensitive, "thin-skinned," low self-esteem, hard on self and others.

13.19. Normal/Healthy Personality

See also Section 25.7, "Checklist of Strengths."

The relevant ICD-9-CM and DSM-IV-TR code is V71.09, No Diagnosis or Condition on Axis I/No Diagnosis on Axis II.

As alternatives to relying on the absence of pathology, here are several options for describing a healthy or highly functional personality–in other words, criteria for positive mental health.

Frisch (1999) offers these 17 areas of life function as assessed by his Quality of Life Inventory:

Health.

Work.

Creativity.

Love relationship.

Community.

Having a stable and adequate standard of living.

Neighborhood safety/aesthetics/naturalness/people.

Realistic self-regard.

Recreation.

Social service to others.

Friendships.

Relationships with relatives.

Having a philosophy of life.

Learning.

Civic action.

Relationships with children.

Having a home.

Positive psychology focuses on the healthy personality. Some resources for clinicians include Frisch (2006), Diener and Biswas-Diener (2008), and Lopez and Snyder (2009).

Freud's famous formula for normality was *"Arbeiten und leben"* (to be able to work and love).

Jahoda (1958) mentions the following:

Awareness, acceptance, and correctness of self-concept.

Mastery of the environment and adequacy in meeting demands of life.

Integration and unity of personality, whole-hearted pursuit of one's goals.

Autonomy and self-reliance.

Perception of reality and social sensitivity.

Continued growth toward self-actualization.

Shoben (1956) describes these characteristics:

Aptitude for capitalizing on past experience.

Self-control.

Ability to envisage ideals.

Social reliability (predictability).

Capacity to act independently while still acknowledging the need for relationships (interdependence).

Finally, W. C. Menninger (1967) offers these criteria for emotional maturity:

The ability to deal constructively with reality.

The capacity to adapt to change.

A relative freedom from symptoms produced by tensions and anxieties.

The capacity to find more satisfaction in giving than in receiving.

The capacity to relate to other people in a consistent manner, with mutual satisfaction and helpfulness.

The capacity to sublimate–to direct one's instinctive hostile energy into creative and constructive outlets.

The capacity to love.

13.20. Obsessive Personality

See Section 13.12, "Compulsive Personality," especially the "Note" there. See also Sections 12.8, "Compulsions," 12.21, "Obsessions," and 13.4, "A and B Personality Types."

The relevant ICD-9-CM and DSM-IV-TR codes are given in Section 13.12.

Cardinal Features

Overideational, worries, overconscientiousness.

Cognitions

See Shapiro (1965).

Ruminates, doubting, balances pro and con, overdeliberateness, "thinks too much," distrusts own judgments, flounders, dithers, ponders endlessly, indecisive, avoids decision situations, reverses decisions, wishy-washy, vacillates.

Must never be irresponsible/careless/unappreciative/bad/imperfect/flawed,[1] overresponsibility, fears making any mistake, overconscientious.

Overdependence on intellect and logic ("lives in head"), overconfidence in own willpower, intolerant of strong affects.

Preoccupation with trivial details, overconcern with technical details, compelled attention to details, "can't see the forest for the trees," "rearranges the deck chairs on the *Titanic*," a "fanatic," a stickler for details, gives unnecessary warnings and reminders.

Preoccupation with the mechanics of efficiency, such as list making/organizing/schedule making/revising/following rules; fears of loss of control.

Perfectionism, demandingness, rigidity, inflexibility, "never good enough," concern with doing things the one right way, judgmental, moralistic, controlled by "tyranny of the shoulds" (Horney), "musterbates" (Ellis).

Religious concerns, scrupulosity, seeking repeated reassurance from spiritual guides, repetition of religious rituals because of their possible invalidation, sense of sinfulness and guilt.

Attention rigidly and narrowly focused on own interests/technical indicators/details, novel stimuli rejected as distractions, discounts/rejects new ideas or data.

Behaviors

Procrastinates, dawdles, delays, avoids, denies, ineffective, important tasks done last, mistakes the immediate for the important.

Exquisite care of belongings/"preciousness," meticulous, preserves worthless items.

Tense activity, effortful, burdened, driven, suffers under deadlines, pressured, racing thoughts.

Mild rituals, ritualistic interests, repeated "incantations," magical thinking (e.g., her/his specialness, innocence, virtue).

Affects

Isolation of affect, loss of spontaneity, stiff and formal in relating, incapable of genuine/intense pleasure in anything, ambivalences, mixed feelings, chronic mild depression.

Terrified of being embarrassed/humiliated, fears being found inadequate/wanting/making a mistake.

Terror of the unknown/uncontrollable/unpredictable.

---

[1]This was suggested by Marcia L. Whisman, MSW, ACSW, of St. Louis, MO.

Detects/discovers feelings through own behaviors (e.g., "I'm crying so I must be sad").

Interpersonal Aspects

Proper, careful, dutiful, stilted, dogmatic, opinionated, inflexible.
Uncomfortable on vacations or unstructured times, forgets to "smell the flowers."
Demanding and controlling but resists others' control.

13.21. Paranoid Personality

See Section 12.24, "Paranoia."

The relevant ICD-9-CM and DSM-IV-TR code is 301.0, Paranoid Personality Disorder.

Cardinal Features

Distrust and vigilance.

Interpersonal Aspects

Distrusts, untrusting, mistrustful of others, overcautious, suspiciousness, unwarranted distrust, expects mistreatment and treachery, distrusts motives of others, suspects manipulations, distrusts previous "allies," questions loyalty of others, believes others are trying to put him/her at a disadvantage/plotting against/manipulating/watching/laughing at/commenting on him/her.

Skeptical/cynical view of others' motives, loyalty, interest in her/him.

Vigilant, sensitive to deception/betrayal/deprecation/slights/"putdowns," listens for insulting/questioning references, hypersensitivity to criticism, seeks signs of trickery/manipulation/treachery.

Guarded, defensive, reinforced expectations lead to isolation/enhancing distrust.

Hostile, belligerent, oppositional, confrontational, argumentative, stubborn, quick to take offense, easily offended, desire to vanquish/humiliate/deprecate, makes disparaging remarks.

Revenge fantasies, preoccupied with/desires to get even, carries grudges, schemes.

Desires to remain independent, no close relationships, refusal to confide, aloof, distant, isolated, withdrawn, retreats, secretive, terror of being controlled, continuous and extreme defense of autonomy, dread of passive surrender, a loner unless in total control of other/group, jealous of others' status.

Made indirect references/hinted/ideas of reference, knowing looks/winks/oblique references, power themes in all conversations.

Difficult, rigid, oppositional, deflects criticism onto others, recognizes no faults in self, denies responsibility or blame, blames others for all negative outcomes and frustrations, externalizes blame, never forgives or forgets, "chip on shoulder."

Carping, hypercritical, fault-finding.

Arrogant, prideful, overbearing, boastful, sensational plans, grandiosity, inflated appraisal of own worth/contacts/power/knowledge, takes a superior posture, disgusted by others' weakness.

Attention is narrowly focused on searching for confirmation/clues, novel stimuli are interpreted for real meanings, immune to contrary/corrective evidence.

Cognitions

See Shapiro (1965).

Projects onto others what is unacceptable about self, distorts the significance of actions and facts, loss of a sense of proportion.

Rigid and repetitive searching for confirmation of suspicions/ideas of reference/personalized meanings, attends only to conforming evidence/clues, belief in own convictions of underlying truth, magnifies minor social events into confirmations of the evil intentions of others and their lying, exaggerating distortions resulting in delusions, flimsy or unfounded reasons produce intense suspicion.

Vigilant, hypersensitive, hyperalert, oversensitive to any changes/the unexpected/anything out of the ordinary, fears of surprises.

Affects

Shallow emotional responses, cold and humorless, absence of tender or sentimental feelings, unemotional, restricted, enigmatic and fixed smile/smug, humorless.

Edgy, rarely relaxes, on guard, tense, anxious, worried, threatened, motor tension, touchy, irascible, jealous/envious of the progress of others.

Self-Image

Bitter, feels mistreated/taken advantage of/tricked/pushed around/overlooked/abused/threatened, collects injustices, suspects being "framed/set up."

Grandiose/self-important.

Sees self as objective, unemotional, rational, careful, "Just doing what's necessary to survive in a tough world."

Delusional System   *See also Section 12.10, "Delusions."*

Belief in unusual or irrational ways of knowing (e.g., reading the future, magical thinking, ExtraSensory Perception).

Delusions of power/status/knowledge/contacts.

Creates a "pseudocommunity" (Cameron & Rychlak, 1968) of persons for and against her/him, schemes, etc.

Other

Auditory hallucinations/voices that command, mock, or threaten.

Litigious tendencies.

Passive Personality   *See Section 13.13, "Dependent Personality."*

13.22. Passive–Aggressive Personality

The relevant ICD-9-CM code is 301.84, Passive–aggressive personality disorder. DSM-IV-TR offers Passive–Aggressive Personality Disorder (Negativistic Personality Disorder) as a diagnosis for further study.

Cardinal Features

Intentional ineffectiveness and unacknowledged hostility.

Interpersonal Aspects

Superficially submissive.

Indirect control of others without taking responsibility for actions or anger, denies/refuses open statements of resistance/maintains own "good intentions."

Cannot say a direct "No," indirectly expressed resistance to demands of others for performance, thwarts/frustrates authority/spouse/partners/relatives.

Intentional but unconscious passivity to hide aggression, denial of/confusion over own role in conflict, gives mixed signals ("Go away and come close"), hostile defiance alternating with contrition.

Overcritical, "left-handed" compliments, subtle attacks, blames, insults, complains to others, critical of boss/all authorities/those with power/control over him/her, carping/fault-finding as defense against intimacy/commitment, unnecessary and prolonged argumentativeness.

Autocratic/tyrannical, demanding, manipulative, harassing, ruminates, troubled/conflictual relationships.

Affects

Denial of most emotions (especially anger, hurt, resentment), hostile motives, deeply and persistently ambivalent, sullen, envious, resentful.

Vocational/Academic Aspects

Intentional inefficiency that covertly conveys hostility, veiled hostility, resents control/demands.

Qualifies obedience with: Tardiness, dawdling, sloppiness, stubbornness, sabotage, "accidental" errors, procrastination, forgetfulness, incompleteness, withholding of critical information/responses/replies, leisurely work pace, fails to meet deadlines.

Not lazy or dissatisfied with job, but spotty employment record/no promotions despite ability.

Psychopathic Personality   *See Section 13.7, "Antisocial Personality."*

13.23. Sadistic Personality

See also Sections 12.19, "Impulse-Control Disorders," 13.6, "Aggressive Personality," 13.7, "Antisocial Personality," and 13.8, "Authoritarian Personality."

Not in ICD-9-CM or DSM-IV-TR.

Cardinal Feature

Cruelty.

Behaviors

Demeaning, aggressive/dominating behavior pattern, embarrasses/humiliates/demeans others.

Brutal, enjoys making others suffer, has lied to make others suffer, intimidates/frightens/terrorizes others to gain own wants, restricts others' autonomy, uses power in harsh manner for discipline or mistreatment, uses threats/force/physical cruelty to dominate others, quickly escalates level of violence to reestablish dominance when challenged, fascinated by violence/injury/torture/weapons/martial arts.

✓ **Note:** According to Weinberg et al. (1984), *consensual* sadomasochistic activities have these characteristics:

1. Agreement about which partner is dominant/submissive ("top/bottom").
2. Shared awareness that they are play-acting ("in scene," "subspace," with costume, bondage equipment/"toys").
3. Informed, voluntary, explicit consent (agreed-upon "safe word" to stop, discussion of and respect for "bottom's" limits).
4. A sexual context.
5. Shared awareness that this behavior is sadomasochistic, "kinky," "BDSM," unusual, etc.

13.24. Schizoid Personality

The relevant ICD-9-CM and DSM-IV-TR code is 301.20, Schizoid Personality Disorder.

Cardinal Features

Social remoteness, emotional constriction.

Social Aspects

Solitary, aloof, social isolation, no close friends, "loner," withdrawn, unobtrusive, "fades into the background," remote, indifferent to others' praise/feelings/criticism, complacent.
Solitary interests, daydreams, self-absorption, may seem "not with it," inaccessible.
Limited social skills, lacking in social understanding, maladroit, says inappropriate things and may immediately apologize, unresponsive, unable to form attachments, peripheral roles, rarely dates or only passively, attends to only the formal and external aspects of relationships.
Normal or below-average work performance and achievement unless work does not require social contact.
Victimized, abused, taken advantage of.

Cognitions

Circuitous thinking, preoccupied with abstract/theoretical ideas, vague and obscure thought processes, unconventional cognitive approach, cryptic.
Intellectualizes, mechanical, impoverished/barren/sterile cognitions.
Vague and indecisive, absent-minded.
Excessive compulsive fantasizing, fantasies are sources of gratification and motivation, hostile flavor to fantasies.

Behaviors

Lethargic, low vitality, lack of spontaneity, sluggish.

Affects

Emotional coldness, limited capacity to relate emotionally, flat, impassive, blunted affect, emotional remoteness, absence of warm emotions toward others, no deep feelings for another, unfeeling, only weak/shallow emotions, weak erotic needs, cold/stark affects.

13.25. Schizotypal Personality

The relevant ICD-9-CM and DSM-IV-TR code is 301.22, Schizotypal Personality Disorder.

Cardinal Features

The interpersonal difficulties of the schizoid personality, plus eccentricities or oddness of thinking/behavior and/or perception.

Behaviors

Idiosyncratic, odd, curious, bizarre.
Odd speech with vague/fuzzy/odd/idiosyncratic expressions.
Odd clothing or personal style.

Cognitions

Magical thinking, superstitiousness, clairvoyance, telepathy, precognition, recurrent illusions, undoing of "evil" thoughts/"misdeeds," sometimes paranoid ideation and style.
Autistic, ruminative, metaphorical; poorly separates personal from objective, fantasy from common realities; dissociations/depersonalizations/derealizations; sees life as empty and lacking in meaning.

Affects

Chronic discomfort, negative affects, painfully shy.

Interpersonal Aspects

Suspicious, tense, wary, aloof, withdrawn, tentative relationships, gauche, eccentric, peripheral, clandestine, dull, uninvolved, apathetic, unresponsive or obliquely reciprocating.

13.26. Self-Defeating Personality

See also Section 13.13, "Dependent Personality."

Not in ICD-9-CM or DSM-IV-TR.

✓ **Note:** Beware of gender bias in the application of this diagnosis. *(See the caution concerning sexism in Section 13.13.)*

Cardinal Features

Chooses situations that will cause him/her to suffer mistreatment, failure, or disappointment.

Interpersonal Aspects

Excessive and unsolicited self-sacrifice, sacrifice induces guilt in others and then avoidance, provokes rejection by others and then feels hurt or humiliated, responds to success with depression/guilt/self-harming behaviors.
Avoids pleasurable or success experiences, does not perform success-producing tasks despite possessing the ability.
Rejects or does not pursue relationships with seemingly caring or needed/helpful individu-

als (e.g., a therapist), undermines self, "snatches defeat from the jaws of victory," chooses unavailable partners, seeks hurt/humiliation, sees those who treat her/him well as boring or unattractive, selects relationships with abusive persons, possibly sexually stimulated in relationships with exploitative or insensitive partners, "masochistic," incites anger/abuse/rejection.

Sociopathic Personality   *See Section 13.7, "Antisocial Personality."*

Tests of Personality   *See Section 13.2, "Assessment Methods."*

Type A and Type B Personalities   *See Section 13.4, "A and B Personality Types."*

C. The Person
in the Environment

The larger world that the client lives in, and how well or poorly he/she functions in it, are matters of concern. Therefore, this subdivision offers ways to describe the client's performance of the basic <u>A</u>ctivities of <u>D</u>aily <u>L</u>iving, his/her involvement in society and community, the extent and qualities of intimate relationships, his/her competence in vocational and academic skills, and other more specialized areas of evaluation.

14

Activities of Daily Living

✓ **Note:** If there are deficits in ADLs or there has been a change generally, indicate the reasons for this situation. And, as applicable, describe behaviors or deficits that limit independent living.

14.1. Assessment

The core ADLs are bathing, dressing–undressing, eating, transferring from bed to chair and back, using the toilet, and walking. Since we all depend on others for some supports, assessment has to take context into account.

Many measures, for different populations, can be found online. Some commonly used ADL assessment tools are listed below. Each entry offers the title of the current edition or version of each test (with acronym, abbreviation, or common name indicated as usual by underlining); its copyright date if known; its current publisher or distributor; and the applicable age range.

> <u>A</u>daptive <u>B</u>ehavior <u>A</u>ssessment <u>S</u>ystem–II (2003), Pearson Assessments, 0–89 years.
> <u>A</u>merican <u>A</u>ssociation on <u>M</u>ental <u>R</u>etardation <u>A</u>daptive <u>B</u>ehavior <u>S</u>cales—School, 2nd ed. (1993), PRO-ED, 3–18:11 years.
> <u>A</u>merican <u>A</u>ssociation on <u>M</u>ental <u>R</u>etardation <u>A</u>daptive <u>B</u>ehavior <u>S</u>cales—Residential and <u>C</u>ommunity, <u>2</u>nd ed. (1993), PRO-ED, 18–80 years.
> <u>A</u>daptive <u>B</u>ehavior <u>I</u>nventory, PRO-ED, 6–18:11 years.
> <u>S</u>cales of <u>I</u>ndependent <u>B</u>ehavior—<u>R</u>evised (1996), Riverside, infancy–80+ years.
> <u>Vineland</u> Adaptive Behavior Scales—II (three versions) (2005), Pearson Assessments, 0–18 years.

✓ Occupational therapists have many tools for assessment of specific ADLs and ways to intervene.

14.2. Assistance Level Required/Degree of Independence

> (↔ *by degree*) Incapable/unable, needs 1:1/hands-on assistance, limited by physical/medical conditions rather than psychiatric ones, only simple tasks, helps spouse/partner/family with chores, participates, needs to be reminded/prompted/monitored/supervised, does with help, finishes unassisted, initiates/independent/autonomous.
> ADLs done by spouse/partner by tradition/agreement/default/because of physical limitations.
> ADLs performed by children/relatives/landlady/landlord/live-in friend/paid helpers/publicly provided aides.

14.3. Child Care

(↔ *by degree*) Abuses, exploits, neglects, feeds regularly/appropriately/healthily, bathes regularly/ safely, changes diapers and clothes, dresses child appropriately for weather and setting, performs routines (bedtimes, up and off to school, mealtimes), is affectionate with, actively interacts with/enjoys child's presence, does not leave alone, babysits, defends, amuses/ entertains, teaches, enjoys child's growth, brags about, disciplines effectively, advocates for.

14.4. Chores/House Care/Domestic Skills

Cleaning

Food cleanup: Sets the table, clears table, washes, dries, puts away, silverware, does pots, uses dishwasher correctly, cleans up kitchen.
Neatens up house: Runs sweeper/vacuum, straightens up bedroom, takes out trash, dusts, mops, cleans bathroom.
(↔ *by degree*) House is immaculate/neat/clean/functional/cluttered/disorganized/chaotic/in disrepair/dangerous, filthy, infested, smells of _____.

Clothing Care

Laundry: Recognizes dirty, collects, separates, washes/runs washer, dries, folds, irons, puts away.
Sews/repairs/replaces.

Other

Maintenance: (↔ *by degree*) Recognizes malfunctioning appliances, recognizes emergencies, calls for help/repair persons, shovels snow, mows lawn, can turn off electricity and water supplies, changes light bulbs, does minor repairs, changes faucets/switches, does major repairs.
Decoration: (↔ *by degree*) Chooses bed covers/rugs, chooses and hangs curtains/slipcovers, paints, wallpapers, remodels.
Plant/pet care: (↔ *by degree*) Cares for plants, fish, cat, dog, safely and effectively.

14.5. Cooking

(↔ *by degree*) Must have all meals prepared and served, eats all meals out, eats only snacks/fast foods/prepared foods/takeout/carryout, prepares boxed or canned foods (e.g., canned soup and sandwiches), no/simple preparation, top-of-stove/light cooking (fries, boils), full menu, nutritionally balanced, uses all kitchen appliances, coordinates foods' types and preparation times, bakes, entertains.

14.6. Financial Skills

See also Section 17.4, "Math Ability."

(↔ *by degree*) Has receptive and expressive recognition of denominations of coins/metal money/ currency/checks, counts, makes change, handles all finances on a cash basis, can perform arithmetic calculations sufficient to allow over-the-counter purchases, buys money orders, uses debit card, has checking account (writes checks, deposits checks, able to do routine banking), saves money for large purchases, has credit card, manages all financial resources.

($\leftrightarrow$ *by degree*) Squanders resources, impulsive/inappropriate/useless/wasteful purchases, easily duped into situations leading to financial risks/difficulty, not able to manage own finances, mathematically/intellectually/emotionally incompetent/incapable, not financially competent, able to handle small sums but not larger sums/own purchases/checking account/bill paying/saving/investing.

14.7. Hazard Recognition and Coping

Traveling

Wanders away from home.
Gets lost; does not recognize route home, streets, or house numbers.
Travels through dangerous places unaware of risks.
Fails to look for approaching traffic.
Does not respond to stop or direction signs when walking.

Fire

Knows how to evacuate home.
Can check and service smoke alarm.
Overuses electrical outlets or extension cords, does not replace frayed/loose wires.
Smokes in bed or reclining chair, careless with matches/candles.
Heats home with oven, lets food burn.
Recognizes smell of gas, but searches for gas leak with a flame.

Home Care

Cannot state what to do about a leaking faucet or pipe.
Cannot keep thermostat at a regular setting.
Leaves doors or windows open inappropriately.
Mixes or misuses cleaning products.
Fails to clean up spills, broken glass, or other risks safely.
Fails to care for pets/plants, causes suffering or death.

Food Preparation

Does not eat healthily (only snacks, meals too small or too few, fails to follow prescribed diet).
Does not store food safe from deterioration, will consume spoiled food.
Fails to set proper cooking temperatures, fails to monitor cooking progress on stove/oven/toaster/microwave.
Leaves refrigerator/oven open, water running, food to burn.

Clothing

Wears loose or otherwise dangerous clothing.
Clothing inappropriate for weather or season.

Illness/Injury

Does not recognize signs of serious illness or injury and respond appropriately (cleaning wound/burn, ointment, bandage, taking medications, seeking professional help).
Does not take medications appropriately or as prescribed, takes wrong doses, wrong schedule.
Does not recognize side effects of medications.

Hazard Recognition: Summary Statements

Cannot be left unattended because simply cannot respond appropriately to environment.
Appears to be completely unaware of dangers, risks, and demands of situation.
Knows functions of police, fire, emergency medical services and how to reach them.

14.8. Living Situation/Level of Support Needed

($\leftrightarrow$ *by degree*) Lives independently in own home/apartment, uses community's support services (e.g., soup kitchen, food bank/community pantry, "Meals on Wheels," homemaker services, special buses), lives with spouse/children/partner/parental family/relatives/friends/roommate, occupies single/sleeping room with/without cooking facilities, lives in monitored individual apartment, attends partial/day hospital/sheltered workshop/day activities center, lives in residential drug/alcohol treatment program, in rehabilitation facility, in a Community Living Arrangement/Community Rehabilitative Residence/group home/supervised group apartment, in a boarding home, in a custodial/domiciliary care facility, in a personal care home/nursing home, in a Skilled Care Facility, in an Acute Care Facility, in a private/community/state/city/Department of Veterans Affairs hospital, in an Intensive Care Unit.

14.9. Quality of Performance

Each area of ADL performance can be evaluated as to its safety, independence, appropriateness, and effectiveness.

Has a history of accidents/is "accident-prone," performance of ADLs is unsafe/self- and other-endangering (e.g., gets lost, burns food).
Is aware/unaware of the large hazards of life and can/cannot avoid them.
($\leftrightarrow$ *by degree*) Makes it worse, disorganized, ineffective, needs to be redone, unacceptable, sloppy, casual, neat, orderly, fussy, fastidious, meticulous, obsessive.

14.10. Self-Care Skills

Eating and Toileting

Feeding: ($\leftrightarrow$ *by degree*) Cannot feed self, assists with own feeding, feeds self.
Eating: Eats ir-/regularly, appetite in-/appropriate, food preferences, good/poor balance/nourishment, restrictions, allergies.
Toileting: Problems with elimination/urination/using toilet, uses laxatives/stool softeners/etc., incontinence (stress, night/day), uses pads.

Grooming   *See also Sections 7.1, "Appearance," and 7.2, "Clothing/Attire."*

Bathing: Bathes ir-/regularly, requires prompting, attends to basic hygiene, uses makeup/shaves, gets haircuts, trims nails.

Dressing: (↔ *by degree*) Dons and doffs clothing, dresses self, dresses appropriately for weather/occasion, does laundry, buys clothing.

Health Care

Exercise: (↔ *by degree*) No activity, stretching, regular exercise, aerobic movements.

Sleep: (↔ *by degree*) Sleeps well, has occasional difficulty, has significant problems. *(See Section 12.37, "Sleep Disturbances.")*

Medications: Takes prescribed medications without prompting, with reminders/prompts/urging/seldom/irregularly/refuses, misuses/takes other's medications, takes many unnecessary over-the-counter medications.

14.11. Shopping

(↔ *by degree*) Unable to shop alone, can for snacks/toiletries/own clothes/simple foods/prepared foods/full menu foods/presents, can run errands for self/others, shops as entertainment, waits for and recognizes bargains/sales, makes major purchases effectively.

Is able to estimate the costs of common foods/items, knows which store sells which kinds of merchandise, can separate needs from wants/can control impulse shopping, is a wise consumer.

14.12. Transportation

(↔ *by degree*) Does not travel at all, needs companion, uses special bus/paratransit/"jitney"/taxi/regular buses/mass transit, gets about by walking/bicycling/hitchhiking, driven by family/friends/spouse/etc., drives with companion, drives alone, vacations independently.

14.13. Caregiver Burden

Needing to feed/toilet/dress/clean up after other.

Time demands, lessened or no privacy, routines disrupted, personal plans and activities disrupted, lessened self-care.

Caregiving is confining, restricts travel/visiting/employment/recreation/church involvement/etc.

Financial losses/costs of care/strains.

Difficulty accessing services.

Disturbed sleep, physical strains, injuries.

Interpersonal emotional disruptions (e.g., arguments, noncooperation, withdrawal, false accusations), loss of life partner without death, feeling overwhelmed.

14.14. Summary Statements

Level of personal independence is adequate, given SocioEconomic Status and lifestyle.

The client has adapted well to reduced circumstances.

ADLs

She is intellectually and psychologically capable of performing ADLs but does not, due to physical limitations/primarily due to physical/medical circumstances.

He is not able to care for his own needs, and so requires _____ support services. *(See also Chapter 22, "Recommendations.")*

She is functional in her current lifestyle/supportive situation, but in a more independent setting (i.e., living independently/alone), she appears to lack adequate self-direction and other resources for maintenance/continued functioning.

For a Child:

He goes to bed by himself and does not need a night light.
She does not go into parents' bed during night.
Child can sleep over at friend's house or visit for a day.
Self-care is age-appropriate.

15

Social/Community Functioning

This chapter covers **social and community activities** only. Descriptors for **interpersonal behavior in the interview** can be found in Chapters 8 and 9, and for **couple and family relationships** in Chapter 16.

✓ **Note:** If social relating has been reduced in any area, try to indicate why and when this happened.

15.1. General Lifestyle

Location

Rural, farm/ranch, suburban, urban, small/medium/large city, commuter, inner city.

Qualities (↔ *by degree*)

nomadic	**unstable**	**solitary**	low variety	**low activity**	comfortable
vagrant	limited by	vegetative	low stress	no productive	independent
wanders	poverty	homebound	low intensity	activities	autonomous
migratory	survival	reclusive	low demand	low ambition	satisfied
roams	marginal		minimal	unproductive	productive
"street person"			mundane	indolent	
panhandles			circumscribed	recumbent	
			constricted		
parasitic			limited		
predatory			regressed		
symbiotic			centers around		
			TV		
chaotic			routine		
			simple		
			monotonous		
			regularity		
			"just killing		
			time"		

SOCIAL
FUNCTIONING

15.2. Involvement in Social/Community Activities

($\leftrightarrow$ *by degree*) The following groupings are sequenced by increasing degree of involvement.

Hermit, recluse, isolated, withdrawn, aloof, avoidant, no interest in social relationships, uninterested in people and relating, no social activities, keeps to self.

Goes only to medical appointments/etc., no outside interests or functioning in any organizations, talks on phone, visited but does not visit, gardening/bird watching/other solitary pursuits, hunts/fishes alone, attends sporting events as spectator.

Window-shops, church attendance only on major holidays, visits/goes out with/drinks with friends, drops in on nearby friends, writes to or calls friends, hangs out with/visits family/neighbors, eats out with others, regular "coffee klatch"/"breakfast club"/"night out," interested/participates in community groups, small outings (church, bingo, bowling, senior center, movies), friends help if he/she is sick, gets along selectively/appropriately with friends/family/authorities/public, shops in a variety of stores for all needs.

Gregarious, actively participates in church/religious group/social club/commercial sports weekly or more often, has out-of-town guests, goes to movies/sports events, visits museums, participates in musical and other cultural activities, votes in elections.

Attends adult school or classes, active in the community, plans life goals/self-improvement, plays team sports, visits out of town alone, does volunteer work, fully participates in society.

✓ **Note:** If client reports "attends church/temple/synagogue/mosque" or "plays cards," inquire what she/he does there, what the name of the clergyperson is, or which games are played. This will enable you to assess level of interests, demands (active or passive, skill or chance), satisfactions, and the quality and intensity of her/his social performance.

For a Child:

✓ Because a child's social activities are usually dependent on a caregiver's efforts, question carefully to separate out child's interests, skills, and performance.

15.3. Problems/Conflicts in Community Relating

Problems at Work   *See also Chapter 17, "Vocational/Academic Skills."*

Warnings, close supervision/monitoring, reprimands, suspensions, firings.
Fighting/arguing with peers, given "cold shoulder," teases/provokes, threatening/disruptive behaviors.

Legal Aspects

Police contacts, warnings, tickets, summary offenses, arrests (indicate for what, when, with whom, and consequences), misdemeanor/felony, trials, convictions, probation, jail/prison time, parole.
History of public drunkenness, <u>D</u>riving <u>U</u>nder the <u>I</u>nfluence/<u>D</u>riving <u>W</u>hile <u>I</u>ntoxicated, assaults.
Evictions, bankruptcies.
Conflicts with neighbors, agency personnel, landlords/landladies, store clerks.
Child/spouse/partner/relative/animal abuse, <u>P</u>rotection <u>F</u>rom <u>A</u>buse orders.

16

Couple and Family Relationships

DSM diagnoses are almost exclusively about individuals, not intimate relationships, situations, or interactions. Yet current understandings of disorders emphasize interactions, stressors and diatheses, family therapy, systems thinking, etc. Therefore this chapter lists several ways to evaluate couple and family relationships and interactional processes, and I would be grateful for your suggestions of more and better ways.

✓ You can record much useful information about couples and families on a genogram. *(See Section 6.6, "Family Genogram/Family Tree/Pedigree.")*

16.1. Systemic Family Constructs

Structure/coupling: Involvement, enmeshed vs. disengaged (Minuchin, 1974), isolation, individuation, power structure.

Boundaries: Rigidity vs. flexibility, closed vs. open, generational boundaries.

Coalitions: Schism, skew (Lidz & Fleck, 1985), pivotal members, dyads, triangles, labels, identifications, mappings, alliances, interfaces, relationship of spouses.

Style: Closed (traditional/authoritarian) vs. open (collaborative/democratic), random (individualistic/permissive) vs. synchronous (perfectionistic/consentient); note family image vs. actual behaviors on these style criteria.

Dynamics:
  How problem works, who is involved, who is served by the problem.
  Motivators, demotivators.
  Strengths.
  Disablement: Who is blocked from which targets, collective failings.

Subsystems:
  Couple system, sibling system, intergenerational system.
  Boundaries, patterns, alliances, ethnic influences, "shoulds," conflict and cooperation, cutoffs.
  Other subsystems: Friends, work, school, church, professionals, agencies.
  Support systems: Relatives, friends, etc.

Other aspects:
  Family lifestyles, themes, myths (security, success, taboos, secrets).
  Pseudomutuality (Wynne, 1988).

247

Scapegoating (Ackerman, 1982): Scapegoat, persecutor, family healer.
Paradoxes, double binds (Bateson, 1972).
Discordance, disturbance, disruption.
Centripetal and centrifugal family interaction patterns (Beavers, 1990).

Formulate hypotheses re: maintenance of symptoms, functional analysis, payoffs, trade-offs, homeostasis.

16.2. Assessment of Families at Intake

✓ Evaluate both current and previous marriages/relationships/families.

Presenting Problem, <u>C</u>hief <u>C</u>omplaint/<u>C</u>oncern, Referral Reason

These are listed in alphabetical order.

Abuse/violence/neglect (spouse/partner, child; sexual, physical).
Adolescent adjustment problem.
Chemical abuse (parent, child).
Child behavior problem/parenting problem.
Child custody.
Divorce mediation/adjustment.
Enrichment (marital, family, personal, relationship).
Health/medical/nutritional/physical conditions.
Legal difficulties (child, parent, other; civil, criminal, misdemeanor, felony; incarceration).
Marital/couple conflict.
Parenting (skill enhancement).
"Poor communication."
School problem (behavior, academic, peer).
Separation/breakup, spouse/partner absence.
Sexual dysfunction/patterns/conflicts.
Time management/conflict/absence. [Ask about each member's daily schedule.]
Truancy/runaway.
Other: Cultural problems, religion, job/financial problems, education, peer problems, relatives.

Who?

Ask these questions:

"Who is seeking treatment? Why?"
"Who is involved in the problem?"
"Who currently resides in the household?"

Perceptions of Problem and Circumstances

Ask:

"What is _____'s (the referrer's) perception of the problem?"
"Why is help being sought now?" (Possible precipitants: Changes, births, illnesses, deaths, re-/marriages, divorces, moves, job changes, departures, other transitions.)
"What is each family member's perception of . . .
    the problem?"
    the major tasks/changes desired/facing the family now?"
    the time frame for improvement?"
    who has the problem (i.e., is the <u>I</u>dentified <u>P</u>atient)?"

Previous Solutions

Find out about the following:

> Efforts/attempts, outcome, ineffective attempts to maintain homeostasis.
> Previous treatment of whom, for what, when; intervention, outcome.

Developmental Issues

Learn about individual development issues for children and adults.

> History of adults' relationship:
> > How met, courtship, each family's attitude.
> > Relationship to grandparents, other relatives.
> > Beginning expectations, satisfaction/fulfillment levels.
> > Children's birth, blended family (if applicable).
> Family stage/life cycle: Courtship, early marriage, child bearing, child rearing, parents of teen-agers, launching, middle years, retirement, transitions.

Legal and Social Status

Ascertain the following:

> Adults' current status—describe as:
> > Never married, "single," living together, People of Opposite Sex Sharing Living Quarters, par-amours, "live-ins," roommates, boyfriend/girlfriend, fiancé/fiancée, common-law mar-riage, civil law partners, married, "commuter marriage," separated/living apart, estranged, divorced, remarried, marriage of convenience/outward appearance of a marriage.
> Previous relationships/cohabitations/marriages: For each, note duration, satisfaction, reasons ended/termination reasons, age and date at termination.
> Number, names, ages, and genders of all children.
> Relationship with spouse/partner, ex-spouse/partner (if applicable), children.
> Adultery/extramarital relations/satellite relationships, expectations of exclusivity/monogamy.
> Whether an adult is in process of divorcing/ex-spouse-to-be/"pre-ex."

Other: Summary Statements

> _____ [name] is ignored by, distanced, never/rarely visited, only fought with, only contacted by phone, estranged, struggling to individuate from family of origin.
> _____ [name] feels he/she gets much/some/no support from spouse/ partner in parenting/child management/child raising/child care, doing chores, handling finances, dealing with relatives, doing home maintenance, supporting household.
> Child rearing is viewed as unsuccessful/overwhelming/stressful/difficult at times.
> A high priority/high risk/danger/matter of great seriousness is _____ (specify).
> _____ is an emergency/crisis/critical need, recurrent crisis/problem requiring only ordi-nary procedures, past crisis/chronic crisis.

16.3. Family Interviewing Method

Questions to Ask Each Member

> "What are the main problems in your family?"
> "What do you have to do in this family to . . .
> > be alone/maintain your privacy?"
> > get others to stop bugging you?"

get attention, appreciation, physical contact, love?"
be listened to?"
get the family together?"
"When do you feel . . .
tense, depressed, upset, worthless?"
best, freest, most worthwhile, proudest, optimistic, loving, loved?"
you have to conceal your feelings/fake it?"
"How do you show your feelings of . . .
anger, disappointment, frustration, sadness, tension?"
affection, love, appreciation?"
"Whom do you depend on?"
    "Whom can you count on to . . . ?"
    "Who helps with . . . ?"
"What big changes/problems have happened in this family?"
"Have you been disappointed in your marriage/family/children/relatives?"

Questions to Ask the Family as a Group

"Do you ever plan things you can all do together?"
"What are your family's biggest goals/plans/fears?"
"What are the strengths in this family?"
    "Who has athletic skills? Manual skills? Academic skills? Musical skills?"
    "Best sense of humor? Smartest? Most faith?"
"Besides you, who else is part of this family?" (Relatives, friends, boarders, pets, etc.?)
"When do you all get together?"
"Who's the boss of this family?"
"Who calls the shots in what areas?"

16.4. Child Rearing/Raising: Aspects

Parental Restrictiveness

Limits: Overprotection/excessive restriction, overpermissiveness/indulgence, unrealistic demands.

Strictness/leniency re: feeding, mobility, interruption by children, table manners, neatness, cleanliness, bedtime, noise, radio and TV, chores, obedience/compliance, aggression.

Restrictiveness regarding sexuality (nudity, modesty, masturbation, sex play), anger, emotionality.

Aggression: Encouraged to fight back/defend self, toward parents/sibs/peers, inhibited, redirected.

Parental differences: High/low ratio of maternal to paternal discipline, mother/father views other parent as overly strict, conflicts over discipline.

Problematic discipline: Lack of discipline, inconsistent discipline, chaotic/harsh/overly severe discipline, fear/hatred of parent, decreased initiative/spontaneity, unstable values.

Parental Acceptance

Warmth: Sympathetic/rejecting response to crying, open/muted/no demonstrations of affection, fun/no fun in child care, great/little/no warmth of bond, playtime initiated by mother/father/no one.

Use of praise: For table manners, for obedience, for nice play/amount of play, no use of praise.

Other: Positive/negative feelings when pregnancy discovered.

16.5. Couple Relationships: Aspects

For questions and descriptors pertaining to sexual aspects of couple relationships, see Sections 3.25, "Sexual History," 6.4, "Adjustment History," and 10.12, "Sexuality." See also Sections 12.1, "Abuse," and 12.5, "Battered-Woman Syndrome."

Dating Intensity (↔ *by degree*)

Never, seldom/rarely, only periodic/special events/holidays, group/car date/dyadic, "gets together with," interested in more dates but ... (specify), frequently, dates compulsively/promiscuous, many dating partners, has many/only brief relationships, "dating" same person for many years, exclusive relationship/"going steady," serial monogomy, progressively better relationships, has a single committed long-term relationship.

Other Qualities (↔ *by degree*)

Physical/verbal/emotional abuse, abusing spouse/partner, abused spouse/partner, neglecting, exploitative, punishing, parasitic, repeatedly unfaithful, avoidant, fragile, distant, boring, stale, stalemate, "truce," unhappy, mismatched, ill-considered, hasty, unhealthy, unsupportive, limiting, unsatisfying, symbiotic, stable, functional, adequate, satisfying, rewarding, close/tight, intimate, enhancing, loving, fulfilling.

16.6. Summary Statement

The family history is positive for _____, _____, and _____ (specify conditions) involving an immediate/nuclear family member.

The V codes in ICD-9-CM and DSM-IV-TR offer many labels for relationship issues and problems. (*See Section 21.21, "V Codes, Etc."*)

RELATIONSHIPS FUNCTIONING

17

Vocational/Academic Skills

This chapter covers much of the information you may need for **disability reports**, as well as other evaluations of vocational and academic functioning.

17.1. Basic Work Skills

Energy Level (↔ *by degree*)

Sickly, easily fatigued, requires frequent rest periods, low energy, adequate/normal, healthy, vital, vigorous, has stamina, excessive, driven.

Motor Skills

Coordination

(↔ *by degree*) Poor coordination, good/adequate/normal dexterity, dexterous, excellent coordination.

✓ Pay particular attention to different types of coordination (eye–hand, cross-body, fingers, etc.), as well as to balance, gait, and other job-relevant aspects of movement.

Fine Motor Skills

Can make fast/repeated movements of fingers/hands/wrists, can use hand/power tools safely and effectively, writing is legible, requires and benefits from _____ as assistive equipment.

Gross Motor Skills

Strong, can stretch/bend/twist/reach/etc. rapidly and effectively, can run/climb/jump, can lift/carry heavy weights, can carry medium weights (suitcase, stepladder, etc.), can hold but not lift/carry objects.

Hearing

No significant limitations, copes with the use of hearing aid/sign language/interpreter/written communications/etc.

Vision

Normal or near-normal vision with/without glasses/contact lenses, some difficulties, requires modification of work setting/equipment/procedures.

Appearance (↔ *by degree*)

Shows minimal/unacceptable regard for personal attire or cleanliness, disheveled and sloppy/wears dirty clothes, needs a bath or shave, adheres to standards of nonoffensive personal cleanliness, is cleanly but inappropriately dressed, appears typical of his/her community's workers in grooming/cleanliness/attire choice.

Concentration (↔ *by degree*)   *See also Section 11.4, "Concentration/Task Persistence."*

Deficiencies of attention/persistence, low frustration tolerance, occasionally distracted, can focus and maintain attention for expected periods.

Motivation to Work (↔ *by degree*)

Refuses, apathetic, indifferent, is minimally motivated/compliant without complaint/positive/eager, willing to work at tasks seen as monotonous or unpleasant.

Memory (↔ *by degree*)

Is unable to retain instructions for simplest of tasks, requires constant/hands-on/one-on-one supervision/continual reminders/prompts/cues/coaching to perform routine tasks, requires reinforcement to retain information from day to day, requires little or no direction after initial instruction or orientation, remembers locations/work procedures/instructions/rules, able to learn job duties/procedures from oral instructions/demonstrations/written directions, carries out short/simple/detailed/multistep instructions.

Mistakes (↔ *by degree*)

Makes an un-/acceptable number of errors that must be corrected by client/coworkers/supervisors, does not notice exceptions/failures, has low/poor/adequate/high inspection skills, monitors own quality, conceptualizes the problem, corrects situation/alters own behavior, quality/accuracy increases (or waste/scrap decreases) with repetition/training/supervision.

Productivity (↔ *by degree*)

Minimal/below expected/equal to _____% of average competitive worker's rate/quantity of work, increased production/productivity by _____% over original measured rate, quantity/productivity increases with practice/repetition/training/supervision, shows acceptance of competitive work norms, able to enter and sustain competitive employment.

Attendance (↔ *by degree*)

Unreliable/inadequate/minimal/spotty/deficient, has unusual/large number of unexcused absences per month/calls in sick, seldom/generally punctual for arrival/breaks/lunch hours, performs without excessive tardiness/rest periods/time off/absences/interruptions from psychological symptoms, dependable, responsible.

VOCATION/
ACADEMICS

Communication (↔ *by degree*)

Seldom communicates beyond the minimum and often misunderstands directions, is misunderstood by peers/supervisors, can comprehend some nonconcrete aspects of work situation, communication is usually understood by others, communications are clear and work-relevant, uses telephone properly, has the ability to ask questions or seek assistance as needed.

Response to Supervision (↔ *by degree*)

Rebels against supervision, is oppositional to requests of supervisor, does not seek supervision when needed, personalizes supervisor–worker relationship, often withdraws/refuses offers of interaction, is difficult to get along/work with, requires firm supervision, asks for unnecessary help/requests excessive supervision, interacts with the general public/coworkers/supervisors without behavioral extremes/appropriately, reports appropriately to supervisor, improves work methods/organization under supervision, works in small/large groups, is helpful to supervisor and peers.

Emotional Responsiveness (↔ *by degree*)

Tends to become emotional/angry/hurt/anxious when corrected/criticized/cannot have own way and is unable to continue work, argues, responds angrily or inappropriately to comments but with counseling or encouragement can remain at work site, verbally denies problems but has an "accident" whenever eligible for promotion or transfer, maintains composure and attention to task, takes corrective action, anticipates others' needs, responds appropriately by adjusting behavior or work habits, apologizes, reacts appropriately to conflict/authorities/peers/coworkers, maintains even temperament.

Adaptability (↔ *by degree*)

"Set in her/his ways," exhibits serious adjustment problems when work environment changes, is unable to cope with job's pressures, displays inappropriate or disruptive behavior only briefly after work changes and is able to return to task with supervisory encouragement, generally adapts to/copes with/tolerates work changes/schedules/deadlines/interruptions/pressures, accepts instructions/criticism/authority/supervision/feedback/rules, relies on own resources, learns from mistakes/instruction/supervision.

Hazard Awareness

Oblivious to/aware of hazards and able to take precautions, seems to be "accident-prone" beyond usual frequency of accidents.

Decision Making (↔ *by degree*)

Cannot make simple decisions to carry out a job, indecisive, confused by choices and criteria, cannot organize himself/herself/prioritize work/arrange materials, becomes paralyzed by decisions, makes correct routine decisions, handles exceptions and disruptions, makes up own mind, effectively sequences steps in a procedure.

Pacing/Scheduling (↔ *by degree*)

Cannot conform to a schedule/tolerate a full workday/perform within a schedule/sustain a routine, shows an uneven/unsteady work pace throughout workday, shows necessary/expected/normal/required stamina, maintains motivation, completes assignments, finishes what she/he starts, continues despite obstacles/opposition/frustrations, works in a time-conscious manner.

Conscientiousness (↔ *by degree*)

Irresponsible, unaware/inconsistently aware of the consequences of own activities, wastes materials/damages equipment, does not adjust/maintain or service/repair/replace equipment and materials as needed, cares for tools/supplies/equipment/products effectively.

Travel to Work (↔ *by degree*)

Will not use available travel options, makes unreliable travel arrangements, travels reliably to work site, uses public transportation effectively, drives to work consistently.

Relationship to Peers/Coworkers (↔ *by degree*)

Avoidant, distant, shy, self-conscious, nervous, conflictual, domineering, submissive, competitive, suspicious, attention-seeking, clowning, immature, provocative, inappropriate, dependent, troublemaker, ridiculing, teasing, <normal>, friendly.

Maladaptive or Odd Behaviors

Too introverted/withdrawn, loud/domineering, manipulative/takes advantage of peers, limits conversation to "yes" or "no" answers, will not look at person he/she is addressing, gossips, will not start a conversation, seeks unwanted/ill-timed/inappropriate physical contacts, has attention-getting odd behaviors/offensive personal hygiene, confuses actual and imagined abilities, makes excessive or unrealistic complaints.

Assessment

The following tests are commonly used for assessment of basic vocational skills and for guidance. Each entry offers the title of the current edition or version of each test (with acronym, abbreviation, or common name indicated as usual by underlining); its copyright date if known; its current publisher or distributor; and the applicable age range.

Differential Aptitude Tests for Personnel and Career Assessment, 5th ed. (1990), Pearson Assessments, grades 7–12 and adults.
Holland Self-Directed Search (1994), *www.self-directed-search.com*, high school and older.
Strong Interest Inventory (1994), Consulting Psychologists Press, adolescents and older.
Kuder Occupational Interest Survey, *www.kuder.com*, adolescents and older.

17.2. History of Work

Ask the following questions:

Has client ever been employed/"worked"/had a wage-earning job outside the home? If so, number/duration/kind of jobs?
Is client currently employed/unemployed/laid off/underemployed/retired? If employed, is employment marginal/labor pool/temporary/seasonal/part-time/full-time?
Is employment history regular/irregular/interrupted/sporadic? Number and reasons for firings? Problems with absenteeism, conflict with customers/peers/coworkers/supervisors?
Any job trials, work attempts, job coaches, job-finding clubs, work-hardening programs?

VOCATION/
ACADEMICS

Have any background factors (e.g., medical, home, school) kept client from benefiting from formal education?

Does client have a history of low productivity/achievement/advancement throughout life?

17.3. Language Skills: Reading and Writing Ability

See also Section 18.4, "Reading Materials."

Reading Comprehension

Test client with a paragraph from a magazine on a current topic, and ask about its meanings.

(↔ *by degree*) Alexic, illiterate, functionally illiterate, lacks basic/survival reading skills.

(↔ *by degree*) Names letters, says simple words, reads out loud/silently, only small sight reading vocabulary, reads signs/directions/labels/instructions/recipes, low/normal comprehension, deciphered word meanings, slow reader, basic functional literacy, no reading for pleasure, usual skills, literate, avid, scholarly.

Summary Statements

His/her reading is limited to a small group of memorized words.

He/she has rudimentary phonetic abilities, but cannot decipher unfamiliar or phonetically irregular words.

His/her poor reading skills prohibit responding to/guidance by written instructions.

She/he worked hard, asked appropriately for assistance, recognized errors, used word attack skills to successfully identify/decipher unfamiliar words on a reading test.

Reading skills are adequate for basic literacy and utilization of written materials for getting directions.

Literacy

"Functional literacy" varies with time and location, because it is the ability to use reading, writing, and computational skills at a level adequate to meet the needs of everyday situations.

(↔ *by degree*) The following three paragraphs are sequenced by increasing degree of functional literacy.

Extremely low literacy: Grammatical errors producing confusion, missing punctuation, misspelling common words, childish word choice, malformed letters, swear words/insults.

Low to low-average literacy: Spelling as words sound, incorrect punctuation, slang terms, vague expressions/terms.

High literacy: Complex sentence structure where appropriate, sophisticated word choice, correct spelling and punctuation, abstract thoughts, powerful metaphors, lucid.

Spelling/Writing

Spelling: (↔ *by degree*) Agraphic, letter–sound relationships are absent/poor/need strengthening, spelling skills are poor/good/excellent, shows/demonstrates a solid grasp of underlying phonetic principles.

Writing from dictation: Reversals, omissions, substitutions, additions, confused attack on letters, labored writing, reckless spelling.

Handwriting: Good/poor quality, problems with upper-/lower-case letters, inversions, reversals, confused one letter with another, degree of effort required, awkward handgrip position/use of the page, size of letters.

Statements of Implications for Vocational/Academic Functioning

Relationship of client's skill level to expected school/work achievement is ... (specify).
Areas of educational strength/weakness/handicap and need for intervention suggest ... (specify).

17.4. Math Ability

See also Section 14.6, "Financial Skills."

($\leftrightarrow$ *by degree*) The following groupings are sequenced by degree of increasing skill.

Anumerate, can say the digits, knows the sequence, holds up the correct number of fingers when asked for a number, counts items, knows which number is larger.

Can do simple tasks of counting and measurement but not computation beyond addition and subtraction.

Can do simple addition and subtraction of single-digit/double-digit numbers but only when borrowing is not involved.

Ability limited to simple computation in orally presented arithmetic problems, can do problems requiring addition/subtraction/multiplication/division.

Can solve problems when regrouping is required.

Can correctly do problems involving decimals/fractions/measurements. Understands prices, counts change, makes change, possesses basic survival math (measurements, portions, percentages, fractions, weights, etc.), knows basic business math/consumer's math, is fully numerate.

17.5. Special Considerations for Disability Reports

✓ If a client has an attorney and is not working, record this in the report.

✓ Note also that in a disability report, you should not state unequivocally that the client is or is not "disabled." This is usually an administrative decision and is based on criteria beyond just your findings.

17.6. Vocational Competence/Recommendations

Overall Competence: Summary Statements

Normal

This client is capable of performing substantial gainful employment at all levels.
There are no psychological barriers to employment.
She can perform in a competitive work setting/in the open labor market.

Somewhat Limited

He is intellectually limited, but not to the extent that would preclude appropriate employment.

She could understand, retain, and follow instructions within the implied limitations of her borderline intellectual functioning/mild mental retardation/mild intellectual disability.

The client is able to understand, retain, and follow only simple, basic instructions.

He would be able/unable to meet the quality standards and production norms in work commensurate with his intellectual level.

She can perform activities commensurate with her residual physical/functional capabilities/capacity.

He is able to relate to coworkers and supervisors, handle the stresses and demands of gainful employment within his intellectual/physical limitations.

Significantly Limited

He/she can function only in a stable setting/sheltered program/very adapted and supportive setting.

The client requires appropriate prevocational experiences/work adjustment training/work-hardening program/diagnostic work study/evaluation of vocational potential.

This person can/can't tolerate pressures of workplace, is un-/used to the regularities and demands of the world of work.

No Residual Functional Capacity for Substantial Gainful Activity.

The cumulative impact of the diagnoses presents a very significant deterrent/obstacle to employment/productivity/substantial gainful activity.

Setting and Tasks Needed

($\leftrightarrow$ *by degree*) The following groupings are sequenced by degree of increasing demand on the client.

Nonstressful/unpressured/noncompetitive setting, simple/basic/repetitive/routine/noncomplex/slow-paced/unpaced/nonspeeded tasks that do not require facility in academics.

Solitary/nonsocial tasks, working alone/no contact with the public.

Closely supervised.

Sheltered/highly supportive, stable.

Part-time/flexible hours, full-time, overtime.

Employment Level ($\leftrightarrow$ *by degree*)

Unskilled/helper/laborer, semiskilled, skilled, professional, managerial, self-employed.

Supervision ($\leftrightarrow$ *by degree*)

Requires continual redirection, repetition of instructions, working under close and supportive supervision, instruction only, monitoring only, occasional overview, can work independently.

Ambition ($\leftrightarrow$ *by degree*)

Avoidant, lethargic, indolent, listless, lackadaisical, self-satisfied, content, eager, persistent, hopeful, ambitious, enterprising, greedy, selfish, opportunistic, pretentious, unrealistic.

Self-Confidence ($\leftrightarrow$ *by degree*)

Highly/counterproductively self-critical, has low opinion of own abilities, normally self-assured, realistic self-appraisal, overconfident, impractical/unrealistic confidence, grandiose.

Job Seeking/Hunting

(↔ *by degree*) The following groupings are sequenced by degree of increasing effort on the client's part.

Poor/low/inadequate knowledge of vocational and educational resources.

Employment is seen as too/highly/moderately/mildly stressful.

Has no actual or realistic history of seeking, efforts have been episodic/half-hearted, efforts have been determined but initiative is now exhausted.

Has job-finding skills/interviewing skills, can identify obstacles to successful completion of training/skill development/employment, has a feasible vocational goal/time frame for actions.

Obstacles to Success: Summary Statements

This client is academically so deficient that he/she cannot find or hold a job.

Engages in excessive off-task behaviors.
She invents excuses for lateness/absences/mistakes/inattention, is irresponsible.
He avoids some essential tasks.
She engages in inappropriate or disruptive behaviors/agitates intentionally.

She does not work effectively when under any/normal/expected pressure.
He responds to criticism with anger/anxiety/hurt/withdrawal.

She uses/overuses offensive language.

The client does not appear disabled, but is not employable because ... (specify).
In the course of his life he has changed jobs to manage his symptoms better.

18

Recreational Functioning

18.1. Entertainment: TV/Radio/Music

(↔ *by degree*) Avoids, dislikes, confused/overstimulated by, just as background/passive listener, aware of news/weather, selective/chooses/plans for particular programs, "Must see my stories/soaps," recalls, actively records/purchases music, attends musical events regularly, plays musical instrument.

18.2. Hobbies

(↔ *by degree*) No hobbies, does puzzles/plays computer games/letter games/board games (cards, checkers, Monopoly), does crafts/needlecrafts, tinkers, paints by numbers/in water/oil/ acrylics, builds models, takes photographs, hunts/fishes, gardens, reads, collects, repairs, plans, travels, builds.

Cares for pets (feeds, exercises, cleans up after, grooms, teaches, consults veterinarian, etc.).

Recreational use of the Internet: Reads magazines/news articles/blogs, e-mails, shops online, uses search functions, is a member of e-mail lists (listservs), writes using word processor, writes a blog.

Plays online games (Sudoku, card games), Multiplayer Online Games such as Second Life.

Uses social networking websites (Facebook, MySpace, Twitter, etc.).

For a Child:

Plays with toys/dolls/miniatures, builds models (airplanes, cars, etc.), has/maintains collections.

18.3. Sports

Specify the sport(s) with which the client is involved.

(↔ *by degree*) Watches on TV, attends/spectates, reads about, discusses, participates in, Special Olympics, bowling league, plays on sports team, has individual sport(s), regularly participates in sport, competitive player.

Exercises regularly, walks, jogs, aerobics, health club, golfs, swims, lifts weights, other.

18.4. Reading Materials

See also Section 17.3, "Language Skills: Reading and Writing Ability."

Newspapers (↔ *by degree*)

Headlines only, comics, horoscopes, simple stories, advertisements/prices, classifieds, news, columnists, editorials, news analyses, arts sections, reviews.

Magazines (↔ *by degree*)

Word-finding magazines, children's books/magazines, comic books, adventure, gossip, supermarket, women's, men's, newsweeklies/current events, crosswords, science fiction, special interest (e.g., war, detective, biker, guns, wrestling, hobby, trade, technical, professional, literary, arts).

Books (↔ *by degree*)

Comics/picture, children's books, graphic novels, romances, short stories, mysteries, novels, Westerns, horror, adventure, science fiction, contemporary literature, poetry, biographies, self-help, nonfiction, texts, classics.

18.5. Participation/Performance Quality

(↔ *by degree*) No recreational activities, nothing for relaxation/fun, very few pleasurable activities, moderate interest in recreation, active and satisfying recreational life, recreation integrated into work and social lives.

(↔ *by degree*) Discontinues, has many unfinished projects, completes but only at a very low quality, takes much longer than usual/previously, is very slow, forgets, neglects/distracted from activities, finishes only the simplest/quickest, usually completes, always finishes, compulsively completes.

For a Child:

(↔ *by degree*) Autistic movements/manipulation, watches/participates passively only, parallel play, stereotyped actions built into toys, has imaginary playmates, takes active part in play/sporting activities, creative, makes own toys, involves others.

19

Other Specialized Evaluations

This chapter covers a variety of other dimensions of functioning that clinicians are often asked to evaluate.

19.1. Coping Ability/Stress Tolerance

See also Section 6.4, "Adjustment History."

Types and Dimensions

Instrumental, affective, and escape coping.
Frustration tolerance, ability to delay gratifications, tolerance for ambiguity/uncertainty/conflict/low information/structure, hardiness.

Coping Skills (↔ *by degree*)

Inept, incompetent, "can't cope," unadaptable, rigid, inflexible, stubborn.

Has developed specific psychological skills: Anger management, assertiveness, rational self-talk, has developed self-soothing techniques.

Uses social support system/friendships/informal consultants.

Resourceful, skilled, "survivor," courageous, realistic, adaptable, flexible, adjusts, conforms, bends, resourceful, "just down on his/her luck," valiant, proud.

Assets/Strengths and Liabilities/Weaknesses   *See Section 25.7, "Checklist of Strengths."*

19.2. Culturally Sensitive Formulations

Culture may include ethnicity, race, religion, social class, gender, age, and similar categories. We all know that culture can affect behaviors, personality, self-image, symptoms, complaints, response to treatment, and other clinical data. These interactions are very complex, usually underestimated, and poorly understood. To add to the complexity, some aspects of culture may affect some clinically interesting phenomena in different ways and to different degrees in different people.

Our ethical guidelines require us to have "cultural sensitivity (i.e., awareness of cultural variables that may affect assessment and treatment) and cultural competence (i.e., translation of this awareness into behaviors that result in effective assessment and treatment" (Paniagua, 2005, p. 8). It is impossible to know well all of the cultures we encounter as clinicians, but we must learn what we can, and we should be constantly aware of our assumptions, expectations, stereotypes, and ethnocentrisms.

DSM-IV-TR (American Psychiatric Association, 2000) offers some guidance. First, what little is known is indicated in the DSM-IV-TR's descriptions of many disorders, under "Specific Culture, Age, and Gender Features." Second, DSM-IV-TR's Appendix I contains a "Glossary of Culture-Bound Syndromes," as well as an extremely useful "Outline for Cultural Formulation," which is adapted (by permission of the American Psychiatric Association) and expanded below. Please consider this only a beginning, and just one formulation of factors to be considered.

1. The client's cultural identity:
   a. Ethnic or cultural reference group as seen in his/her preferred self-descriptions.
   b. Degree of involvement with the culture of origin and host culture.
   c. Language abilities and preferences, ability to switch between standard English and the language used with family and friends, preference of idioms, etc.
   d. Other aspects of communication, such as interpersonal distance and eye contact.
   e. Other behaviors, such as clothing choices, food preferences, and religious practices.

2. The individual's cultural explanation for the illness:
   a. The "idioms of distress through which the symptoms ... are communicated (e.g., 'nerves,' possessing spirits, somatic complaints, inexplicable misfortune)."
   b. The "meaning and perceived severity of ... symptoms in relation to norms of the cultural reference group."
   c. The explanatory models of causation offered by the culture.
   d. Expectations about the course and outcome of the disorder.
   e. The use of any culture-bound syndrome diagnoses (see the "Glossary" in Appendix I of DSM-IV-TR).

3. "Cultural factors related to psychosocial environment and levels of functioning." These include culturally relevant interpretations of the following:
   a. Social stressors of all kinds and sources. These may include traumatic experiences of losses, deaths, torture, dislocation, separation, flight, etc., due to war, disaster, persecution, or other experiences unfamiliar to you as the clinician. Attend to racial and ethnic prejudice, victimization, oppression, and rejection.
   b. Supports of all kinds, including ones the clinician may not use. DSM-IV-TR suggests investigating the "role of religion and kin networks in providing emotional, instrumental, and informational support." Also investigate individual coping strategies, defenses, and attitudes toward helpers.
   c. The resulting levels of functioning and disability, again within the client's culture's expectations. Also, inquire into the client's history of higher and lower functioning.

4. "Cultural elements of the relationship between the individual and the clinician":
   a. Differences in social status.
   b. Racial, ethnic, religious, and other differences.
   c. Any "problems that these differences may cause in diagnosis and treatment (e.g., difficulty in communicating in the individual's first language, in eliciting symptoms or understanding their cultural significance, in negotiating an appropriate relationship or level of intimacy, in determining whether a behavior is normative or pathological)."
   d. The patient's current preferences for and past experiences with professional and culturally sanctioned sources of care and about expectations for treatment.

The best and most readily available introductory books in this area are by Sue and Sue (2008), Pedersen et al. (2008), Ponterotto et al. (2010), Tseng (2003), and Paniagua (2005).

19.3. Developmental Stages

Erikson's (1963) "eight stages of man" are highly psychosocial and hopeful. Each stage presents a challenge to the ego to learn new adaptive skills or suffer limitations on ego identity.

Psychosexual stage	Crisis/conflict	Strength, virtue
Oral–sensory	Basic trust vs. mistrust	Drive, hope
Muscular–anal	Autonomy vs. shame, doubt	Self-control, will
Locomotor–genital	Initiative vs. guilt	Direction, purpose
Latency	Industry vs. inferiority	Method, competence
Puberty and adolescence	Identity vs. role confusion	Devotion, fidelity
Young adulthood	Intimacy vs. isolation	Affection, love
Adulthood	Generativity vs. stagnation	Production, care
Maturity	Ego integrity vs. despair	Renunciation, wisdom

Mahler's (1975) stages: **Normal autism, normal symbiosis, separation–individuation (subphases: differentiation, practicing, rapprochement, individuality, and emotional object constancy). Splitting, reintegration vs. fragmentation.**

Piaget's stages (see Gruber & Von Eiche, 1977): **Sensorimotor, preoperational, concrete operations, formal operations. Assimilation, accommodation, conservation.**

Freud's stages: **Oral, anal, phallic, latency, genital.**

Maslow's (1962) hierarchy of needs: **Physiological, safety, belongingness/social, esteem, cognitive, aesthetic, self-actualization, peak experiences.**

In Kohlberg's (1984) stages of the development of moral reasoning, morality is defined as follows at each stage:

Premoral level	1	Obedience to avoid punishment.
	2	Gains reward. Instrumental purpose and exchange.
Conventional level	3	Gains approval and avoids disapproval of others. Interpersonal accord and conformity.
	4	Defined by rigid codes of "law and order." Social accord and system maintenance.
Principled level	5	Defined by a "social contract" agreed upon for the public good. Utility and individual rights.
	6	Personal moral code based on universal, abstract ethical principles.

19.4. Financial Competence/Competence to Manage Funds

See also Section 14.6, "Financial Skills," and 14.11, "Shopping."

✓ **Note:** "Incapacitated" is currently preferred to "incompetent," as it is less sweeping and focuses on receiving and evaluating information, which are more capable of accurate evaluation.

Standards/Criteria

Ability to manage own property/likelihood of dissipating own property.
Likelihood of becoming the victim of designing persons.
Ability to make or communicate decisions about the use and management of entitlements.

Components of Financial Competence Assessment

Psychological/psychiatric evaluation/<u>M</u>ental <u>S</u>tatus <u>E</u>valuation/data base of testing of orientation, memory, judgment, reading ability, emotional disturbance, intelligence. Address issues like these:

- This person's orientation to time, place, person, common items.

- Presence or absence of adequate memory functions, social judgment, test judgment, control of emotions.

- Quality of person's reality contact (delusions, hallucinations, thought disorder, disordered thought processes, etc.).

- Person's ability to recognize currency, make change, identify values/costs of several common items, do simple/basic arithmetic, perform relevant calculations.

- Person's factual knowledge of the source and extent of her/his assets, understanding of financial terms and concepts.

- Person's functional ability/behavior, such as observed/historical ability to conduct transactions/conserve assets, competent performance of financial management/responsibilities, perception of situations of potential exploitation.

Summary Statements

On the basis of the present evaluation, this person is considered to be ...
   incapacitated in all financial areas.
   able to manage only small amounts of money, about $_____ to $_____.
   able/not able to manage his/her property, likely/unlikely to dissipate/squander his/her property.
   able/unable to manage benefits/entitlements, and make long-range financial decisions autonomously, responsibly, and effectively.
   likely/unlikely to fall victim to/become the victim of designing persons, be exploited.
   able/unable to make/communicate responsible decisions about the use and management of his/her entitlements and assets.
   likely/unlikely to hoard funds rather than make necessary purchases.
If benefits are awarded, this person would use the money for drugs/alcohol/gambling or disorganized/impulsive purchases, and therefore he/she may/will/should not be the best recipient of funds for his/her management.

19.5. Homosexual Identity: Stages of Formation

Coming out to oneself, family, and others is a difficult, continuing, and universal struggle. There are several models in use, but the most widely accepted is this set of seven stages about identity, partly quoted and partly adapted from Cass (1979).

   Confusion: Conscious awareness that homosexuality has relevance to oneself: "My behavior may be called homosexual. Does this mean that I am a homosexual?" → turmoil, alienation, searching → denial of personal relevance, antihomosexual stance, or inhibition of homosexual behaviors → foreclosure.
   Comparison: "I may be homosexual" → "I'm different, I don't belong to society at large," "I do not want to be different."
   Tolerance: "I am probably a homosexual."
   Acceptance: "I am a homosexual."

Pride: "Gay is good," "Gay and proud."

Activism: Confrontation activities, disclosure as a strategy. "How dare you presume I'm heterosexual?" Also, "them and us"—"Homosexual is good, heterosexual is bad."

Synthesis: "There are some heterosexual others who accept (my) homosexual identity as I do." At this stage homosexual identity is no longer "seen as *the* identity, it is now given the status of being merely one aspect of self."

19.6. Impairment's Effects on a Person

($\leftrightarrow$ *by degree*) Has become psychotic, suicidal, decompensated, devastated, catastrophic reaction, regressed, denial of event or its consequences, overwhelmed, maladaptive, deteriorating, marginal functioning, depressed, adjustment disorder, prolonged/delayed mourning, saddened, adjusting to disability/losses, adequate/fair functioning, functional, adapting, assimilating, accepting, accommodating, using psychological coping mechanisms, compensating, has devised compensatory/prosthetic/mnemonic/coping devices, successful, mature, is challenged, is growing, overcompensating.

Summary Statement

The cumulative impact/effect of this client's emotional and physical impairments results in no/insignificant/mild/significant/moderate/severe/crippling limitations.

19.7. Puberty

Puberty is physical; adolescence is social.

Tanner Staging System

Several decades ago, Tanner (1962) defined the stages of puberty as follows:

Stage	Pubic hair	Breast	Penis	Testes
I	Preadolescent	Preadolescent	Preadolescent	Preadolescent
II	Sparse, long, lightly pigmented, downy, straight hair	Breast bud; breast and papilla elevated, with increased areolar diameter	Slight enlargement	Enlarged scrotum, pink, texture roughened
III	Increased pigmentation, more curly	Enlarged breast and areola with no contour separation	Increased length	Increased size
IV	Adult type, but less	Areola and papilla form secondary mound	Glans enlarged, increased breadth	Enlarged, scrotum darker in color
V	Adult distribution with spread to medial thighs	Nipple elevated, areola contour continuous with breast	Adult size	Adult size

Tanner's data were based on European children and on North American children of European descent. There are variations between ethnic groups; for example, people of African ancestry tend to begin puberty 1–2 years earlier. Moreover, with better nutrition, the age of puberty is decreasing for all ethnic groups. Precocious puberty is defined as follows: male, genital stage II before age 9½ years; female, breast or pubic hair development before age 8 years. The sequence of hair development is pubic first, then axillary, then facial. About 40% of girls will have menarche by stage II and 90% by stage IV. The median age for first ejaculation in boys is between 12½ and 14 years in the United States, and is affected by psychological and cultural as well as hereditary and biological factors. First ejaculation usually occurs about 1 year after the accelerated penile growth. Gynecomastia is common (up to 70%) in young adolescent boys and usually resolves within 1 year.

19.8. The Refugee Process

This material is adapted by permission from Gonsalves (1992).

Phases of the Process

> Preflight: Mounting anxiety, sense of abandonment, "victim of fate," "no one cares."
> Flight: Traumatizing experiences, varying in intensity, duration, and number; returning as intrusive memories, often on anniversary dates.
> Resettlement: Complex; a lifetime process of coping with different language, traditions, etc.

Stages of Resettlement

Early Arrival

From 1 week to 6 months after their arrival in the new country, refugees learn the surroundings/"lay of the land"; remain involved with their homeland; and experience disorientation, low energy, sadness/loss, anger, guilt, relief, and excitement. Examiners should be alert to possible PTSD symptoms.

Destabilization

From 6 months to 3 years after arrival, refugees acquire survival tools; develop a support group; and learn the language/social customs/culture due to economic pressures. They may experience great stress and pain, hostile withdrawal from the new culture, resistance to the new culture, or uncritical compliance with the new culture. They generally view the old country as better, feel lonely, and show denial.

Exploration and Restabilization

From 3 to 5 years after arrival, refugees usually develop more flexible culture-learning methods, and often experience marital conflict and adjustment. They may also resist further adaptation; remain linked to other refugees; experience anger at their lowered status, fear of failure, and isolation; and/or undergo premature culture or identity closure.

Return to Normal Life

From 5 to 7 years after arrival, refugees generally maintain flexible cultural accommodation while retaining some old values; develop realistic expectations for new generations; develop a positive identity; and expect these personality changes to last. They may also show delayed grief reactions, and experience rigidity and intergenerational conflict.

Decompensation

Some refugees may decompensate at any time from 1 week to 7 years after arrival, as they struggle to meet survival needs; modify identity; enter the new culture; continue family commitments; and connect to the past, present, and future. They may experience psychosis, identity disorders, depression, and existential crises.

19.9. Religious and Spiritual Concerns

The relevant DSM-IV-TR and ICD-9-CM code is V62.89. *(See Section 21.21, "V Codes, Etc.")*

✓ **Note:** It can be very difficult to distinguish a religious crisis from a manic episode, delusions from personalized beliefs or overvalued ideas, or obsessive scrupulousness from piety. Different religious traditions raise different spiritual issues, so please use your knowledge to modify these points for the evaluation of religious and spiritual concerns.

History

Ask about the following:

Role of religion during childhood, adolescence, adulthood; church attendance, praying, holidays.

Spiritual concerns during these periods: Existential concerns, search for life-guiding values, spiritual health.

Past and present religious affiliations/membership, attendance, involvement in activities such as individual and communal prayer, meditation, meeting with a spiritual leader, study of scripture, etc.

Frequency of religious observance—describe as:
Only in crises, holidays/with family, routine, daily.

Attitude/devotion/commitment—describe as:
Compulsive, pious, observant, routine, agnostic, hostile, atheistic.

Perception of Higher Power/God/prophets.

Concerns about Morality

Conflicts among moral/ethical behavior of self or others, values, religious training, society.

Excessive or minimal guilt, feelings of being punished, need to atone, inability to feel forgiven.

Confusion about sin/evil, right vs. wrong, responsibility, practices.

Concerns Related to the Loss or Questioning of Faith

Differences/conflicts/problems with a church/organization, teachings, clergy, scripture/sacred texts/prayers (e.g., hypocrisy).

Doubts because of injustice/suffering/illness/deaths/unfulfilled prayers.

Anger, fears, or distrust of Higher Power.

Doubts because of loss of control/illness/losses/despite religious conformity or sinlessness.

Difficulty believing in or getting closer to a Higher Power.

Conflicts between concepts of a Higher Power as judgmental and demanding vs. accepting, loving, and forgiving.

Concerns Related to Conversion from or Marriage into a Different Faith

Difficulties with initiation procedures into new faith.

Being considered apostate/unchurched/lost/dead by family/members of former faith.

Questions about arrangements of marriage, handling of ceremonies/holidays, religious training of children.

Concerns about Death and Suicide

Fears about dying (e.g., unfinished spiritual business, arrangements for funeral/burial).
Beliefs about what happens after death (e.g., reunion with decedents/never-ending sleep/darkness, judgment after death, an afterlife in Heaven or Hell, reincarnation, etc.).
Religious beliefs against suicide.

Religious Experiences

Responses to prayer or effects of praying.
A vocation/call.
Special revelations.
Demonic possession, being the Messiah/a prophet/etc.
Abandonment by God.

Other Concerns

Demand for a therapist of client's faith.

19.10. Testamentary Competence/Competence to Make a Will

The individual must understand (1) the nature and extent of her/his property; (2) the identity and relationships of the usual beneficiaries; and (3) the nature and (4) effects of making a will. The book by Melton et al. (2007) covers testamentary competence in detail.

D. Completing the Report

The chapters in this last subdivison of Part II flow logically. They start with a pulling together of your findings and observations, so that you can offer a diagnosis that is a professional shorthand version of your conclusions. From these two summaries of your understanding of the client, you are in a position to make meaningful recommendations for treatment or other services. Then you can offer a statement of expected outcomes—a prognosis. The last chapter addresses the issues of closing the report and contains the standard language.

20

Summary of Findings and Conclusions

20.1. Overview

The summary of findings and conclusions is the place to offer your integration of history, findings, or observations, and your understanding of the client's functioning in the areas most relevant to the referrer's or reader's needs. If there is a referral question, it is likely to be answered here. However, for referral questions seeking a disposition, a separate "recommendations" section may be a more appropriate heading for such an answer *(see Chapter 22, "Recommendations")*. A summary is the appropriate place to review the episode of therapy you have conducted or the conclusions you have drawn from an evaluation you have conducted. Diagnostic statements are usually also in a separate section *(see Chapter 21, "Diagnostic Statement/Impression")*. But if there are no changes to a previous diagnosis, that statement can be included in the summary.

Because there will always be readers who need or want to read only a brief summary, be sure to include the information or conclusions with the most important implications for the client.

20.2. Beginning the Summary

Open the summary with one of these phrases or a similar version:

> **In summary/In short/To summarize** ...
> **In my professional opinion, and with a reasonable degree of professional/medical certainty** ...

Then give a brief description of the client's demographics:

> **(Name of client)/this (age), (gender), (any other decision-related factors, such as marital status or parental status) client/patient/consumer/etc.** ...

Under the "Attributions" heading, "Getting Oriented to the *Clinician's Thesaurus*" provides other terms to use for variety in referring to a client.

20.3. Summary of Previous Information

Condense the background information and history *(see Chapter 6)* and the referral reasons *(see Chapter 5)* into a few sentences or a short paragraph.

20.4. Relevant Findings and/or Conclusions

In a separate paragraph, or as part of the summary of previous information, offer only the most referral-relevant three or four major findings or conclusions. For treatment summaries, offer the most important themes of the therapy process, with an eye to assisting the client's next therapist. For other situations, tailor the list of your findings to your understanding of the report's audience.

For testing reports, findings should be organized by topic (integrating the results of different tests)—such as cognitive functioning, emotional controls, interpersonal relations, etc., depending on the referral questions. A reliability statement is also needed (*see Section 4.6, "Reliability/Validity Statements"*).

> *If the psychological symptoms presented may be due to a medical condition, see Chapter 29, "Psychiatric Masquerade of Medical Conditions."*

20.5. Diagnostic Statement

Generally a diagnostic statement is in a separate section of a report, following the summary of findings and conclusions. However, if the diagnosis is simple or does not alter current treatments or previous diagnoses, it can be included in this summary section. (*For more on diagnoses, see Chapter 21, "Diagnostic Statement/Impression."*)

20.6. Consultations and Further Evaluations

Record the following about all outside consultations performed on the client: reasons/need; type of evaluation; name(s) of consultant(s); date(s) performed; conclusions and recommendations; and, if not apparent, the locations and dates of the original copies of those consultations (so that they can be requested by others).

If your suggestions for further evaluations are simple or routine for your setting, they can be included here; if they are more complex, describe them more fully in the recommendations section of your report (*see Chapter 22, "Recommendations"*).

20.7. Summarizing Treatment

Services Provided

Record the types of services rendered (consultation, assessment, evaluation, treatment, etc.), as well as the number of sessions (including those missed, as relevant) and the dates of the first and last sessions.

Termination

Note the source of the decision to terminate (client, therapist, client and therapist together, agency, managed care, other), as well as the reason(s) for termination. Descriptors for termination reasons include:

> **Refused services, excessive/unexplained no-shows, little/no progress, planned pause in treatment, successful completion of program/achievement of goals, transfer to another therapist or service provider because ...** (specify), **referred elsewhere, no longer eligible for services because ...** (specify), **other** (specify).

Outcome Summary Statements

Treatment has been a complete/partial/minimal success.
Some/the majority of/nearly all goals were exceeded/achieved/not achieved.

This patient has followed a productive hospital course.
He is in good remission due to medications/is in good chemical remission.
She has received maximum benefit from treatment/hospitalization/services.

Treatment received has had no success/been ineffective in removing/reducing symptoms.
Treatment has had a negative outcome for this patient.
This patient's condition has shown adverse reactions/worsened/stayed the same/shown no improvement.

Disposition

Describe the disposition of the case as appropriate (inactive, closed, transfer, aftercare, referral).

21

Diagnostic Statement/Impression

Although they are not so tightly tied to treatment in the mental health field as in medicine, diagnoses are a kind of professional shorthand for integrating many kinds of data. In most cases, your diagnosis should follow from and sum up the data you have reported earlier. A diagnosis also orients your reader to the recommendations and treatment planning that follow it.

Generally offer only the most important one or two diagnoses, unless diagnosing was the reason for the referral, you are in training, or your setting's culture requires a fuller listing. You should include all five axes of a DSM-IV-TR (or ICD-9-CM) diagnosis and any "Rule-Outs" or other qualifications (*see Section 21.1, below*). Offer a "diagnostic impression" if you are not qualified to offer a DSM-IV-TR diagnosis or if you are quite uncertain.

21.1. Qualifiers for Diagnosis

A DSM-IV-TR diagnosis may be described or qualified with one of the following terms:

> Initial, deferred, principal, additional/comorbid, Rule Out ..., admitting, tentative, working, final, discharge, in remission, quiescent.

DSM-IV-TR offers these qualifiers: If the criteria are currently met for a diagnosis, Mild, Moderate, or Severe; or if the criteria are no longer met, In Partial Remission, In Full Remission, or Prior History. Not Otherwise Specified is used when not all the criteria are met.

ICD-9-CM does not have qualifiers that apply broadly across diagnoses, but, like DSM-IV-TR it offers qualifiers for some specific conditions.

21.2. ICD Versions

Currently the United States uses both DSM-IV-TR (2000; *see Section 21.3*) and the *International Classification of Diseases*, 9th revision, Clinical Modification (1980, but updated yearly). The ICD-9-CM was made the official standard for medical records and payment for health care by the Health Insurance Portability and Accountability Act of 1996, which was implemented in 2003. ICD-10 (World Health Organization, 1992) is used in the rest of the world and is due to become the standard in the United States in October 2013 (as required by the Department of Health and Human Services). More information on all of these can be found at the website of the Centers for Disease Control and

Prevention (*www.cdc.gov/nchs*). In the lists that follow, the abbreviation cce means <u>C</u>onditions <u>C</u>lassified <u>E</u>lsewhere (usually medical, not psychiatric, disorders).

21.3. DSM-IV-TR

The current U.S. reference for mental disorder diagnoses is the *<u>D</u>iagnostic and <u>S</u>tatistical <u>M</u>anual of Mental Disorders*, <u>Fourth</u> Edition, <u>T</u>ext <u>R</u>evision (American Psychiatric Association, 2000).

The DSM-IV-TR system is **multiaxial**. The five axes are as follows:

Axis I: Clinical Disorders (but not Personality Disorders) and Other Conditions That May Be a Focus of Clinical Attention (most V codes; *see Section 21.21*).
Axis II: Personality Disorders (long-standing patterns, in adults) and Mental Retardation.
Axis III: General Medical Conditions.
Axis IV: Psychosocial and Environmental Problems. *(See Section 21.22.)*
Axis V: <u>G</u>lobal <u>A</u>ssessment of <u>F</u>unctioning Scale. *(See Section 21.23.)*

The major categories and the diagnoses presented in the bulk of this chapter are given in order from the most to the least commonly used. The listing is almost complete (except for some rare substance use conditions) and is a "crosswalk" of the diagnostic labels and code numbers from DSM-IV-TR and ICD-9-CM. It is offered only as a convenient reference for the knowledgeable clinician. If there is any uncertainty about the choice of diagnosis, the DSM-IV-TR or ICD-9-CM should be consulted. The DSM and ICD systems are not identical. The DSM-IV-TR codes and diagnoses are given in the left-hand column; the right-hand column contains what I believe to be the corresponding ICD-9-CM codes and their diagnostic labels.

The DSM-IV-TR codes are reprinted with permission from the *Diagnostic and Statistical Manual of Mental Disorders,* Fourth Edition, Text Revision. Copyright 2000 American Psychiatric Association.

21.4. Anxiety Disorders

See Sections 21.6 for codes for Acute Stress Disorder, <u>P</u>ost<u>T</u>raumatic <u>S</u>tress <u>D</u>isorder, and Adjustment Disorders; see Section 21.12 for codes for Substance-Induced Anxiety Disorders.

DSM-IV-TR		ICD-9-CM	
300.00	Anxiety Disorder NOS	300.00	Anxiety state, unspecified
300.01	Panic Disorder Without Agoraphobia	300.01	Panic disorder without agoraphobia
300.02	Generalized Anxiety Disorder	300.02	Generalized anxiety disorder
		300.09	Anxiety states: Other
		300.10	Hysteria, unspecified
		300.20	Phobia, unspecified
300.21	Panic Disorder With Agoraphobia	300.21	Agoraphobia with panic disorder Panic disorder with agoraphobia
300.22	Agoraphobia Without History of Panic Disorder	300.22	Agoraphobia without mention of panic attacks
300.23	Social Phobia	300.23	Social phobia
300.29	Specific Phobia	300.29	Other isolated or specific phobias
300.3	Obsessive–Compulsive Disorder	300.3	Obsessive–compulsive disorders

Mixed Anxiety–Depressive Disorder is a diagnosis proposed for further study; see Appendix B of DSM-IV-TR.

799.2	Nervousness

21.5. Mood Disorders

See Sections 21.6 for codes for Adjustment Disorders, and 21.12 for codes for Substance-Induced Mood Disorders.

The following specifiers can be applied to various DSM-IV-TR mood disorder diagnoses: Chronic, With Catatonic Features, With Melancholic Features, With Atypical Features, With Postpartum Onset, With Seasonal Pattern, With Rapid Cycling, With/Without Full Interepisode Recovery.

DSM-IV-TR		ICD-9-CM	
300.4	Dysthymic Disorder Specify if: Early/Late Onset, With Atypical Features	300.4	Dysthymic disorder. Reactive depression
		296.xx	Episodic mood disorders (*Use the following 5th digits for the 296 conditions: 0, unspecified; 1, mild; 2, moderate; 3, severe, without mention of psychotic behavior; 4, severe, specified as with psychotic behavior; 5, in partial or unspecified remission; 6, in full remission*)
296.20	Major Depressive Disorder, Single Episode, Unspecified	296.20	Major depressive disorder, single episode: Unspecified
296.21	Major Depressive Disorder, Single Episode, Mild	296.21	Major depressive disorder, single episode: Mild
296.22	Major Depressive Disorder, Single Episode, Moderate	296.22	Major depressive disorder, single episode: Moderate
296.23	Major Depressive Disorder, Single Episode, Severe Without Psychotic Features	296.23	Major depressive disorder, single episode: Severe, without mention of psychotic behavior
296.24	Major Depressive Disorder, Single Episode, Severe With Psychotic Features	296.24	Major depressive disorder, single episode: Severe, specified as with psychotic behavior
296.25	Major Depressive Disorder, Single Episode, In Partial Remission	296.25	Major depressive disorder, single episode: In partial or unspecified remission
296.26	Major Depressive Disorder, Single Episode, In Full Remission	296.26	Major depressive disorder, single episode: In full remission
296.30	Major Depressive Disorder, Recurrent, Unspecified	296.30	Major depressive disorder, recurrent: Unspecified
296.31	Major Depressive Disorder, Recurrent, Mild	296.31	Major depressive disorder, recurrent: Mild
296.32	Major Depressive Disorder, Recurrent, Moderate	296.32	Major depressive disorder, recurrent: Moderate
296.33	Major Depressive Disorder, Recurrent, Severe Without Psychotic Features	296.33	Major depressive disorder, recurrent: Severe, without mention of psychotic behavior
296.34	Major Depressive Disorder, Recurrent, Severe With Psychotic Features	296.34	Major depressive disorder, recurrent: Severe, specified as with psychotic behavior

DSM-IV-TR		**ICD-9-CM**	
296.35	Major Depressive Disorder, Recurrent, In Partial Remission	296.35	Major depressive disorder, recurrent: In partial or unspecified remission
296.36	Major Depressive Disorder, Recurrent, In Full Remission	296.36	Major depressive disorder, recurrent: In full remission
296.00	Bipolar I Disorder, Single Manic Episode, Unspecified	296.00	Bipolar I disorder, single manic episode: Unspecified Hypomania (mild) NOS, Hypomanic psychosis. Mania (monopolar)
296.01	Bipolar I Disorder, Single Manic Episode, Mild	296.01	Bipolar I disorder, single manic episode: Mild
296.02	Bipolar I Disorder, Single Manic Episode, moderate	296.02	Bipolar I disorder, single manic episode: Moderate
296.03	Bipolar I Disorder, Single Manic Episode, Severe Without Psychotic Features	296.03	Bipolar I disorder, single manic episode: Severe, without mention of psychotic behavior
296.04	Bipolar I Disorder, Single Manic Episode, Severe With Psychotic Features	296.04	Bipolar I disorder, single manic episode: Severe, specified as with psychotic behavior
296.05	Bipolar I Disorder, Single Manic Episode, In Partial Remission	296.05	Bipolar I disorder, single manic episode: In partial or unspecified remission
296.06	Bipolar I Disorder, Single Manic Episode, In Full Remission	296.06	Bipolar I disorder, single manic episode: In full remission
		296.10	Manic disorder, recurrent episode: Unspecified
		296.11	Manic disorder, recurrent episode: Mild
		296.12	Manic disorder, recurrent episode: Moderate
		296.13	Manic disorder, recurrent episode: Severe, without mention of psychotic behavior
		296.14	Manic disorder, recurrent episode: Severe, specified as with psychotic behavior
		296.15	Manic disorder, recurrent episode: In partial or unspecified remission
		296.16	Manic disorder, recurrent episode: In full remission
296.40	Bipolar I Disorder, Most Recent Episode Manic, Unspecified	296.40	Bipolar I disorder, most recent episode (or current) manic: Unspecified
296.40	Bipolar I Disorder, Most Recent Episode Hypomanic		
296.41	Bipolar I Disorder, Most Recent Episode Manic, Mild	296.41	Bipolar I disorder, most recent episode (or current) manic: Mild
296.42	Bipolar I Disorder, Most Recent Episode Manic, Moderate	296.42	Bipolar I disorder, most recent episode (or current) manic: Moderate

DSM-IV-TR		**ICD-9-CM**	
296.43	Bipolar I Disorder, Most Recent Episode Manic, Severe Without Psychotic Features	296.43	Bipolar I disorder, most recent episode (or current) manic: Severe, without mention of psychotic behavior
296.44	Bipolar I Disorder, Most Recent Episode Manic, Severe With Psychotic Features	296.44	Bipolar I disorder, most recent episode (or current) manic: Severe, specified as with psychotic behavior
296.45	Bipolar I Disorder, Most Recent Episode Manic, In Partial Remission	296.45	Bipolar I disorder, most recent episode (or current) manic: In partial or unspecified remission
296.46	Bipolar I Disorder, Most Recent Episode Manic, In Full Remission	296.46	Bipolar I disorder, most recent episode (or current) manic: In full remission
296.50	Bipolar I Disorder, Most Recent Episode Depressed, Unspecified	296.50	Bipolar I disorder, most recent episode (or current) depressed: Unspecified
296.51	Bipolar I Disorder, Most Recent Episode Depressed, Mild	296.51	Bipolar I disorder, most recent episode (or current) depressed: Mild
296.52	Bipolar I Disorder, Most Recent Episode Depressed, Moderate	296.52	Bipolar I disorder, most recent episode (or current) depressed: Moderate
296.53	Bipolar I Disorder, Most Recent Episode Depressed, Severe Without Psychotic Features	296.53	Bipolar I disorder, most recent episode (or current) depressed: Severe, without mention of psychotic behavior
296.54	Bipolar I Disorder, Most Recent Episode Depressed, Severe With Psychotic Features	296.54	Bipolar I disorder, most recent episode (or current) depressed: Severe, specified as with psychotic behavior
296.55	Bipolar I Disorder, Most Recent Episode Depressed, In Partial Remission	296.55	Bipolar I disorder, most recent episode (or current) depressed: In partial or unspecified remission
296.56	Bipolar I Disorder, Most Recent Episode Depressed, In Full Remission	296.56	Bipolar I disorder, most recent episode (or current) depressed: In full remission
296.60	Bipolar I Disorder, Most Recent Episode Mixed, Unspecified	296.60	Bipolar I disorder, most recent episode (or current) mixed: Unspecified degree
296.61	Bipolar I Disorder, Most Recent Episode Mixed, Mild	296.61	Bipolar I disorder, most recent episode (or current) mixed: Mild
296.62	Bipolar I Disorder, Most Recent Episode Mixed, Moderate	296.62	Bipolar I disorder, most recent episode (or current) mixed: Moderate
296.63	Bipolar I Disorder, Most Recent Episode Mixed, Severe Without Psychotic Features	296.63	Bipolar I disorder, most recent episode (or current) mixed: Severe, without mention of psychotic behavior

DSM-IV-TR		**ICD-9-CM**	
296.64	Bipolar I Disorder, Most Recent Episode Mixed, Severe With Psychotic Features	296.64	Bipolar I disorder, most recent episode (or current) mixed: Severe, specified as with psychotic behavior
296.65	Bipolar I Disorder, Most Recent Episode Mixed, In Partial Remission	296.65	Bipolar I disorder, most recent episode (or current) mixed: In partial or unspecified remission
296.66	Bipolar I Disorder, Most Recent Episode Mixed, In Full Remission	296.66	Bipolar I disorder, most recent episode (or current) mixed: In full remission
296.7	Bipolar I Disorder, Most Recent Episode Unspecified	296.7	Bipolar I disorder, most recent episode (or current) unspecified
296.80	Bipolar Disorder NOS	296.80	Bipolar disorder, unspecified.
		296.81	Atypical manic disorder
		296.82	Atypical depressive disorder
296.89	Bipolar II Disorder Specify (current or most recent episode): Hypomanic/Depressed	296.89	Other and unspecified Bipolar II disorder Bipolar Disorders: Other Manic–depressive psychosis, mixed type
296.90	Mood Disorder NOS	296.90	Unspecified episodic mood disorder Affective psychosis NOS Melancholia NOS
		296.99	Other specified episodic mood disorder Mood swings: brief, compensatory, rebound
301.13	Cyclothymic Disorder	301.13	Cyclothymic disorder Cyclothymic personality
293.83	Mood Disorder Due to ... [Indicate the General Medical Condition] Specify if: With Depressive Features/Major Depressive-Like Episode/Manic Features/Mixed Features		
311	Depressive Disorder NOS	311	Depressive disorder, not elsewhere classified

Premenstrual Dysphoric Disorder, Recurrent Brief Depressive Disorder, Minor Depressive Disorder, and Mixed Anxiety–Depressive Disorder are diagnoses proposed for further study; see Appendix B of DSM-IV-TR.

For clients who have recently lost someone close to them, consider the V code V62.82, Bereavement (in DSM-IV-TR) or Bereavement, uncomplicated (in ICD-9-CM).

DIAGNOSIS

21.6. Stress and Adjustment Disorders

See also Section 21.9, "Childhood Disorders," and the V codes in Section 21.21.

DSM-IV-TR		ICD-9-CM	
		308.0	Predominant disturbance of emotions
			Emotional crisis or Panic state as acute reaction to exceptional (gross) stress
		308.1	Predominant disturbance of consciousness. Fugues
		308.2	Predominant psychomotor disturbance
			Agitation or stupor
308.3	Acute Stress Disorder	308.3	Other acute reactions to stress
		308.4	Mixed disorders as reaction to stress
		308.9	Unspecified acute reaction to stress
309.0	Adjustment Disorder With Depressed Mood	309.0	Adjustment disorder with depressed mood. Grief reaction
		309.1	Prolonged depressive reaction
		309.2	Adjustment reaction with predominant disturbance of other emotions
		309.21	Separation anxiety disorder
		309.22	Emancipation disorder of adolescence and early adult life
		309.23	Specific academic or work inhibition
309.24	Adjustment Disorder With Anxiety	309.24	Adjustment disorder with anxiety
309.28	Adjustment Disorder With Mixed Anxiety and Depressed Mood	309.28	Adjustment disorder with mixed anxiety and depressed mood
		309.29	Adjustment reaction: Other Culture shock
309.3	Adjustment Disorder With Disturbance of Conduct	309.3	Adjustment disorder with disturbance of conduct
			Conduct Disorder or Destructiveness as adjustment disorder
309.4	Adjustment Disorder With Mixed Disturbance of Emotions and Conduct	309.4	Adjustment disorder with mixed disturbance of emotions and conduct
		309.8	Other specified adjustment reactions
309.81	Posttraumatic Stress Disorder	309.81	Posttraumatic stress disorder
			Posttraumatic stress disorder NOS or chronic
		309.82	Adjustment reaction with physical symptoms
		309.83	Adjustment reaction with withdrawal

DSM-IV-TR		ICD-9-CM	
		309.89	Other specified adjustment reaction: Other
309.9	Adjustment Disorder, Unspecified	309.9	Unspecified adjustment reaction

In DSM-IV-TR, for all Adjustment Disorders, specify Acute/Chronic.

21.7. Personality Disorders

Code all of these (except V71.01 and 310.1) on Axis II of DSM-IV-TR.

DSM-IV-TR		ICD-9-CM	
301.0	Paranoid Personality Disorder	301.0	Paranoid personality disorder
		301.10	Affective personality disorder, unspecified
		301.11	Chronic hypomanic personality disorder
		301.12	Chronic depressive personality disorder
		301.13	Cyclothymic disorder
301.20	Schizoid Personality Disorder	301.20	Schizoid personality disorder, unspecified
		301.21	Introverted personality [Note: not a disorder]
301.22	Schizotypal Personality Disorder	301.22	Schizotypal personality disorder
		301.3	Explosive personality disorder Aggressiveness Emotional instability (excessive) Pathological emotionality Quarrelsomeness
301.4	Obsessive–Compulsive Personality Disorder	301.4	Obsessive–compulsive personality disorder
301.50	Histrionic Personality Disorder	301.50	Histrionic personality disorder, unspecified
		301.51	Chronic factitious illness with physical symptoms Hospital addiction syndrome Multiple operations syndrome Munchausen syndrome
		301.59	Other histrionic personality disorder
301.6	Dependent Personality Disorder	301.6	Dependent personality disorder
301.7	Antisocial Personality Disorder	301.7	Antisocial personality disorder
		301.8	Other personality disorders
301.81	Narcissistic Personality Disorder	301.81	Narcissistic personality disorder
301.82	Avoidant Personality Disorder	301.82	Avoidant personality disorder
301.83	Borderline Personality Disorder	301.83	Borderline personality disorder
		301.84	Passive–aggressive personality disorder
		301.89	Other personality disorder

DSM-IV-TR		ICD-9-CM	
301.9	Personality Disorder NOS	301.9	Unspecified personality disorder
310.1	Personality Change Due To … [Indicate the General Medical Condition]		
V71.01	Adult Antisocial Behavior	V71.01	Gang activity without manifest psychiatric disorder

Passive–Aggressive Personality Disorder (Negativistic Personality Disorder) and Depressive Personality Disorder are diagnoses proposed for further study; see Appendix B of DSM-IV-TR.

21.8. Impulse-Control Disorders Not Elsewhere Classified

See also "Behavior and Conduct Disorders" in Section 21.9, below.

DSM-IV-TR		ICD-9-CM	
312.30	Impulse-Control Disorder NOS	312.30	Impulse control disorder, unspecified
312.31	Pathological Gambling	312.31	Pathological gambling
312.32	Kleptomania	312.32	Kleptomania
312.33	Pyromania	312.33	Pyromania
312.34	Intermittent Explosive Disorder	312.34	Intermittent explosive disorder
		312.35	Isolated explosive disorder
312.39	Trichotillomania	312.39	Disorders of impulse control, not elsewhere classified: Other Trichotillomania

21.9. Childhood Disorders

Mental Retardation

All of these are coded on Axis II of DSM-IV-TR.

DSM-IV-TR		ICD-9-CM	
V62.89	Borderline Intellectual Functioning (IQ 71–84) [Note: not Mental Retardation]		
317	Mild Mental Retardation (IQ 50–55 to approximately 70)	317	Mild mental retardation (IQ 50–70)
318.0	Moderate Mental Retardation (IQ 35–40 to 50–55)	318.0	Moderate mental retardation (IQ 35–49)
318.1	Severe Mental Retardation (IQ 20–25 to 35–40)	318.1	Severe mental retardation (IQ 20–34)
318.2	Profound Mental Retardation (IQ less than 20–25)	318.2	Profound mental retardation (IQ < 20)
319	Mental Retardation, Severity Unspecified (Not testable)	319	Unspecified mental retardation

Pervasive Developmental Disorders

DSM-IV-TR		ICD-9-CM	
		(For the codes below, enter the 5th digit as follows: 0, current or active state; 1, residual state)	
299.00	Autistic Disorder	299.0x	Autistic disorder Kanner's syndrome
299.10	Childhood Disintegrative Disorder	299.1x	Childhood disintegrative disorder
299.80	Asperger's Disorder	299.8x	Other specified pervasive developmental disorders
299.80	Schizophrenia, childhood type, NOS		
299.80	Rett's Disorder		
		299.9	Unspecified pervasive developmental disorder Pervasive developmental disorder NOS

Movement Disorders

DSM-IV-TR		ICD-9-CM	
307.20	Tic Disorder NOS	307.20	Tic disorder, unspecified Tic disorder NOS
307.21	Transient Tic Disorder Specify if: Single Episode/Recurrent	307.21	Transient tic disorder
307.22	Chronic Motor or Vocal Tic Disorder	307.22	Chronic motor or vocal tic disorder
307.23	Tourette's Disorder	307.23	Tourette's disorder
307.3	Stereotypic Movement Disorder Specify if: With Self-Injurious Behavior	307.3	Stereotypic movement disorder
315.4	Developmental Coordination Disorder	315.4	Developmental coordination disorder

Behavior and Conduct Disorders

DSM-IV-TR		ICD-9-CM	
		(Options for the 5th digit of 312.0, 312.1, and 312.2: 0, unspecified; 1, mild; 2, moderate; 3, severe)	
		312.0x	Undersocialized conduct disorder, aggressive type
		312.1x	Undersocialized conduct disorder, unaggressive type
		312.2x	Socialized conduct disorder
		312.3x	Disorders of impulse control, not elsewhere classified

DSM-IV-TR		ICD-9-CM	
		312.4	Mixed disturbance of conduct and emotions
312.81	Conduct Disorder, Childhood-Onset Type	312.81	Conduct disorder, childhood onset type
312.82	Conduct Disorder, Adolescent-Onset Type	312.82	Conduct disorder, adolescent onset type
312.89	Conduct Disorder, Unspecified Onset	312.89	Other conduct disorder
312.9	Disruptive Behavior Disorder NOS	312.9	Unspecified disturbance of conduct Juvenile delinquency Disruptive behavior disorder NOS
313.81	Oppositional Defiant Disorder	313.81	Oppositional defiant disorder

V71.02, Child or Adolescent Antisocial Behavior (in DSM-IV-TR) or Childhood or adolescent anti-social behavior (in ICD-9-CM), should be considered when antisocial behavior in a youth does not appear to be due to a mental disorder.

Disturbance of Emotions Specific to Childhood and Adolescence

DSM-IV-TR		ICD-9-CM	
		313.0	Overanxious disorder
		313.1	Misery and unhappiness disorder
		313.2	Sensitivity, shyness, and social withdrawal disorder
		313.21	Shyness disorder of childhood
		313.22	Introverted disorder of childhood
313.23	Selective Mutism	313.23	Selective mutism
		313.3	Relationship problems. Sibling jealousy
		313.8	Other or mixed emotional disturbances of childhood or adolescence
309.21	Separation Anxiety Disorder Specify if: Early Onset	309.21	Separation anxiety disorder
313.82	Identity Problem	313.82	Identity disorder Identity problem
313.89	Reactive Attachment Disorder of Infancy or Early Childhood Specify type: Inhibited/ Disinhibited Type	313.89	Reactive attachment disorder of infancy or early childhood Other or mixed emotional disturbances of childhood or adolescence: Other
313.9	Disorder of Infancy, Childhood, or Adolescence NOS	313.9	Unspecified emotional disturbance of childhood or adolescence

Learning and Developmental Disorders

DSM-IV-TR		ICD-9-CM	
315.00	Reading Disorder	315.00	Developmental reading disorder, unspecified
		315.01	Alexia
		315.02	Developmental dyslexia
		315.09	Other specific developmental reading disorder
315.1	Mathematics Disorder	315.1	Developmental mathematics disorder
315.2	Disorder of Written Expression	315.2	Other specific developmental learning difficulties Disorder of written expression
		315.5	Mixed development disorder
		315.8	Other specified delays in development
315.9	Learning Disorder NOS	315.9	Unspecified delay in development Learning disorder NOS
		313.83	Academic underachievement disorder
		309.23	Specific academic or work inhibition

Communication Disorders

DSM-IV-TR		ICD-9-CM	
307.0	Stuttering	307.0	Stuttering
307.9	Communication Disorder NOS	307.9	Other and unspecified special symptoms or syndromes, not elsewhere classified
315.31	Expressive Language Disorder	315.31	Expressive language disorder Developmental aphasia Auditory processing disorder
315.32	Mixed Receptive–Expressive Language Disorder	315.32	Mixed receptive–expressive language disorder
		315.34	Speech and language developmental delay due to hearing loss
315.39	Phonological Disorder	315.39	Developmental speech or language disorder: Other Dyslalia
313.23	Selective Mutism	313.23	Selective mutism

A̲ttention-D̲eficit(/H̲yperactivity) D̲isorder

	DSM-IV-TR		ICD-9-CM
314.00	Attention-Deficit/Hyperactivity Disorder Predominantly Inattentive Type	314.00	Attention deficit disorder: Without mention of hyperactivity
314.01	Attention-Deficit/Hyperactivity Disorder, Predominantly Hyperactive–Impulsive Type or Combined Type	314.01	Attention deficit disorder: with hyperactivity, predominantly hyperactive, impulsive type
		314.1	Hyperkinesis with developmental delay
		314.2	Hyperkinetic conduct disorder
		314.8	Other specified manifestations of hyperkinetic syndrome
314.9	Attention-Deficit/Hyperactivity Disorder NOS	314.9	Unspecified hyperkinetic syndrome

21.10. Eating and Elimination Disorders

In DSM-IV-TR, the first three of these disorders have their own section; the others are grouped with the Disorders Usually First Diagnosed in Infancy, Childhood, or Adolescence.

	DSM-IV-TR		ICD-9-CM
307.1	Anorexia Nervosa Specify type: Restricting or Binge-Eating/Purging Type	307.1	Anorexia nervosa
307.50	Eating Disorder NOS	307.50	Eating disorder, unspecified
307.51	Bulimia Nervosa Specify type: Purging/Nonpurging Type	307.51	Bulimia nervosa
307.52	Pica	307.52	Pica
307.53	Rumination Disorder	307.53	Rumination disorder
		307.54	Psychogenic vomiting
307.59	Feeding Disorder of Infancy or Early Childhood	307.59	Other and unspecified disorders of eating: Other
307.6	Enuresis (Not Due to a General Medical Condition) Specify type: Nocturnal Only/Diurnal Only/Nocturnal and Diurnal	307.6	Enuresis Specify: Primary or secondary
307.7	Encopresis, Without Constipation and Overflow Incontinence	307.7	Encopresis Specify: Continuous or discontinuous
787.6	Encopresis, With Constipation and Overflow Incontinence		

Binge-Eating Disorder is a diagnosis proposed for further study; see Appendix B of DSM-IV-TR.

21.11. "Organic" Cognitive Conditions

DSM-IV-TR no longer uses the term "organic" for these conditions, but the descriptor is still widely used in practice and in ICD-9-CM.

<u>DSM-IV-TR</u>		<u>ICD-9-CM</u>	
		290.0	Senile dementia, uncomplicated *Excludes: Dementia due to alcohol (291.0–291.2) and dementia due to drugs (292.82)*
290.10	Dementia of the Alzheimer's Type, With Early Onset, Without Behavioral Disturbance	290.10	Presenile dementia, uncomplicated
290.10	Dementia of the Alzheimer's Type, With Late Onset, Without Behavioral Disturbance		
290.11	Dementia of the Alzheimer's Type, With Early Onset, With Behavioral Disturbance	290.11	Presenile dementia with delirium
290.11	Dementia of the Alzheimer's Type, With Late Onset, With Behavioral Disturbance		
		290.12	Presenile dementia with delusional features (paranoid type)
		290.13	Presenile dementia with depressive features
		290.20	Senile dementia with delusional features
		290.21	Senile dementia with depressive features
		290.3	Senile dementia with delirium
		290.4	Vascular dementia
290.40	Vascular Dementia, Uncomplicated	290.40	Vascular dementia, uncomplicated
290.41	Vascular Dementia, With Delirium	290.41	Vascular dementia with delirium
290.42	Vascular Dementia, With Delusions	290.42	Vascular dementia with delusions
290.43	Vascular Dementia, With Depressed Mood For all Vascular Dementias, specify if: With Behavioral Disturbance	290.43	Vascular dementia with depressed mood
		290.8	Other specified senile psychotic conditions
		290.9	Unspecified senile psychotic condition
293.0	Delirium Due to ... [Indicate the General Medical Condition]	293.0	Delirium due to CCE
780.09	Delirium NOS		
		293.1	Subacute delirium
293.81	Psychotic Disorder Due to ... [Indicate the General Medical Condition], With Delusions	293.81	Psychotic disorder with delusions in CCE

DSM-IV-TR		ICD-9-CM	
293.82	Psychotic Disorder Due to … [Indicate the General Medical Condition], With Hallucinations	293.82	Psychotic disorder with hallucinations in CCE
293.83	Mood Disorder Due to [Indicate the General Medical Condition]	293.83	Mood disorder in CCE
293.84	Anxiety Disorder Due to [Indicate the General Medical Condition]	293.84	Anxiety disorder in CCE
293.89	Catatonic Disorder Due to … [Indicate the General Medical Condition]	293.89	Other specified transient mental disorders due to CCE: Other
293.9	Mental Disorder NOS Due to … [Indicate the General Medical Condition]	293.9	Unspecified transient mental disorder in CCE
294.0	Amnestic Disorder Due to … [Indicate the General Medical Condition]	294.0	Amnestic syndrome in CCE Korsakoff's Psychosis or Syndrome
294.10	Dementia Due to … [Indicate the General Medical Condition], Without Behavioral Disturbance	294.10	Dementia in CCE without behavioral disturbance
294.11	Dementia Due to … [Indicate the General Medical Condition], With Behavioral Disturbance	294.11	Dementia in CCE with behavioral disturbance Dementia of the Alzheimer's type
294.8	Amnestic Disorder NOS	294.8	Other persistent mental disorders due to CCE
294.8	Dementia NOS		Amnestic disorder NOS Dementia NOS
294.9	Cognitive Disorder NOS	294.9	Unspecified persistent mental disorders due to CCE
		310	Specific nonpsychotic mental disorders due to organic brain damage
		310.0	Frontal lobe syndrome
310.1	Personality Change Due to … [Indicate the General Medical Condition]	310.1	Personality change due to CCE
		310.2	Postconcussion syndrome (*see note in left column re: the DSM-IV-TR equivalent*)
		310.8	Other specified nonpsychotic mental disorders following organic brain damage Mild memory disturbance
		310.9	Unspecified nonpsychotic mental disorder following organic brain damage

780.9   Age-Related Cognitive Decline

In DSM-IV-TR, Postconcussional Disorder and Mild Neurocognitive Disorder are diagnoses proposed for further study; see Appendix B of the manual.

21.12. Substance-Related Disorders

There are also diagnoses not included here related to the use of amphetamines, hallucinogens, inhalants, phencyclidine, sedatives/hypnotics/anxiolytics, and unknown substances.

Note: Possible DSM-IV-TR dependence specifiers for substance-related diagnoses include **With Physiological Dependence** (evidence of tolerance or withdrawal) and **Without Physiological Dependence** (no evidence of tolerance or withdrawal). Remission specifiers are as follows: **Early Full Remission** (no criteria met for at least 1 month, but for less than 12 months); **Early Partial Remission** (one or more criteria met for 1 month but for less than 12 months); and **Sustained Full Remission** (no abuse or dependence criteria met for 12 months); **Sustained Partial Remission** (one or more abuse or dependence criteria met during 12-month period, but full criteria for dependence not met in that period). Other specifiers are **On Agonist Therapy** (taking an agonist medication [e.g., Antabuse] and with no criteria for abuse or dependence met for 1 month); **In a Controlled Environment** (in a setting in which access to substances is restricted, with no criteria met for 1 month); **With Onset During Intoxication**; and **With Onset During Withdrawal.**

Alcohol-Related Disorders

DSM-IV-TR		ICD-9-CM	
291.0	Alcohol Intoxication or Withdrawal Delirium	291.0	Alcohol withdrawal delirium (including delirium tremens)
291.1	Alcohol-Induced Persisting Amnestic Disorder	291.1	Alcohol-induced persisting amnestic disorder
291.2	Alcohol-Induced Persisting Dementia	291.2	Alcohol-induced persisting dementia
291.3	Alcohol-Induced Psychotic Disorder, With Hallucinations	291.3	Alcohol-induced psychotic disorder with hallucinations
		291.4	Idiosyncratic alcohol intoxication
291.5	Alcohol-Induced Psychotic Disorder, With Delusions	291.5	Alcohol-induced psychotic disorder with delusions
291.81	Alcohol Withdrawal Specify if: With Perceptual Disturbances	291.81	Alcohol withdrawal
		291.82	Alcohol-induced sleep disorder
291.89	Alcohol-Induced Anxiety Disorder, Mood Disorder, Sexual Dysfunction, or Sleep Disorder	291.89	Other specified alcohol-induced mental disorders: Other
291.9	Alcohol-Related Disorder NOS	291.9	Unspecified alcohol-induced mental disorders

(Note: ICD-9-CM uses the following 5th digits for all 303, 304, and 305 conditions: 0, unspecified; 1, continuous; 2, episodic; 3, in remission.)

DSM-IV-TR		ICD-9-CM	
303.00	Alcohol Intoxication	303.0x	Acute alcoholic intoxication
303.90	Alcohol Dependence	303.9x	Other and unspecified alcohol dependence
305.00	Alcohol Abuse	305.0x	Nondependent alcohol abuse

Other Substance-Related Disorders

Except in the diagnoses for intoxication, dependence, and abuse, ICD-9-CM does not distinguish the other drugs by code number, but by an additional E code for External cause (including drugs). Unless noted otherwise, the following categories can apply to cannabis, cocaine, hallucinogens, inhalants, opiates, phencyclidine, sedatives/hypnotics/anxiolytics, amphetamines, and other or unknown substances.

DSM-IV-TR		ICD-9-CM	
292.0	Withdrawal [State Class of Drug, or Other or Unknown Substance]	292.0	Drug withdrawal
292.11	Substance-Induced Psychotic Disorder, With Delusions [State Class of Drug, or Other or Unknown]	292.11	Drug-induced psychotic disorder, with delusions
292.12	Substance-Induced Psychotic Disorder With Hallucinations [State Class of Drug or Other or Unknown Substance]	292.12	Drug-induced psychotic disorder, with hallucinations (excludes brief states, "bad trips")
		292.2	Pathological drug intoxication (for brief states)
292.81	[Class of Drug, or Other or Unknown Substance] Intoxication Delirium	292.81	Drug-induced delirium
292.82	[Class of Drug, or Other or Unknown Substance]-Induced Persisting Dementia	292.82	Drug-induced persisting dementia
292.83	Sedative, Hypnotic, or Anxiolytic [or Other or Unknown Substance]-Induced Persisting Amnestic Disorder	292.83	Drug-induced persisting amnestic disorder
292.84	[Class of Drug, or Other or Unknown Substance]-Induced Mood Disorder	292.84	Drug-induced mood disorder
292.89	[Class of Drug, or Other or Unknown Substance]-Induced Anxiety, Sexual, or Sleep (specify) Disorder	292.89	Other specified drug-induced mental disorders: Other Drug-induced anxiety disorder, sexual dysfunction, sleep disorder, or drug intoxication
292.9	[Class of Drug, or Other or Unknown Substance]-Related Disorder NOS	292.9	Unspecified drug-induced mental disorder

Caffeine-Related Disorders

DSM-IV-TR		ICD-9-CM	
292.89	Caffeine-Induced Anxiety or Sleep Disorder		
292.9	Caffeine-Related Disorder NOS		
305.90	Caffeine Intoxication	305.9x	Caffeine intoxication

Caffeine Withdrawal is a diagnosis proposed for further study; see Appendix B of DSM-IV-TR.

Cannabis-Related Disorders

DSM-IV-TR		ICD-9-CM	
292.11	Cannabis-Induced Psychotic Disorder, With Delusions		
292.12	Cannabis-Induced Psychotic Disorder, With Hallucinations		
292.81	Cannabis Intoxication Delirium		
292.89	Cannabis-Induced Anxiety Disorder		
292.89	Cannabis Intoxication Specify if: With Perceptual Disturbances		
292.9	Cannabis-Related Disorder NOS		
304.30	Cannabis Dependence	304.3x	Cannabis dependence
305.20	Cannabis Abuse	305.2x	Nondependent cannabis abuse

Cocaine-Related Disorders

DSM-IV-TR		ICD-9-CM	
292.0	Cocaine Withdrawal		
292.11	Cocaine-Induced Psychotic Disorder, With Delusions		
292.12	Cocaine-Induced Psychotic Disorder, With Hallucinations		
292.81	Cocaine Intoxication Delirium		
292.84	Cocaine-Induced Mood Disorder		
292.89	Cocaine-Induced Anxiety Disorder, Sexual Dysfunction, or Sleep Disorder		
292.89	Cocaine Intoxication Specify if: With Perceptual Disturbances		
292.9	Cocaine-Related Disorder NOS		
304.20	Cocaine Dependence	304.2x	Cocaine dependence
305.60	Cocaine Abuse	305.6x	Nondependent cocaine abuse

Nicotine-Related Disorders

DSM-IV-TR		ICD-9-CM	
292.0	Nicotine Withdrawal		
292.9	Nicotine-Related Disorder NOS		
305.1	Nicotine Dependence	305.1	Nondependent tobacco use disorder. Tobacco dependence

Opioid-Related Disorders

DSM-IV-TR		ICD-9-CM	
292.0	Opioid Withdrawal		
292.11	Opioid-Induced Psychotic Disorder, With Delusions		
292.12	Opioid-Induced Psychotic Disorder, With Hallucinations		
292.81	Opioid Intoxication Delirium		
292.84	Opioid-Induced Mood Disorder		
292.89	Opioid-Induced Sexual Dysfunction or Sleep Disorder		
292.89	Opioid Intoxication Specify if: With Perceptual Disturbances		
292.9	Opioid-Related Disorder NOS		
304.00	Opioid Dependence	304.0x	Opioid type dependence
305.50	Opioid Abuse	305.5x	Nondependent opioid abuse

Miscellaneous Substance-Related Conditions

DSM-IV-TR		ICD-9-CM	
304.10	Sedative, Hypnotic, or Anxiolytic Dependence	304.1x	Sedative, hypnotic, or anxiolytic dependence
		304.7x	Drug dependence: Combinations of opioid type drug with any other
304.80	Polysubstance Dependence	304.8x	Combinations of drug dependence, excluding opioid type drug
305.90	Inhalant, Phencyclidine, Other, or Unknown Abuse		
305.30	Hallucinogen Abuse	305.3x	Hallucinogen abuse
305.40	Sedative, Hypnotic, or Anxiolytic Abuse	305.4x	Nondependent sedative, hypnotic, or anxiolytic abuse
304.50	Hallucinogen Dependence	304.5x	Hallucinogen dependence
305.70	Amphetamine Abuse	305.7x	Nondependent amphetamine or related-acting sympathomimetic abuse
304.40	Amphetamine Dependence	304.4x	Amphetamine and other psychostimulant dependence

DSM-IV-TR		ICD-9-CM	
304.60	Inhalant or Phencyclidine Dependence	304.6x	Other specified drug dependence Inhalant dependence Phencyclidine dependence Glue sniffing
		305.8x	Nondependent antidepressant type abuse
		304.9x	Unspecifed drug dependence
		305.9x	Nondependent other, mixed, or unspecified drug abuse Caffeine intoxication Inhalant abuse Phencyclidine abuse Nonprescribed use of drugs or patent medicinals

21.13. Psychotic Disorders

See Section 21.12 for codes for Substance-Induced Psychotic Disorders.

In DSM-IV-TR, for all subtypes of Schizophrenia, use these longitudinal course specifiers: **Episodic with Interepisodal Residual Symptoms, Episodic with No Interepisodal Residual Symptoms, Single Episode in Partial Remission, Single Episode in Full Remission, Other or Unspecified Pattern.** For the first three of these specifiers, also specify if: **With Prominent Negative Symptoms.**

DSM-IV-TR		ICD-9-CM	
		(Use the following 5th digits: 0, unspecified; 1, subchronic; 2, chronic; 3, subchronic with acute exacerbation; 4, chronic in acute exacerbation; 5, in remission.)	
		295.0x	Simple type schizophrenia
295.10	Schizophrenia, Disorganized Type	295.1x	Disorganized type schizophrenia
295.20	Schizophrenia, Catatonic Type	295.2x	Catatonic type schizophrenia
295.30	Schizophrenia, Paranoid Type	295.3x	Paranoid type schizophrenia
295.40	Schizophreniform Disorder Specify if: With/Without Good Prognostic Features	295.4x	Schizophreniform disorder
		295.5x	Latent schizophrenia
295.60	Schizophrenia, Residual Type	295.6x	Residual type schizophrenia Chronic undifferentiated schizophrenia
295.70	Schizoaffective Disorder Specify type: Bipolar/Depressive Type	295.7x	Schizoaffective disorder

DSM-IV-TR		ICD-9-CM	
		295.8x	Other specified types of schizophrenia
295.90	Schizophrenia, Undifferentiated Type	295.9x	Unspecified schizophrenia Schizophrenia, undifferentiated type
		297.0	Paranoid state, simple
297.1	Delusional Disorder Specify type: Erotomanic/Grandiose/ Jealous/Persecutory/Somatic/ Mixed/Unspecified Type	297.1	Delusional disorder
		297.2	Paraphrenia Involutional paranoid state
297.3	Shared Psychotic Disorder	297.3	Shared psychotic disorder Folie à deux
		297.8	Other specified paranoid states
		297.9	Unspecified paranoid state
		298.0	Depressive type psychosis
		298.1	Excitative type psychosis
		298.2	Reactive confusion
		298.3	Acute paranoid reaction
		298.4	Psychogenic paranoid psychosis
298.8	Brief Psychotic Disorder Specify if: With/Without Marked Stressors, With Postpartum Onset	298.8	Other and unspecified reactive psychosis Brief psychotic disorder
298.9	Psychotic Disorder NOS	298.9	Unspecified psychosis

21.14. Sleep Disorders

See Sections 12.37 for different diagnoses, and 21.12 for codes for Substance-Induced Sleep Disorders.

Dyssomnias

DSM-IV-TR		ICD-9-CM	
		307.40	Nonorganic sleep disorder, unspecified
		307.41	Transient disorder of initiating or maintaining sleep
307.42	Primary Insomnia Specify if: Recurrent	307.42	Persistent disorder of initiating or maintaining sleep
307.42	Insomnia Related to ... [Indicate the Axis I or II Disorder]		
		307.43	Transient disorder of initiating or maintaining wakefulness
307.44	Hypersomnia Related to ... [Indicate the Axis I or II Disorder]	307.44	Persistent disorder of initiating or maintaining wakefulness
307.44	Primary Hypersomnia Specify if: Recurrent		
307.45	Circadian Rhythm Sleep Disorder	307.45	Circadian rhythm sleep disorder

DSM-IV-TR	**ICD-9-CM**
Specify type: Delayed Sleep Phase/ Jet Lag/Shift Work/Unspecified Type	
307.47 Dyssomnia NOS	307.47 Other dysfunctions of sleep stages or arousal from sleep
347 Narcolepsy	347.0 Narcolepsy
780.52 Sleep Disorder Due to ... [Indicate the General Medical Condition], Insomnia Type	
780.54 Sleep Disorder Due to ... [Indicate the General Medical Condition], Hypersomnia Type	
780.59 Sleep Disorder Due to ... [Indicate the General Medical Condition], Mixed Type	
780.59 Sleep Disorder Due to ... [Indicate the General Medical Condition], Parasomnia Type	
780.59 Breathing-Related Sleep Disorder	
	V69.4 Lack of adequate sleep. Sleep deprivation
	V69.5 Behavioral insomnia of childhood

Many more sleep-disordered patterns are included in ICD-9-CM under 327.xx. Organic sleep disorders. Sleep disturbances (due to a medical condition) are classified under 780.5x codes.

Parasomnias

DSM-IV-TR	**ICD-9-CM**
307.46 Sleep Terror Disorder	307.46 Sleep arousal disorder
307.46 Sleepwalking Disorder	Night terror disorder
	Night terrors
	Sleep terror disorder
	Sleepwalking
	Somnambulism
307.47 Nightmare Disorder	
307.47 Parasomnia NOS	307.47 Other dysfunctions of sleep stages or arousal from sleep
	Nightmare disorder
	Parasonmia NOS
	307.48 Repetitive intrusions of sleep
	307.49 Other specific disorders of sleep of nonorganic origin
	Subjective insomnia complaint

21.15. Somatoform Disorders

DSM-IV-TR		ICD-9-CM	
		300.5	Neurasthenia
300.11	Conversion Disorder	300.11	Conversion disorder
	Specify type: With Motor Symptom or Deficit/With Seizures or Convulsions/With Sensory Symptom or Deficit/With Mixed Presentation		
300.7	Body Dysmorphic Disorder		
300.7	Hypochondriasis	300.7	Hypochondriasis
	Specify if: With Poor Insight		
300.81	Somatization Disorder	300.81	Somatization disorder
300.82	Somatoform Disorder NOS		
300.82	Undifferentiated Somatoform Disorder	300.82	Undifferentiated somatoform disorder
		300.89	Other somatoform disorders

21.16. Psychological Factors Affecting a Medical Condition

DSM-IV-TR		ICD-9-CM	
		306.xx	Physiological malfunction arising from mental factors
		306.0	Musculoskeletal
		306.1	Respiratory
		306.2	Cardiovascular
		306.3	Skin
		306.4	Gastrointestinal
		306.5	Genitourinary
		306.50	Psychogenic genitourinary malfunction, unspecified
		306.6	Endocrine
		306.7	Organs of special sense
		306.8	Other specified psychophysiological malfunction
		306.9	Unspecified psychophysiological malfunction
307.80	Pain Disorder Associated With Psychological Factors Specify if: Acute/Chronic	307.80	Psychogenic pain, site unspecified
		307.81	Tension headache
307.89	Pain Disorder Associated With Both Psychological Factors and a General Medical Condition Specify if: Acute/Chronic	307.89	Pain disorders related to psychological factors: Other

DIAGNOSIS

DSM-IV-TR	**ICD-9-CM**
	307.9 Other and unspecified special symptoms or syndromes, not elsewhere classified. Nail biting, hair plucking, lalling, masturbation, thumb-sucking
316 ... [Specified Psychological Factor] Affecting ... [Indicate the General Medical Condition] (Choose one of the following for [Specified Psychological Factor]: Mental Disorder, Psychological Symptoms, Personality Traits or Coping Style, Maladaptive Health Behaviors, Stress-Related Physiological Response, and Other or Unspecified Psychological Factors)	316 Psychic factors associated with diseases classified elsewhere *(Use additional code to identify the associated physical condition.)*

21.17. Dissociative Disorders

DSM-IV-TR	**ICD-9-CM**
300.12 Dissociative Amnesia	300.12 Dissociative amnesia
300.13 Dissociative Fugue	300.13 Dissociative fugue
300.14 Dissociative Identity Disorder	300.14 Dissociative identity disorder
300.15 Dissociative Disorder NOS	300.15 Dissociative disorder or reaction, unspecified
300.6 Depersonalization Disorder	300.6 Depersonalization disorder Derealization

Dissociative Trance Disorder is a diagnosis proposed for further study; see Appendix B of DSM-IV-TR.

21.18. Sexual Dysfunctions and Disorders

See Section 21.12 for codes for Substance-Induced Sexual Dysfunctions.

Sexual Dysfunctions

In DSM-IV-TR, specify type: Lifelong/ Acquired/Generalized/Situational Type, Due to Psychological Factors/Due to Combined Factors.

DSM-IV-TR	**ICD-9-CM**
302.70 Sexual Dysfunction NOS	302.70 Psychosexual dysfunction, unspecified
302.71 Hypoactive Sexual Desire Disorder	302.71 Hypoactive sexual desire disorder

DSM-IV-TR		ICD-9-CM	
302.72	Female Sexual Arousal/Male Erectile Disorder	302.72	Psychosexual dysfunction with inhibited sexual excitement Female sexual arousal disorder Male erectile disorder
302.73	Female Orgasmic Disorder	302.73	Female orgasmic disorder
302.74	Male Orgasmic Disorder	302.74	Male orgasmic disorder
302.75	Premature Ejaculation	302.75	Premature ejaculation
302.76	Dyspareunia (Not Due to . . . a General Medical Condition)	302.76	Dyspareunia, psychogenic
302.79	Sexual Aversion Disorder	302.79	Psychosexual dysfunction: With other specified psychosexual dysfunctions Sexual aversion disorder
306.51	Vaginismus (Not Due to . . . a General Medical Condition)	306.51	Psychogenic vaginismus
		306.52	Psychogenic dysmenorrhea
		306.53	Psychogenic dysuria
		306.59	Physiological malfunction arising from mental factors: Genitourinary: Other
607.84	Male Erectile Disorder Due to . . . . . . [Indicate the General Medical Condition]		
608.89	Male Dyspareunia Due to . . . . . . [Indicate the General Medical Condition]		
608.89	Male Hypoactive Sexual Desire Disorder Due to . . . . . . [Indicate the General Medical Condition]		
608.89	Other Male Sexual Dysfunction Due to . . . . . . [Indicate the General Medical Condition]		
625.0	Female Dyspareunia Due to . . . . . . [Indicate the General Medical Condition]		
625.8	Female Hypoactive Sexual Desire Disorder Due to . . . . . . [Indicate the General Medical Condition]		
625.8	Other Female Sexual Dysfunction Due to . . . . . . [Indicate the General Medical Condition]		

Gender and Sexual Identity Disorders

DSM-IV-TR		ICD-9-CM	
		302.0	Ego-dystonic sexual orientation Sexual orientation conflict disorder
302.6	Gender Identity Disorder in Children Gender Identity Disorder NOS	302.6	Gender identity disorder in children Gender identity disorder NOS

DSM-IV-TR		ICD-9-CM	
302.85	Gender Identity Disorder in Adolescents or Adults Specify if: Sexually Attracted to Males/Females/Both/Neither	302.85	Gender identity disorder in adolescents or adults

Paraphilias

DSM-IV-TR		ICD-9-CM	
		302.1	Zoophilia
302.2	Pedophilia Specify if: Sexually Attracted to Males/Females/Both, Limited to Incest, Exclusive/Nonexclusive Type	302.2	Pedophilia
302.3	Transvestic Fetishism Specify if: With Gender Dysphoria	302.3	Transvestic fetishism
302.4	Exhibitionism	302.4	Exhibitionism
		302.50	Trans-sexualism: With unspecified sexual history
		302.51	Trans-sexualism: With asexual history
		302.52	Trans-sexualism: With homosexual history
		302.53	Trans-sexualism: With heterosexual history
302.81	Fetishism	302.81	Fetishism
302.82	Voyeurism	302.82	Voyeurism
302.83	Sexual Masochism	302.83	Sexual masochism
302.84	Sexual Sadism	302.84	Sexual sadism
302.89	Frotteurism	302.89	Other specified psychosexual disorders: Other Frotteurism
302.9	Sexual Disorder NOS Paraphilia NOS	302.9	Unspecified psychosexual disorder Paraphilia NOS Sexual disorder NOS

21.19. Factitious Disorders

DSM-IV-TR		ICD-9-CM	
300.16	Factitious Disorder with Predominantly Psychological Signs and Symptoms	300.16	Factitious disorder with predominantly psychological signs and symptoms
300.19	Factitious Disorder with Predominantly Physical Signs and Symptoms		

DSM-IV-TR		ICD-9-CM	
300.19	Factitious Disorder with Combined Psychological and Physical Signs and Symptoms	300.19	Other and unspecified factitious illness
			Factitious disorder NOS
300.19	Factitious Disorder NOS		
		301.51	Chronic factitious illness with physical symptoms
			Munchausen Syndrome

21.20. Medication-Induced Movement Disorders

DSM-IV-TR		ICD-9-CM	
332.1	Neuroleptic-Induced Parkinsonism	332.1	Secondary Parkinsonism
333.1	Medication-Induced Postural Tremor	333.1	Essential and other specified forms of tremor
333.7	Neuroleptic-Induced Acute Dystonia	333.7	Acquired torsion dystonia
333.82	Neuroleptic-Induced Tardive Dyskinesia		
		333.85	Subacute dyskinesia due to drugs
333.90	Medication-Induced Movement Disorder NOS	333.90	Unspecified extrapyramidal disease and abnormal movement disorder
333.92	Neuroleptic Malignant Syndrome	333.92	Neuroleptic malignant syndrome
333.99	Neuroleptic-Induced Acute Akathisia		
995.2	Adverse Effects of Medication NOS	995.2	Other and unspecified adverse effect of drug, medicinal and biological substance (due to correct medicinal substance properly administered)

21.21. V Codes, Etc.

In ICD-9-CM and DSM-IV-TR, "V codes" are assigned to conditions that are not themselves attributable to a mental disorder but that may be a focus of attention or treatment. This section covers most V codes, as well as some additional numerical codes.

Relational Problems; Problems Related to Abuse or Neglect
See also Chapter 16, "Couple and Family Relationships."

DSM-IV-TR		ICD-9-CM	
V61	Family Disruption		
		V61.01	Family disruption due to family member on military deployment.
		V61.02	Family disruption due to return of family member from military deployment.

DSM-IV-TR		ICD-9-CM	
		V61.03	Family disruption due to divorce or legal separation
		V61.04	Family disruption due to parent–child estrangement
		V61.05	Family disruption due to child in welfare custody
		V61.06	Family disruption due to child in foster care or in care of non-parental family member
		V61.09	Other family disruption
V61.10	Partner Relational Problem	V61.10	Counseling for marital and partner problems, unspecified
		V61.11	Counseling for victim of spousal and partner abuse (use with 995.81, Physical abuse of adult; or 995.83 Sexual abuse of adult)
V61.12	Physical Abuse of Adult (if focus of clinical attention is on perpetrator and abuse is of partner)	V61.12	Counseling for perpetrator of spousal and partner abuse (use with 995.81, Physical abuse of adult; or 995.83, Sexual abuse of adult)
	Sexual Abuse of Adult (if focus of clinical attention is on perpetrator and abuse is of partner)		
V61.20	Parent–Child Relational Problem	V61.20	Parent–child relational problem
V61.21	Physical Abuse of Child (use 995.4 if focus of attention is on victim)	V61.21	Counseling for victim of child abuse (use with 995.52, Child neglect [nutritional]; 995.53, Child sexual abuse; or 995.54, Child physical abuse)
	Sexual Abuse of Child (use 995.3 if focus of attention is on victim) Neglect of Child (use 995.52 if focus of attention is on victim)		
		V61.22	Counseling for perpetrator of parental child abuse (use with 995.52, Child neglect [nutritional]; 995.53, Child sexual abuse; or 995.54, Child physical abuse)
		V61.29	Parent–child problems: Other
		V61.3	Problems with aged parents or in-laws
		V61.7	Other unwanted pregnancy
V61.8	Sibling Relational Problem	V61.8	Other specified family circumstances
V61.81	Relational Problem NOS		
V61.9	Relational Problem Related to a Mental Disorder or General Medical Condition	V61.9	Unspecified family circumstance

DSM-IV-TR	ICD-9-CM
V62.83 Physical Abuse of Adult (if focus of clinical attention is on perpetrator and abuse is not by partner; use 995.81 if focus is on victim) Sexual Abuse of Adult (if focus of clinical attention is on perpetrator and abuse is not by partner; use 995.83 if focus is on victim)	V62.83 Counseling for perpetrator of physical/sexual abuse (of a child or an adult)

Additional Conditions That May Be a Focus of Clinical Attention

DSM-IV-TR	ICD-9-CM
V15.81 Noncompliance with Treatment	V15.81 Noncompliance with medical treatment
V62.2 Occupational Problem	V62.2 Other occupational circumstances or maladjustment
	V62.21 Personal current military deployment status. Individual (civilian or military) currently deployed in theater or in support of military war, peacekeeping and humanitarian operations
	V62.22 Personal history of return from military deployment. Individual (civilian or military) with past history of military war, peacekeeping and humanitarian deployment (current or past conflict)
	V62.29 Other occupational circumstances or maladjustment: Other Career choice problem Dissatisfaction with employment Occupational problem
V62.3 Academic Problem	V62.3 Educational circumstances
V62.4 Acculturation Problem	V62.4 Social maladjustment
V62.82 Bereavement	V62.82 Bereavement, uncomplicated
V62.89 Phase of Life Problem Religious or Spiritual Problem Borderline Intellectual Functioning (coded on Axis II)	V62.89 Other psychological or physical stress, not elsewhere classified: Other (includes Phase of life problem, Religious or spiritual problem, Borderline intellectual functioning)
V65.2 Malingering	V65.2 Person feigning illness Malingering
	V65.4 Other counseling, not elsewhere classified
	V65.5 "Worried well"
V71.09 No Diagnosis (or Condition) on Axis I or II	V71.09 Observation of other suspected mental condition

DSM-IV-TR		ICD-9-CM	
799.9	Diagnosis (or Condition) Deferred on Axis I or II	799.9	Other unknown and unspecified cause of morbidity and mortality
300.9	Unspecified Mental Disorder (nonpsychotic)	300.9	Unspecified nonpsychotic mental disorder
		307.9	Other and unspecified special symptoms or syndromes, not elsewhere classified
		780.79	Other malaise and fatigue
		780.95	Excessive crying of child, adolescent, or adult

21.22. Axis IV: Psychosocial and Environmental Problems

DSM-IV-TR Axis IV categories (reprinted by permission of the American Psychiatric Association) include the following:

Problems with primary support group.
Problems related to the social environment.
Educational problems.
Occupational problems.
Housing problems.
Economic problems.
Problems with access to health care services.
Problems related to interaction with the legal system/crime.
Other psychosocial and environmental problems.

✓ **Note:** Describing the specific stressors experienced by the client, usually over the last year, is more clinically useful than using just the categories above (Segal & Hutchings, 2007).

21.23. Axis V: Global Assessment of Functioning Scale

This is an abbreviated version and does not list examples. It is adapted by permission from DSM-IV-TR.

Ratings are made for current level of psychological/social/physical functioning and for highest level in past year.

91–100	Superior functioning in a wide range of areas; no symptoms.
81–90	No or minimal symptoms; generally good functioning in all areas; no more than everyday problems or concerns.
71–80	Transient, slight symptoms that are reasonable responses to stressful situations; no more than slight impairment in social, occupational, or school functioning.
61–70	Mild symptoms, or some difficulty in social, occupational, or school functioning.
51–60	Moderate symptoms, or moderate difficulties in social, occupational, or school functioning.
41–50	Serious symptoms, or any serious impairment in social, occupational, or school functioning.

31–40	Serious difficulties in thought or communication, or major impairment in several areas of functioning.
21–30	Behavior influenced by psychotic symptoms, or serious impairment in communication or judgment, or inability to function in almost all areas.
11–20	Dangerous symptoms, or gross impairment in communication.
1–10	Persistent danger to self or others, or persistent inability to maintain hygiene.
0	Inadequate information.

The equivalent Children's Global Assessment Scale is available online (see, e.g., *www.kidsmental-health.org/documents/CGAS.pdf*).

22

Recommendations

Making recommendations is usually the chief aim of report construction. If treatment is appropriate, its indicators and urgency must be presented to justify it. Selecting treatments from the hundreds of interventions available requires extensive knowledge of the structure and method of each intervention, its demands on client and therapist, and its likely outcomes for different syndromes and personalities. While treatment-to-client matching is beyond this book's scope, the sections here provide a large checklist of services to address the client's needs.

22.1. Need for Treatment

Your description of the need for treatment should include the justifications/reasons/clinical rationales/indications for the medical necessity (if any) of, and the risks and benefits of, each proposed treatment choice/option/alternative (including those you did not recommend).

Indication(s) for Hospitalization/Intensification of Treatment Efforts: Summary Statements

This patient, with a history of severe and/or prolonged psychiatric illness, is showing significant decompensation.

His disorder remains severe or persistent, despite appropriate outpatient treatment.

She is exhibiting suicidal ideation/threats/gestures/attempts, or is (considered) a physical danger to herself.

There is severe loss of appetite/weight, and/or sleep disturbance, considered to be detrimental to physical health.

He is believably threatening to act/acting in a physically destructive manner toward others or property.

She is demonstrating bizarre, antisocial, or risky behaviors that will progress unless she is hospitalized.

There is evidence of cognitive disorders, dementia, or organic brain syndrome requiring psychiatric, neuropsychological, or medical evaluation, which can only be provided in an inpatient setting.

I am/Dr. _____ is starting or modifying psychopharmacological treatments that require continuous monitoring and evaluation because of the type of medication or the presence of other medical conditions or complicating factors.

The patient's substance abuse is of such intensity and persistence that hospitalization is required to control or prevent the severe physical and psychiatric consequences of withdrawal.

Precautions are needed to prevent assault/elopement/homicide/suicide.

Urgency

($\leftrightarrow$ *by degree*) The following groupings are sequenced by degree of decreasing urgency.

Emergency, act without delay, immediate intervention required to preserve life or health.

Critical/serious disruption of functioning, act today/within 24 hours.

Patient is suffering, treatment/evaluation is needed, act soon.

Routine intake/evaluation/referral.

Wait for _____ (specify).

Estimate of Treatability

Although currently out of fashion, the issue of treatability is often worth considering, especially when resources are limited. In estimating treatability, weigh these characteristics of the patient:

Motivators/pain; demotivators/anxieties/avoidances/resistances.
Support needed and availability.
Barriers (financial, logistical, cultural, intellectual).
Openness to new experiences/the intimacy of therapy/strong affects/new perspectives.
Psychological-mindedness, willingness to work, ego strength.
Probability of remaining in treatment.

22.2. Treatments of Choice

Although it is clear from meta-analyses that psychotherapy benefits most clients, it is also well documented that very few therapists have used research on the effectiveness of methods of therapy to guide their practices. Of the perhaps 400 "brand-name" therapies, however, only a few dozen have been properly evaluated for effectiveness for any kind of outcomes, and fewer have been empirically supported (in medicine this is called "evidence-based practice").

Variation in treatment practices accounts for about a quarter of the variance in outcomes. Variation in the client–therapist relationship accounts for most of the rest, and yet this has been less studied. These "common factors" (meaning common across different treatment techniques) are comprehensively reviewed in Norcross (2002) and are well worth pursuing.

Summaries of the comparative evaluations of treatments can be found in several places. A list of Empirically Supported Treatments with relevant treatment manuals and training resources can be found online at the Website on Research-Supported Psychological Treatments maintained by the Society of Clinical Psychology, Division 12 of the American Psychological Association (*www.psychology.sunysb.edu/eklonsky-/division12*). (*See Chapter 27 for more on treatment resources for specific concerns and disorders.*)

Several books contain much useful guidance to the outcome research on treatments. These include Roth and Fonagy (2005), Nathan and Gorman (2007), and, for children, Christophersen and Mortweet (2001). The treatments discussed in these books are primarily behavioral and cognitive, because these have been properly investigated. Many common therapies do not generate empirically testable or falsifiable hypotheses. Also, therapist variables such as competence in and adherence to the techniques of a treatment, personality, allegiance, and similarity to the client have all been shown to be important determinants of outcome. See especially Norcross (2002) on this. We really need more research to answer the question framed by Gordon Paul in 1966 as follows: "Which treatment, administered by whom, for what diagnosis/problem, in what kind of person, has what outcome?"

22.3. Treatment Options/Case Disposition

See also Chapter 25, "Treatment Planning and Treatment Plan Formats."

General Statements

Continue current treatment(s).
Add further/concurrent treatments (specify).
Refer/transfer patient to a different hospital/program/therapist (specify).
Discharge to be followed by/at _____ [treater or agency] with first appointment on _____ [date] at _____ [time].

Counseling or Psychotherapy   *See Chapter 25 for goals and methods.*

Medication Statement

The patient and I have had a full and free discussion of the risks and benefits of the proposed medication, and he/she agrees to this regimen. He/she will start _____ [trade or generic name] at a dose of _____, ____ times per day, for a period of _____ and then will increase/decrease/taper/stop this medication at a dose of _____, ____ times per day, for a period of _____. We have discussed benefits and risks, expectations, ways to deal with problems, etc. This regimen will be supervised/administered by the patient/family/clinic staff/school nurse/other (specify).

Referrals

Further evaluations/diagnostic studies: physical/medical, intellectual, personality, neuropsychological, custody, family, forensic, speech/language, audiological, educational/academic, occupational/vocational/rehabilitative (specify).
To a nutritional education program and recommend dietary change.
To an exercise education program/exercise program.
To recreation counseling, have him/her change social/recreational, etc. activities to _____ (specify), increase activities outside the home/family, take on volunteer activities such as _____ (specify).

22.4. Types of Therapies/Services

Types of therapies and services are listed alphabetically, both to reflect the fact there is no accepted hierarchy and to encourage consideration of the many options available.

Aftercare services, case management and monitoring, liaison, intensive outpatient treatment, partial hospital.
Behavior modification methods[1]: Contingency management, contingency contracting, stimulus control, convert sensitization, time out, token economy, modeling, self-control methods, covert aversion therapy, Stress Inoculation Training, etc.
Behavior therapies: Systematic desensitization, flooding, implosion, Eye Movement Desensitization and Reprocessing.
Behavior referral: Self-control training, anger management, parenting skills/child management training, Parent Effectiveness Training (Gordon, 2000), assertiveness training, antivictimization program.

---

[1]Kratochwill and Bergan (1990) provide excellent guidance to the implementation of behavioral programs as a consultant.

Bibliotherapy, self-help (see Norcross et al., 2003), and patient education.

Body–mind awareness: Primal (scream), Rolfing, bioenergetics, Autogenic Training, gestalt, Functional Integration, biofeedback, the Alexander method, shiatsu, many kinds of yogas, martial arts training programs, tai chi, etc.

Case management (intensive and tailored to client), Assertive Community Treatment.

Cognitive and cognitive-behavioral therapies of many kinds, narrative therapies, interpersonal therapies, Dialectical Behavior Therapy, Motivational Interviewing, Acceptance and Commitment Therapy, etc.

Crisis intervention and management.

Expressive therapies: Art, music, dance/movement, journaling, poetry writing.

Family support: Crisis care, staff monitoring and ongoing evaluations and interventions, respite care, in-home/mobile therapy, individual behavior support and training, etc.

Psychological growth: Transactional Analysis, psychoanalysis, encounter/marathon/Open Encounter groups, Morita therapy, Reality Therapy, Psychosynthesis, narrative therapies.

Relationship and communication: Sex therapy, Marriage Encounter, Relationship Enhancement.

Residential services: Foster care, "group homes," community living arrangements, community residential services, "halfway house," structured/supportive living arrangement, transitional services, protective services, domiciliary care, etc.

Schooling: High school, General Equivalency Diploma classes, local college/general studies/evening classes, vocational/trade schools.

Skill-building groups: Toastmasters International, parenting skills/child management training, PET, anger management, assertiveness training, dating skills, antivictimization program, etc.

Support groups (see also Norcross et al., 2003):

Grief counseling, victim support services, Mothers Against Drunk Driving, Parents of Murdered Children, Compassionate Friends (parents of children who died), Candlelighters (children with cancer), Make Today Count (those with fatal illnesses).

Encore Plus (women with breast cancer), Reach for Recovery (women who have had breast cancer surgery).

Parents Anonymous (parents who abuse children), Sojourn (battered women), Daughters and Sons United (sexually abused children).

Resolve (infertility), Adoptees Liberty Movement Association (adult adoptees and birth parents), Tough Love (parents of difficult adolescents), Single Parent Network.

Recovery (people with nervous and mental problems), Take Off Pounds Sensibly, HELP (herpes), Mutual Friends (ex-Jehovah's Witnesses), Dignity (gay and lesbian Catholics), etc.

Twelve-Step programs for many addictive behaviors: Alcohol/Cocaine/Narcotics/Families/Overeaters/Gamblers Anonymous, Al-Anon, Alateen.

Work adjustment training, work hardening program, work placement, internship program. *(See Chapter 17, "Vocational/Academic Skills.")*

✓ **Note:** You may want to create and insert here a reference list of additional or specific services, and their providers, available in your community or system.

For a Child:

Special Education

In-school supportive services for various disabilities/impairments (lists of eligible disabilities are readily available online) and of various types (physical support, speech and language support, life skills support, etc.).

Other supportive services: In-home, "cyberschool," alternative schools, Residential Treatment Facilities, inpatient services, etc.

Intensity of services:
Itinerant: Special education personnel inside or outside a regular classroom for part of school day.
Resource: As above, but provided in a resource classroom.
Part-time special education in the regular classroom: Special education services provided outside the regular classroom but in the regular school for most of the day.
Full-time special education class: Full-day special education classes with some participation in nonacademic and extracurricular activities inside or outside a regular school.
Counseling, medical/psychiatric/medication evaluation/consultation, play and expressive therapy, child management skills training, parent–staff conference, social skills training (remedial/adaptive/for acceptance), etc.

There is endless information on the Internet about educational issues and methods. One good resource on effective practices for children with (and without) disabilities is provided by the National Dissemination Center for Children with Disabilities (*www.nichcy.org/EducateChildren/Pages*). A good list of modifications can also be found online (*www.trumbullps.org/policies/IGBG_modifications.pdf*).

23

Prognostic Statements

A model for coming to a prognosis is to list separately and evaluate (1) predisposing factors, (2) precipitating factors, (3) protective factors.

23.1. General Prognostic Statement

This is a general format for a prognostic statement, with blanks to be filled in using the options below:

> **The prognosis for this client's _____ [type of outcome] is _____ [prognosis descriptor]. The course is/is expected to be _____ [course descriptor], because the client is/appears to be _____ [client descriptor].**

Types of Outcomes

Improvement, full/partial recovery.
Employment (competitive/supportive/sheltered workshop), return to original job/alternative work placement at _____ level.
Community/family/structured/institutional placement, or other.

Prognosis Descriptors (↔ *by degree*)

Excellent/good/positive/uncertain because ... (specify)/variable/unknown/guarded/poor/precarious/negative/grave/terminal.

Course Descriptors (↔ *by degree*)

Benign, acute, waxing and waning, stepwise, fluctuating, with remissions and exacerbations, steady, protracted recovery, chronic, static, intractable, unchanging with or without treatment, arduous, declining, worsening rapidly, unrelenting despite our best efforts, malignant, fulminating.

Client Descriptors (↔ *by degree*)

Recuperating/convalescent, making good progress, reaching a steady state, symptoms continue to disrupt daily functioning, hard to treat, refractory to treatment, suffering from a virulent form of the disorder, failing despite all appropriate treatment.

23.2. Other Statements

This client's eventual prognosis for success in later life will be a function of how well the situational demands match his/her individual profile of abilities.

The severity and chronicity of her/his symptoms indicate a poor prognosis.

His/her course so far has been downhill, and his/her prognosis therefore must be considered negative unless ... (specify).

This outcome/result of treatment is expected only if (specify) services are received, and progress is expected to be slow and difficult with many reversals.

The probable duration of treatment is _____ with these goals of therapy ... (specify).

The client needs the structure of various social agencies with which she/he is involved.

Due to the chronicity of his condition, the present treatment and goals are being maintained.

The client reports full/partial/variable/intermittent compliance/adherence with the regimen and/or medications prescribed.

24

Closing Statements

24.1. Value of the Information

I hope this information will be useful to you as you consider this case's/person's/client's needs, and will aid you in your tasks/evaluation/treatment/decisions.
I hope this information will be sufficient for you to judge this patient's situation.
In the hope that these data will prove of assistance ...

24.2. Thanking the Referrer

Thank you for the opportunity/privilege of being able to evaluate your patient/this most interesting/challenging/pleasant patient/person/man/woman.
We appreciate your sending _____ to us/inviting us to assist in the care of _____/asking us to see _____.
Thanks again for the opportunity to participate in _____'s care.
Thanks for the chance to help take care of _____ with you.
I consider it a privilege to have been able to care for this patient.

It goes almost without saying that I appreciate your trust in allowing me to assist in the care of this/your patient.
My colleagues and I appreciate ... (specify).
As always, thank you very much for your kind referrals.

24.3. Continued Availability

I trust that this is the information you desire/require, but if it is not ...
Please feel free to contact me if I can supplement the information in this report/if other questions or issues arise.
Please let me know if you have any other thoughts about this person's condition(s).
If there are further questions I may address as a result of/on the basis of my examination of this individual, please contact me at your convenience.
I will make myself/am available for further information/consultation regarding this client's needs.
With an appropriate release of information, I will be happy to discuss this case further with individuals who are involved with the person's care.
If I can be of further benefit to you with this case, do not hesitate to contact me.

If I can be of any further assistance with reference to this patient's treatment or problem or any patient's treatment, it certainly will be my pleasure to assist you.

If clarification is needed, I can best be reached on _____ [days] from _____ to _____ [times] at _____ [phone number].

Should additional examination/evaluation/testing/clarification/information/treatment be needed, I am/am not willing to provide it.

I am/am not willing to perform additional examinations/evaluations on this person.

I will see this client again in _____. I am certainly available sooner should problems arise.

I remain available to this patient to provide care should it be needed.

The client requires no further/active follow-up from our standpoint, but he/she is aware that he/she can contact us should further problems arise.

I am returning her/him to your care regarding . . . (specify).

As always, I shall keep you informed of my further contacts with/interactions with/treatment of your patient via/by means of copies of my progress notes, with the patient's full consent.

24.4. Signature, Etc.

Always sign a report with your personal signature, degree, and title, preceded by "Yours truly/Sincerely/Respectfully." Add any of these statements as appropriate:

I authorize that my name may be mechanically affixed to this report.

Dictated but not read, to facilitate mailing to you.

Typed and mailed in the doctor's absence.

If my initials do not follow this sentence, this printed report has not been reviewed/edited by me and may contain errors of typing or words that I would have changed.

24.5. Disclaimer

The reader should understand that this report is based upon all the information available to the writer at the time of this assessment. Other information that may be pertinent but is presently unavailable, or information that may be received after this report is completed, is of course not included. Any such other information that may be supplied to the reader may alter the findings or recommendations in the current report.

Part III

Useful Resources

25

Treatment Planning
and Treatment Plan Formats

Treatment plans are simply one step in an episode of treatment: Do a comprehensive evaluation; plan treatment thoughtfully; do the treatment consistently, compassionately, and conscientiously; write complete progress notes; evaluate your efforts and outcomes; and write a closing summary.

25.1. The Flow and Nature of Treatment Planning

The sequence of clinical thinking in treatment planning follows four steps: assessment, diagnosis, goals, and only then intervention plans.

Treatment planning begins with **assessment** of the client's presenting problem/Chief Complaint, presenting symptoms, mental status, risks, history (especially of treatment), and expectations of treatment and outcomes. This leads to **diagnosis making**. Do all of this with the client, ask about all areas of functioning, and prioritize problems jointly and realistically.

The planning process then continues with a consideration of **outcomes**—goals, objectives, and benefits. Ask, "If we wish to achieve this goal by this date, what steps need to be taken before then?" Select and prioritize goals.

Now planning can proceed to **treatment design and selection**—the choice of interventions, efforts, methods, and means. Consider the resources available and the limitations imposed by reality, time, finances, etc. *(See Section 22.2, "Treatments of Choice.")*

25.2. Some Advice on Writing Treatment Plans

- Spending the time to develop a plan jointly and collaboratively with the client requires the kind of thoughtful, comprehensive, insightful efforts that will ensure successful therapy. It is not a waste of therapy time but rather a productive focusing of it. A preliminary step could be to list, with the client, the major problems and related effects of these problems on his/her life. Review all the areas of functioning. Then inquire about expectations of treatment and of change for this problem list. Some see goal setting as the client's job, while selecting and implementing the means are the contributions of the therapist/professional.

Much of this chapter is adapted from my book *The Paper Office* (4th ed.). Copyright 2008 by Edward L. Zuckerman. Adapted by permission.

- Berg and Miller (1992) offer these criteria for "well-formed treatment goals":
  They must be important to the client.
  They should be concrete, behavioral, and specific [and memorable].
  They should focus on the presence rather than the absence of something.
  They must focus on the first small steps, on what to do first, on a beginning rather than an end.
  They should be realistic and achievable within the context of the client's life.
  They should be perceived as requiring "hard work" [like Jay Haley's Prescribed Ordeal Therapy; see Haley (1984)].

- A symptom does not have to be absent completely, or for months, in order for a client to demonstrate recovery. It only has to be not significantly interfering with or limiting life functions.

- Treatment planning should logically include the ending of treatment and the client's proceeding with her/his life trajectory, which may have been interrupted by the disorder. Therefore, an integral aspect of treatment planning is preparation for ending treatment. <u>M</u>anaged <u>C</u>are <u>O</u>rganizations may ask what steps have been taken or will be taken to prepare the patient or family for discharge from treatment.

- Let your writings reflect that you considered all options, rationales, and decisions at each stage of treatment, so that you can review and revise from a solid basis, communicate with peers and patients, evaluate and learn from your outcomes, and protect yourself from malpractice accusations.

- In writing plans, you may find yourself struggling between writing a plan that is too specific and will require continual revisions, and a plan that is too general and is an empty exercise because it offers no guidance for treatment. The overly precise plan requires either following it rigidly or constantly revising it in light of the vicissitudes of actual clinical practice.

- A caution for writing treatment plans: Avoid jargon, especially words understood only by professionals of a particular orientation. MCO reviewers are usually nurses or counselors untrained in more specific techniques and suspicious of ones with idiosyncratic and obscure terminology. Use common-language translations of theory or focus elsewhere.

- I see writing treatment plans as an ethical as well as a clinical responsibility for us as therapists. If we don't write our plans down, our human nature will convince us that we intended to get to wherever we ended up. Treatment plans keep us honest.

- Much research comparing novices and experts points to the novices' lack of the large internal list of options that experts have developed. Novice treatment planners find it very difficult to design goals and generate methods. Experts may have a parallel difficulty: articulating what has become a "second-nature" understanding of goals and methods. These difficulties have led to the popularity of books and software on treatment planning, but with a little mental effort any clinician can generate perfectly satisfactory plan statements. For more details on how the contents of this book can be of assistance, see the relevant parts of the sections on MCO plans and outcomes, below.

25.3. Various Formats for Treatment Plans

The Tabular Model

Each clinician, agency, funder, and monitor seems to have a different preferred format for treatment plans. Many of them use a page turned sideways and divided into columns. If you wish to use this approach, offered below are four commonly used headings for the columns (and some optional others). For each column heading, I have supplied a series of terms used to express a similar idea. From these, you can choose headings that best fit your way of practicing and your setting.

The first column is the "Goal" column. Alternative terms:

Problem, Aim,[1] Behaviors to Be Changed, Focus of Treatment, Long-Term Goal, Diagnosis-Related Symptoms.

The second is the "Outcome" column. Alternative terms:

Objective, Subgoal, Outcome Sought/Desired/Expected,[2] Observable Indicators of Improvement,[3] Symptom-Related Goals, Short-Term Goal, Discharge Level of Problem Behavior, Performance, Operationalization.

The third is the "Intervention" column. Alternative terms:

Resources to Be Employed, Methods, Treatments, Means, Strategies, Tactics, Efforts, Inputs.

This column should answer these questions: Who is going to do what, where, when, how often and for how long, with whom, and supervised by whom when?

The last column is the "Time Frame" column.[4] Alternative terms:

Date of Evaluation, Date of Initiation, Target Date, Completion Date, Expected Number of Sessions to Achieve Objective, Date of Review/Reevaluation/Progress Evaluation.

Other columns may include the following:

Intensity, Frequency, Duration of Treatment.
Client's Related Strengths or Assets, Degree of Involvement.
Liabilities, Resistances/Barriers to Change (in the client or elsewhere).
Priorities, Sequence of Objectives.
Documentation of Involvement (of client, providers, payors, family, others).

Wilson's Social Work Model

From social work (Wilson, 1980), this model describes:

The ideal means of meeting the needs of this client.
What you can do realistically to meet these needs.
The client's willingness and ability to carry out these treatment plans.
Progress made or not made since the plan was written.
What you will now do differently.

---

[1] This term is used by Makover (2004).

[2] <u>G</u>oal <u>A</u>ttainment <u>S</u>caling is built on rating the expected outcomes. See Kiresuk et al. (1994) and Section 25.8 below.

[3] This excellent phrasing was introduced, as far as I know, by Levenstein (1994).

[4] If you can, write the target for this column in terms of treatment sessions, because clients may miss meetings during a specified time period. Similarly, it is preferable to offer a review date rather than an achievement/completion date.

The Analytical Thinking Model

Using this model (also described by Wilson, 1980) to think about a client can be a productive exercise.

1. Review in your mind everything you know about the case.
2. Make a list of the 10–15 key facts of the case.
3. Imagine what feelings the client might have about his/her situation.
   a. At whom or what might the feelings be directed?
   b. Why might he/she feel that way?
   c. What would be the behavioral manifestations of those feelings?
4. Who are the client's "significant others"?
5. Develop a treatment plan:
   a. List all the possible outcomes of treatment (whether realistic or not).
   b. Label each as realistic or not.
   c. For each realistic goal, list the subgoals or objectives to be achieved, and put them in any necessary sequence.
   d. State the exact treatment techniques that would accomplish the subgoals.
   e. Rank the goals in a time sequence so you know where to start.
   f. Estimate the time needed to achieve each goal.

Write a summary of the main thoughts of steps 2 through 4, and discard all the material except this and the lists developed in step 5.

A Children's Residential Agency Model

Identifying information: Name, date of birth, date of admission, agency, primary worker.
Data and needs.
1. Education.
2. Medical/physical.
3. Contacts: Legal, family, etc.
4. Personal development (goals).
   a. Personal hygiene.
   b. Peer relationships.
   c. Adult relationships.
   d. Group relationships.
   e. Specialized treatments/therapies/support.
   f. Specific events.
Treatment/program adjustments (to methods).
1. Major incidents.
2. Routine adjustments.
3. Level changes (levels of programming).
4. Attitude and motivation.
5. Target summary (and changes in targets).
Family.

Multimodal Therapy Model

Arnold A. Lazarus (1997) has developed a model of assessment in which treatments of choice (those whose effectiveness for a specific problem has been supported by empirical research) are matched to each problem, analyzed at each of seven levels. The acronym for the levels is BASIC ID. There are no limitations on the methods of treatment that can be used, and so it can fit any paradigm. Proper diagnosis/problem specification is crucial to this model.

Assessment area/Problematic behaviors	*Interventions*
<u>B</u>ehavior	
<u>A</u>ffect	
<u>S</u>ensation	
<u>I</u>magery (fantasies, expectations)	
<u>C</u>ognition (beliefs)	
<u>I</u>nterpersonal relations	
<u>D</u>rugs/biology (included here are all medical conditions and nutrition, exercise, and hygiene)	

The Levels-of-Functioning Model

Kennedy (2003) offers an inventive, different approach to planning interventions. Using Axis V of DSM-IV-TR *(see Section 21.23)*, he has built numerous master treatment plans around levels of functioning in the seven areas of psychological impairment, social skills, dangerousness, <u>A</u>ctivities of <u>D</u>aily <u>L</u>iving/occupational skills, substance abuse, and medical and ancillary impairments.

The Stages-of-Change Model

Prochaska et al. (1992) have proposed a set of five stages through which everyone goes when making any kind of behavior change. It addresses a client's readiness or openness to change, with or without professional help. It has been widely used in addictions treatment.

Precontemplation

No intention to change in the foreseeable future. Client doesn't see that he/she has a problem. In "denial." Presenting for treatment due to pressure from others.

Contemplation

Also known as "ambivalence" because of weighing of pros and cons. Aware of a problem—"Something is wrong." Some commitment to action in next 6 months—"Not quite ready."

Preparation

Attempting to put thoughts about change into actions. Some change in behavior (e.g., "cutting down" on substance use, but not abstinent). Cycling in and out of pathological behaviors. Less debate of pros and cons, and more actual decisions or plans. May present for voluntary treatment at this stage.

Action

More overt behaviors in the direction of change. Some "successes." Behavior change (e.g., abstinence) at least for a period of time, but less than 6 months.

Maintenance

Behavior change for at least 6 months. Efforts are made to continue the change. In therapy, the goals are stabilizing the changed behaviors and avoiding relapse. The pattern of change is not linear. Some relapses should be expected and planned for.

Treatment Implications

Treatment must be matched with the client's stage of change, and progress is a function of the pretreatment stage of change, so some interventions are not appropriate. Treatment should focus on the transition points between stages. Strike (only) while (and where) the iron is hot. Watch out for your countertransference reactions at each stage of change. Change can involve 10 processes: Consciousness raising, self-reevaluation, environmental evaluation, self-liberation, counterconditioning, stimulus control, reinforcement management, helping relationships, dramatic relief, and social liberation.

25.4. A Treatment Plan Format for Case Conceptualization

Although MCO's demands for oversight and cost containment were the major motivators for formalizing written treatment plans, they have great value as an aid to case conceptualization. For those who need a brief, checklist-formatted plan, an efficient form can be found in *The Paper Office*, 4th ed. (Zuckerman, 2008). However, to structure the fuller evaluation of a client's history and situation and assist in comprehensive case formulation, working through Form 2 is recommended. You may photocopy and adapt it for your work with clients without obtaining written permission, but may not use it for teaching, writing, or any commercial venture without written permission. More guidance on treatment plans can be found in *The Paper Office*. For space considerations, this version eliminates the lines you will need to enter your findings, and it limits the number of responses in each instance to three.

Authorization: The Report's Purpose When an MCO Is the Reader

Treatment plans are submitted to obtain authorization for reimbursement (payment after delivery) for mental health services. A form such as Form 2 documents the need for mental health services and the plans to deliver them. On the basis of these statements, an MCO will decide to authorize or deny payment for the services of providers. This form is completed at intake and, if treatment is initially authorized, again toward the expiration of the (small) number of authorized sessions ("concurrent review"). This micromanagement is still a common format, despite its costs to all involved. See also the comments below under "III. A. Progress in current treatment to date."

For simplicity, again, the presentation here is confined to the end product—a plan written in a format suitable for and required by MCOs, as illustrated in Form 2. The meanings and rationale of each heading in this form from II onward are discussed below, and advice is offered.

II. Case formulation/overview

A. Presenting problem(s)/Chief complaint/Chief concern

The client comes in with a "complaint" (his/her formulation) or distress (psychic pain), and the clinician inquires, tests, weighs evidence, and reinterprets this into a "diagnosis" (in a medical model), a "concern" (in a patient-centered approach), or a "problem" (in common language and MCO terms).

- *For questions to ask, see Chapters 2, "Mental Status Evaluation Questions/Tasks," and 3, "Questions about Signs, Symptoms, and Other Behavior Patterns."*

- *For referral reasons in children, see Chapter 5, "Referral Reasons."*

B. History of presenting problem(s) and current situation

Mental health clinicians usually subscribe to an interacting biopsychosocial model for comprehensiveness, and to a "diathesis (vulnerability) plus stressor (demand for change) yields symptomatic behavior" model to explain abnormal behaviors. All the elements needing clinical attention are conceived of as either stressors, diatheses, or abnormal behaviors. In turn, behaviors may become new stressors.

Individualized Behavioral/Mental Health Treatment Plan

This is for ❑ Preauthorization for initial certification ❑ Concurrent review for reauthorization of care

I. Identification

Client's name: _____ Soc. Sec. #: _____ ID #: _____

Membership #: _____ Date of birth: _____ Sex: _____

Group name/#: _____ Certificate #: _____

Name of subscriber/member, and address (if other than client): _____

Release-of-records form(s) signed: ❑ Yes ❑ Not yet

II. Case formulation/overview

A. Presenting problem(s)/Chief complaint/Chief concern/Reasons for referral or seeking treatment/ crisis(es):

Problem	Severity[1]	Duration
1.		
2.		
3.		

B. History of presenting problem(s) and current situation (precipitants, motivations, stressors and resources/coping skills, comorbid conditions, living conditions, relevant demographics):

C. Previous treatments:

Name	Location/phone	Type of services and dates

D. Brief summary of abnormal or unusual mental status evaluation results:

_____   *(cont.)*

[1]Code for rating the severity of disruption or decreased performance of life routines and personal effectiveness: Mi = Mild, Mod = Moderate, S = Severe, VS = Very severe, or use GAF ratings from Axis V of DSM-IV-TR.

FORM 2. Individualized Behavioral/Mental Health Treatment Plan. Adapted from Zuckerman (2008). Copyright 2008 by Edward L. Zuckerman. Adapted by permission in *Clinician's Thesaurus,* 7th ed., by Edward L. Zuckerman. Permission to photocopy this form is granted to purchasers of this book for personal use only (see copyright page for details).

E. Functional limitations and impairments (descriptions and ratings of severity of limitation):

1. Self-care and ADLs—severity[1]:

2. Academic/occupational—severity[1]:

3. Intimate relationships/marriage/children/family of origin—severity[1]:

4. Social relationships—severity[1]:

5. Other areas—severity[1]:

F. Strengths:

1.

2.

3.

Code #
❑ DSM-IV-TR
G. Diagnoses—Current best formulation: Name (indicate which is primary diagnosis with "P"): or ❑ ICD?

Axis I _____ _____

Axis II _____ _____

Axis III—Significant and relevant medical conditions, including allergies and drug sensitivities:

Condition	Treatment/medication (regimen)	Provider	Status
1. _____	_____	_____	_____
2. _____	_____	_____	_____
3. _____	_____	_____	_____

Axis IV—Psychosocial and environmental problems in last year; overall severity rating: _____
❑ Problems with primary support group   ❑ Problems related to the social environment
❑ Educational problems   ❑ Occupational problems
❑ Housing problems   ❑ Economic problems
❑ Health care access problems   ❑ Other problems: _____
❑ Problems related to interaction with the legal system/crime

Axis V—Global Assessment of Functioning (GAF) rating: Currently: ____   Highest in past year: ____

V Codes—Other problems that may be a focus of clinical attention: _____

_____

(cont.)

TREATMENT
PLANS

H. Current assessment of foreseeable risks:

1. *Self-neglect or damage:* ❏ None ❏ Poor self care ❏ Significant self-neglect ❏ Self-abuse

   Specifics:

2. *Suicide:* ❏ No evidence ❏ Ideation only ❏ Plan ❏ Intent without means ❏ Intent with means

3. *Homicide:* ❏ No evidence ❏ Ideation only ❏ Plan ❏ Intent without means ❏ Intent with means

4. *Impulse control:* ❏ Sufficient ❏ Inconsistent ❏ Minimal ❏ Explosive

5. *Treatment compliance:* ❏ Fully compliant ❏ Variable ❏ Passive noncompliance ❏ Resistive

6. *Substance use:* ❏ None/normal use ❏ Abusing ❏ Unstable remission ❏ Dependence

7. *Physical or sexual abuse:* ❏ No evidence ❏ Yes ❏ Not reportable ❏ Date reported: _____

8. *Child or elder abuse or neglect:* ❏ No evidence ❏ Yes ❏ Not reportable ❏ Date reported: _____

   If yes, client is ❏ Victim ❏ Perpetrator ❏ Both ❏ Neither, but abuse exists in family

9. *If risk(s) exists:* Client ❏ can ❏ cannot meaningfully agree to a contract not to harm ❏ self ❏ others
   ❏ both

III. Treatment concerns

A. Progress in current treatment to date—Gains made and current level of severity of problems, reasons for continuing treatment: ❏ No treatment yet

B. Treatment plan—A recommended program of coordinated liaisons, consultations, evaluations, and treatment services:

1. Based on the current clinical evaluation, these **additional consultations or evaluations** are necessary:

Concern or question	Consultant
a.	
b.	
c.	

2. **Treatment's objectives and goals:** Significant improvement is to be expected, with treatment specified, for:

   Problem: _____

   - Behaviors to be changed:

   - Interventions (who does what, how often, with what resources; modality, frequency, duration):

   - Observable indicators of improvement (behaviors, reports):
     - Expected number of visits to achieve each indicator:

   - Discharge level of problem behaviors:
     - Review date:

   [✓ Item 2 is repeated for each additional problem.]

(cont.)

TREATMENT
PLANS

3. **Other current treating professionals:**

Name	Location/phone	Treatments provided

4. **My signature means** that I have participated in the formulation of my treatment plan, that I understand and approve of it, and that I accept the responsibility to fully carry out my parts of the plan.

Client: _____ Date: _____

Service provider: _____ Date: _____

5. **Additional comments, plans, or information:**

As a clinician, you can focus on symptoms, complaints, problems, goals, functioning level, behavioral excesses and deficits, recovery by stressor reduction, growth and learning to cope, alteration of family dynamics/homeostasis, crisis management, etc. How you understand the problem—its cause, dynamics, and goals—depends on your paradigm and training.

C. Previous treatments

MCOs want to know about previous treatment so that they may exclude payment for the treatment of preexisting conditions, since as *in loco* insurers they appear to believe that a previous insurer should pay for services for disorders that continue to exist or have reappeared.

Previous treaters are vitally important to you as a clinician for two reasons: (1) Misdiagnosing or mistreating a condition of which you were not aware but should have been (because all good clinicians always get old records) is a major source of malpractice vulnerability; and (2) you should learn what has and has not worked in the past, in order to make your own treatment more effective.

D. Brief summary of abnormal or unusual mental status evaluation results

Conducting MSEs is a traditional skill area of clinicians, and you should strive to be a sophisticated evaluator. Here, write a summary of your abnormal findings and disregard all normal findings.

- *Chapter 2 presents the world's largest collection of MSE questions.*
- *Chapter 11 offers thousands of descriptors for writing up the MSE.*
- *Section 2.25 offers a form for recording your findings (Form 1).*

E. Functional limitations and impairments

Which areas of function to evaluate and how to label them are controversial topics. For individual clients, you might add or substitute "Affective functioning" (e.g., emotional paralysis from continuing grieving or depression with suicidal preoccupations), "Physical functioning" (e.g., chronic fatigue, dizziness, and incontinence resulting in social isolation), or combinations of these areas.

The areas of functioning listed in Form 2 are the only ones of concern to MCOs. If the client has discontinued working, returning her/him to employment is the most valuable service you can provide in the eyes of MCO personnel (who, after all, work for the client's employer).

- *For ADL evaluation, see Chapter 14.*
- *For relationships in society, see Chapter 15.*
- *For couple and family relationships, see Chapter 16.*
- *For the criteria for work or school functioning, see Chapter 17.*

Legal problems can go under "Social" or "Occupational"; leisure/recreational losses under Other, etc. Do not obsess over the best choice of category for each limitation; it doesn't matter to anyone else. Similarly, the titles of the categories themselves don't matter greatly ("Work," "Vocational," "Occupational," "Employment," and "Military" are functional equivalents).

MCOs are almost uninterested in some clinical areas, such as sexual dysfunctions, traumatic early experiences, and eating disorders, unless they can be shown to have a significant impact on work functioning. MCOs interpret learning disorders and other academic dysfunctions as educational/school problems rather than health problems, and refuse to pay for their assessment or treatment. Only lip service is paid to spiritual/religious, cultural/ethnic, and recreational aspects.

A key principle of MCO work is that therapy's goal is just to restore the client to an immediately previous (premorbid) level of functioning. Therapy with any aim higher than recovery to this level (perhaps healthier functioning, understanding, personality change, prevention of relapse, or even reduced costs of further treatment) is simply not the financial responsibility of the MCO.

I suggest a simple rating scale for severity of impairments. The GAF numbers provide both vague anchors for judgments and the illusion of precision.

- *See Section 21.23, "Axis V: <u>G</u>lobal <u>A</u>ssessment of <u>F</u>unctioning Scale," for the anchoring statements.*

F. Strengths

We clinicians focus to a great (indeed, excessive) extent on deficits and defects, and yet nothing can be built on deficits or absences. MCOs, the <u>J</u>oint <u>C</u>ommission on <u>A</u>ccreditation of <u>H</u>ealthcare <u>O</u>rganizations, and others rightly demand that we consider the client's resources as a foundation for growth and as a font of ideas about previous successes that might be inspirational or repeatable. Therapies such as the "solution-focused approach" and the "miracle cure" deliberately utilize these successes, and you may find that a thorough inquiry into resources makes your job easier.

- *Sections 2.24 and 19.1 may help you assess coping ability. See also Section 25.7, "Checklist of Strengths."*

G. Diagnoses

We all know that diagnosis, impairment, and treatment are not tightly related in the mental health area; we don't treat a diagnosis, but a client with patterns and pains. However, the shorthand of a diagnostic label conveys important information about what is and is not present to the professionally educated. MCOs demand that we offer diagnoses based on certain widely acknowledged standards, even when other aspects are the foci of intervention and the diagnoses fail to address interactive or interpersonal aspects.

MCOs are also reluctant to pay for treatment of Axis II diagnoses, because they seem to believe that therapy for personality disorders is ineffective. Nevertheless, make sure to record any Axis II conditions present. You are not paid by the number of diagnoses, and great precision is not required these days. However, you must be correct, so careful differential diagnosing *is* required. Morrison (2001, 2006) will teach you all you need to know.

- *Chapter 21 contains almost all of the DSM-IV-TR and ICD-9-CM titles and codes.*

H. Current assessment of foreseeable risks

For their finality, impacts, and legal consequences, homicide, violence, and suicide are risks of greatest concern to both clinicians and MCOs. Of only slightly less concern to MCOs are substance abuse and dependence.

- *Section 12.40 will help you evaluate suicide potential.*
- *Sections 13.6 and 12.41 may help you evaluate potential for violence.*

Form 2 offers simple checkoffs, but if you suspect that any of these risks are of significance or you are unsure and anxious, consult with others and elaborate on your concerns in a narrative. From a malpractice point of view, demonstrating that you were professionally thoughtful before a tragic incident is more important than accurately predicting it (which you generally cannot do).

III. Treatment concerns

A. Progress in current treatment to date

This item is completed when you seek reauthorization for a continuation of your services. These "concurrent reviews" function like progress reports. They do not *have* to be positive to justify services, but should be thoughtful. If the client has returned to a previous level of functioning, continued services will usually be deemed unnecessary, generally without regard to the stability of the recovery. If little or no progress has been demonstrated, you should consider adding treatments (medications, family meetings, drug and alcohol evaluation, psychoeducational community groups) or changing your approach. This is both a financial consideration and an ethical one in the face of little or no progress after sincere and appropriate efforts.

B. Treatment plan

- *Chapter 22, "Recommendations," has a long list of therapeutic services from which to select.*

1. ADDITIONAL CONSULTATIONS OR EVALUATIONS

Although these questions are often missing from MCOs' forms, it is logical and clinically justifiable to ask them: What else do we need to know, and how can we find this out?

MCOs have gutted the assessment function, with the rationale that the treater learns all that is necessary to guide treatment by doing treatment. This is not necessarily the case, nor is it efficient. Although testing can be overused, it can still be valuable to know what kind of personality a depressed person has or what other problems are not being currently demonstrated to you during therapy. It is even more clear that treating a person with dementia for depression, no matter how well validated the methods, is unlikely to result in full recovery. I recommend that all therapists learn how to use and interpret at least a few screening tests and whatever instruments they intend to use for outcome assessment.

2. TREATMENT'S OBJECTIVES AND GOALS

To conserve space, only one problem is shown on Form 2. As indicated there, you should repeat this format as many times as necessary, based on your conceptualization of the case. Only a few problems should be listed, in order for you and your client to remain focused. Select ones tightly related to the diagnosis and the limitations of function, and present them in order of priority.

Behaviors to be changed

This is essentially a restatement of the problem in terms of the behaviors demonstrating its dynamics—its signs and symptoms or behavioral manifestations. If you can't specify the behaviors, you may need to do a more thorough investigation and interview of the client. But some may remain unarticulated and ineffable.

Interventions

You can specify interventions by asking yourself questions like these: What approaches have been shown to work for this problem? *(See Section 22.2, "Treatments of Choice.")* What are you trained to do with these kinds of problems? (If you lack skill in these areas, do not try to fake it. Get training or refer the client.) What techniques address the symptoms presented? How are these implemented? (How often? For how long? With what tools?) What will you expect your patient to do? Generic, goalless, unfocused treatment is unethical. Avoid experimental or faddish techniques for most clients, and get fully informed consent.

Offer descriptors of the mode of therapy (individual, group, family, etc.), the orientation or modality (cognitive, interpersonal, psychodynamic, structural, etc.), and specific techniques ("hot seat," "covert sensitization," "relapse prevention"). Indicate the clinical focus of these, such as "traumatic experiences in marriage" or "depressogenic thought patterns."

MCOs seem fond of interventions with low or no costs to them. Try to include (where appropriate) community support groups, psychoeducational efforts by others, bibliotherapy, etc.

Goals

You may have noticed that there is no heading "Goals" on Form 2. That is deliberate. Instead, the form offers "Observable indicators of improvement" and "Discharge level of problem behaviors," both of which are more easily understood and stated than the more popular "Goals." However, for generalizability, I use the word "goal" in the discussion to follow.

Goals are usually understood as long-term destinations, and objectives are the steps needed to reach those goals. But because there is no agreement in the field over the exact meaning of objectives, you need not be precise in differentiating them from goals. Objectives are usually more behavioral and concrete than goals. Objectives are also shorter-term and more easily measurable. They are usually described in terms of the client's performance ("The client will be able to … "). Identifying long-term goals or changes makes little sense when treatment will be limited to 10–12 sessions. Much effort has been spent in distinguishing goals from objectives, describing the actions of therapy as methods, and devising ways of articulating measurable outcomes. We clinicians have usually been more anxious and precise than is necessary. Take a problem, consider how it might change with therapy, and then state some goals.

Observable indicators of improvement

Being able to assess change is absolutely crucial. Write desired outcomes in behavioral language. This means what a camera would see (actions and expressions), not the invisible emotions, cognitive processes, history, and intentions. Consider the manifestations of these, and not your well-trained formulations and shorthands for them.

Avoid very broad terms like "communication skills" or "depression," because the client and reviewer will not be able to know what counts as change. Tie each indicator of change (objective or step toward the goal or longer-range outcome) to the presenting limitations of function. Make these observable objectives measurable or at least quantifiable. Frequency, duration, intensity, and latency are the classic dimensions for describing changes in symptomatic behaviors. This objectification allows impartial evaluation.

Avoid steps of change that are too difficult (so as not to reinforce failure, anxiety, or low confidence) or too easy (so as to make reaching them irrelevant and unmotivating) to achieve.

Because you cannot observe the client in her/his life circumstances, accept and use "client reports" of the new behaviors, as necessary. It would be best if you could get confirmation of changes from someone else who observes the client frequently (this person, you, and the client would then create an elegant "triadic" assessment).

Expected number of visits to achieve each indicator

You may notice that no time frames or dates are offered, because sessions may be missed or other issues may arise. Besides, payment is based on services rendered, not calendar time.

Discharge level of problem behaviors

This is another way of saying "long-term goals," but for MCOs it is the criterion of recovery of function. There is no specific mention here of dates for evaluation of progress or more formal reevaluations of the client's status, which would normally be part of the treatment plan.

3. OTHER CURRENT TREATING PROFESSIONALS

You need this information to coordinate treatment; to prevent the loss of information crucial to your or another's treatment of the client (e.g., side effects of medications); perhaps to receive medical oversight to treat a client; to indicate supervision; to reduce duplication of services; to obtain backup in an emergency; to consult in regard to problems; etc.

4. MY SIGNATURE MEANS ...

Fully informed consent is an ethical necessity. Treatment is seen more these days as a contractual arrangement between a capable client and a professional, and not as a process taking place between a passive patient and an active expert. If treatment is a shared adventure, both parties must know about and voluntarily agree to it.

It may be very therapeutically productive to share the planning with the client, and not to treat this document as simply a burden required for payment.

5. ADDITIONAL COMMENTS, PLANS, OR INFORMATION

This is self-explanatory and is included mainly to remind you of any other less tidy details.

25.5. Treatment Plan Components for Clients with Substance Abuse

See also "Responses to Treatment" under Section 12.39, "Substance Use, Abuse, and Dependence."

The lists below of goals and methods are derived from statements from the literature and are designed to be comprehensive but not exhaustive. They should, of course, be tailored to each client.

Treatment Goals

Abstinence: Obtain and maintain sobriety, live a chemical-free life, cope with life without chemicals.
Controlled drinking: Follow patterns of use that reduce harm. (See below.)

Stabilize one's health, finances, vocation/school, employment, living arrangements.
Complete a physical examination as prescribed, and comply with medical advice.
Enhance health and fitness. Get medical checkups. Take medications as prescribed; report on adherence to regimen/schedule, effectiveness, and side effects.
Resolve and avoid legal problems.
Develop sober leisure skills.

Stabilize one's intimate relationships, marriage, family.
Include significant others such as spouse/partner, children, relatives, friends, etc., in the recovery program as prescribed.
Improve social skills, assertiveness, emotional expression, communication.
Improve social support, friendships, social pursuits.

Deal/cope with/resolve emotional problems/feelings such as rejection, depression, unresolved grief/mourning, shame, guilt, abandonment.
Improve coping skills, stress management skills, relaxation abilities, self-control.
Enhance self-esteem, confidence, and self-acceptance.
Accept responsibility for the consequences of one's behavior.
Improve problem-solving ability, setting of priorities, persistence, frustration tolerance.

Be an active participant in the treatment program by attending/participating in:
Scheduled education classes about chemical dependency and the process of recovery.
Scheduled counseling, psychotherapy, and educational groups (e.g., spirituality groups, men's and women's groups).

Recreational activities to expand pleasures of physical activity, healthy competition, skill acquisition, socializing, interest areas, etc.

Alcoholics Anonymous/Narcotics Anonymous/etc. groups to develop a sober support fellowship in the community.

The design and carrying out of a discharge plan that includes plans for employment, a place to live, sobriety.

Become a sponsor, substance educator, role model.

Offer and receive effective constructive feedback in groups.

Assume leadership roles in the community.

Methods

Education

Learn about the following (alternate phrasings can include "be exposed to," "understand," "appreciate," "apply," and "explain"):

The disease concept of addiction.

The consequences of accepting one's identity as having alcoholism/drug abuse.

Cross-addiction, multiple addictions, dual diagnoses.

Addictive behavior not involving chemicals, etc.

The nature and processes of addiction and recovery.

The issues of dysfunctional families, codependence, Adult Children Of Alcoholic Parents, cycles.

Write and share one's chemical history, the progression of addiction, and the consequent problems.

Read recommended books and discuss their contents.

Therapeutic Activities

Define, in one's own words, all the words in one of the Twelve Steps.

Interview five peers on powerlessness, their understanding of the Twelve Steps, etc.

List five examples of one's personal unmanageableness.

Identify specific negative consequences of one's substance use.

Keep a "feelings journal" and make at least two entries a day.

Interview counselors on how to deal with anger.

Interview peers about a positive and a negative quality of oneself.

Write a "feelings letter" to one's parents (about feelings of inadequacy, history of emotional/physical/sexual abuse or neglect, abandonment, etc.).

Identify and practice other ways to achieve the benefits previously obtained from substance abuse.

List five things to be grateful for each day.

Therapeutic Planning

Prepare an aftercare plan, including a daily plan, home group meetings, and attendance at (#) of meetings per week for a total of (#) meetings/weeks/days.

Prepare a plan to cope with typical triggers of relapse: Hungry, Angry, Lonely, Tired. For more triggers, see a fine list online (*www.psychpage.com/learning/library/assess/relapse*).

Relapse prevention (Marlatt & Donovan, 2005): Learn about the abstinence violation effect statements and develop counters to these; identify high-risk situations, warning signs, and triggers; rehearse coping responses; write a relapse prevention plan for oneself; teach relapse prevention to others.

TREATMENT PLANS

Develop multiple alternatives to chemical use for high-risk situations (e.g., recreation skills, time management planning, calling on one's support system); use <u>S</u>tress <u>I</u>noculation <u>T</u>raining (Meichenbaum, 1996).

Learn and utilize harm reduction approaches (Marlatt, 1998; Denning, 2000; and Tatarsky, 2002).

25.6. Treatment Plan Components for Crisis Interventions

Acknowledge/appreciate/validate/take seriously the subject's distress.
Encourage ventilation of feelings.
Reassure subject/family of your continued availability.
Reinforce/support all positive responses.
Reinforce/support problem-solving efforts.
Offer alternative methods of coping.
Negotiate a contract of not doing anything to worsen the situation for a period of time.
Negotiate what to do during periods when feeling bad.
Provide assured and continual support.

25.7. Checklist of Strengths

Partly in reaction to the pathology-based focus of most clinical work, the search to articulate, evaluate, and build upon the strengths of humans has gained momentum in recent years. See especially Peterson and Seligman (2004) and two websites (*www.ppc.sas.upenn.edu* and *www.authentichappiness.com*).

Related terms worth researching include these:

Resilience, posttraumatic growth, wellness, competence, human strengths, protective factors, optimism, empowerment, self-efficacy, salutogenesis.

Social/Community

Has multiple, extensive, and accessible support systems.
Productive member of viable groups or communities.
Has endeared self to a large number of people and enjoys their company quite frequently.
Has long-term relationships; a supportive, capable partner/spouse, relatives, close friends.
Social life remains intact.
Pursues justice/fairness, is brave/courageous.

Interpersonal

Socially skilled/competent, intelligent, popular, likable, works on a team.
Assertive, strong, powerful, dominant, acts as a leader, decisive.
Respectful, tolerant, offers and accepts feedback.
Friendly, comfortable, outgoing, extroverted, has good sense of humor, playful, shares, helpful.
Socially sensitive, aware of own impact on others, empathetic, good listener, concerned for others, compassionate.
Sensitive to the examiner's needs and the social demands of the examination.
Supports/provides for others, nurturing, generous, kind, loving, merciful, forgives appropriately.
Maintains appropriate boundaries, prudent, cautious, discreet.

Occupational/Educational

Good adjustment, normal, well adjusted, happy, satisfied.

High task motivation, ambitious, hard-working, persistent, diligent, industrious, school/career success, skilled at problem solving.

History of triumphs over challenges, nonavoidance/counterphobic, coped effectively with losses, benefited from previous counseling, no substance abuse.

Consistent employment/vocation/career.

Has adequate income, financial resources, savings, insurance. Manages finances well.

Knowledgeable, well-informed, loves learning.

Personality

Shows integrity/honesty, trustworthy, accepts responsibility for own behavior, dependable, reliable, stable.

Resilient, hardy, coping skills, adaptable, flexible, able to self-correct.

Self-confident and has self-esteem, accurate self-perceptions, positive self-regard.

Can attend/concentrate/focus for long periods.

Can recall well.

Spiritual, has religious faith, hopeful, optimistic, attitude of gratitude, thankful.

Understands interactions of cognitions, affects, and behaviors, understands own motivations, insightful, psychological-minded, sophisticated.

Curious, rational, skillful, intellectually competent, flexible.

Creative, imaginative, ingenious, inventive, artistic in any medium, talented, appreciates beauty and excellence, feels awe.

Wise, has good judgment, keeps perspective, good reality testing, accurate appraisal of demands, realistic, open-minded.

Affective

Aware and comfortable with feelings in self and others, expressive, shows a range of affects.

Self-disciplined/regulated/controlled, modulates impulses, thinking and feeling are integrated.

Tolerates painful emotions.

Emotionally intelligent.

Has zest and enthusiasm.

Physical

Healthy, energetic, vital.

Has stamina, athletic, exercises.

Sleeps well, good hygiene, satisfying recreation, sexually satisfied.

Adapts to physical limitations and losses.

25.8. Outcome Measures/Goal Achievements

The evaluation of the effects of one's work is a professional and ethical as well as a scientific obligation. As part of the privilege of being in clinical practice, we owe our current and future patients the most effective care, and we owe ourselves the feedback to guide the development of our skills. For the clinician who wishes to evaluate his/her own practice, much guidance is available in Clement (1999), Wiger and Solberg (2001), and Ogles et al. (2002). An example of a comprehensive package is OQ-Analyst from OQ Measures (*www.oqmeasures.com/site*).

Many aspects of treatment can be evaluated. Clients and MCOs focus most on the goal of symptom reduction. This book contains much detail about particular symptoms from which to develop goals: Emotional/affective symptoms are presented in Chapter 10, cognitive ones in Chapter 11, personality disorder symptoms in Chapter 13, and most of the other symptoms in Chapter 12. In addition, Chapter 5, "Referral Reasons," describes many symptomatic behaviors. Use the index for more specific areas. For the goals of increasing functionality, Chapter 14 covers ADLs, Chapter 15 social/community functioning, Chapter 16 relationships, and Chapter 17 vocational and academic functioning.

Common Foci of Outcome Evaluations

Clinicians and MCOs define outcomes from very different perspectives. Clinicians tend to focus on building realistic self-esteem; providing a supportive context for the exploration of feelings/history; bolstering defenses and preventing further decompensation; improving insight; increasing behavior controls, coping skills, and the tolerance of stressors at work/home; improving sexual adjustment; etc. The most common focus of MCOs is client satisfaction with services. This has most often been defined in its more easily measured but less clinical aspects, such as physical accessibility, scheduling/availability, comfort of setting, etc. More recently, MCOs have been asking clients whether they would return for care or recommend the service to another, about their comfort with level of autonomy/control, and about their relationship with the providers (including respect, trust, competence, availability, etc.). Obviously, these additional factors are difficult to assess, and so the measurements are open to interpretation.

The larger picture of assessing the role of therapy in improving the quality of life; reducing other health care costs; lengthening lifespan; and increasing human happiness, satisfaction, and productivity has yet to be addressed by MCOs. However, Frisch (1999) has made an excellent start.

<u>G</u>oal <u>A</u>ttainment <u>S</u>caling

The strengths of GAS, a little-known method for assessing outcomes, are its simplicity and flexibility: Any kind of goal, in any paradigm, in any area, with any definition can be used. All that is needed is the ability to specify five levels of outcome (least favorable likely outcome, less than expected, expected, more than expected, and most favorable likely outcome), in observable terms, for each of at least five goals. Each level is given a relative weight. At review time the current status of each goal is assessed, and a simple mathematical formula determines the success of the intervention. For more information, see Kiresuk et al. (1994).

26

Formats for Reports, Evaluations, and Summaries

This chapter offers templates, formats, or outlines for many kinds of reports to organize and convey your information for specific audiences or purposes. Although neuropsychological, forensic, developmental, vocational, rehabilitation, and some other specialized psychiatric nursing and psychosocial evaluations are beyond the scope of this book, you will find guidance here for common reports and some examples of uncommon but heuristic alternatives.

26.1. A Standard Format for Reports of Evaluations

The sequential structure of Part II of this book can be used. *(See also Table 1 in "Getting Oriented to the* Clinician's Thesaurus.*")*

Use your agency's letterhead, or your own letterhead with credentials of relevance. Give the title or type of report as the heading. Then provide the following:

Name of person to whom report is being sent.
Name of subject of report; case/identification number; subject's gender and age.
Date(s) of examination(s) and report.
Evaluator's name (if not the same as the name on the letterhead).

A report should meet the needs of the reader, not the writer. The 12 content areas below, with my specifics, are recommended by Rivas-Vasquez et al. (2001) for the initial evaluation. You should select from these and expand on the ones most relevant to the purpose and audience of your report.

1. Identifying information.
2. Chief Complaint or Concern.
    In the client's language.
    Referral source and reason.
3. History of present illness.
    Symptoms, treatments, conflicts.
4. Medical history.
    Conditions, medications, treatments, treaters, nutrition.
5. Prior psychiatric history.
6. Substance abuse history.
7. Family psychiatric and substance abuse histories.

8. Psychosocial history.
   Traumas, educational and vocational functioning, legal issues.
9. <u>M</u>ental <u>S</u>tatus <u>E</u>xamination.
   Appearance, behavioral observations.
   Mood and affect.
   Cognitive functioning.
10. Psychometric data base (when applicable).
    Summary of findings.
11. Diagnostic impression.
    Case formulation/summary.
    Reliability or cautions.
    Diagnoses.
12. Treatment plan or recommendations.
    Referrals.
    Resources.
    Motivation and barriers.

Rivas-Vasquez et al. (2001) state: "The outline presented above is intended to allow clinicians to structure the documentation of the initial diagnostic evaluation in order to produce a clinical and legal record that can attest to the work that was performed. It will also serve to outline the psychologist's diligence and thoroughness, serve as a communication between health care providers, and satisfy reimbursement requirements for third party payers" (p. 199).

In a follow-up, Lewis (2002) points out that since the purposes of consultations differ, so should the content of reports, and that most often a limited number of the items listed above is more appropriate. He adds that the accepted practice in a given setting shapes the content.

26.2. Format for Psychodynamic Evaluations: Developmental Model

Huber (1961) offers an outline for what he calls the "sequential report," which combines the chronological (to understand causation) with the topical (to understand the presentation) and frames the questions of dynamics.

1. Intellectual functioning.
   Level of present functioning, comparison with his/her group.
   Level of capacity.
   Reasons for failure to function up to capacity.
   Areas of strength and weakness.
2. Dynamics.
   What is he/she attempting to accomplish with her/his present mode of behavior?
   What thoughts and feelings is she/he having?
   What events or people produce conflict? Anxiety?
   Major and minor conflicts.
   People with whom the conflicts are manifested.
   Times and places where the conflicts arise.
   How did her/his present situation arise? What pressures and supports were given by significant
      figures? What was the sequence of learning the defenses, symptoms, adaptations, etc.?
3. Methods of handling conflicts.
   Overt behavior manifesting anxiety, defense mechanisms, symptoms.
4. Strengths and weaknesses in relation to goals.
   Needs and wishes, both manifest and latent.
   Strengths for pursuing them: What are the pressures, supports, and strengths (environmen-

tal and intrapsychic) that can change her/his life?

   Weaknesses: What can produce dangerous and/or crippling behaviors (suicide, psychotic reactions, psychosomatic difficulties, antisocial acts)?

   What does she/he need to function more effectively?

   How much impairment is there? What is the nature of the impairment?

 5. Recommendations.

   Therapy/no therapy, environmental change.

   Form(s) of therapy.

   Predictions about therapy.

26.3. The Psychodynamic Diagnostic Manual

The PDM (PDM Task Force, 2006) represents the most sophisticated, comprehensive, research-based, current, psychodynamic approach to case conceptualization. Using it allows integration of symptoms and personality with functioning and adaptability. Codes and descriptions for adults are assigned along three axes: Personality type and dynamics; Mental functioning and adaptability; and Symptom patterns that address the person's subjective experiences. There are equivalent axes for children and adolescents; the P, M, and S codes are used with the suffix CA. For infants and young children, there are additional codes addressing Interactive disorders, Regulatory–Sensory Processing disorders, Neurodevelopmental disorders, and other patterns appropriate for their life stages. These diagnoses have multiply supported causative, functional, and treatment implications, as described in the PDM. (See also R. Gordon, 2010.)

26.4. Themes for Evaluations from an Existential Perspective

   Enhancing the capacity for self-awareness so as to make choices and live more fully.

   Acceptance of responsibility: Because we are free to act, we must accept responsibility for our actions. We cannot change without accepting this responsibility.

   Striving for an identity from within rather than based on others' expectations.

   The continuous search for the meaning of one's life: "What do I want from this life? Where is my source of meaning?"

   Acceptance of anxiety as a normal, inescapable part of living.

   Fuller awareness of death and nonbeing.

26.5. Adlerian Evaluations[1]

Life Style Analysis

   Activity level and radius: Friendships, social life, occupation, recreation, love, and sex.

   Degree of cooperation and social interest: Thinking about needs and feelings of others, actions to help others.

   Courage and conquests.

   Discouragements and stopping points.

   Excesses and omissions.

   Level and type of intelligence.

   Emotions and feelings: Conjunctive and disjunctive, depth and range.

[1]These are courtesy of Henry T. Stein, PhD, of San Francisco, CA.

Scheme of apperception: Antithetical scheme of apperception, perceived minus and plus situations.

Use of capabilities: Intelligence (social purpose), abilities and talents (socially useful and useless), feelings and emotions (move ahead or stop), and memory and imagination (encouragement/discouragement).

Pattern of dealing with tasks and difficulties: Childhood prototype, adolescent experimentation, repetitive adult style.

Inferiority feelings, compensatory goal, and style of life: Inferiority feelings (what to avoid, painful insecurity); fictional goal of superiority (imagined compensation, security and success); style of life (how to get to goal and deal with life's major tasks: social relationships, occupation, love, and sex); connection of presenting problem with life style and goal; use of symptoms to excuse avoidance of normal tasks.

Theory

Interpersonal focus: Social beings moving through and interacting with their environments.

Goals of psychotherapy: Expansion of the individual, self-realization, enhancement of social interest, enhancement of choices (ability to choose to shape the internal and external environment, and to choose posture adopted toward life's stimuli).

Terms and Concepts

Inferiority, superiority, and their complexes.
Compensation, overcompensation.
Life style, style of life.
Confluence and transformation of drives.
Masculine protest.
Fictionalism, fictional finalisms.
Striving for perfection, self-enhancement.
Social embeddedness, social interest.
Early/first recollections.

26.6. Transactional Analysis[2]

Almost all clinical models examine only the individual. Eric Berne's (1964) TA combines interactional and psychodynamic perspectives.

Ego states: Parent, Child, Adult; contaminations, exclusions; critical, nurturing; defining/structuring.

Adapted Child, Natural Child, Little Professor.

Strokes: Stroke Economy, Stroke Hunger, for being/doing, conditional/unconditional, discounting, compromise.

Transactions: Complementary, crossed, ulterior, congruent, angular, duplex.

Relationships: Companionate, intimate, symbiotic.

Scripts, counterscript, script injunction, positive script decisions, messages.

Ways of structuring time: Withdrawal, intimacy, ritual, activities, pastimes, games, rackets.

Pastimes: PTA, Psychiatry, Small Talk (General Motors, Who Won?, Grocery, Kitchen, Wardrobe, How To?, How Much?, Do You Know?, Ever Been?, What Became Of?, Morning After, Martini).

---

[2]Resources for TA materials include these: For information, International Transactional Analysis Association, 436 14th St., Suite 1301, Oakland, CA 94612-2710; (510) 625-7720; *www.itaa-net.org*.

Games:

Degrees of games: Hard, soft, ulterior transactions.

Elements of games: Steps, Gambits, Moves, Payoffs.

Types of games:

Alcoholic games: Roles for the game of Alcoholic include Alcoholic, Patsy, Connection, Rescuer, Persecutor. (Variations of this game include Drunk and Proud; Lush; Wino; High and Proud; etc.—for these and other games people with alcoholism play, see Steiner, 1971.)

Marital games: Corner; Courtroom; Frigid Woman; Frigid Man; Harried; If It Weren't for You; Look How Hard I've Tried; Sweetheart.

Sexual games: Let's You and Him Fight; Perversion; Rapo; Stocking Game; Uproar.

Party games: Ain't It Awful; Blemish; Schlemiel; Anti-schlemiel; Why Don't You–Yes, But; You Got Me into This; You Got Yourself into This; There I Go Again.

Underworld games: Cops and Robbers; How Do You Get Out of Here; Let's Pull a Fast One on Joey.

Consulting room games: Greenhouse; Stupid; Wooden Leg; Do Me Something; Indigence; Peasant; I'm Only Trying to Help You; Psychiatry.

Good games: Busman's Holiday; Cavalier; Happy to Help; Homely Sage; They'll Be Glad They Knew Me.

Other games: Kick Me; Harass; I Am Blameless; NIGYSOB (<u>N</u>ow <u>I</u>'ve <u>G</u>ot <u>Y</u>ou, <u>S</u>on <u>O</u>f a <u>B</u>itch); See What You Made Me Do; Debtor; Creditor.

Rackets: Stamp Collecting, Nobody Loves Me.

26.7. Nursing Diagnoses and Treatment Planning[3]

Each profession approaches the facts of abnormal behavior from its own perspective, history, and traditions. Many clinicians are surprised to find that nursing thinks clearly and comprehensively (nursing diagnoses—NANDA International, 2003) and productively (nursing care plans) about psychological conditions, and that many nurses are trained and certified as psychiatric specialists. The basic psychiatric credential is <u>C</u>ertified <u>S</u>pecialist, which requires 2 years of supervised practice beyond the <u>M</u>aster of <u>S</u>cience in <u>N</u>ursing level. With courses in medication, etc., nurses are called <u>A</u>dvanced <u>P</u>ractice <u>R</u>egistered <u>N</u>urses and can prescibe in 42 states as of late 2009.

Nursing diagnoses tend to be quite behavior specific and can add "potential for" additional behaviors of concern, such as suicide or substance abuse.

26.8. Vocational and Nonclinical Personality Evaluations

Huber (1984) quotes these skeletal industrial/organizational report outlines:

From Roher, Hibler, and Replogle:

1. Intelligence.
2. Emotional control.
3. Skill in human relations.
4. Insight and self-criticism.
5. Organization and planning ability, direction of others.
6. Recommendations and prognosis (for candidates) or conclusions and prognosis (for noncandidates).

---

[3]I am most grateful to Patricia Hurzeler, MS, APRN, CS, of Bloomfield, CT, for these suggestions.

From Fear (1958):

1. Test results: Mental ability, numerical ability, verbal ability, clerical aptitude (or other appropriate testing), social intelligence.
2. Evaluation: Work history, education and training, early home background, present social adjustment, personality, motivation, and character.
3. Summary of assets and liabilities.
4. Summary.

From Richardson, Bellows, Henry, and Co.:

1. Intellectual functioning.
2. Relations with others.
3. Work characteristics.
4. Aspirations and drive.
5. Interests and values.
6. Personal adjustment.
7. Family background.
8. Potential and recommendations.

Huber (1961) also suggests asking the reader or recipient of the report these questions:

"Describe the characteristics of the most satisfactory/ideal candidate in this job."
"What characteristics of this person stand in the way of your hiring him/her without any hesitation?"
"What specific questions keep coming into your mind about this candidate?"
"What do you not want to see in a candidate for this job?"

26.9. Formats for Therapy Notes

First decide on the answers to these questions: (1) To/for whom am I writing? (2) For what purpose am I making these notes? (3) What is my system for recording data?

Include the content (facts, actions, words) and some interpretations, and keep these distinguished.

There is no universally accepted standard for therapy notes, and it appears that the <u>H</u>ealth <u>I</u>nsurance <u>P</u>ortability and <u>A</u>ccountability <u>A</u>ct of 1996's rules will become the default for most records. HIPAA delineates "<u>P</u>sychotherapy <u>N</u>otes" whose content *excludes* medication prescription and monitoring, as well as these elements of the counseling session: starting and stopping times, the modalities of treatment (individual, family, etc.), the frequency of sessions, and summaries of the following: symptoms, diagnosis/es, the treatment plan, functional status, progress to date, prognosis, and results of clinical tests. By default, the items just mentioned become the elements of what are customarily called "Progress Notes." Simply, the Progress Notes can be, under HIPAA, released to other Covered Entities (other treaters, insurance companies, and billers) for almost any purpose. In contrast, PNs are for the personal use of the clinician and are not to be released, so they are the place for speculations, discussions with oneself, comments on the relationship, etc. HIPAA-defined PNs need not be kept (or at least not on every patient), but should be clearly marked as protected by or compliant with HIPAA to prevent their accidental unauthorized release. The mechanics of implementing HIPAA are complex, and so you might want to look into Zuckerman (2006; see also *www.hipaahelp.info*).

See also Zuckerman (2008) for guidance, forms, and examples of formats, and Wiger (1998) for suggestions and examples of good and bad notes.

FORMATS
FOR REPORTS

A Simple Format

Huber (1961) suggests this format. The tips in brackets indicate my way of noting various elements.

Content (or behavior): What each did and said. [I record these with no modifiers.]

What the therapist thought and felt about the content and may have said to the patient. [I put these in parentheses.]

What the therapist thought and felt about the patient, the interview, the content—and probably did not tell the patient. [I put these comments in square brackets, along with my observations and hypotheses about games played, emotional and cognitive styles, etc.]

Outside: Anything bearing on the therapy that happened outside the interview. Menninger (1952) adds to this: Compliance with the therapeutic program, steps taken to overcome the patient's resistance and who took them, telephone calls, consultations with colleagues and the results.

Plans for the next interview (promises made, what to pursue, questions). [I use the headings "HW" for work to be done by either of us, and "RX" for topics to be followed up.]

27

Treatments for Specific Disorders and Concerns

This chapter is a listing of resources on treatments for many of the disorders and concerns discussed elsewhere in this book.

27.1. Abuse/Aggression/Violence/Impulsive Behaviors

Deffenbacher, J., & McKay, M. (2000). *Overcoming situational and general anger* (2nd ed.). Oakland, CA: New Harbinger.

Dutton, D. G. (2007). *The abusive personality: Violence and control in intimate relationships* (2nd ed.). New York: Guilford Press.

Gottlieb, M. M. (1999). *The angry self: A comprehensive approach to anger management.* Phoenix, AZ: Zeig, Tucker.

Kassinove, H., & Tafrate, R. C. (2002). *Anger management: The complete treatment guidebook for practitioners.* San Luis Obispo, CA: Impact.

Webster, C. D., & Jackson, M. A. (Eds.). (1997). *Impulsivity: Theory, assessment, and treatment.* New York: Guilford Press.

A guide to domestic violence: Risk assessment, risk reduction, and safety plan. Retrieved from *www.police.nashville.org/bureaus/investigative/domestic/stalking.asp.*

Violence Against Women Online Resources. Available at *www.vaw.umn.edu.*

27.2. Anorexia Nervosa and Bulimia Nervosa

Fairburn, C. G. (2008). *Cognitive behavior therapy and eating disorders.* New York: Guilford Press.

Grilo, C. M., & Mitchell, J. E. (Eds). (2009). *The treatment of eating disorders: A clinical handbook.* New York: Guilford Press.

Le Grange, D., & Lock, J. (2007). *Treating bulimia in adolescents: A family-based approach.* New York: Guilford Press.

Lock, J., Le Grange, D., Agras, W. S., & Dare, C. (2001). *Treatment manual for anorexia nervosa: A family-based approach.* New York: Guilford Press.

Werne, J. (1996). *Treating eating disorders.* San Francisco: Jossey-Bass.

Gurze Books is a publisher that specializes in eating disorders. Available at *www.bulimia.com.*

27.3. Antisocial Personality Disorder

Hervé, H., & Yuille, J. C. (Eds.). (2007). *The psychopath: Theory, research, and practice*. Mahwah, NJ: Erlbaum.
Reid, W. (Ed.). (1986). *Unmasking the psychopath: Antisocial personality and related syndromes*. New York: Norton.

27.4. Anxiety Disorders

See also Sections 27.15, "*Obsessive–Compulsive Disorders,*" 27.17, "*Phobias,*" and 27.18, "*PostTraumatic Stress Disorder.*"

Butler, G., Fennell, M., & Hackmann, A. (2008). *Cognitive-behavioral therapy for anxiety disorders: Mastering clinical challenges*. New York: Guilford Press.

27.5. Asperger Syndrome

Gaus, V. L. (2007). *Cognitive-behavioral therapy for adult Asperger syndrome*. New York: Guilford Press.

27.6. Attention-Deficit/Hyperactivity Disorder

Barkley, R. A. (2005). *Attention-deficit hyperactivity disorder: A handbook for diagnosis and treatment* (3rd ed.). New York: Guilford Press.
Barkley, R. A., & Murphy, K. R. (2005). *Attention-deficit hyperactivity disorder: A clinical workbook* (3rd ed.). New York: Guilford Press.
Barkley, R. A., Murphy, K. R., & Fischer, M. (2008). *ADHD in adults: What the science says*. New York: Guilford Press.
DuPaul, G. J., & Stoner, G. (2003). *ADHD in the schools: Assessment and intervention strategies* (2nd ed.). New York: Guilford Press.
Goldstein, M. (1998). *Managing attention deficit hyperactivity disorder in children: A guide for practitioners* (2nd ed.). New York: Wiley.
Tuckman, A. (2007). *Integrative treatment for adult ADHD: A practical, easy-to-use guide for clinicians*. Oakland, CA: New Harbinger.

27.7. Bipolar I Disorder

Basco, M. R. (2006). *The bipolar workbook: Tools for controlling your mood swings*. New York: Guilford Press.
Basco, M. R., & Rush, A. J. (2005). *Cognitive-behavioral therapy for bipolar disorder* (2nd ed.). New York: Guilford Press.
Frank, E. (2005). *Treating bipolar disorder: A clinician's guide to interpersonal and social rhythm therapy*. New York: Guilford Press.
Lam, D. H., Jones, S. H., Hayward, P., & Bright, J. A. (1999). *Cognitive therapy for bipolar disorder: A therapist's guide to concepts, methods and practice*. New York: Wiley.
Bipolar (manic–depressive) disorder. Retrieved from *www.psycom.net/depression.central.bipolar.html*.

27.8. Body Dysmorphic Disorder

Phillips, K. (2009). *The broken mirror: Understanding and treating body dysmorphic disorder* (rev. and expanded ed.). New York: Oxford University Press.
Wilhelm, S. (2006). *Feeling good about the way you look: A program for overcoming body image problems*. New York: Guilford Press.
Zerbe, K. J. (2008). *Integrated treatment of eating disorders: Beyond the body betrayed*. New York: Norton.

27.9. Borderline Personality Disorder

Layden, M. A., Newman, C. F., Freeman, A., & Morse, S. B. (2002). *Cognitive therapy of borderline personality disorder*. Boston: Pearson, Allyn & Bacon.

Linehan, M. M. (1993). *Cognitive-behavioral treatment of borderline personality disorder*. New York: Guilford Press.

27.10. Dementia

Zarit, S. H., & Zarit, J. M. (2007). *Mental disorders in older adults: Fundamentals of assessment and treatment* (2nd ed.). New York: Guilford Press.

27.11. Dissociative Identity Disorder

Krakauer, S. (2001). *Treating dissociative identity disorder: The power of the collective heart*. London: Routledge.

Putnam, F. W. (1989). *Diagnosis and treatment of multiple personality disorder*. New York: Guilford Press.

Spira, J. L. (Ed.). (1996). *Treating dissociative identity disorder*. San Francisco: Jossey-Bass.

27.12. Dual Diagnosis

Evans, K., & Sullivan, J. M. (2001). *Dual diagnosis: Counseling the mentally ill substance abuser* (2nd ed.). New York: Guilford Press.

Mueser, K. T., Noordsy, D. L., Drake, R. D., & Fox, L. (2003). *Integrated treatment for dual disorders: A guide to effective practice*. New York: Guilford Press.

Watkins, T. R., Lewellen, A., & Barrett, M. C. (2000). *Dual diagnosis: An integrated approach to treatment*. Thousand Oaks, CA: Sage.

27.13. Gambling, Pathological

Ciarrocchi, J. W. (2002). *Counseling problem gamblers: A self-regulation manual for individual and family therapy*. San Diego, CA: Academic Press.

Ladouceur, R., & Lachance, S. (2007). *Overcoming pathological gambling: Therapist guide*. New York: Oxford University Press.

McCown, W. G., & Howatt, W. A. (2007). *Treating gambling problems*. New York: Wiley.

Whelan, J. P., Meyers, A. M., & Steenbergh, T. A. (2007). *Problem and pathological gambling*. Cambridge, MA: Hogrefe & Huber.

Gamblers Helpline. Available at (888) LAST BET (527-8238).

National Council on Problem Gambling. Available at (800) 522-4700 and *www.ncpgambling.org*.

27.14. Hypochondriacal Personality

Furer, P., Walker, J. R., & Stein, M. B. (2007). *Treating health anxiety and fear of death: A practitioner's guide*. New York: Springer.

Taylor, S., & Asmundson, G. J. G. (2004). *Treating health anxiety: A cognitive-behavioral approach*. New York: Guilford Press.

Woolfolk, R. L., & Allen, L. A. (2007). *Treating somatization: A cognitive-behavioral approach*. New York: Guilford Press.

27.15. Obsessive–Compulsive Disorders

Antony, M., Purdon, C., & Summerfeldt, L. J. (Eds.). (2007). *Psychological treatment of obsessive–compulsive disorder: Fundamentals and beyond.* Washington, DC: American Psychological Association.
Clark, D. A. (2004). *Cognitive-behavioral therapy for OCD.* New York: Guilford Press.
March, J. S., & Mulle, K. (1998). *OCD in children and adolescents: A cognitive-behavioral treatment manual.* New York: Guilford Press.
Steketee, G. (1999). *Overcoming obsessive–compulsive disorder* [Therapist protocol and client manual]. Oakland, CA: New Harbinger.

27.16. Pain, Chronic

Caudill, M. A. (2009). *Managing pain before it manages you* (3rd ed.). New York: Guilford Press.
Eimer, B., & Freeman, A. (1998). *Pain management psychotherapy: A practical guide.* New York: Wiley.
Thorn, B. E. (2004). *Cognitive therapy for chronic pain: A step-by-step guide.* New York: Guilford Press.
Turk, D. C., & Gatchel, R. J. (Eds.). (2002). *Psychological approaches to pain management: A practitioner's handbook* (2nd ed.). New York: Guilford Press.
Turk, D. C., & Melzack, R. (Eds.). (2001). *Handbook of pain assessment* (2nd ed.). New York: Guilford Press.

27.17. Phobias

Bourne, E. J. (1998). *Overcoming specific phobias* [Therapist protocol and client manual]. Oakland, CA: New Harbinger.
Craske, M. G., Antony, M. M., & Barlow, D. H. (2006). *Mastering your fears and phobias: Therapist guide* (2nd ed.). New York: Oxford University Press.
Hope, D. A., Heimberg, R. C., & Turk, C. L. (2010). *Managing social anxiety: A cognitive-behavioral therapy approach. Therapist guide* (2nd ed.). New York: Oxford University Press.

27.18. PostTraumatic Stress Disorder

Foa. E. B., Keane, T. M., Friedman, M. J., & Cohen, J. A. (Eds.). (2009). *Effective treatments for PTSD: Practice guidelines from the International Society for Traumatic Stress Studies* (2nd ed.). New York: Guilford Press.
Najavits, L. M. (2002). *Seeking safety: A treatment manual for PTSD and substance abuse.* New York: Guilford Press.
Smyth, L. (1999). *Overcoming post-traumatic stress disorder* [Therapist protocol and client manual]. Oakland, CA: New Harbinger.
Taylor, S. (2006). *Clinician's guide to PTSD: A cognitive-behavioral approach.* New York: Guilford Press.
Zayfert, C., & Becker, C. B. (2007). *Cognitive-behavioral therapy for PTSD: A case formulation approach.* New York: Guilford Press.
David Baldwin's Trauma Pages. Available at *www.trauma-pages.com.*
National Center for PTSD. Available at *www.ncptsd.org.*

27.19. Religious and Spiritual Concerns

Dowd, E. T., & Nielsen, S. L. (2006). *The psychologies in religion: Working with the religious client.* New York: Springer.
Pargament, K. I. (2001). *The psychology of religion and coping: Theory, research, practice.* New York: Guilford Press.
Richards, P. S., & Bergin, A. E. (Eds.). (2000). *Handbook of psychotherapy and religious diversity.* Washington, DC: American Psychological Association.

Spilka, B., Hood, R. W., Jr., Hunsberger, B., & Gorsuch, R. (2003). *The psychology of religion: An empirical approach* (3rd ed.). New York: Guilford Press.

27.20. Schizophrenia and Psychosis

Burns, T., & Firn, M. (2002). *Assertive outreach in mental health: A manual for practitioners.* New York: Oxford University Press.

Corrigan, P. W., Mueser, K. T., Bond, G. R., Drake, R. E., & Solomon, P. (2008). *Principles and practice of psychiatric rehabilitation: An empirical approach.* New York: Guilford Press.

Hofmann, S. G., & Tompson, M. C. (Eds.). (2002). *Treating chronic and severe mental disorders: A handbook of empirically supported interventions.* New York: Guilford Press.

Rapp, C. A., & Goscha, R. J. (2006). *The strengths model: Case management with people with psychiatric disabilities.* New York: Oxford University Press.

Stein, L. I., & Santos, A. B. (1998). *Assertive community treatment of persons with severe mental illness.* New York: Norton.

Torrey, E. F. (2006). *Surviving schizophrenia: A manual for families, consumers, and providers* (5th ed.). New York: Harper Paperbacks.

27.21. Sleep Disturbances

Edinger, J. D., & Carney, C. E. (2008). *Overcoming insomnia: A cognitive-behavioral therapy approach: Therapist guide.* New York: Oxford University Press.

Morin, C., & Espie, C. A. (2003). *Insomnia: A clinician's guide to assessment and treatment.* New York: Springer.

Perlis, M. L., Jungquist, C., Smith, M. T., & Posner, D. (2005). *Cognitive behavioral treatment of insomnia: A session-by-session guide.* New York: Springer.

27.22. Stalking

Meloy, J. R. (Ed.). (1998). *The psychology of stalking: Clinical and forensic perspectives.* San Diego, CA: Academic Press.

Pinals, D. A. (Ed.). (2007). *Stalking: Psychiatric perspectives and practical approaches.* New York: Oxford University Press.

Stalking Resource Center. Available at *www.ncvc.org/src.*

27.23. Substance Abuse

Beck, A. T., Wright, F. D., Newman, C. F., & Liese, V. S. (2001). *Cognitive therapy of substance abuse.* New York: Guilford Press.

Connors, G. J., Donovan, D. M., & DiClemente, C. D. (2001). *Substance abuse treatment and the stages of change: Selecting and planning intervention:* New York: Guilford Press.

Denning, P. (2000). *Practicing harm reduction psychotherapy: An alternative approach to addictions.* New York: Guilford Press.

Johnson, S. L. (2003). *Therapists' guide to substance abuse intervention.* San Diego, CA: Academic Press.

Martin, P. R., Weinberg, B. A., & Bealer, B. K. (2007). *Healing addiction: An integrated pharmacopsychosocial approach to treatment.* New York: Wiley.

Miller, W. R., & Rollnick, S. (2002). *Motivational interviewing: Preparing people for change* (2nd ed.). New York: Guilford Press.

Monti, P. M., Kadden, R. M., Rohsenow, D. J., Cooney, N. L., & Abrams, D. B. (2002). *Treating alcohol dependence: A coping skills training guide* (2nd ed.). New York: Guilford Press.

Rotgers, F., Morgenstern, J., & Walters, S. T. (Eds.). (2003). *Treating substance abuse: Theory and technique* (2nd ed.). New York: Guilford Press.

SPECIFIC DISORDERS

Velasquez, M. M., Maurer, G. G., Crouch, C., & DiClemente, C. D. (2001). *Group treatment for substance abuse: A stages-of-change therapy manual.* New York: Guilford Press.

HabitSmart Treatment. Available at *www.habitsmart.com.*

National Institute on Drug Abuse. Available at *www.nida.nih.gov.*

SMART Recovery. Available at *www.smartrecovery.org.*

27.24. Types of Therapies

Barlow, D. H. (Ed.). (2008). *Clinical handbook of psychological disorders: A step-by-step treatment manual* (4th ed.). New York: Guilford Press.

Christophersen, E. R., & Mortweet, S. L. (2001). *Treatments that work with children: Empirically supported strategies for managing childhood problems.* Washington, DC: American Psychological Association.

Lambert, M. J. (Ed.). (2004). *Bergin and Garfield's handbook of psychotherapy and behavior change* (5th ed.). New York: Wiley.

Norcross, J. C. (Ed.). (2002). *Psychotherapy relationships that work: Therapist contributions and responsiveness to patients.* New York: Oxford University Press.

Norcross, J. C., Santrock, J. W., Campbell, L. F., Smith, T. P., Sommer, R., & Zuckerman, E. L. (2003). *Authoritative guide to self-help resources in mental health* (rev. ed.). New York: Guilford Press.

Weisz, J. R. (2004). *Psychotherapy for children and adolescents: Evidence-based treatments and case examples.* New York: Cambridge University Press.

28

Listing of Common Psychiatric and Psychoactive Drugs

28.1. List of Medications by Trade and Generic Names

See also Section 12.36, "Side Effects of Psychotropic Medications/Adverse Drug Reactions."

A majority of mental health clients are taking some kind of psychoactive medication, and since such medications are likely to affect their assessment and treatment, clinicians should have some awareness of these drugs. Much information is available online *(see Section 28.4)* but a printed list can be handy.

The following is a checklist of dosages and uses for over 100 medications commonly used in psychiatry. Drugs are listed in the alphabetical order of their trade names, followed by their generic names. The list is updated several times a year at *www.TheCliniciansToolBox.com* (click on "Free Tools" for the latest version). The present version is copyright 2010 by Edward L. Zuckerman, PhD, and Dan Egli, PhD. See the "Disclaimer" at the end for conditions governing the use of the list.

Name			Usual adult		
Trade	Generic	Drug class	daily dosage (range in mg)	FDA-approved indication(s)	Common "Off-label" uses, if any
Abilify	aripiprazole	Atypical	10–15	Schizophrenia, Bipolar, adjunctive Tx adult MDD, Agitation	
Adderall, XR	D- & L-amphetamine	Stimulant	5–40	ADHD, Narco	
Ambien, CR	zolpidem	Nonbenzo. hypnotic	5–12.5	DFA, SCD (short-term use)	
Anafranil	clomipramine	Tricyclic AD	100–250	OCD	
Antabuse	disulfiram	Alcohol antagonist	125–500	Manage chronic alcoholism	
Aplenzin	bupropion	DNRI	174–522	MDD	

| Name | | | Usual adult | | Common |
Trade	Generic	Drug class	daily dosage (range in mg)	FDA-approved indication(s)	"Off-label" uses, if any
Aricept	donepezil	Cholinesterase inhibitor	5–10	Mild/moderate/severe dementia	
Artane	trihexyphenidyl	Antidyskinetic	1–15	Anti-Parkinson's	Extrapyramidal symptoms
Ativan	lorazepam	Benzodiazepine	2–6	Anxiety	Alcohol withdrawal, Seizures, Insomnia
Aventyl/ Pamelor	nortriptyline	Tricyclic AD	25–100	MDD	Depr
BuSpar	buspirone	Antianxiety	15–60	GAD	
Campral	acamprosate	Alcohol antagonist	1332–1998	Alcohol dependence	
Catapres, TTS	clonidine	Antihypertensive	.1–.3	Hypertension	Drug detox, Pain, Impulse, ADHD
Celexa	citalopram	SSRI	20–40	MDD	Depr, PmDD, PTSD, BDD, Soc. Anxiety
Centrax	prazepam	Benzodiazepine	30–60	Anxiety	Alcohol withdrawal, Seizures
Chantix	varenicline	Nicotinic receptor agonist	0.5–2	Smoking cessation	
Cialis	tadalafil	PDE-5 inhibitor	5–20	Erectile dysfunction	
Clozaril/ FazaClo	clozapine	Atypical	300–450	Schizophrenia	Bipolar
Cogentin	benztropine	Antidyskinetic	1–8	Anti-Parkinson's	Extrapyramidal symptoms
Cognex	tacrine	Cholinesterase inhibitor	40–160	Mild/moderate dementia	
Concerta	methylphenidate	Stimulant	18–54	ADHD	
Cymbalta, DR	duloxetine	SNRI	20–80	MDD, GAD, Neuropathic pain, Fibro	Depr, PmDD, PTSD, Soc. Anxiety
Dalmane	flurazepam	Benzodiazepine	15–30	Insomnia (short-term use)	
Daytrana, TTS	methylphenidate	Stimulant	10–27	ADHD (ages 6–12)	
Depakote/ -ene/-con	divalproex	Anticonvulsant	750–3000	Bipolar, Epilepsy, Migraine	

PSYCHOACTIVE MEDICATIONS

Name		Drug class	Usual adult daily dosage (range in mg)	FDA-approved indication(s)	Common "Off-label" uses, if any
Trade	*Generic*				
Deplin	L-methylfolate	Medical food	7.5	Augment antidepressant in MDD, T-R Depr	
Desoxyn	methamphetamine	Stimulant	5–25	ADHD, Anorexiant	EDS, Narco
Desyrel	trazodone	SARI	150–400	MDD	Depr, Hypn
Dexedrine	dextroamphetamine	Stimulant	5–40	ADHD, Narcolepsy	EDS
Doral	quazepam	Benzodiazepine	7.5–15	Insomnia (short-term use)	
Edluar	zolpidem	Nonbenzo. hypnotic	5–10	Insomnia	
Effexor, XR	venlafaxine	SNRI	75–375	MDD, GAD, Panic	Depr, PTSD, Soc. Anxiety, PmDD
Elavil	amitriptyline	Tricyclic AD	75–150	MDD	Depr
Eldepryl	selegiline	MAOI	5–10	Anti-Parkinson's	Depr, Smoking cessation
Emsam, TTS	selegiline	MAOI	6–12	MDD	
Equetro, ER	carbamazepine	Anti-manic	200–1600	Bipolar	
Eskalith/ Lithobid	lithium carbonate	Anti-manic	900–1800	Bipolar	
Exelon, patch	rivastigmine	Cholinesterase inhibitor	3–12	Mild/moderate dementia, Parkinson's dementia	
Fanapt	iloperidone	Atypical	12–24	Schizophrenia	
Focalin, XR	dexmethylphenidate	Stimulant	5–20	ADHD	
Gabitril	tiagabine	Anticonvulsant	4–32	Epilepsy	Bipolar
Geodon	ziprasidone	Atypical	40–160	Schizophrenia, Bipolar	
Halcion	triazolam	Benzodiazepine	.25–.50	Insomnia (short-term use)	
Inderal	propranolol	Antihypertensive	10–80	Hypertension	Anxiety, Alcohol withdrawal, Akathisia, Panic
Intuniv, ER	guanfacine	Antihypertensive	1–4	ADHD	
Invega, ER	paliperidone	Atypical	3–12	Schizophrenia (acute and chronic)	
Kemadrin	procyclidine	Antidyskinetic	7.5–20	Anti-Parkinson's	
Keppra, XR	levetiracetam	Anticonvulsant	1000–3000	Epilepsy	Bipolar

Name			Usual adult daily dosage (range in mg)	FDA-approved indication(s)	Common "Off-label" uses, if any
Trade	*Generic*	*Drug class*			
Klonopin, wafers	clonazepam	Benzodiazepine	.25–40	Seizures, Panic	GAD, Hypn
Lamictal, ODT	lamotrigine	Anticonvulsant	100–200	Epilepsy, Bipolar	
Levitra	vardenafil	PDE-5 inhibitor	5–20	Erectile dysfunction	
Lexapro	escitalopram	SSRI	10–20	MDD (down to ages 12–17), GAD	BDD, PTSD, Soc. Anxiety, Depr, PmDD
Librium	chlordiazepoxide	Benzodiazepine	5–100	Anxiety, Alcohol withdrawal	
Ludiomil	maprotiline	Tetracyclic AD	75–225	MDD	Depr
Lunesta	eszopiclone	Nonbenzo. hypnotic	2–3	Insomnia (≤6 months use)	
Luvox, CR	fluvoxamine	SSRI	50–300	OCD, Soc. Anxiety	MDD, PTSD, PmDD, BDD
Lyrica	pregabalin	Anticonvulsant	300–600	Seizures, Neuropathic pain, Fibro	GAD
Marplan	isocarboxazid	MAOI	20–60	MDD	
Meridia	sibutramine	Anorexiant	10–15	Obesity	
Metadate, CR, ER	methylphenidate	Stimulant	20–60	ADHD	
Methylin	methylphenidate	Stimulant	20–60	ADHD, Narco	
Mirapex	pramipexole	Dopamine agonist	1.5–4.5	Anti-Parkinson's, RLS	T-R Depr
Namenda	memantine	NMDA antagonist	5–20	Moderate/ severe dementia	
Narcan	naloxone	Opioid antagonist	.4–2	Opioid overdose	
Nardil	phenelzine	MAOI	45–90	MDD	
Neurontin	gabapentin	Anticonvulsant	900–1800	Epilepsy	Bipolar
Niravam	alprazolam, ODT	Benzodiazepine	.3–5	Panic, GAD	
Nuvigil	armodafinil	Wakefulness promoter	150–250	Sleep apnea, Narco, SWSD	
Parnate	tranylcypromine	MAOI	30–60	MDD	
Paxil, CR/ Pexeva	paroxetine	SSRI	20–60	MDD, GAD, OCD, Panic, Soc. Anxiety, PTSD	Depr, Anxiety, PmDD
Pristiq	desvenlafaxine	SNRI	50	MDD	
ProSom	estazolam	Benzodiazepine	1–2	Insomnia (short-term use)	

PSYCHOACTIVE MEDICATIONS

Name		Drug class	Usual adult daily dosage (range in mg)	FDA-approved indication(s)	Common "Off-label" uses, if any
Trade	Generic				
Provigil	modafinil	Wakefulness promoter	100–400	EDS, OSA, SWSD	ADHD, MDD
Prozac/ Sarafem	fluoxetine	SSRI	20–80	OCD, Panic, PmDD, MDD, PTSD, Bulimia	Depr, Soc. Anxiety, Anxiety, BDD
Razadyne, ER	galantamine	Cholinesterase inhibitor	8–32	Mild/moderate dementia	
Remeron/ SolTab	mirtazapine	Tetracyclic AD	15–45	MDD	Depr
Requip, XL	ropinirole	Dopamine agonist	.75–3	Anti-Parkinson's, RLS	T-R Depr
Restoril	temazepam	Benzodiazepine	15–30	Insomnia, short-term use	
Revia/Revex	naltrexone/ nalmefene	Opioid antagonist	50	Opioid dependence	Alcohol dependence
Risperdal/ Consta	risperidone	Atypical	1–8	Bipolar & Schizophrenia (in adults and teens), Irritability (in autism)	
Ritalin	methylphenidate	Stimulant	20–60	ADHD, Narco	EDS
Rozerem	ramelteon	Hypnotic	8	Insomnia	
Sabril	vigabatrin	Anticonvulsant	1000–4000	Bipolar, Epilepsy	
Serax	oxazepam	Benzodiazepine	30–120	Anxiety, Alcohol withdrawal	Anti-itch, Seizures, Hypn
Seroquel, XR	quetiapine	Atypical	150–800	Schizophrenia, Bipolar, T-R Depr	
[Serzone]	nefazodone	SNRI + 5HT2a	300–600	MDD	Anxiety, PTSD
Sinequan/ Adapin	doxepin	Tricyclic AD	150–300	MDD	Depr
Sonata	zaleplon	Nonbenzo. hypnotic	5–10	Insomnia (short-term use)	
Stavzor, DR	valproic acid	Anticonvulsant	250–750	Bipolar, Seizures, Migraine	
Strattera	atomoxetine	Non-stimulant	40–100	ADHD	
Suboxone	buprenorphine & naloxone	Opioid agonist	12–16	Opioid dependence	
Subutex	buprenorphine	Opioid agonist	12–16	Opioid dependence	
Symbyax	olanzapine & fluoxetine	Atypical & SSRI	6/25–12/50	Bipolar	Schizophrenia

Name		Drug class	Usual adult daily dosage (range in mg)	FDA-approved indication(s)	Common "Off-label" uses, if any
Trade	Generic				
Tegretol	carbamazepine	Anticonvulsant	400–1200	Epilepsy	Bipolar
Tenex	guanfacine	Antihypertensive	.5–3	Hypertension	Drug withdrawal
Tofranil/IM	imipramine	Tricyclic AD	75–200	MDD, Enuresis	Depr
Topamax	topiramate	Anticonvulsant	400–1600	Epilepsy, Migraine	Bipolar
Tranxene	clorazepate	Benzodiazepine	15–60	Anxiety, Seizures	
Trileptal	oxcarbazepine	Anticonvulsant	600–1200	Epilepsy	Bipolar
Valium	diazepam	Benzodiazepine	4–40	Anxiety, Muscle spasm, Seizures	
Viagra/ Revatio	sildenafil	PDE-5 inhibitor	25–100	Erectile dysfunction	
Vivitrol, IM	naltrexone	Opioid antagonist	190–380/ mo.	Alcohol/Opioid dependence	
Vyvanse	lisdexamfetamine	Stimulant	30–70	ADHD (child & adult)	
Wellbutrin/ Zyban/ Budeprion, ER	bupropion	DNRI	200–450	MDD, Smoking cessation, SAD	
Xanax, XR	alprazolam	Benzodiazepine	.25–40	Panic	Anxiety
Xenical/Alli	orlistat	Lipase inhibitor	360	Obesity	
Xyrem	sodium oxybate	Stimulant	3–9 g	EDS, Cataplexy	
Zoloft	sertraline	SSRI	50–200	Panic, OCD, MDD, PTSD, Soc. Anxiety, PmDD	BDD, Depr, Anxiety
Zonegran	zonisamide	Anticonvulsant	100–400	Epilepsy	Bipolar
Zyprexa/ Zydis, IM	olanzapine	Atypical	5–30	Schizophrenia, Bipolar	

Key: [ ] means trade drug withdrawn from market by manufacturer, but still available as generic.

Drug name and class: Anorexiant = Drug used to treat obesity. Antidyskinetic = Drug used to treat Parkinson's disease and extrapyramidal effects of antipsychotics. Atypical = Newer antipsychotic/neuroleptic (The conventional, older antipsychotics/neuroleptics are now rarely used and so are not listed). DNRI = Dopamine–Norepinephrine Reuptake Inhibitor. MAOI = Monoamine Oxidase Inhibitor. PDE-5 inhibitor = Phosphodiesterase type 5 inhibitor. SARI = Serotonin-2 Antagonist/Serotonin Reuptake Inhibitor. SNRI = Serotonin–Norepinephrine Reuptake Inhibitor. SSRI = Selective Serotonin Reuptake Inhibitor. Tetracyclic AD = Tetracyclic Antidepressant. Tricyclic AD = Tricyclic Antidepressant (almost replaced by SSRIs, and thus few are listed). IM = Intramuscular. ODT = Orally Disintegrating Tablet. TTS = Transdermal Therapeutic System (a skin patch). CR, DR, ER, XL, XR = Slowed release.

Indications and "off-label" uses: ADHD = Attention-Deficit/Hyperactivity Disorder. Anorexiant = For exogenous obesity. Anxiety = Anxiety Disorder NOS. BDD = Body Dysmorphic Disorder. Bipolar = Bipolar I Disorder (manic). Depr = Depression (see MDD). DFA = Difficulty Falling Asleep. EDS = Excessive Daytime Sleepiness. EMA = Early Morning Awakening. Fibro = Fibromyalgia. GAD = Generalized Anxiety Disorder.

Hypn = Hypnotic (sleep inducer) for many sleep disorders. Impulse = Impulse-Control Disorders. MDD = Major Depressive Disorder (not Dysthymia or Depression NOS). Narco = Narcolepsy. OCD = Obsessive–Compulsive Disorder. OSA = Obstructive Sleep Apnea. Panic = Panic Disorder, with or without Agoraphobia. PmDD = Premenstrual Dysphoric Disorder. PTSD = Posttraumatic Stress Disorder. RLS = Restless Leg Syndrome. SAD = Seasonal Affective Disorder. SCD = Sleep Continuity Disturbance. SWSD = Shift Work Sleep Disorder. Soc. Anxiety = Social Anxiety/Social Phobia. T-R Depr = Treatment-Resistant Depression.

Disclaimer: The information presented here is intended as general health information and as an educational tool, but is not precise enough for making prescription decisions and is not to be construed as medical advice. The indications/diagnoses are not exclusive, exhaustive, or precise. We have tried to be accurate, but errors may exist here. Listing here is in no sense an endorsement by us of the use of any medication for any treatment purpose. The dosages offered here are for maintenance, and authorities differ on these. Starting doses may be lower, and for some people higher (supratherapeutic) dosages are warranted. All trade names are the property of their respective manufacturers, distributors, and copyright holders. Noncommercial copying and distribution of this list are permitted as long as NO changes are made to it. Any other uses require written permission.

28.2. Finding Street Drugs' Names

The commonly used names of street drugs—increasingly, medicines obtained and sold illegally, as well as illegal and abusable substances—vary by location and change frequently, but here are some websites:

> *www.watton.org/drugsinfo/a-z*
> *www.soberrecovery.com/alcoholdrugtreatment/category/drug-street-names*
> *www.whitehousedrugpolicy.gov/streetterms* (**Note:** This site offers thousands of names in a downloadable list.)

28.3. Results of Medication Treatment: Descriptors

Good/fluctuating/poor adherence/compliance.
Tolerated without difficulty, rapid and dramatic improvement, abatement of symptoms, symptomatology improved.
No signs of addiction, diversion, misuse, or excessive use.
Highly sensitive to all medications, multiple/distressing side effects, quite difficult to find a medication regimen that was tolerated, distressing and extreme reactions to all medications tried despite changes in dosage and schedule, adverse drug reactions.
Contraindicated, use not advisable because ... (specify).
Polypharmacy, more than one/several/multiple drugs being taken, drug interactions, drug augmentation.

28.4. Drug Resources for the Clinician

Books

Although books' information often cannot be completely current, the books listed below have been recently revised and provide extensive information. (See *www.psychmeds.info* for current materials.)

Information on current uses, adverse effects, and interactions of medications can be found in the latest editions of the *Physicians' Desk Reference* and the *PDR Guide to Drug Interactions, Side Effects, and Indications* (both 2010 at this writing).

Diamond, R. J. (2009). *Instant psychopharmacology* (3rd ed.). New York: Norton.
     All the basics are here, as well as advice on compliance and the relationship with the patient, prices, side effects, and interactions. A fine starting place.
Patterson, J., Albala, A. A., McCahill, M. E., & Edwards, T. M. (2006). *The therapist's guide to psychopharmacology: Working with patients, families, and physicians to optimize care.* New York: Guilford Press.
     An ideal introduction to the subject for those working with prescibers.
Preston, J. D., O'Neal, J. H., & Talaga, M. C. (2010). *Handbook of clinical psychopharmacology for therapists* (5th ed.). Oakland, CA: New Harbinger.
     Practical, user-friendly, and comprehensive.
Stahl, S. (2009). *Stahl's essential psychopharmacology: The prescriber's guide* (3rd ed.). New York: Cambridge University Press.
     Rich in expertise, pragmatic, current, and comprehensive.
Virani, A. S., Bezchlibnyk-Butler, K., & Jeffries, J. (2009). *Clinical handbook of psychotropic drugs* (18th rev. ed.). Cambridge, MA: Hogrefe & Huber.
     Lots of objective data displayed in tables for easy access, and organized by disorder. No narrative explanation or interpretation, but bits of advice on interactions, comparisons, side effects, etc.
Wilens, T. E. (2009). *Straight talk about psychiatric medications for kids* (3rd ed.). New York: Guilford Press.
     Comprehensive; like listening to a wise and informed counsel or sharing his wealth.

There are many other books, and new ones come out monthly, so just visit your favorite bookstore or website for the most current information.

Online Drug Information

www.rxlist.com (Very extensive information on each drug, somewhat like the PDR.)
www.drugs.com (Extensive information in a Q&A format, and some useful tools.)
online.epocrates.com (Lists of every drug and of medical conditions; drug interactions checker; images; pictures of pills; printable handouts; etc. Requires free registration.)

Two valuable resources for report writers are available at *www.TheCliniciansToolBox.com* under the "Free Tools" tab: a list of drugs' generic and trade names (a periodically updated version of the list in Section 28.1, as noted earlier), and a list of all the terms used in the diagnostic labels. Why download them? Copy and paste them into a new document in your word processor, and run your spelling checker to teach it these spellings, and you will never misspell any of these again.

PSYCHOACTIVE MEDICATIONS

29

Psychiatric Masquerade of Medical Conditions

29.1. Introduction

The well-trained and responsible clinician must consider all possible causes of a client's symptoms: developmental, dynamic, existential, learned, cultural, and medical/physiological.

"Psychiatric masquerade" is the commonly accepted term for the situation in which a patient presents to the clinician with psychological or psychiatric symptoms caused by a medical condition or illness that is not immediately (and, sadly, sometimes never) recognized. In other words, it is the case in which a medical condition wears the "mask" of a psychiatric condition. Adams (1991) notes that calling it "psychiatric masquerade" focuses on the presentation; if we were to focus on the causation, we would call it "medical masquerade." It is not to be confused with malingering *(see Section 12.20)* or the somatoform disorders.

Although there are numerous excellent articles and books that describe the psychological effects of medical conditions or of medications, they are useless to the professional who sees only the patient presenting with psychiatric symptoms, unaccompanied by a medical diagnosis. However, as clinicians, all of us have the ethical obligation to be sensitive to the possibility of masquerade and to investigate any such possibilities appropriately.

Common causes of the presentation of psychiatric symptoms are the side effects and interactions of prescribed drugs with each other and with herbals, dietary supplements, Over-The-Counter (nonprescription) drugs, and abusable substances. Because this is a complex and changing area, consultations with experts, current books, and online data bases are necessary to achieve clarity. The individual clinician can do his/her part by making a comprehensive inventory of all substances the client takes in.

Good guides to this complex area are Pincus and Tucker (2003), Lishman (1998), Morrison (1997), and Taylor (2007). Surprisingly, the last two are quite accessible and are recommended to the nonmedical clinician. Especially for children and adolescents is Reed's (2005) list.

29.2. Anxiety

See Section 10.3, "Anxiety/Fear."

Medications/Substances That May Induce Anxiety

✓ Stimulants and sympathomimetics: Amphetamines, cocaine, amethylphenidate, pemoline, ephedrine, pseudoephedrine, phenylpropanolamine, xanthine derivatives (caffeine, theobromine, theophylline).

Withdrawal states (especially from alcohol, sedatives, narcotics).
Anticholinergics and antihistamines.
Antidepressants: Fluoxetine and other <u>S</u>elective <u>S</u>erotonin <u>R</u>euptake <u>I</u>nhibitors, <u>M</u>ono<u>A</u>mine <u>O</u>xidase <u>I</u>nhibitors, tricyclic antidepressants (especially early in therapy).
Benzodiazepines (paradoxical reactions, withdrawal states).
Euphoriants and hallucinogens: Cannabis, LSD, mescaline, psilocybin, phencyclidine (PCP).
Hormones: Androgens, estrogens, progesterones, corticosteroids, thyroid supplements.
Others: Cycloserine, metrizamide, quinacrine, nasal decongestant sprays.

Medical Conditions That May Present as/with Anxiety

<u>M</u>itral <u>V</u>alve <u>P</u>rolapse, adrenal tumor, alcoholism, carcinoid syndrome, <u>C</u>entral <u>N</u>ervous System degenerative diseases, Cushing's disease, coronary insufficiency, delirium, hypoglycemia, hyperthyroidism, Meniere's disease (early stages), postconcussion syndrome, chronic obstructive lung disease, AIDS, diabetes, fibromyalgia.

29.3. Sexual Dysfunction

Many common medications may cause sexual dysfunctions (difficulties with arousal or orgasm). A good source of information is the book by Segraves and Balon (2003).

29.4. Depression

See Section 10.7, "Depression."

Medications/Substances That May Induce Depression

Antiarrhythmics: Digitalis, disopyramide, nifedipine.
Antihypertensives: Clonidine, guanethidine, hydralazine, methyldopa, prazosin, propranolol, and other β-blockers; reserpine; trichloromethiazide.
Antimicrobials: Cycloserine, isoniazid, metronidazole, nalidixic acid.
Anti-Parkinsonian agents: Levodopa, amantadine, carbidopa.
Chemotherapeutic agents: Asparaginase, vinblastine, vincristine.
Hormone preparations: Corticosteroids, oral contraceptives, thyroid supplements.
Sedatives: Alcohol, barbiturates, benzodiazepines, hypnotics, marijuana, hallucinogens.
Withdrawal states (especially from cocaine and other stimulants, amphetamines).
Other: Cimetidine, ranitidine, disulfiram, levodopa, α-methyldopa, carbidopa, metoclopramide, metrizamide, cholinesterase inhibitors, insecticides. Interferon treatment of hepatitis almost always causes significant depression.

PSYCHIATRIC MASQUERADE

Diseases That May Present as/with Depression

Influenza, tuberculosis, general paresis/tertiary syphilis, hypothyroidism, Cushing's disease, Addison's disease, Parkinson's disease, Systemic Lupus Erythematosus, Rheumatoid Arthritis, stroke, Multiple Sclerosis, End-Stage Renal Disease (with hemodialysis),[1] cerebral tumors, sleep apnea, early stages of dementing diseases, epilepsy, diabetes, brain trauma, Lyme disease, pancreatic cancer.

29.5. Mania

See Section 10.9, "Mania."

Medications/Substances That May Induce Mania

Amphetamines, bromides, cocaine, isoniazid, procarbazine, corticosteroids, levodopa, MAOI and tricyclic antidepressants, methylphenidate, OTC stimulants/appetite suppressants, vitamin deficiencies, excess of fat-soluble vitamins.

Diseases That May Present as/with Mania

Influenza, general paresis/tertiary syphilis, St. Louis encephalitis, Q fever, thyrotoxicosis, rheumatic chorea, stroke, MS, cerebellar/diencephalic/third-ventricle tumors, hyperthyroidism, Cushing's disease, hyperparathyroidism.

29.6. Organic Brain Syndrome/Dementia

See Section 11.7, "Dementia."

Medications/Substances That May Induce Delirium, Hallucinations, or Paranoia

Antiarrhythmics: Digitalis, lidocaine, procainamide, quinacrine.
Anticholinergics.
Antimicrobials, antiparasitics, antivirals: Amantadine, amphotericin B, metronidazole, thiabendazole, cycloserine, isoniazid, chloroquine, hydroxychloroquine, dapsone, penicillin G procaine.
Antihistamines: H_2 blockers (cimetidine, rantidine).
β-blockers.
Chemotherapeutic agents (especially intrathecal administration): Asparaginase, cisplatin, vincristine.
Euphoriants and hallucinogens: Cannabis, LSD, mescaline, psilocybin, PCP.
Hormone preparations: Corticosteroids.
Sedatives: Alcohol, barbiturates, benzodiazepines, hypnotics.
Stimulants and sympathomimetics: Amphetamines, cocaine, methylphenidate, pemoline.
Withdrawal states (especially from alcohol, sedatives).
Other: Albuterol, bromides, bromocriptine, disulfiram, levodopa, carbidopa, methyldopa, methysergide, metrizamide.

✓ The most frequent causes of demented/delirious presentations, especially in elderly persons, are these: drug–drug, drug–food, drug–OTC medication, and drug–herbal interactions; alcohol abuse; polypharmacy or over-, under-, and misuse of medication; diabetes; depression; and, for paranoia, partial deafness.

---

[1] I am grateful to Renee F. Bova-Collis of Richmond, VA, for pointing this out.

Neurological Conditions That Commonly Exhibit Psychological Symptoms

Bondi (1992) offers this basic orienting information about this issue:

Neurological conditions have a base rate of 2.5% of general population.

General symptoms: Paranoia, attentional deficits, mood swings, euphoria, sleep disturbance, personality changes, depression, impaired memory, anxiety, apathy, violence.

Temporal lobe epilepsy/complex partial seizure disorder → global diminution in sexual behavior, impulsive–irritable behaviors, especially in a context of hyperethical and hyperreligious history, hypergraphia, and overconcern and overemphasis on the trivial.

Frontal lobe damage → apathy (empty indifference as contrasted with the depressive's preoccupation with worry), total loss of initiative, euphoria, lack of adult restraint/tact, incontinence.

<u>T</u>raumatic <u>B</u>rain <u>I</u>njury → like frontal lobe damage as well as depression (psychomotor retardation, apathy, lack of initiative, blunted or flat affect), and memory dysfunction.

Huntington's disease → intermittent mood disorder with onset before the chorea and dementia. Besides the affective components, there may be paranoia, delusions, hallucinations, and mood swings. Always seek a family history.

Hypothyroidism → progressive cognitive deterioration, insidious onset, sluggishness, lethargy, poor attention and concentration, memory disturbances.

MS → muscle weakness, fatigue, double vision, numbness, paresthesia, pain, bowel and bladder dysfunction, sexual disturbance. Euphoria and/or depression, "conversion" symptoms.

Headache:

- If it is the worst ever experienced by the patient, a new type of headache, or accompanied by neurological signs, it is much more likely to be organic than one that is dull, generalized, familiar, or present for a year.
- Tumor-caused headaches have no one quality. They may occur on awakening and recede during the day; they are often bifrontal or bioccipital, lateralized or localized, and ameliorated or exacerbated by changes in body position.

Some Clues Suggestive of Organic Mental Disorder

The following is adapted by permission from Hoffman and Koran (1984).

Psychiatric symptom onset after age 40.

Psychiatric symptoms beginning ...
    a. during a major illness.
    b. while taking drugs known to cause mental symptoms (see above).
    c. suddenly, in a patient without prior psychiatric history or known stressors.

A history of ...
    a. alcohol or drug abuse.
    b. a physical illness impairing a major organ's function (e.g., hepatitis).
    c. taking multiple medications (prescribed or OTC).
    d. poor response to apparently adequate psychiatric treatment.

A family history of ...
    a. degenerative or inheritable brain disease.
    b. metabolic disease (diabetes, pernicious anemia, etc.).

Mental signs including ...
    a. altered level of consciousness.
    b. fluctuating mental status.
    c. cognitive impairment.
    d. episodic, recurrent, or cyclic course.
    e. visual, tactile, or olfactory hallucinations.

Physical signs that include …
   a. signs of organ malfunction that can affect the brain.
   b. focal neurological deficits.
   c. diffuse subcortical dysfunction (slowed speech/mentation/movement, ataxia, incoordination, tremor, chorea, asterixis, dysarthria, etc.).
   d. cortical dysfunction (dysphasia, apraxias, agnosia, visuospatial deficits, or defective cortical sensation, etc.).

Treatable/Possibly Reversible Causes of OBS

The following list is adapted by permission from Slaby et al. (1994):

Addison's disease, some angiomas of the cerebral vessels, anoxia secondary to chronic cardiac or respiratory disease, cerebral abscess, some cerebral neoplasms, chronic subdural hematomas, electrolyte imbalance, endogenous toxins (as with hepatic or renal failure), exogenous toxins such as carbon monoxide, hypothyroidism, hypoglycemia, cerebral infections (such as tuberculosis, syphilis, parasites, or yeasts), intracranial aneurysms, normal-pressure hydrocephalus, pseudodementia (e.g., in schizophrenia or depression), vitamin deficiencies, Wilson's disease.

Irreversible Causes of OBS

The following list is reprinted by permission from Slaby et al. (1994):

Alcoholic encephalopathy, Alzheimer's disease, arteriosclerosis, cerebral metastases, some primary cerebral neoplasms, Creutzfeldt–Jakob disease, dementia pugilistica, familial myoclonic epilepsy, Friedreich's ataxia, Huntington's chorea, Kuf's disease, Marchiafava–Bignami disease, multiple myeloma, MS, collagenoses, Parkinsonism/dementia complex of Guam, Pick's disease, presenile dementia with motor neuron disease, presenile glial dystrophy, primary parenchymatous cerebellar atrophy with dementia, primary subcortical gliosis, progressive supranuclear palsy, sarcoidosis, Schilder's disease, senile dementia.

29.7. Psychosis

Medications/Substances That May Induce Psychosis

Sympathomimetics (e.g., cocaine, "crack," many OTC cold medications).
Antinflammatory drugs: Steroids.
Anticholinergics: Anti-Parkinsonian agents (especially levodopa, in patients with schizophrenia).
Hallucinogens.

The top 10 drugs or drug classes associated with hallucinations, based on reports received by the West Midlands Centre for Adverse Drug Reaction Reporting (*www.yccwm.org.uk/factsheets/hallucinations.pdf*), are as follows:

SSRIs, tramadol, bupropion, venlafaxine, quinolones, proton pump inhibitors, clarithromycin, zopiclone, ropinirole, beta-adrenoreceptor antagonists.

Medical Conditions That May Present as/with Psychosis

Addison's disease, CNS infections, CNS neoplasms, CNS trauma, Cushing's disease, folic acid deficiency, Huntington's chorea, MS, myxedema, pancreatitis, pellagra, pernicious anemia, porphyria, SLE, temporal lobe epilepsy, thyrotoxicosis.

PSYCHIATRIC
MASQUERADE

29.8. Medication-Induced Psychiatric Conditions

See also Section 12.36, "Side Effects of Psychotropic Medications ... "

Medication-induced psychiatric conditions can be due to mistaken failure to research known interactions and risks; to unknowable misadventure; or to anticipated and accepted risks that are outweighed by the benefits, either actual or anticipated. There is a peculiar lack of current books on this subject. A British website, the Adverse Psychiatric Reactions Information Link (*www.april.org. uk*) has many links to articles and lists.

Appendices

A

Abbreviations
in Common Use

Throughout the book, initials of common acronyms are capitalized and underlined. The abbreviations presented below include many in common use, as well as some I personally find useful. In the columns below, the abbreviation is given on the left and the full term on the right.

A.1. Clinicians/Mental Health Professionals

Academic Degrees

BSW	Bachelor of Social Work	DO	Doctor of Osteopathy
MA	Master of Arts	EdD	Doctor of Education
MS	Master of Science	MD	Doctor of Medicine
MSW	Master of Social Work	PhD	Doctor of Philosophy
		PsyD	Doctor of Psychology

Psychology

The two most widely recognized credentials in the field of psychology beyond the PhD/PsyD and state licensure are entry into the National Register of Health Service Providers in Psychology and receipt of a diploma in any of 13 specialty areas from the American Board of Professional Psychology. In particular, the ABPP diploma is awarded only after an extensive evaluation of clinical skills and expertise. Beware: There are dozens of "vanity boards" and "diploma mills" conferring impressive-sounding and -looking credentials, whose standards of experience and skill are nonexistent or too low to impress those of your peers who have earned their credentials.

Social Work

Titles may differ by state.

ACSW	Academy of Certified Social Workers
CSW	Clinical or Certified Social Worker
LCSW	Licensed Certified Social Worker
LGSW	Licensed Graduate Social Worker
LICSW	Licensed Independent Clinical Social Worker
LSW	Licensed Social Worker
LSWA	Licensed Social Work Associate

Counseling

Again, titles may vary.

CAS	Certified Addictions Specialist
LPC	Licensed Professional Counselor
NBCC	National Board for Certified Counselors
NCC	National Certified Counselor

Nursing

APRN	Advanced Practice Registered Nurse
BSN	Bachelor of Science in Nursing
CNA	Certified Nursing Assistant
CRNP	Certified, Registered Nurse Practitioner
LPN	Licensed Practical Nurse
MSN	Master's of Science in Nursing
RN	Registered Nurse
RNCS	Registered Nurse, Certified Specialist
PHN	Public Health Nurse

Other

AT	Art Therapist
CAC	Certified Alcoholism Counselor
CCC	Certificate of Clinical Competence (speech and language pathologist)
COTA	Certified Occupational Therapist Assistant
LMFT	Licensed Marriage and Family Therapist
NCSP	Nationally Certified Speech Pathologist
OTR or OTR/L	Occupational Therapist, Registered or Licensed
PA	Physician's Assistant
PT	Physical Therapist
SLP	Speech and Language Pathologist

A.2. Treatment

IV	Interview	P/T	Psychotherapy	P/A	Psychoanalysis
Σ	Summary	Rx, Tx	Treatment	Th	Therapist
Hx	History	Px	Prognosis	h/o	History of
HW	Homework	Sx	Symptom	d/c	Discontinue/ed
NOS	Not otherwise specified	Dx	Diagnosis	d/ch	Discharge/ed
WNL	Within normal limits	AMA	Against medical advice	PTA	Prior to admission

A.3. Diagnoses and Conditions

Needless to say, only a small sampling of the many possible abbreviations in this category can be provided here.

<u>A</u>	Anxiety	h/a	Headache
AOD	Alcohol and other drugs	H/A	Heart attack
Bip	Bipolar disorder	HBP	Hypertension/high
CHI	Closed head injury		blood pressure
COPD	Chronic obstructive	LBP	Low back pain
	pulmonary disease	MCA	Motorcycle accident
CUS or CUSc	Chronic undifferentiated	MVA	Motor vehicle accident
	schizophrenia	MVP	Mitral valve prolapse
CVA	Cerebral vascular accident	<u>P</u>	Panic
<u>D</u>	Depression	Pa	Paranoia
D+A	Drug and alcohol	R/O	Rule out
D+H	Delusions and hallucinations	SI	Suicidal ideation
DM	Diabetes mellitus	sz	Seizures
GAD	Generalized anxiety disorder	TBI	Traumatic brain injury
GSW	Gunshot wound	tt	Temper tantrum
		TT	Toilet training

A.4. Relations

B	Brother	gf	Girlfriend	s	Son
bf	Boyfriend	GP[1]	Grandparent	S	Sister
bil	Brother-in-law	H	Husband	sil	Sister-in-law
d	Daughter	HH	Household	W	Wife
Fa	Father	Mo	Mother		

A.5. General Aids to Recording

$\bar{a}$	Before (*ante*)	FTKA	Failed to keep	× 3	Times 3
@	At		appointment	~	Approximate
AO	Anyone	NO	No one	Δ	Change
c.	About (*circa*)	$\bar{p}$ or s/p	After, by history	↓	Decreasing/-ed
$\bar{c}$	With (*cum*)		(*post*)	↑	Increasing/-ed
d or d/	Divorced	Q, ?	Question	<	Less, lesser,
D	Died	RTC	Return to clinic		smaller
d/o	Disorder	RTW	Return to work	>	More, greater,
DNKA	Did not keep	$\bar{s}$ or w/o	Without (*sine*)		larger
	appointment	S+S	Signs and	∅ or ⊖	Not present,
DNS	Did not show		symptoms		absent
DOB	Date of birth	w/d	Withdrawal/	#	Number
DOD	Date of death		withdrew	⊕	Present,
EO	Everyone	w/i or $\bar{c}$/in	Within		positive for
f	Frequency	1°	Primary	∴	Therefore
		2°	Secondary		

[1]Grandparents may be further specified as follows: maternal grandmother/grandfather, MGM/MGF; paternal grandmother/grandfather, PGM/PGF.

A.6. Legal Terms

CMM	Corrupting the morals of a minor	IVDU	Intravenous drug use
IA	Indecent assault	UAD	Underage drinking
IDSI	Involuntary deviate sexual intercourse		

A.7. Medication Regimens

b.i.d.	Twice a day	p.c.	After meals	q.q.h.	Every 4 hours
h.s.	At night/bedtime (hours of sleep)	p.o.	By mouth	q.s.	As much as required
		p.r.n.	Whenever needed	Sig.	Schedule
i.m.	Intramuscular				
i.v.	Intravenous	q.d.	Every day	t.i.d.	Three times a day
o.m.	Every morning	q.i.d.	Four times a day		

A.8. Educational Services

In this section, acronyms for disability categories are linked by arrows with acronyms for the appropriate services.

A	Autism	→	AS	Autism support
ER	Evaluation report			
HI	Hearing impairment	→	SIS	Sensory impairment support
ID	Intellectual disability	→	LS or LSS	Learning support or life skills support (as appropriate)
IEP	Individualized education program		NORA	Notice of recommended assignment
LD	Learning disability	→	LS	Learning support
MDT	Multidisciplinary team		MDE	Multidisciplinary evaluation
MR	Mental retardation	→	LS or LSS	Learning support or life skills support (as appropriate)
SEM/SED	Social and emotional maladjustment/disturbance	→	ES	Emotional support
SLI	Speech and language impairment	→	SLS	Speech and language support
VI	Visual impairment support	→	SIS	Sensory impairment

See also Section 22.4, "Types of Therapies/Services."

B

Annotated Readings in Assessment, Interviewing, and Report Writing

Assessment

Antony, M. M., & Barlow, D. H. (Eds.). (2002). *Handbook of assessment and treatment planning for psychological disorders.* New York: Guilford Press.

>The value of this book lies in the successful integration of assessment into clinical care. It is organized by diagnosis, not by test, and the number of assessment tools for each is impressive.

Clement, P. W. (1999). *Outcomes and incomes: How to evaluate, improve, and market your psychotherapy practice by measuring outcomes.* New York: Guilford Press.

>This book offers dozens of assessment tools specially designed to show changes in symptoms and other client aspects of therapeutic interest. Using one or two of these with each client allows the therapist to document initial levels, change in therapy, and further benefits. Clement also provides all the assistance needed to easily use his tools to evaluate one's clinical practice.

Fischer, J., & Corcoran, K. (2007). *Measures for clinical practice: A sourcebook* (4th ed.). New York: Oxford University Press.

>If you need a questionnaire for your clinical work and want one with reliability and validity studies, it is probably in here.

Groth-Marnat, G. (2009). *Handbook of psychological assessment* (5th ed.). Hoboken, NJ: Wiley.

>*The* current standard concerning testing and evaluation. Comprehensive, up-to-date, solid data-based weighing of the tests. Strong on integrating data from different sources. For the beginner through the skilled clinician.

Hebben, N., & Milberg, W. (2009). *Essentials of neuropsychological assessment* (2nd ed.). Hoboken, NJ: Wiley.

>A basic book that covers administration, scoring, and interpretation of the common tests; the populations tested; and ways of constructing a good report.

Lezak, M. D., Howieson, D. B., Loring, D. W., Hannay, J., & Fisher, J. S. (2004). *Neuropsychological assessment* (4th ed.). New York: Oxford University Press.

>*The* standard in this area. For the beginner through the skilled clinician.

Meehl, P. (1996). *Clinical vs. statistical prediction: A theoretical analysis and a review of the evidence.* Northvale, NJ: Aronson. (Original work published 1954)

>Still in print because it tells the truth: Mechanical formulas weighing objective data are more accurate than any clinician using his/her favorite test, etc. We clinicians don't like to hear that as we become more experienced, our confidence in our judgments rises, but the judgments do not become more valid. Read this before you go much further.

Interviewing

Greenspan, S. I., & Greenspan, N. T. (2003). *The clinical interview of the child* (3rd ed.). Washington, DC: American Psychiatric Press.

> This classic text covers how to interview all ages, what to observe, how to interpret it, how to formulate a developmental profile in a biopsychosocial framework, and how to select diagnoses. It includes full case examples.

Lukas, S. (1993). *Where to start and what to ask: An assessment handbook.* New York: Norton.

> She starts the beginner or student out right, with specific tools and usable guidance for gathering the information and integrating it into a coherent assessment.

MacKinnon, R. A., Michels, R., & Buckley, P. J. (2006). *The psychiatric interview in clinical practice* (2nd ed.). Washington, DC: American Psychiatric Publishing.

> Besides describing in detail how to interview, it covers psychodynamics, the major clinical syndromes, special situations, and even note taking and use of e-mail.

Morrison, J. (2001). *DSM-IV made easy: The clinician's guide to diagnosis* (rev. ed.). New York: Guilford Press.

> Do not go to DSM-IV to learn to diagnose. All that you need is easily accessible right here. It is like looking over the shoulder of a superb clinician, diagnostician, and interviewer at work. Just paging through it, even over familiar terrain, makes me feel smarter. For example, the discussions of "rule-outs" expand my understanding of dynamics, and the discussions of medical disorders that might be present sharpen my skills. Hundreds of perfectly constructed vignettes invite practice and consideration.

Morrison, J. (2008). *The first interview* (3rd ed.). New York: Guilford Press.

> If you are less interested in diagnosing and more interested in the dynamics of the interview, get ready to enjoy Morrison's gifts as a teacher. This book gives especially good advice on handling the many kinds of difficult interview situations clients can present. Rich with perfectly structured cases.

Morrison, J., & Anders, T. F. (1999). *Interviewing children and adolescents: Skills and strategies for effective DSM-IV diagnosis.* New York: Guilford Press.

> The subtitle is accurate: This book is a step-by-step guide to building rapport, gathering information (for all ages), and constructing a useful report. Detailed diagnostic information is provided on all the disorders of children and the "adult" disorders seen in children. The book is clearly written, with many teaching tools and excellent examples. Perhaps it is the child equivalent of Lukas's book, with more on clinical presentations and diagnoses.

Rogers, R. (2001). *Handbook of diagnostic and structured interviewing.* New York: Guilford Press.

> Interviewing has low reliability and therefore low validity. Structured interviews are the answer, and this book is a readable and reliable guide to selecting the most appropriate ones available for each disorder.

Segal, D. L., & Hersen, M. (Eds.). (2010). *Diagnostic interviewing* (4th ed.). New York: Springer.

> The next step up from Lukas. Covers the basics, as well as various special and difficult situations.

Shea, S. C. (1998). *Psychiatric interviewing: The art of understanding.* Philadelphia: Saunders.

> A big book (750 pages) but not intimidating. Absolutely comprehensive, yet simple and clear.

Trzepacz, P. T., & Baker, R. W. (1993). *The psychiatric mental status examination.* New York: Oxford University Press.

> Just on the MSE, and under 200 pages, but everything you need to know on doing and interpreting it.

Report Writing

Braaten, E. (2007). *The child clinician's report-writing handbook.* New York: Guilford Press.

> The whole language of child mental health evaluations.

Goldfinger, K., & Pomerantz, A. M. (2010). *Psychological assessment and report writing.* Thousand Oaks, CA: Sage.

> Concise. Covers many tests for gathering relevant information.

Harvey, V. S. (2006). Variables affecting the clarity of psychological reports. *Journal of Clinical Psychology, 62,* 5–18.

> Provides solid guidelines for writers.

Lichtenberger, E. O., Mather, N., Kaufman, N. L., & Kaufman, A. S. (2004). *Essentials of assessment report writing*. Hoboken, NJ: Wiley.

Comprehensive, extensive, perfectly clear advice and guidance. The "gold standard" text for students.

Michaels, M. (2006). Ethical considerations in writing psychological assessment reports. *Journal of Clinical Psychology, 62*, 47–58.

PsychAssessment is a very practical webpage generously provided for graduate students by Richard Niolon, PhD (*www.psychpage.com/article_index.html#PsychAssessment*).

Feedback Solicitation Form

Dear Fellow Clinician,

I created this book to meet my needs as a clinician writing reports and gave it my best shot. I really would appreciate your best shot too, so that it may be further developed to aid all of us. New versions can be designed to meet our needs better if we work together. If you will send your suggestions, modifications, and ideas (perhaps by photocopying the relevant pages), and they are adopted, I will give you credit in the revised editions and send you a free copy of the next edition.

> *Ed Zuckerman*
> *P.O. Box 222, Armbrust, PA 15616*
> *E-mail: edwardzuckerman@gmail.com*

Would you answer a few questions for me so I can better understand your professional life, please?

Your name: _____

Your professional title: _____

Years in practice when you bought this book: _____ Today's date: _____

Your mailing address: _____

_____

Your phone/fax numbers: _____

Your e-mail address(es): _____

How often do you refer to this book? (Check one.)

❏ Whenever I evaluate people.　　❏ Fairly often, when I need some specific ideas and wording choices.

❏ Every time I write a report.　　❏ Never now, but it was useful when I was learning to write reports.

❏ Other times: _____

How do you use it?

❏ I use it for questions in evaluating people.　　❏ I use it to teach evaluation or report writing.

❏ I use it to structure my report writing.　　❏ I refer to it for specific information and wording choices.

❏ Other use(s): _____

What is your overall evaluation of the *Clinician's Thesaurus,* 7th Edition, in just a few words?

_____

_____

I would suggest the following changes:

Increase these sections: _____

_____

Add coverage of the following: _____

_____

Decrease or eliminate these sections: _____

_____

As a clinician, I really wish there were a "tool" to: _____

_____

About the *Clinician's Electronic Thesaurus, Version 7.0*

If you write your reports on a computer and find this book helpful, the *Clinician's Electronic Thesaurus, Version 7.0* (CET 7.0) can make your report writing even easier. CET 7.0 is an easy-to-use computer program, available on CD-ROM, that is filled with terms, standard phrasings, and common concepts—as found in Part II of this book. The program is also fully searchable and fully compatible with any Windows-based word-processing software. Terms can be quickly found, copied, and then pasted into your own word-processing documents. As with the book version, the computerized thesaurus covers the appropriate terms to describe almost any clinical situation from intake and diagnostic workup to psychological evaluations, psychosocial narratives, treatment plans, progress notes, case summaries, and closings.

- *CET 7.0 is a text library.* You will never need to type the same paragraph again.

- *CET 7.0 can store all of your favorite wordings so you can use them repeatedly.* You can store your technical terms, localized referral statements, complex treatment plans, test interpretation statements, or any other text. Then with only a few mouse clicks you can find them under your own choice of headings.

- *CET 7.0 is completely customizable by you for you.* You can move text around or delete it (and reinstall it from the CD-ROM if you need it later). You can add new chapters, sections, and subsections to what is already present in the book. You can also change the fonts, font sizes, and formatting to highlight your preferred word choices in the text windows.

Additional Productivity Features

- Easy-access definitions of numerous mental health and drug/alcohol terms.

- Ability to copy and paste more than one item at a time from the thesaurus into your document.

- **Find** command that searches the whole thesaurus to locate key words. You can then find similar words nearby.

- Fully compatible with Windows XP and all newer versions.

CET 7.0 is very simple to learn and use. It has a foolproof installation with our custom installer. Technical support is provided by Guilford by phone, fax, and e-mail. CET 7.0 works with your word processor's resources, including spell-check, page formatting, and printing. A full set of Help files is available within the program under the Help menu. Witty documentation with many examples and tips is included with the CD-ROM.

Hardware Requirements

- PC with a Pentium chip or above.

- A hard disk with at least 11 megabytes (MB) of available space.

- At least 128 MB of RAM.

- A CD-ROM drive of any speed.

Software Requirements

- Microsoft operating system of Windows XP or higher.

- Any word-processing program running under Windows.

Want to see how this program can make your life easier? You can download a demonstration of the software at *www.guilford.com/cet7*.

References

Ackerman, N. (1982). *The strength of family therapy.* New York: Brunner/Mazel.

Adams, D. (1991). Factitious disorders and malingering: Choosing the appropriate role for the psychologist. *American Psychological Association Division 29 Newsletter,* pp. 10–13.

Adorno, T. W., Frenkel-Brunswik, E., Levinson, D. J., & Sanford, R. N. (1993). *The authoritarian personality.* New York: Norton. (Original work published 1950)

American Academy of Sleep Medicine. (2005). *International classification of sleep disorders: Diagnostic and coding manual* (2nd ed.). Westchester, IL: Author.

American Psychiatric Association. (2000). *Diagnostic and statistical manual of mental disorders* (4th ed., text rev.). Washington, DC: Author.

Babcock, M., & McKay, M. C. (Eds.). (1995). *Challenging codependency: Feminist critiques.* Toronto: University of Toronto Press.

Barkley, R. A. (2005). *Attention-deficit hyperactivity disorder: A handbook for diagnosis and treatment* (3rd ed.). New York: Guilford Press.

Barkley, R. A., & Murphy, K. R. (2005). *Attention-deficit hyperactivity disorder: A clinical workbook* (3rd ed.). New York: Guilford Press.

Bateson, G. (1972). *Steps to an ecology of mind.* San Francisco: Chandler.

Beavers, R. W. (1990). *Successful families.* New York: Norton.

Beck, A. T., Rush, A. J., Shaw, B. F., & Emery, G. (1979). *Cognitive therapy of depression.* New York: Guilford Press.

Beck, J. C. (1990). The potentially violent patient: Clinical, legal and ethical implications. In E. Margenau (Ed.), *The encyclopedic handbook of private practice.* New York: Gardner Press.

Benjamin, L. S. (1996). *Interpersonal diagnosis and treatment of personality disorders* (2nd ed.). New York: Guilford Press.

Berg, I. K., & Miller, S. D. (1992). *Working with the problem drinker.* New York: Norton.

Bernard, S. D. (1991). A substance use checklist. In P. Keller & S. R. Heyman (Eds.), *Innovations in clinical practice: A source book* (Vol. 10). Sarasota, FL: Professional Resource Exchange.

Berne, E. (1964). *Games people play.* New York: Grove Press.

Bernstein, E. M., & Putnam, F. W. (1986). Development, reliability, and validity of a dissociation scale. *Journal of Nervous and Mental Disease, 174,* 727–735.

Blakiston's Gould medical dictionary (3rd ed.). (1972). New York: McGraw-Hill.

Bleuler, E. (1968). *Dementia praecox, or the group of schizophrenias* (J. Zinkin, Trans.). New York: International Universities Press. (Original work published 1911)

Bondi, M. (1992). Distinguishing psychological disorders from neurological disorders: Taking Axis III seriously. *Professional Psychology: Research and Practice, 23*(4), 306–309.

Bongar, B. (2002). *The suicidal patient: Clinical and legal standards of care* (2nd ed.). Washington, DC: American Psychological Association.

Bornstein, R. (1997). Dependent personality disorder in the DSM-IV and beyond. *Clinical Psychology: Science and Practice, 4*(2), 175–187.

Braaten, E. (2007). *The child clinician's report-writing handbook.* New York: Guilford Press.

Brenner, E. (2003). Consumer-focused psychological assessment. *Professional Psychology: Research and Practice, 34*(3), 240–247.

Breznitz, S. (1988). The seven kinds of denial. In C. Spielberger et al. (Eds.), *Stress and anxiety* (Vol. 2). Washington, DC: Hemisphere.

Broverman, I. D., Broverman, D. M., Clarkson, F. E., Rosencrantz, P. S., & Vogel, S. R. (1970). Sex-role stereo-types and clinical judgements of mental health. *Journal of Consulting and Clinical Psychology, 34,* 1–7.

Brown, M. L., & Rounsley, C. A. (2003). *True selves: Understanding transsexualism—for families, friends, coworkers, and helping professionals.* San Francisco: Jossey-Bass.

Brown, W. A. (2006, May 26). Acknowledging preindustrial patterns of sleep may revolutionize approach to sleep dysfunction. *Psychiatric Times.* Retrieved from *www.psychiatrictimes.com/display/article/10168/56881.*

Burgess, T., & Holmstrom, B. (1974). Rape trauma syndrome. *American Journal of Psychiatry, 131*(9), 981–986.

Burns, D. D. (1999). *Feeling good: The new mood therapy, revised and updated.* New York: Harper.

Cameron, N., & Rychlak, J. F. (1968). *Personality and psychopathology.* Boston: Houghton Mifflin.

Campbell, R. J. (2009). *Campbell's psychiatric dictionary* (9th ed.). New York: Oxford University Press.

Cass, V. C. (1979). Homosexual identity formation: A theoretical model. *Journal of Homosexuality, 4*(3), 219–235.

Cheyne, J. A., Newby-Clark, I. R., & Rueffer, S. D. (1999). Relations among hypnagogic and hypnopompic experiences associated with sleep paralysis. *Journal of Sleep Research, 8*(4), 313–317.

Christophersen, E. R., & Mortweet, S. L. (2001). *Treatments that work with children: Empirically supported strategies for managing childhood problems.* Washington, DC: American Psychological Association.

Cleckley, H. M. (1976). *The mask of sanity* (5th ed.). St. Louis, MO: C. V. Mosby.

Clement, P. W. (1999). *Outcomes and incomes: How to evaluate, improve, and market your psychotherapy practice by measuring outcomes.* New York: Guilford Press.

Coons, P. M., & Milstein, V. (1986). Psychosexual disturbances in multiple personality: Characteristics, etiology, and treatment. *Journal of Clinical Psychiatry, 47,* 107–110.

Costa, P. T., Jr., & McCrae, R. R. (1995). *NEO-PI-R professional manual.* Odessa, FL: Psychological Assessment Resources.

Costa, P. T., Jr., & Widiger, T. A. (2002). *Personality disorders and the five-factor model of personality* (2nd ed.). Washington, DC: American Psychological Association.

Coulehan, J., & Block, M. (1987). *The medical interview: A primer for students of the art.* Philadelphia: Davis.

Courtois, C. (2004). Complex trauma, complex reactions: Assessment and treatment. *Psychotherapy: Theory, Research, Practice, and Training, 41*(4), 412–425.

Davis, T. C., Long, S. W., Jackson, R. H., et al. (1993). The Rapid Estimate of Adult Literacy in Medicine: A shortened screening instrument. *Family Medicine, 25,* 391–395.

Denning, P. (2000). *Practicing harm reduction psychotherapy: An alternative approach to addictions.* New York: Guilford Press.

Derogatis, L. R. (1994). *The Symptom Checklist—90—Revised (SCL-90-R).* Minneapolis: Pearson Assessments.

DiClemente, C. D. (2003). *Addiction and change: How addictions develop and addicted people recover.* New York: Guilford Press.

Diener, E., & Biswas-Diener, R. (2008). *Happiness: Unlocking the mysteries of psychological wealth.* Malden, MA: Blackwell.

Drum, D. J., Browson, C., Denmark, A. B., & Smith, S. E. (2009). New data on the nature of suicidal crises in college students: Shifting the paradigm. *Professional Psychology: Research and Practice, 40*(2), 213–222.

DuPaul, G. J. (2003). Assessment of ADHD symptoms: Comment on Gomez et al. *Psychological Assessment, 15*(1), 115–117.

Durkheim, E. (1966). *Suicide: A study in sociology* (J. Spaulding & G. Simpson, Trans.). New York: Free Press. (Original work published 1897)

Dutton, D. G. (2007). *The abusive personality: Violence and control in intimate relationships* (2nd ed.). New York: Guilford Press.

Ebert, B. W. (1987). Guide to conducting a psychological autopsy. *Professional Psychology: Research and Practice, 18*(1), 52–56.

Edinger, J. D., & Carney, C. E. (2008). *Overcoming insomnia: A cognitive-behavioral therapy approach. Therapist guide.* New York: Oxford University Press.

Ellis, A. E., & Dryden, W. (Eds.). (1997). *The practice of rational emotive behavior therapy* (2nd ed.). New York: Springer.

Erikson, E. (1963). *Childhood and society* (rev. ed.). New York: Norton.

Esser, T. J. (1974). *Effective report writing in vocational evaluation and work adjustment training.* (Available from Materials Development Center, Department of Rehabilitation and Manpower, University of Wisconsin, Menomonie, WI 54751)

Farberow, N. (Ed.). (1980). *The many faces of suicide: Indirect self-destructive behavior.* New York: McGraw-Hill.

Fear, R. A. (1958). *The evaluation interview: Predicting job performance in business and industry.* New York: McGraw-Hill.

Firestone, L. (1991). *Firestone Voice Scale for Self-Destructive Behavior.* (Available from The Glendon Association, 2049 Century Park East, Suite 3000, Los Angeles, CA 90067)

Folstein, M. F., Folstein, S. E., & McHugh, P. R. (1975). Mini-Mental State: A practical method for grading the cognitive state of patients for the clinician. *Journal of Psychiatric Research, 12,* 189–198.

Frisch, M. B. (1999). Quality of life therapy and assessment in health care. *Clinical Psychology: Science and Practice, 5*(1), 19–40.

Frisch, M. B. (2006). *Quality of life therapy: Applying a life satisfaction approach to positive psychology and cognitive therapy.* Hoboken, NJ: Wiley.

Gardner, H. (1999). *Multiple intelligences: New horizons.* New York: Basic Books.

Gardner, H. (2004). *Frames of mind: The theory of multiple intelligences.* New York: Basic.

Garner, D. M., & Garfinkel, P. E. (1979). The Eating Attitudes Test: An index of the symptoms of anorexia nervosa. *Psychological Medicine, 9,* 273–279.

Geller, J. A. (1992). *Breaking destructive patterns.* New York: Free Press.

Gibbs, R. W., & Beitel, D. (1995). What proverb understanding reveals about how people think. *Psychological Bulletin, 118*(1), 133–154.

Gill, D. J., Freshman, A., Blender, J. A., & Ravina, B. (2008). The Montreal Cognitive Assessment as a screening tool for cognitive impairment in Parkinson's disease. *Movement Disorders, 23*(7), 1043–1046.

Goldberg, L. R. (1992). The development of markers for the Big Five factor structure. *Psychological Assessment, 4,* 26–42.

Goleman, D. (1988, November 1). Narcissism looming larger as root of personality woes. *The New York Times,* pp. C1, C16.

Gonsalves, C. (1992). Psychological stages of the refugee process: A model for therapeutic interventions. *Professional Psychology: Research and Practice, 23*(5), 382–389.

Goodman, A. (2005). Sexual addiction: Nosology, diagnosis, etiology, and treatment. In J. H. Lowinson, P. Ruiz, R. B. Millman, & J. G. Langrod (Eds.), *Substance abuse: A comprehensive textbook* (4th ed., pp. 504–539). Philadelphia: Lippincott Williams & Wilkins.

Goodman, A. (2009, May 26). Sexual addiction update: Assessment, diagnosis, and treatment. *Psychiatric Times, 26*(6). Available at *www.psychiatrictimes.com/display/article/10168/1416827.*

Goodman, W. K., Rasmussen, S. A., Price, L. H., Mazure, C., Heninger, C. R., & Charney, D. S. (1989). *Yale–Brown Obsessive Compulsive Scale.* (Available from Clinical Neuroscience Research Unit, Connecticut Mental Health Center, 34 Park Street, New Haven, CT 06508).

Gordon, R. (2010). The Psychodynamic Diagnostic Manual. In I. Weiner & E. Craighead (Eds.), *Corsini's encyclopedia of psychology.* Hoboken, NJ: Wiley.

Gordon, T. (2000). *Parent effectiveness training: The proven program for raising responsible children.* New York: Three Rivers Press.

Grant, I., & Atkinson, J. (1995). Psychiatric aspects of acquired immune deficiency syndrome. In H. I. Kaplan & B. J. Sadock (Eds.), *Comprehensive textbook of psychiatry* (6th ed., Vol. 2, Sect. 29.2, pp. 1644–1669). Baltimore: Williams & Wilkins.

Gratz, K. (2003). Risk factors for and functions of deliberate self-harm: An empirical and conceptual review. *Clinical Psychology: Science and Practice, 10*(2), 192–205.

Greenwood, D. U. (1991). Neuropsychological aspects of AIDS dementia complex: What clinicians need to know. *Professional Psychology: Research and Practice, 22*(5), 407–409.

Greist, J. H., Jefferson, J. W., & Marks, I. M. (1986). *Anxiety and its treatment: Help is available.* Washington, DC: American Psychiatric Press.

Groth-Marnat, G. (2009). *Handbook of psychological assessment* (5th ed.). Hoboken, NJ: Wiley.

Group for the Advancement of Psychiatry (GAP). (1990). *Casebook in psychiatric ethics.* New York: Brunner/Mazel.

Gruber, H. E., & Von Eiche, J. J. (1977). *The essential Piaget.* New York: Basic Books.

Hagen, C., Malkmus, D., & Durham, P. (1979). Levels of cognitive functioning. In *Rehabilitation of the head injured adult: Comprehensive physical management.* Downey, CA: Los Amigos Research & Education Institute, Rancho Los Amigos National Rehabilitation Center.

Haley, J. (1984). *Ordeal therapy.* San Francisco: Jossey-Bass.

Hamilton, M. (1960). A rating scale for depression. *Journal of Neurology, Neurosurgery and Psychiatry, 23,* 56–62.

Harder, D. W., & Greenwald, D. F. (1999). Further validation of the shame and guilt scales of the Harder Personal Feelings Questionnaire-2. *Psychological Reports, 85,* 271–281.

Hare, R. D. (1999). *Without conscience: The disturbing world of the psychopaths among us.* New York: Guilford Press.

Harvey, V. S. (1997). Improving readability of psychological reports. *Professional Psychology: Research and Practice, 28*(3), 271–274.

Heinik, J., & Shaikewitz, D. (2009). The Clock Drawing Test—Modified and Integrated Approach (CDT-MIA) as an instrument for detecting mild cognitive impairment in a specialized outpatient setting. *Journal of Geriatric Psychiatry and Neurology, 22*(3), 171–180.

Heinik, J., & Solomesh, I. (2007). Validity of the Cambridge Cognitive Examination—Revised new executive function scores in the diagnosis of dementia: Some early findings. *Journal of Geriatric Psychiatry and Neurology, 20*(1), 22–28.

Hersen, M., & Turner, S. (Eds.). (2003). *Diagnostic interviewing* (3rd ed.). New York: Plenum Press.

Hoffman, R. S., & Koran, L. M. (1984). Detecting physical illness in patients with mental disorders. *Psychosomatics, 25,* 654–660.

Holt, J., Hotto, S., & Cole, K. (1994). *Demographic aspects of hearing impairment: Questions and answers* (3rd ed.). Washington, DC: Center for Assessment and Demographic Studies, Gallaudet University. Retrieved from *http://gri.gallaudet.edu/Demographics/factsheet.html.*

Horvath, A. T. (1993). Enhancing motivation for treatment of addictive behavior: Guidelines for the psychotherapist. *Psychotherapy, 30,* 473–480.

Huber, J. T. (1984). *Report writing in psychology and psychiatry.* New York: Harper and Row.

Hyler, S. E., & Spitzer, R. T. (1978). Hysteria split asunder. *American Journal of Psychiatry, 135,* 1500–1504.

Jackson, H., Philip, E., Nutall, R. L., & Diller, L. (2002). Traumatic brain injury: A hidden consequence for battered women. *Professional Psychology: Research and Practice, 33*(1), 39–45.

Jahoda, M. (1958). *Current concepts of positive mental health.* New York: Basic Books.

Jellinek, E. M. (1960). *The disease concept of alcoholism.* New Haven, CT: Hillhouse Press.

Jobes, D. A. (2006). *Managing suicidal risk: A collaborative approach.* New York: Guilford Press.

Juby, A. (1999). Correlation between the Folstein Mini-Mental State Examination and three methods of clock drawing scoring. *Journal of Geriatric Psychiatry and Neurology, 12*(2), 87–91.

Kalichman, S. C. (2003). *The inside story on AIDS: Experts answer your questions.* Washington, DC: American Psychological Association.

Kanfer, F. H., & Saslow, K. (1965). Behavioral analysis: An alternative to diagnostic classification. *Archives of General Psychiatry, 12,* 529–538.

Kaplan, H. S. (1983). *The evaluation of sexual disorders: Psychological and medical aspects.* New York: Brunner/Mazel.

Kaslow, F. (1995). *Projective genogramming.* Sarasota, FL: Professional Resources Press.

Kennedy, J. A. (2003). *Fundamentals of psychiatric treatment planning* (2nd ed.). Washington, DC: American Psychiatric Press.

Kiresuk, T. J., Smith, A., & Cardillo, J. E. (Eds.). (1994). *Goal Attainment Scaling: Applications, theory, and measurement.* Hillsdale, NJ: Erlbaum.

Klonsky, E. D., & Glenn, C. R. (2009, Summer). Non-suicidal self-injury: What independent practitioners should know. *Independent Practitioner: Newsletter of Division 42 of the American Psychological Association,* pp. 147–150.

Kohlberg, L. (Ed.). (1984). *The psychology of moral development: The nature and validity of moral stages.* San Francisco: Harper & Row.

Korkman, M., Kirk, U., & Kemp, S. (2007). *NEPSY—Second edition.* San Antonio, TX: Psych Corp/Pearson.

Kovacs, M. (1992). *Children's Depression Inventory.* San Antonio, TX: Psychological Corporation.

Kral, V. A. (1978). Benign senescent forgetfulness. In R. Katzman, R. F. Terry, & K. L. Bick (Eds.), *Alzheimer's disease: Senile dementia and related disorders.* New York: Raven Press.

Kratochwill, T., & Bergan, J. (1990). *Behavioral consulting in applied settings: An individual guide.* New York: Plenum Press.

Kübler-Ross, E. (1969). *On death and dying.* New York: Macmillan.

Langer, E. J. (1989). *Mindfulness.* Reading, MA: Addison-Wesley.

Lawson, G., Lawson, A. W., & Rivers, P. C. (2001). *Essentials of chemical dependency counseling* (3rd ed.). Austin, TX: PRO-ED.

Lazarus, A. A. (1997). *Brief but comprehensive psychotherapy: The multimodal way.* New York: Springer.

Leary, T. (2004). *Interpersonal diagnosis of personality: A functional theory and methodology for personality evaluation.* Eugene, OR: Resource Publications. (Original work published 1957)

Lesieur, H. R., & Blume, S. E. (1987). South Oaks Gambling Screen (SOGS): A new instrument for the identification of pathological gamblers. *American Journal of Psychiatry, 144,* 1184–1188.

Levenstein, J. (1994). Treatment documentation in private practice: I. The PIC Treatment Plan. *Independent Practitioner, 14,* 181–185.

Levine, S. B. (2006, August). How to take a sexual history (without blushing). Retrieved from *nursinglink.monster.com/training/articles/1245.*

Lewinsohn, P. M., Rohde, P., & Seeley, J. R. (1996). Adolescent suicidal ideation and attempts: Prevalence, risk factors, and clinical implications. *Clinical Psychology: Science and Practice, 3*(1), 25–46.

Lewis, B. L. (2002). Second thoughts about documenting the psychological consultation. *Professional Psychology: Research and Practice, 33*(2), 224–225.

Lichtenberger, E. O., Nather, N., Kaufman, N., & Kaufman, A. S. (2004). *Essentials of assessment report writing.* New York: Wiley.

Lidz, T., & Fleck, S. (1985). *Schizophrenia and the family* (2nd ed.). New York: International Universities Press.

Lishman, W. (1998). *Organic psychiatry: The psychological consequences of cerebral disorder* (3rd ed.). Oxford: Blackwell Scientific.

Logue, M. B., Sher, K. J., & Frensch, P. A. (1992). Purported characteristics of adult children of alcoholics: A possible "Barnum effect." *Professional Psychology: Research and Practice, 23*(3), 226–232.

Lopez, S., & Snyder, C. R. (2009). *Oxford handbook of positive psychology* (2nd ed.). New York: Oxford University Press.

Lukas, C., & Seiden, H. M. (2007). *Silent grief: Living in the wake of suicide* (rev. ed.). Philadelphia: Jessica Kingsley.

Lykken, D. T. (1995). *The antisocial personalities.* Hillsdale, NJ: Erlbaum.

Mahler, M. (1975). *The psychological birth of the human infant.* New York: Basic Books.

Makover, R. B. (2004). *Treatment planning for psychotherapists* (2nd ed.). Washington, DC: American Psychiatric Publishing.

Maris, R. W., Berman, A. L., Maltsberger, J. T., & Yufit, R. I. (Eds.). (1992). *Assessment and prediction of suicide.* New York: Guilford Press.

Marlatt, G. A. (Ed.). (1998). *Harm reduction: Pragmatic strategies for managing high-risk behaviors.* New York: Guilford Press.

Marlatt, G. A., & Donovan, D. M. (Eds.). (2005). *Relapse prevention: Maintenance strategies in the treatment of addictive behaviors* (2nd ed.). New York: Guilford Press.

Maslow, A. H. (1962). *Toward a psychology of being.* Princeton, NJ: Van Nostrand.

McCloskey, K., & Grigsby, N. (2005). The ubiquitous clinical problem of adult intimate partner violence: The need for routine assessment. *Professional Psychology: Research and Practice, 36*(3), 264–275.

McGoldrick, M., Gerson, R., & Petry, S. (2008). *Genograms: Assessment and intervention* (3rd ed.). New York: Norton.

McIntosh, J. L. (1995). Suicide prevention in the elderly (age 65–99). *Suicide and Life-Threatening Behavior, 25*(1), 180–192.

Meichenbaum, D. (1996). Stress inoculation training for coping with stressors [Electronic version]. *The Clinical Psychologist, 49,* 4–7. Retrieved from *www.apa.org/divisions/div12/rev_est/sit_stress.html#top.*

Melton, G. B., Petrila, J., Poythress, N. G., & Slobogin, C. (2007). *Psychological evaluations for the courts: A handbook for mental health professionals and lawyers* (3rd ed.). New York: Guilford Press.

Menninger, K. A. (1952). *A manual for psychiatric case study.* New York: Grune & Stratton.

Menninger, W. C. (1967). *Psychiatrist for a troubled world.* New York: Viking Press.

Michaels, M. (2006). Ethical considerations in writing psychological assessment reports. *Journal of Clinical Psychology, 62,* 47–58.

Milgram, S. (1974). *Obedience to authority.* New York: Harper & Row.

Miller, S. G. (1994). Borderline personality disorder from the patient's perspective. *Hospital and Community Psychiatry, 45*(12), 1215–1219.

Miller, W. R., & Rollnick, S. (2002). *Motivational interviewing: Preparing people for change* (2nd ed.). New York: Guilford Press.

Millon, T., Millon, C. M., Meagher, D., Meagher, S., & Grossman, S. (2004). *Personality disorders in modern life* (2nd ed.). New York: Wiley.

Minuchin, S. (1974). *Families and family therapy.* Cambridge, MA: Harvard University Press.

Monahan, J. (1981). *Predicting violent behavior: An assessment of clinical techniques.* Beverly Hills, CA: Sage.

Morgan, J. F., Reid, F., & Lacey, H. (1999). The SCOFF questionnaire: Assessment of a new screening tool for eating disorders. *British Medical Journal, 319*(7223), 1467–1468.

Morin, C., & Espie, C. A. (2003). *Insomnia: A clinician's guide to assessment and treatment.* New York: Springer.

Morrison, J. (1997). *When psychological problems mask medical disorders: A guide for psychotherapists.* New York: Guilford Press.

Morrison, J. (2001). *DSM-IV made easy: The clinician's guide to diagnosis* (rev. ed.). New York: Guilford Press.

Morrison, J. (2006). *Diagnosis made easier: Principles and techniques for mental health clinicians.* New York: Guilford Press.

Morrison, J. (2008). *The first interview* (3rd ed.). New York: Guilford Press.

Mosher, D. L. (1988). Revised Mosher Guilt Inventory. In C. M. Davis, W. C. Yarber, & R. S. L. Davis (Eds.), *Sexuality-related measures* (pp. 75–88). Lake Mills, IA: Davis.

Mueller, J. (1995). The mental status examination. In H. H. Goldman (Ed.), *Review of general psychiatry* (4th ed.). Los Altos, CA: Lange.

Mullen, P. E., Pathe, M., Purcell, R., & Stuart, G. W. (1999). Study of stalkers. *American Journal of Psychiatry, 156*(8), 1244–1249.

NANDA International. (2003). *Nursing diagnoses: Definitions and classification 2003–2004.* Philadelphia: Author.

Nathan, P. E., & Gorman, J. M. (Eds.). (2007). *A guide to treatments that work* (3rd ed.). New York: Oxford University Press.

National Institute on Alcohol Abuse and Alcoholism. (2000). *10th special report to the U.S. Congress on alcohol and health: Highlights from current research.* Bethesda, MD: Author.

NiCarthy, G., & Davidson, S. (1989). *You can be free: An easy to read handbook for abused women.* Seattle, WA: Seal Press.

Nietzel, M. T., & Himelein, M. J. (1987). Crime prevention through social and physical environmental change. *Behavior Analyst, 10*(1), 69–74.

Norcross, J. C. (Ed.). (2002). *Psychotherapy relationships that work: Therapist contributions and responsiveness to patients.* New York: Oxford University Press.

Norcross, J. C., Santrock, J. W., Campbell, L. F., Smith, T. P., Sommer, R., & Zuckerman, E. L. (2003). *Authoritative guide to self-help resources in mental health* (rev. ed.). New York: Guilford Press.

O'Connor, L. E., Berry, J. W., Weiss, J., Bush, M., & Sampson, H. (1997). Interpersonal guilt: The development of a new measure. *Journal of Clinical Psychology, 53*(1), 73–89.

Ogles, B. J., Lambert, M. J., & Fields, S. A. (2002). *Essentials of outcome assessment.* New York: Wiley.

Ownby, R. L. (1997). *Psychological reports: A guide to report writing in professional psychology* (3rd ed.). New York: Wiley.

Paniagua, F. (2005). *Assessing and treating culturally diverse clients: A practical guide* (3rd ed.). Thousand Oaks, CA: Sage.

Paul, G. L. (1966). *Insight vs. desensitization in psychotherapy: An experiment in anxiety reduction.* Stanford, CA: Stanford University Press.

PDM Task Force. (2006). *Psychodynamic diagnostic manual.* Silver Spring, MD: Alliance of Psychoanalytic Organizations.

PDR guide to drug interactions, side effects, and indications (64th ed.). (2010). Montvale, NJ: Thomson Healthcare.

Pedersen, P. B., Draguns, J. G., Lonner, W. J., & Trimble, J. E. (Eds.). (2008). *Counseling across cultures* (6th ed.). Thousand Oaks, CA: Sage.

Pelonero, A. L., Levenson, J. L., & Pandurangi, A. K. (1998). Neuroleptic malignant syndrome: A review. *Psychiatric Services, 49*(9), 1163–1172.

Perlis, M. L., Jungquist, C., Smith, M. T., & Posner, D. (2005). *Cognitive behavioral treatment of insomnia: A session-by-session guide.* New York: Springer.

Peruzzi, N., & Bongar, B. (1999). Assessing risk for completed suicide in patients with major depression: Psychologists' views of critical factors. *Professional Psychology: Research and Practice, 30*(6), 576–680.

Peterson, C., & Seligman, M. E. P. (2004). *Character strengths and virtues: A handbook and classification.* New York: Oxford University Press.

Phillips, K. A. (2004). Body dysmorphic disorder: Recognizing and treating imagined ugliness. *World Psychiatry, 3*(1), 12–17. Retrieved from *www.ncbi.nlm.nih.gov/pmc/articles/PMC1414653*

Phillips, K. A. (2009). *The broken mirror: Understanding and treating body dysmorphic disorder* (rev. and expanded ed.). New York: Oxford University Press.

Physicians' desk reference (64th ed.). (2010). Montvale, NJ: Thomson Healthcare.

Pies, R. (1993). The psychopharmacology of PTSD. *Psychiatric Times, 10*(6), 21–24.

Pincus, H. H., & Tucker, G. J. (2003). *Behavioral neurology* (4th ed.). New York: Oxford University Press.

Ponterotto, J., Casas, J. M., Suzuki, L. A., & Alexander, C. M. (Eds.). (2010). *Handbook of multicultural counseling* (3rd ed.). Thousand Oaks, CA: Sage.

Potter-Effron, R. T. (1989). Shame and guilt: Definitions, processes, and treatment issues with AODA clients. In R. T. Potter-Effron & P. S. Potter-Effron (Eds.), *The treatment of shame and guilt in alcoholism counseling.* New York: Haworth Press.

Prochaska, J. P., DiClemente, C. C., & Norcross, J. (1992). In search of how people change: Applications to addictive behaviors. *American Psychologist, 47*(9), 1102–1114.

Putnam, F. W. (1989). *Diagnosis and treatment of multiple personality disorder.* New York: Guilford Press.

Putnam, F. W. (1991). Recent research on multiple personality disorder. *Psychiatric Clinics of North America, 14*(3), 489–502.

Putnam, F. W. (1997). *Dissociation in children and adolescents.* New York: Guilford Press.

Radloff, L. S. (1977). The CES-D scale: A self-report depression scale for research in the general population. *Applied Psychological Measurement, 1,* 385–401.

Ramsey, S. E., Engler, P. A., & Stein, M. D. (2005). Alcohol use among depressed patients: The need for assessment and intervention. *Professional Psychology: Research and Practice, 36*(2), 203–207.

Reed, W. J. (2005). Medical conditions that may present as psychological disorders. In G. P. Koocher, J. C. Norcross, & S. S. Hill III (Eds.), *Psychologists' desk reference* (2nd ed., pp. 447–453). New York: Oxford University Press.

Reimer, T., Brink, P. J., & Saunders, J. M. (1984). Cultural assessment: Content and process. *Nursing Outlook, 32*(2), 78–82.

Reisberg, B., Ferris, S., deLeon, M. J., & Crook, T. (1982). The Global Deterioration Scale for assessment of primary degenerative dementia. *American Journal of Psychiatry, 139*(9), 1136–1139.

Resnick, R. J. (2000). *The hidden disorder: A clinician's guide to attention deficit hyperactivity disorder in adults.* Washington, DC: American Psychological Association.

Rivas-Vasquez, R. A., Blais, M. A., Rey, G. J., & Rivas-Vasquez, A. A. (2001). A brief reminder about documenting the psychological consultation. *Professional Psychology: Research and Practice, 32*(2), 194–199.

Rivas-Vasquez, R. A., Saffa-Biller, D., Ruiz, I., Blais, M. A., & Rivas-Vasquez, A. (2004). Current issues in anxiety and depression: Comorbid, mixed, and subthreshold disorders. *Professional Psychology: Research and Practice, 35*(1), 74–83.

Rogers, R. (1984). Toward an empirical model of malingering and deception. *Behavioral Science and the Law, 2,* 544–559.

Rogers, R. (2001). *Handbook of diagnostic and structured interviewing.* New York: Guilford Press.

Rogers, R. (Ed.). (2008). *Clinical assessment of malingering and deception* (3rd ed.). New York: Guilford Press.

Roid, G. (2003). *Stanford–Binet Intelligence Scales, Fifth Edition.* Itasca, IL: Riverside.

Rosenthal, N. E. (2005). *Winter blues: Everything you need to know to beat seasonal affective disorder* (rev. ed.). New York: Guilford Press.

Ross, C. A. (1997). *Dissociative identity disorder* (2nd ed.). New York: Wiley.

Ross, C. A., Miller, S. D., Reagar, P., Bjornson, L., Fraser, G. A., & Anderson, G. (1990). Structured interview data on 102 cases of multiple personality disorder from four centers. *American Journal of Psychiatry, 147,* 596–601.

Ross, M. W., Channon-Little, L. D., & Rosser, B. R. S. (2000). *Sexual health concerns: Interviewing and history taking for health practitioners* (2nd ed.). Philadelphia: Davis.

Roth, A., & Fonagy, P. (2005). *What works for whom?* (2nd ed.). New York: Guilford Press.

Rudd, M. D., Joiner, T. E., Jr., & Rajab, H. (2001). *Treating suicidal behavior: An effective, time-limited approach.* New York: Guilford Press.

Ruiz, M. A., Drake, E. B., Glass, A., Marcotte, D., & van Gorp, W. G. (2002). Trying to beat the system: Misuse of the Internet to assist in avoiding the detection of psychological symptom dissimulation. *Professional Psychology: Research and Practice, 33*(3), 294–299.

Rüsch, N., Corrigan, P. W., Bohus, M., Brueck, R., Lieb, K., & Jacob, G. A. (2007). Measuring shame and guilt by self-report questionnaires: A validation study. *Psychiatry Research, 150*(3), 313–325.

Samenow, S. (2004). *Inside the criminal mind* (rev. and updated ed.). New York: Crown.

Sattler, J. M., & Hoge, R. D. (2005). *Assessment of children* (5th ed.). San Diego, CA: Jerome M. Sattler.

Schaef, A. W. (1986). *Codependency: Misunderstood—mistreated.* San Francisco: Harper & Row.

Schneider, K. (1959). *Clinical psychopathology.* New York: Grune & Stratton.

Segal, D. L., & Hutchings, P. S. (2007). Writing up the intake interview. In M. Hersen & J. C. Thomas (Eds.), *Handbook of clinical interviewing with adults* (pp. 114–132). Thousand Oaks, CA: Sage.

Segraves, R. T., & Balon, R. (2003). *Sexual pharmacology: Fast facts.* New York: Norton.

Shapiro, D. (1965). *Neurotic styles.* New York: Basic Books.

Shea, C. S. (2002). *The practical art of suicide assessment: A guide for mental health professionals and substance abuse counselors.* New York: Wiley.

Sher, K. J. (1991). *Children of alcoholics: A critical appraisal of theory and research.* Chicago: University of Chicago Press.

Sherin, K. M., Sinacore, J. M., Li, X. Q., Zitter, R. E., & Shakil, A. (1998). HITS: A short domestic violence screening tool for use in a family practice setting. *Family Medicine, 30*(7), 508–512.

Shneidman, E. S. (Ed.). (1980). *Death: Current perspectives.* Palo Alto, CA: Mayfield.

Shneidman, E. S., & Collins, J. (2004). *Autopsy of a suicidal mind.* New York: Oxford University Press

Shoben, E. J. (1956). *The psychology of adjustment: A dynamic and experiential approach to personality and mental hygiene.* Boston: Houghton Mifflin.

Slaby, A. E., Liev, J., & Tancredi, L. R. (1994). *Handbook of psychiatric emergencies* (4th ed.). Norwalk, CT: Appleton & Lange.

Smith, T., Gildeh, N., & Holmes, C. (2007). The Montreal Cognitive Assessment: Validity and utility in a memory clinic setting. *Canadian Journal of Psychiatry/Revue Canadienne de Psychiatrie, 52*(5), 329–332.

Stedman's medical dictionary (28th ed.). (2006). Philadelphia: Lippincott Williams & Wilkins.

Stedman's psychiatry words (4th ed.). (2007). Baltimore: Wolters Kluwer Health/Lippincott Williams & Wilkins.

Steinem, G. (1980). Erotica and pornography: A clear and present difference. In L. Lederer (Ed.), *Take back the night: Women on pornography.* New York: Morrow.

Steiner, C. (1971). *Games alcoholics play.* New York: Grove Press.

Sternberg, R. J., & Grigorenko, E. L. (1997). Are cognitive styles still in style? *American Psychologist, 52*(7), 700–712.

Stone, W. F., Lederer, G., & Christie, R. (Eds.). (1993). *Strength and weakness: The authoritarian personality today.* New York: Springer-Verlag.

Sue, D. W., & Sue, D. W. (2008). *Counseling the culturally diverse: Theory and practice* (5th ed.). Hoboken, NJ: Wiley.

Tangney, J. P., & Dearing, R. L. (2002). *Shame and guilt.* New York: Guilford Press.

Tanner, J. M. (1962). *Growth at adolescence* (2nd ed.). Oxford: Blackwell Scientific.

Tatarsky, A. (Ed.). (2002). *Harm reduction psychotherapy: A new treatment for drug and alcohol problems.* Northvale, NJ: Jason Aronson.

Taylor, R. L. (2007). *Distinguishing psychological from organic disorders: Screening for psychological masquerade* (3rd ed.). New York: Springer.

Teasdale, G., & Jenvet, B. (1974). Assessment of coma and impaired consciousness. *Lancet, 2*(7872), 81–83.

Tedeschi, R. G., & Kilmer, R. P. (2005). Assessing strengths, resilience, and growth to guide clinical interventions. *Professional Psychology: Research and Practice, 36*(3), 230–237.

Trzepacz, P. T., & Baker, R. W. (1993). *The psychiatric mental status examination.* New York: Oxford University Press.

Tseng, W.-S. (2003). *Clinician's guide to cultural psychiatry.* Amsterdam: Academic Press.

Tuckman, A. (2007). *Integrative treatment for adult ADHD: A practical, easy-to-use guide for clinicians.* Oakland, CA: New Harbinger.

Tyrer, P., Fowler-Dixon, R., Ferguson, B., & Keleman, A. (1990). A plea for the diagnosis of hypochondrical personality disorder. *Journal of Psychosomatic Research, 34*(6), 637–642.

U.S. Department of Health and Human Services. (1980). *International classification of diseases* (9th rev.), *clinical modification: Chapter 5. Mental disorders* (DHHS Publication No. PHS 80-1260). Washington, DC: U.S. Government Printing Office.

Wechsler, D. (1998). *Manual for the Wechsler Memory Scale—Third Edition.* San Antonio, TX: Psychological Corporation.

Wechsler, D. (2003). *Manual for the Wechsler Intelligence Scale for Children—Fourth Edition.* San Antonio, TX: Pearson Assessments.

Wechsler, D. (2008). *Manual for the Wechsler Adult Intelligence Scale—Fourth Edition.* San Antonio, TX: Pearson Assessments.

Weinberg, T. S., Williams, C. T., & Moser, C. (1984). The social constituents of sadomasochism. *Social Problems, 31,* 379–389.

Westen, D., & Shedler, J. (2007). Personality diagnosis with the Shedler–Westen Assessment Procedure (SWAP): Integrating clinical and statistical measurement and prediction. *Journal of Abnormal Psychology, 116*(4), 810–822.

Westen, D., Shedler, J., & Bradley, R. (2006). A prototype approach to personality disorder diagnosis. *American Journal of Psychiatry, 163*(5), 846–856.

White, L., Harvey, P. D., Opler, L., & Lindenmayer, J. P. (1997). Empirical assessment of the factorial structure of clinical symptoms in schizophrenia: A multisite, multimodel evaluation of the factorial structure of the Positive and Negative Syndrome Scale. The PANSS Study Group. *Psychopathology, 30,* 263–274.

Wiger, D. (1998). *The psychotherapy documentation primer.* New York: Wiley.

Wiger, D. E., & Solberg, K. B. (2001). *Tracking mental health outcomes: A therapist's guide to measuring client progress, analyzing data, and improving your practice.* New York: Wiley.

Wilson, S. J. (1980). *Recording guidelines for social workers.* New York: Free Press.

World Health Organization. (1992). *International classification of diseases* (10th rev.): *Chapter V. Mental and behavioral disorders.* Geneva: Author.

Wynne, L. C. (Ed.). (1988). *The state of the art in family therapy research.* New York: Family Process Press.

Zimmerman, I. L., & Woo-Sam, J. M. (1973). *Clinical interpretation of the Wechsler Adult Intelligence Scale.* New York: Grune & Stratton.

Zuckerman, E. L. (2006). *HIPAAHelp: A compliance manual for mental health professionals.* Armbrust, PA: Three Wishes Press. (Also available at *www.hipaahelp.info*)

Zuckerman, E. L. (2008). *The paper office* (4th ed.). New York: Guilford Press.

Zung, W. W. (1965). A self-rating depression scale. *Archives of General Psychiatry, 12,* 63–70.

Index